THE LIFE AND WORK
—OF—
DWIGHT L. MOODY

Presented to the Christian World as
A Tribute to the Memory
of the Greatest Apostle of the Age

—BY—

Rev. J. Wilbur Chapman, D.D.

FOR MANY YEARS A CO-WORKER WITH MR MOODY, AND VICE PRESIDENT OF THE BIBLE INSTITUTE, OF WHICH MR. D. L. MOODY WAS PRESIDENT

Profusely Illustrated with reproductions from Original Photographs and Rare Old Prints, including several Authentic Portraits of Mr. Moody, some of which are here published for the first time.

R. E. WHITMAN & CO.
ELMIRA, N. Y.

Copyright, 1900
by
W. E. Scull

Many of the illustrations in this book are made from copyright photographs, and all persons are warned not to reproduce them without permission.

MR. MOODY IN THE GROVE AT NORTHFIELD.

PREFACE.

NUMEROUS invitations have come to me recently, to write concerning the life and work of D. L. Moody, all of which were declined. I have, however, accepted the invitation of the publishers of this volume for several reasons.

First. Because they have made it possible for me in so doing to make a generous contribution to some benevolent or educational work, which I may select, my hope being that I might in this way contribute to the work for which Mr. Moody gave his life.

Second. Because very many friends have urged upon me the propriety of my so doing; they presented it to me as a call to duty as well as a privilege, they told me it was a golden opportunity to speak of his life to many people who might not read the particulars of it elsewhere, and I was convinced that a subscription book would reach thousands of homes, which might not otherwise be influenced. They told me that my work as an evangelist made it fitting that I should write of him, who was known as the greatest evangelist of the generation.

Third. I write because I loved him, and I felt that I might in this way pay tribute to the most consistent Christian man I have ever known. I am confident that there has not been in these latter days a man who was more truly filled with the Holy Ghost than he.

In view of all this my contract was made with the publishers, and it was made before I knew what other books might be written; but even then I was assured by those who knew that my book had a field of its own, and could not be considered as in competition with any other, for I would write from an entirely different standpoint.

This book is sent forth with the prayer that God may make it a blessing to its readers everywhere. It is my purpose, in using such facts as I may legitimately claim, to present Mr. Moody, not only in his early life, and tell the story of his conversion, but to present him as a public character, as a man of God, as a Prince among evangelists, and give to my readers such a view of him as may not be found in other books. He was a man of great faith in God, and of mighty power in life and in prayer; he was a devout student of the Bible, he was a great preacher, and he moved men as it has been given few men to do. He reached more people during his lifetime than any other man, possibly in the world's history. He was, in the judgment of a distinguished Scotch Christian, the greatest educator of his day. He had a victorious life, and a triumphant death. It is the purpose of this book to give a review of all this, in as personal and practical a way as possible.

Letters have been written me by many of his old friends, giving me even a better knowledge of him than my more than twenty years' acquaintance could afford.

So I write with pleasure, and thanking God that it is my privilege. He was the best friend I have ever known, and whether I think of him as a preacher, and a great leader of men, or just as a humble follower of God, in his home as I frequently saw him, he was the most thoroughly consecrated man, and the most Christ-like of any one I have ever known. Among those who rise up to call him blessed, I thank God I stand.

J Wilbur Chapman

New York, January, 1900.

N. B. I desire to record my grateful appreciation of assistance rendered me in preparing, this book by Rev. Ford C. Ottman, and other friends.

J. W. C.

LIST OF CHAPTERS AND SUBJECTS.

CHAPTER.   PAGE.

I. INTRODUCTORY CHAPTER. 17
       Early Acquaintance with Mr. Moody—A Most Profound Influence—A Master in Moving Men—The Power of God on His Work—The Last Picture of the Evangelist—Professor Drummond on Moody.

II. NORTHFIELD, ... 35
       Northfield Not a Modern Town—The First Settlers—The Second Settlement—After the Revolution—The House in Which Moody was Born—The Character of the Town.

III. MR. MOODY'S EARLY LIFE, ... 45
       The Death of His Father—Mrs. Moody's Struggle—Incidents from Moody's Early Days—His Rudimentary Education—Departure from Home—Looking for Work.

IV. HIS MOTHER, ... 57
       A Picture Never To Be Forgotten—His Mother's Blessing—Her Puritan Ancestry—Her Conversion—D. L. Moody's Tribute to His Mother—Verses She Had Marked.

V. HIS CONVERSION, ... 74
       First Acquaintance With Mr. E. D. Kimball—Just Ready for the Light—Mr. Moody's Probation—Admitted To the Church—A Changed Life—He Seeks His Future In the West.

VI. SUNDAY SCHOOL WORK, ... 87
       Preparation for Future Work—Recruiting For the Church and For Sunday Schools—The School on "the Sands"—Muscular Christianity—The North Market Mission—President Lincoln's Visit—Incidents of the Work.

LIST OF CHAPTERS AND SUBJECTS

CHAPTER.   PAGE.

VII. THE YOUNG MEN'S CHRISTIAN ASSOCIATION AND THE CHICAGO AVENUE CHURCH 100

First work with the Young Men's Christian Association—The Illinois Street Church—Elected President of the Young Men's Christian Association—Dedication of the New Building—A Great Religious Centre—The North Side Tabernacle—Development of the Chicago Avenue Church.

VIII. GIVING UP BUSINESS 109

Moody as a Commercial Traveler—"God will Provide"—He Gives Up Business—His Means Exhausted—Friends Come with Unsolicited Aid—Marriage—His Wife and Her Influence—Mr. Moody's Family.

IX. MOODY AND SANKEY 122

Mr. Sankey's First Singing at a Moody Meeting—A Sudden Proposition—A Street Service—Mr. Sankey Joins Mr. Moody—The Effect of Mr. Sankey's Singing—A Blessed Partnership.

X. EVANGELISTIC WORK IN ENGLAND, IRELAND AND SCOTLAND 139

The Discouraging Outlook—Sunderland—Revival Fire Kindled at Newcastle—Edinburgh—The Work in Scotland Continued—The Evangelists go to Ireland—The Return to England—Various Meetings—The London Revival.

XI. EVANGELISTIC WORK IN THE UNITED STATES . . . 158

The Gospel Campaign in Brooklyn—The Campaign in Philadelphia—The Great Meetings in New York—Glorious Enthusiasm for the Lord—In Baltimore, 1878.

XII. MR. MOODY IN TWO WARS 175

The Sanitary and Christian Commissions—Mr. Moody's Zeal—Experiences from the War—The Revival at Camp Douglas—Work in the War with Spain—On Sea and Land—Striking Illustrations—"God Keep Us From War."

XIII. THE SPIRITUAL SIDE OF NORTHFIELD, ... 190

A Blessed Town—Northfield Dear to Mr. Moody—Mr. Moody's Love of Nature—Dr. A. J. Gordon—Rev. F. B. Meyer at Northfield—A Star In the Midnight Darkness.

LIST OF CHAPTERS AND SUBJECTS

CHAPTER.		PAGE.
XIV.	THE NORTHFIELD SCHOOLS, ...	203

Marvelous Educational Work—The Beginnings of Northfield Seminary—Three Great Ends in View—Mt. Hermon—The Northfield Training School.

XV. THE NORTHFIELD CONFERENCE AND THE STUDENT VOLUNTEERS, ... 215

Various Bible Conferences—The Pre-Eminence of Northfield—The Beginnings and the Growth of the Conference—The Student Volunteers—Missionary Interest Awakened.

XVI. THE CHICAGO BIBLE INSTITUTE, ... 229

The Need of the Institution—The Practical Nature of the Work—Touching Requests for Prayer—The Rev. R. A. Torrey—The Women's Department.

XVII. THE WORLD'S FAIR CAMPAIGN, ... 245

The First Meeting—How Mr. Moody Vivified the Work—The Reports of Co-Workers—The Monday Conferences—Meetings For Children.

XVIII. THE LAST CAMPAIGN 257

Mr. Moody Goes to Kansas City—The Great Convention Hall—Inspiring Opening Services—The Beginning of the End—Mr. Moody Breaks Down—Back to Northfield.

XIX. MR. MOODY AS AN EVANGELIST 269

D. L. Moody an Evangelist in the Truest Sense of the Word—Especially Adapted to His Work—His Dread of Notoriety—His Views on Sudden Conversion.

XX. HIS BIBLE 283

A Book More Than Precious to Him—The Advice of Harry Moorehouse—Mr. Moody's Ideas Concerning the Way to Use God's Word.

XXI. HIS CO-WORKERS 289

Ira David Sankey—Paul P. Bliss—Major Whittle—Henry Varley—John McNeill—George C. Stebbins—Ferdinand Schiverea—H. M. Wharton—R. A. Torrey—A. C. Dixon—Henry Drummond—G. Campbell Morgan—George H. Macgregor—F. B. Meyer.

LIST OF CHAPTERS AND SUBJECTS

Chapter		Page
XXII.	THREE CHARACTERISTIC SERMONS	307

Characteristics of the Three Sermons—God's Love—The Excuses of Men—Reaping Whatsoever We Sow.

XXIII.	HIS BEST ILLUSTRATIONS	346

The Fervor of His Eloquence—"Let the Lower Lights Be Burning"—"For Charlie's Sake"—A Penalty Necessary—Calling on God—One Year's Record.

XXIV.	REVIVAL CONVENTIONS	367

A Typical Convention—What is Evangelistic Service?—We Want New Hymns—Apt Replies to Questions.

XXV.	HOW TO STUDY THE BIBLE, ...	376

A Characteristic Bible Reading—Helpful Auxiliaries to Bible Study—Jesus the Key to the New Testament—The Fou Gospels—Six Things Worth Knowing—How Christ Dealt With Sinners.

XXVI.	HIS CREED—THREE CARDINAL TRUTHS, ...	396

His View Concerning the Word of God—The Second Coming of Christ—The Work of the Holy Ghost—A Blessed Experience.

XXVII.	THE FUNERAL, ...	414

Mr. Moody's Last Moments—A Triumphant Passing Away—Funeral Services—Addresses by Dr. Scofield, Dr. Weston, Dr. Chapman, Bishop Mallalieu, Mr. Torrey, and others.

XXVIII.	ROUNDTOP, WHERE MR. MOODY LOVED TO SPEAK AND WHERE HE WAS BURIED, ...	439

Mr. Moody's Remains Taken to Roundtop—A Place of Blessing—Roundtop Particularly Identified With Mr. Moody.

XXIX.	MEMORIAL SERVICES, ...	456

The Great Meeting in New York—Impressive Addresses—Estimates of Mr. Moody by Dr. Greer, Mr. John R. Mott, Mr. Cutting, Dr. Buckley, and others who knew and loved him.

LIST OF CHAPTERS AND SUBJECTS   xi

CHAPTER.   PAGE.

XXX. APPRECIATIONS BY EMINENT FRIENDS, ... 485

Testimony to Mr. Moody's Wonderful Personality—The Opinions of Prominent Men who Knew Him and His Work—The Universal Regard in Which He Was held.

XXXI. EDITORIAL ESTIMATES OF HIS CHARACTER, ... 503

Important Tributes from the Secular and Religious Press—All Men Eager to Admit Mr. Moody's Greatness—What He Accomplished for the Betterment of Mankind.

XXXII. THE PERSONAL SIDE OF MR. MOODY, ... 517

Personal Characteristics—His Hold Upon His Friends—His Charming Social Side—His Kindliness, Modesty and Unselfishness.

XXXIII. PERSONAL REMINISCENCES OF D. L. MOODY, ... 537

By Rev. H. M. Wharton, D.D. An Estimate of Mr. Moody, based on intimate association with him and long knowledge of his work.

XXXIV. A MONTH WITH MR. MOODY IN CHICAGO, ... 546

By Rev. H. M. Wharton, D.D. Mr. Moody as He Appeared to one of his Prominent Co-Workers during the World's Fair Campaign.

"The Biggest Human I Ever Knew"

By Henry Drummond

WERE once asked what on the human side were the effective ingredients in Mr. Moody's sermons, one would find the answer difficult. Probably the foremost is the tremendous conviction with which they are uttered. Next to that are their point and direction. Every blow is straight from the shoulder and every stroke tells. Whatever canons they violate, whatever faults the critics may find with their art, their rhetoric, or even with their theology, as appeals to the people they do their work with extraordinary power.

If eloquence is measured by its effect upon an audience and not by its balanced sentence and cumulative periods, then there is eloquence of the highest order. In sheer persuasiveness, Mr. Moody's has few equals, and, rugged as his preaching may seem to some, there is in it a pathos of a quality which few otators have ever reached, and appealing tenderness which not only wholly redeems it, but raises it not unseldom almost to sublimity.

In largeness of heart, in breadth of view, in single-eyedness and humility, in teachableness and self-obliteration, in sheer goodness and love, none can stand beside him.

"The Last of the Great Group."

By Newell Dwight Hillis.

WHEN long time hath passed, some historian, recalling the great epochs and religious teachers of our century, will say, "There were four men sent forth by God; their names Charles Spurgeon, Phillips Brooks, Henry Ward Beecher and Dwight L. Moody." Each was a herald of good tidings; each was a prophet of a new social and religious order. God girded each of these prophets for his task, and taught him how to "dip his sword in Heaven."

In characterizing the message of these men we say that Spurgeon was expositional, Phillips Brooks devotional, Henry Ward Beecher prophetic and philosophical, while Dwight L. Moody was a herald rather than teacher, addressing himself to thecommon people—the unchurched multitudes. The symbol of the great English preacher is a lighted lamp, the symbol of Brooks a flaming heart, the symbol of Beecher an orchestra of many instruments, while Mr. Moody was a trumpet, sounding the advance, sometimes through inspiration and sometimes through alarm.

The first three were commanders, each over his regiment, and worked from fixed center, but the evangelist was the leader of a flying band who went everywhither into the enemy's country, seeking conquests of peace and righteousness. Be the reasons what they may, the common people gladly heard the great evangelist.

Moody as a Prophet.

By Rev. F. B. Meyer, B. A.

GOD'S best gifts to man are men. He is always sending forth men. When the time is ripe for a man, God sends him forth. When for a moment the race seems to be halting in its true progress, then, probably from the ranks of the common people, rises he who leads a new advance. "There came a man sent from God." Yes, God constantly sends men. But the greatest gift is a prophet.

When New Testament times dawned the touch of the priest had lost its power forever, but around those times prophets have gathered—John the Baptist, Savonarola, Luther, Latimer, Whitefield, Wesley, Spurgeon, and it is not fulsome flattery which includes the name of Moody.

What is a Prophet?

A prophet is one who sees God's truth by a distinct vision; who speaks as one upon whose eyeballs has burned the Light of the Eternal, and, thus speaking, compels the crowd to listen; he is one whose strong, elevated character is a witness to the truth in which he believes and which he declares. These are the three necessary conditions of a prophet. It matters not in what diction he speaks, whether in the rough, unpolished tongue of the people, or in the choice, well-balanced language of the schools. A man who possesses those three qualities is a prophet, and has a mission from God. Such a one was Moody.

There were certain traits in the prophets and in John the Baptist which we recognize also for the most part in Moody. For instance, the prophet generally rises from the ranks of the people. Again and again from the common people have been supplied the leaders of men. Those in the upper grades of society, from whom we should naturally expect the most, would seem very largely to have worn themselves out with luxury and self-indulgences. History is full of the stories of prophets who came from a lowly stock. And Moody was the child of humble New England parents. His father died early, and Moody's boyhood was spent face to face with privation. He had to fight his way from the ranks of the people. We have to thank this fact for the strong common sense which distinguished him. Moody had the practical insight to humor which belong especially to those who toil upon the land. And this man, with his close relationship to the life of the people, came to be able to hold ten thousand of them spellbound in the grasp of his powerful influence.

Taught of God's Spirit

Again, it will generally be found that a prophet is not learned in the teaching of the schools. John the Baptist received his college education in the desert, amid the elements of Nature. These were his great kindergarten, in which his soul was prepared for its great work. When men go to the conventional colleges they learn to measure their language with the nicest accurateness. Was Moody's lack in this and in similar directions a loss to him? Nay, he was taught of God's Spirit. He bathed himself in a book, in that one volume which is in itself a library, the intimate knowledge of which is alone sufficient to make men cultured.

There is often a brusqueness about the prophet. We see that in John the Baptist. He was not a man to be found in king's courts. Without veneer, brusque, gaunt, strong, he lived and

RESIDENCE OF D. L. MOODY, NORTHFIELD, MASS.

labored. Moody partook the same characteristics. It is not unlikely, however, that he assumed a certain attitude of brusqueness because he felt afraid of being made an idol of the people. Having seen the evils of popularity, he wished to avoid them. To timid, friendless women, to individual sinners, he was wonderfully gentle and kind in manner. Amongst his grandchildren, whose simple playmate he became, he was tenderness itself. The brusqueness belonged only to the rind, to the character which had known deep experiences.

Moody had very distinct experiences. The manner of his conversion led him to expect immediate decisions in the souls of others. Under his Sunday school teacher's influence he had been led on the moment to give himself to Christ, and he looked for others to do nothing less, nothing more tardy.

His Baptism of the Holy Ghost

Again, the prophet has known a touch of fire. Mr. Moody once told me that a number of poor women in Chicago who heard him speak said one day, "You are good; but there is something you have not got; we are praying that it may come." Later, one afternoon in New York, he was walking along, when an irresistible impulse came upon him to be alone. He looked around. Where could he go? What was to be done? He remembered a friend living not far away. So into his house he rushed, and demanded a room where he could be alone. There he remained several hours, and there he received the baptism of the Holy Ghost. When he returned to Chicago and began to speak, the godly women who had spoken to him beforetime said, "You have it now." And the wonderful power which Moody henceforward exercised over his fellow-men he owed to that touch of fire. It never left him. People were attracted. What happened when he visited England, happened wherever he went. The prophet had the real ring about him. He dealt with things as they are.

There was genuine greatness of heart in Mr. Moody, and it constantly triumphed over sect differences. When his mother died three years ago the Roman Catholics of the neighborhood asked that they might be pallbearers.

A prophet, of course, has his message. His office is not so much that of teacher or preacher as of herald. He sounds the alarm and cries "fire." With Moody it was not repentance because of hell-fire. The love of God was his proclamation. And how he could speak about that! I have seen him break down, as with trembling voice and tears in his eyes he pleaded with men for the love of God's sake to be reconciled with Him. A prophet is humble. In this respect Moody was true to the type. He seemed the one person who did not know there was a Moody. He did not know half so much about himself as the newspapers told. This is true greatness.

And now he has gone. My world is very much thinner. A great tree has fallen. One more throbbing voice is silent. Spurgeon is gone. Moody is gone. The voices are dying. Listen to-day to the voice of the Son of God.

REV. J. WILBUR CHAPMAN, D.D.

CHAPTER I.

Introductory Chapter

"I DO not know whether I dare say what I am now about to speak to you. I asked a brother minister this afternoon, and he would not take the responsibility, but after thinking it over I will say it. I believe if Christ had actually lived in the body of our dear brother and had been subject to the same limitations that met him, he would have filled up his life much as D. L. Moody filled up his, and for that reason I say, after the most careful thought, I had rather be D. L. Moody lying dead in his coffin than to be the greatest man alive in the world to-day." This remarkable tribute was paid by Dr. H. G. Weston, of the Crozier Theological Seminary, Chester, Pa., and when he had finished it, there was a wave of sympathetic expression and approval which swept over the entire audience, and his remarkable utterance was greeted with quiet Amens and suppressed sobs.

I question if this generation has known a man who was more Christlike than D. L. Moody. That he sometimes made mistakes his best friends will allow, but that he was ready to undo these mistakes when they were made, and to make acknowledgment when that was necessary, all who knew him well will testify.

Early Acquaintance With Mr. Moody

I have heard his name since infancy. First of all from my mother's lips when I was a child. For it was at that time his name was being spoken with approval by ministers and Christian workers, and also at that time that the newspapers were making frequent reference to his increasing usefulness and power.

I am naturally a hero worshipper. There are certain names that have always stirred me and certain personalities that have ever been my inspiration. No name, however, has ever been more sacred among the names of men than that of Moody, and no character has ever so taken hold of my very being, as his.

When first I felt called to preach the Gospel, I determined there were certain men whom I must hear. In my list of names I had Henry Ward Beecher, and I shall ever recall with grateful appreciation the opportunity of hearing him in the Plymouth Church when his text was: "Except your righteousness exceed the righteousness of the scribes and Pharisees ye shall in no wise enter into the kingdom." And when his prayer reminded me of nothing so much as the running of a mountain stream over the rocks as it hurried on its way to the sea, I came away feeling that I had had a great privilege, not only in hearing Mr. Beecher preach, but in being lifted up to Heaven by his prayer.

A Most Profound Influence

The second name in importance on my list was that of Dr. John Hall, and possibly the deepest impression of my life was made, when he was preaching from the text in I. Timothy iv : 6: " Thou shalt be a good minister of Jesus Christ." He closed his sermon by leaning over the pulpit and saying, "I have only one supreme ambition, and that is that I might close my ministry here and have you say concerning me, "he was a good minister of the Gospel of Jesus Christ," and I came away saying that I had had such an uplift as rarely comes to a young minister.

Written in large letters on my list was the name of Charles H. Spurgeon, and it has ever been the regret of my ministry that before it was given to me to cross the sea, God had called him to cross over into the better land.

But of all the names written, none stood out so plainly as that of D. L. Moody. I had somehow made up my mind from what I had heard of him, and from what the newspapers had printed of his work, that he was to move me more mightily than any other man in the world, and I bear glad testimony to the fact that the after-years proved my expectation to be true. He exercised the most profound influence over me from the very first moment I met him, an influence which only increased with the passing years, and still abides, although he is in the presence of his God.

At The World's Fair Meetings in Chicago

In the providence of God I was frequently with him in services; notably, at the World's Fair Meetings in Chicago, when he was not only the genial host of the workers with whom he was surrounded, but was the leader of a great force of Christian ministers and laymen, commanding the city for God with as great genius as ever an officer commanded and led his soldiers against the enemy on the field of battle.

He invited me to be with him in Pittsburg in 1898, and one of the most tender memories of my life is that which I have of him in connection with the meetings held in the Exposition Building.

I saw him in frequent conferences when I was pastor in Philadelphia, when his great heart yearned over the cities in the East, much as did the heart of the Master when looking down upon the City of his love, he said, "O Jerusalem, Jerusalem!"

I was with him in the special campaign in New York, when from early morning till late at night in the Grand Central Palace, he not only preached himself, but had called to his assistance workers and friends from many other cities.

It was my great privilege to be frequently at Northfield where Mr. Moody showed not only his great heart, but his great power as a leader as in no other place in the country, and intimately as I knew him, and devotedly as I loved him, I never came in contact with him that my heart did not beat a little faster and my pulses throb a little more quickly.

Moody Conducting Meetings

I used to love to watch him in the meetings he conducted. His eyes were always open to take in the most minute detail of the services, and things to which other men would be blind he was ever seeing. I frequently almost lost the message he was giving in my admiration for the messenger. While he was sitting in the first part of the service, he would make a dive into his pocket, take out a little piece of paper and write a message to some of his workers, put down an illustration or record something which was to be the seed thought for a future sermon. Sometimes you would scarcely think he was noticing what was going on, and suddenly he would be on his feet announcing a hymn, and while he could not sing himself, yet he was superb in his power to make other people sing, "Isn't that magnificent" he would say, as voice after voice took up the great chorus. "Now the galleries sing, that is my choir up in the gallery, now show the people what you can do; now the men, now the women, now altogether," until it would seem as if greater singing one had never heard in all his life.

He was ever on the alert in every service. I have heard him many times relate, however, one instance to the contrary, when George O. Barnes was being greatly used in evangelistic effort. Mr. Moody had taken him around to several appointments, and the evening service came so quickly upon them that they did not have time to eat anything except a hasty lunch which they took somewhere together, the principal article of which Mr. Moody said was bologna. When Mr. Barnes arose to speak in the evening, the room was very hot, and Mr. Moody said that that, together with the lunch he had taken, made him very drowsy; he pinched himself to keep awake, but at last he fell asleep. Mr. Barnes did everything he could to arouse him, and when he had failed he stopped preaching, and Mr. Moody said, turned to his audience to say, "This is the first time I have ever seen D. L, Moody defeated, but the devil and bologna sausage seem to have gotten the best of him." I have heard him tell it over and over. No one enjoyed a joke better than himself, even though he might be the subject of it.

He seemed to know what the people wanted and what they would take, and the things that other men would turn away from he would present with great power. I remember a meeting in Albany, New York, years ago, when short conferences were being held through the country by Mr. Moody and his co-workers, when he turned to Dr. Darling, then of Schenectady, now of Auburn Seminary, and said, "Doctor, tell them the story you told me this morning;" and then the distinguished preacher gave an illustration which he might have thought too simple to use in a crowded assemblage, but which swayed the great audience.

A Master in Moving Men

"He was a master in moving men. I can shut my eyes now and see him, with tears rolling down his face, as he plead with men to turn to Christ; sobs breaking his utterance as he told of the love of God to men and of God's special love to himself. He was as sincere a man as ever stood on the platform to preach, and it was for this reason that people of all classes and grades believed in him. When the New York Dailies came out with great headlines saying, "Moody is dead," a Jew in one of the courts turned to a friend of mine to say, " He was a good man," and when his death was being discussed in one of the great clubs in the City of New York, a man who was an infidel said, " I think he was the best man this generation has known, and if I should ever be a Christian I should want to be one just like Moody, if I could."

There were times when he was more than eloquent, when every gesture was a sermon. Who can ever forget his description of Elijah going up by a whirlwind into heaven. When carried away by the power of his own emotions, he lifted his hands while his audience seemed to be lifted with him, and raising them higher and higher, I can hear him say the words, " Up, up, up, I can see Elijah going, and I see heaven open to receive him as he rises." The impression on his audience was profound.

A Blessing To Have Known Him

To have known him at all was a blessing, but to have known him with any degree of intimacy was one of the rarest privileges of a minister's life. I would not say that I knew him better than other men, for hundreds knew him far more intimately and for a far longer time than I ; but if love, since I have known him, can make up for the years in which I was not acquainted with him, then these recent years with their increasing admiration and love will give me the right to speak and write. Dr. Pierson says concerning George Müller, " A human life filled with the presence and power of God, is one of God's choicest gifts to His church and to the world."

"Things which are unseen and eternal seem, to the carnal man, distant and indistinct, while what is seen and temporal is vivid and real. Practically, any object in nature that can be seen or felt is thus more real and actual to most men than the living God. Every man who walks with God, and finds Him a present help in every time of need; who puts His promises to the practical proof and verifies them in actual experience; every believer who with the key of faith unlocks God's mysteries, and with the key of prayer unlocks God's treasuries, thus furnishes to the race a demonstration and an illustration of the fact that 'He is a Rewarder of them that diligently seek Him.'

"Death Has no Terror to Me"

"George Müller was such an argument and example incarnated in human flesh. He was a man of like passions as we are, and tempted in all points like as we are, but who believed God and was established by believing; who prayed earnestly that he might live a life and do a work which should be a convincing proof that God hears prayer and that it is safe to trust Him at all times; and who has furnished just such a witness as he desired Like Enoch, he truly walked with God, and had abundant testimony borne to him that he pleased God. And when, on the tenth day of March, 1898, it was told us of George Müller that 'he was not,' we knew 'God had taken him;' it seemed more like a translation than death," the same thing can be said of Mr. Moody. He used to say, "Sometime you will pick up a paper and will read of D. L. Moody's death; don't believe a word of it; I may be asleep, but I I shall not be dead; death has no terror to me," and his words were a prophecy of his triumphant passing into the presence of God. The telegram written by Mr. A. P. Fitt, his son-in-law, to Mr. Louis Klopsch, of the *Christian Herald*, is a confirmation of this:

"East Northfield, Mass., Dec. 22.

"Mr. Moody had a triumphant entry into Heaven at noon.

"As early as 8 o'clock, A. M., he said: 'Earth is receding and Heaven is opening. God is calling me.'

"He was perfectly conscious to the last, and showed the same courage and faith, unselfishness and thought for his wife and children and his schools as always.

"His doctor says it was 'a pure case of heart failure, due to absolute loss of bodily strength.'

"In leaving us he gave unflinching testimony to the truths he taught.

A. P. Fitt."

A Wonderful Life

His was a wonderful life. In one of Tissot's pictures there is seen a great multitude of people lame and halt and blind in the way along which Jesus of Nazareth is to come, and then there is a view representing him passing, and as he moves along, only those before Him are sick, while all behind him are well. This was Mr. Moody's life. All that was behind him felt the touch of his power. The Chicago Bible Institute has become an object lesson to Christian workers everywhere. Northfield is a center of influence forth from which streams of blessing flow to the very ends of the earth. England, Ireland and Scotland have felt the touch of his consecrated life, and millions of lives the world over thank God that he ever lived, those who were lame, halt and blind spiritually now leap and praise God that D. L. Moody ever lived.

His home life, in the testimony of those who knew it best, was most beautiful. On that memorable day when his body was lying in the casket in the Congregational Church in Northfield, when other speakers had paid their tribute to his distinguished father, Mr. William R. Moody, his eldest son, rose to say: "As a son I want to say a few words of him as a father. We have heard from his pastor, his associates and friends, and he was just as true a father. I don't think he showed up in any way better than when, on one or two occasions, in dealing with us as children, with his impulsive nature, he spoke rather sharply. We have known him to come to us and say: 'My children, my son, my daughter, I spoke quickly; I did wrong; I want you to forgive me.' That was D. L. Moody as a father.

"He was not yearning to go; he loved his work. Life was very attractive; it seems as though on that early morning as he had one foot upon the threshold it was given him for our sake to give us a word of comfort. He said: 'This is bliss; it is like a trance. If this is death it is beautiful.' And his face lighted up as he mentioned those whom he saw.

"We could not call him back; we tried to for a moment, but we could not. We thank God for his home life, for his true life, and we thank God that he was our father, and that he led each one of his children to know Jesus Christ."

A Beautiful Home

There was ever a holy atmosphere about this home to me in the few times I was permitted to pass its portals. Mr. Moody used to tell a story of a sick child whose father one day came into his room and to whom the child said, "lift me up," and the father lifted him gently, and he said, "lift me higher," and he lifted him yet a little higher; "higher," said the child, faintly, and he lifted him just as high as his arms could reach, and when he took him down he was dead. "I believe," said Mr. Moody, "that he lifted him into the arms of Christ," and then his great kindly face glowed, and as the tears rolled down his cheeks he said, "I would rather have my children say that about me than to have a monument of gold that would pierce the clouds," and his home life clearly bore out the fact that he not only said this in words, but he put it into every action in his home. His personality was charming; he was the center of every group everywhere. It was a most ordinary thing to see representative men from many parts of the world in his home, but none were ever so prominent as to dim the brightness of his greatness, and yet he was as modest as a woman and as humble as a little child. Who that ever sat about his table can forget his laugh. It was as hearty a laugh as one has ever heard. He knew just how to put every man at his best. His questions always brought forth that which would make a man appear to the best advantage before his hearers. "Morgan," he would say, speaking to the Rev. G. Campbell Morgan, "tell that story about Joseph Parker;" and then although he might have heard it before he was the most interested listener; his eyes would gleam and his face light up as the inimitable story teller painted the picture of London's greatest preacher.

Thoughtful of Others

He was so very thoughtful of other people. The last time I rode with him to Mt. Hermon, he stopped to talk a few minutes with the men at the old ferry, asked them about their homes and spoke a cheering word concerning their work, and said as he drove on, "I want them to know that I am interested in them."

Driving up from the station at the last students' conference at Northfield, he stopped every student trudging along with his baggage and took the bag into his buggy until it was piled up with luggage, and the greater the number of men whose burdens he lifted, the happier he became.

Walking across his lawn one day when his conversation was, as ever, the evangelizing of the great cities, he turned quickly and said, "Chapman, how many children have you?" and when I told him two, as I had then, he turned quickly about and said "come with me," and he pointed out to me some white turkeys and some ducks of a very rare breed and said, "I will send a pair of these to the children," and when only a few days had elapsed, sure enough the turkeys and the ducks came safely to my country home, and my children took particular delight in feeding and caring for the ducks and turkeys that came from Mr. Moody's house.

Driving along the country road with Dr. Wilton Merle Smith, of New York, when the conversation had been general, he stopped his horse under the shade of a great tree, and, said Dr. Smith, "he poured out his soul in such prayer as I have rarely heard."

"I Just Wanted to be With You"

I shall ever remember one of his illustrations. He had told one of his children that he was not to be disturbed in his study, and after a little while the door of the study opened and the child came in. "What do you want," said the father, and the little fellow looking up into his father's face said, "I just wanted to be with you," and the tears started into the great evangelist's eyes as he said, "it ought to be like that between us and our God." I can well understand how his little child would want to be with him every minute of his time, for there are many of us who counted it our special privilege to be in fellowship with this godly man.

The first time I saw him is a memorable day in my life. I was a student at Lake Forest University, and he was to speak in Chicago, I think it was in 1878. Four times he preached the Gospel that day and I was in every service; but the service of all services was that of the afternoon in old Farwell Hall; it was for men only. The place was filled to overflowing with men; the singing was superb, so said my friends, but I lost the power of the music in the sight of this man of God of whom I had heard so much. His text was, "Be not deceived, God is not mocked; whatsoever a man soweth, that shall he also reap." The sermon is remembered because, under God, it has been used to lead so many to Christ. Under the power of it I saw my own heart, and then I saw the Saviour who was waiting to make it clean. I halted around with others if only I might have the chance to touch his hand. Just in front of me went a man who held Mr. Moody's attention for a little time, and who said to him, as he afterwards told me, "I am a defaulter, I have taken money which is not my own, I am a fugitive from justice, what must I do?" And Mr. Moody told him he must take the money back, even though it meant punishment, and he did it; was sent to the penitentiary, was pardoned out just before he died of quick consumption.

"He Has Forgiven Me!"

Before the pardon Mr. Moody made his way across the country that he might stand in his cell, and as he entered, the young man sprang to his feet and putting his arms out to Mr. Moody said, "He has forgiven me, He has forgiven me." His evangelistic life was filled with just such incidents. In the evening of that great first day I saw him once again and followed him into the after meeting where I had the privilege of a moment's conversation. I had been in doubt for a long time on the subject of assurance. I did not know certainly whether I was a Christian or not, and Mr. Moody said, when I asked him to help me, "do you believe this verse?" and he quoted the Fifth Chapter of John and the 24th verse, "Verily, verily, I say unto you, He that heareth my word, and believeth on Him that sent me, hath everlasting life, and shall not come into condemnation; but is passed from death unto life." I said, "certainly I believe it." "Are you saved," he said, and I said, "sometimes I think I am, other times I feel I am not." He put his hand on my shoulder and said but one sentence, and then he left me; "young man," said he, "whom are you doubting?" and then he left me, and it flashed across my mind in an instant that, in my lack of assurance, I was doubting Christ; from that moment to this I have never doubted.

The Power of God on His Work

The next impression was in connection with the brief conferences held throughout the country when five days were spent in Albany and Troy, and the meetings were held in the First Reformed Church of which I afterwards became pastor. I came down from my country church with many other ministers from different parts of the State. The great church was crowded; I was obliged to stand in the aisle, but I forgot all discomfort in the impression that was made upon me by this mighty man of God. I followed him from one city to another and then went back to my own church to preach to my people on the story of the Moody meetings. The power of God was not only on his work, but was on the very mention of it, so that my church officers came together and said that this work must go on, and more than a hundred people came to Christ because of it. In the day when rewards are given for service, I am very sure that my dear friend will share in the glory of these who came to Christ indirectly through his ministry.

When I became an evangelist his word was always the cheeriest; I never met him that he did not have some word to say concerning the work at large. If ever there was a perplexity in my mind, or any doubt as to what my course of action should be, in settling any problem, Mr. Moody was the first to give advice and always the wisest of all advisers. The last time I saw him was in Boston, in the days when Admiral Dewey was to be welcomed to the New England Metropolis. He was there that the people might have the privilege of hearing Campbell Morgan. I heard him say, "some people think we ought to give the meetings up because of the excitement outside, but I believe," he said "that Christ is more attractive to the people than anything in all this world." The very morning of the parade when Mr. Morgan was obliged to be away and other speakers could not delay, some of his friends suggested that he at least give up this meeting. But he was never easily discouraged and he positively refused to yield in the least, and he preached himself with his old time vigor to a great company of people in Tremont Temple.

The Last Picture of the Evangelist

The last picture of him is drawn by the Hon. John Wanamaker. He was on his way to Kansas City, and, as Mr. Wanamaker said, he had turned away from his comfortable home and was going away into the far West, when he might have had all the rest of his home and help of his family, only for the joy of preaching the Gospel. Mr. Wanamaker met him at one of the railroad stations. It just so happened at this time that he was alone ; he purchased his own ticket, checked his baggage, then said, "we will have a little time now together," and they sat down in another railway station when Mr. Moody poured out his heart to his old friend concerning some of the interests that were dear to him, and then as they parted he said, with his face flushed and his eyes filled with tears, "if I could only get hold of one more Eastern city I should be grateful to God." These two friends said good-bye, the one to go into all the comforts of the presence of his loved ones, and the other to hurry away across the country that he might hold his last service, preach his last sermon, and then go from the very thick of the fight into the presence of his God.

D. L. Moody is dead. Men say it with sobs, and the old world seems lonely without him, but D. L. Moody is in heaven, we say it with thanksgiving, and we can just imagine the joy which rang through all the arches of the heavenly land when he entered in through the gates into the city. So is it strange that many can say the words of Dr. Weston with which this chapter began, "I would rather be D. L. Moody lying dead in his coffin than to be the greatest man alive in the world to-day."

Professor Drummond on Moody

In his day no one was closer to Mr. Moody, than Prof. Drummond, and a few years ago he said this of his friend: "Whether estimated by the moral qualities which go to the making up of a personal character, or the extent to which he has impressed these upon communities of men on both sides of the Atlantic, there is, perhaps, no more truly great man living than D. L. Moody. By moral influences in this connection, I mean the influence which, with whatever doctrinal accompaniment, leads men to better lives and higher ideals. I have never heard Mr. Moody defend any particular church. I have never heard him quoted as a theologian. But I know of large numbers of men and women of all churches and creeds, of many countries and ranks, from the poorest to the richest, and from the most ignorant to the most wise, upon whom he has placed an ineffaceable moral mark."

MAIN STREET OF EAST NORTHFIELD, WHICH MR. MOODY CALLED THE MOST BEAUTIFUL STREET IN THE WORLD.

CHAPTER II.

Northfield.

IT is pleasant to think that the privilege should have been given to Mr. Moody of absorbing his earlier training and of associating his later work with so charming a place naturally as Northfield. God's children are not denied the fair, the beautiful things of Nature. It is just like our Heavenly Father to give the best to one who walked so close to Him as did this dear friend.

Those of us who knew Mr. Moody well remember how he loved beautiful things. The song of the brook was music to his soul; the coming of the leaves and flowers of spring was a parable; and his own dear Northfield was beloved by him to the end. He was perfectly happy when driving about through the beauties of the surrounding country.

In view of his love for Nature, and the unusual beauty of his early environment, it is, perhaps, not surprising that the first doubts to assail the faith of the boy Moody, after his conversion, were pantheistic. He himself has related how a pantheist approached him and told him of God as Nature, and how it troubled him. But his doubts resolved themselves into a firmer belief in Nature, not as God, but as God's handiwork.

Northfield is not a Modern Town.

Its elms whisper a long story of days when men who sought to worship God in freedom of conscience martyred themselves by denial of the comforts of their homes in the old world and faced the terrors of bitter want and of crafty savage foes in the wildernesses of New England.

Long before this particular spot in the valley of the Connecticut was occupied by the white man, large tribes of Indians dwelt there, living upon the fruits of a generous lowland soil and the trophies of the chase.

The streams abounded in shad and salmon. The plenty of fish gave the place its Indian name, Squakheag, which signifies, in the Indian tongue, a place for spearing salmon. Wigwams clustered on nearly every knoll and bluff, and along the banks of the river ran the narrow trail of the aborigines.

A little way back from either side the river, and following its windings, extends a range of hills. Brush Mountain, one of these hills, was regarded by the Indians with a superstitious veneration, as the abode of their Great Spirit. Did not his breath come forth every spring, from a cleft in the rock, and melt the snow? To-day the traveler who climbs Brush Mountain will be shown an opening whence comes a blast of air, warm enough in the winter to keep the snow from accumulating in the immediate vicinity.

The First Settlers.

In 1669 a small party of whites, following the trail along the Connecticut northward from Northampton, came upon the lands of the Squakheags. The natives had suffered severely a few years before from the raid of a large party of Mohawks, who had come from the West, laying waste their fields and destroying their villages. To the eyes of the white men the land seemed very fair. About Northampton the tillable soil had been quite completely taken up, and the Squakheag region seemed to offer a good situation for a new settlement. As the Indians were not unwilling to part with their lands, a petition was made to the General Court of

Massachusetts by thirty-three settlers, for permission to purchase the land from the Indians. The permission was granted on the condition that not less than twenty families should settle there within eighteen months after the first move.

The settlers took up the land in 1673, and for two years lived in amicable relations with their Indian neighbors. Then, when King Philip's war broke out, the Squakheags were moved by the rude eloquence of the chief's emissaries to take part in the uprising. One morning they attacked the whites in the fields, killing many, and driving those who remained to seek refuge within the stockade. The position of the sixteen families in the fort was perilous. A relief expedition from Deerfield was ambushed while on the way, and fled home with great loss. Another company succeeded in reaching Northfield and rescuing the beleaguered ones, who left the settlement and returned to their former homes.

The Second Settlement

Not for seven years did the proprietors of the land take steps towards its re-occupation. Then about twenty families returned. Houses were built along a main street, and were protected by two forts. In 1688 eleven Indians, sent on the warpath by the French in Canada, murdered six persons in Northfield, and so alarmed the rest that more than one-half left the settlement. This so weakened the town that it was abandoned by those who remained.

The final settlement was made in 1713, and Northfield now prospered, although in 1723 it was again exposed to attacks from savages, who had been incited to make depredations upon the New England villages by the French Governor of Canada. It is said that men were then able to harvest their crops only in armed parties of forty or more. A fort was built a few miles up the river, and a cannon was placed there, that its voice might give warning of the approaching enemy. Peace came after the death of the Governor of Canada.

The existence of the hamlet continued for a long time precarious, for it was an outpost among the settlements, and therefore especially exposed to danger from the savages. During the French and Indian War Northfield was in constant terror. Thereafter such dangers gradually disappeared, and time was given to develop the natural resources of the place. Northfield sent her quota to take part in the War of the Revolution, nor did she hesitate to assert the principles of liberty, even to the extent of forcing her parson, against his first desire, to omit from his prayer the usual petition for blessing on "his majesty," the King of Great Britian.

After the Revolution

After the war the town rapidly acquired a certain culture. A hotel building, erected in 1798, was purchased by a company of citizens in 1829, and made into an academy which did honorable service for education during many years. About this same time the town was deeply affected by the wave of Unitarianism, which was then spreading throughout New England. Schisms arose in the village church, and a new parish was formed.

Northfield lies where three States meet—Massachusetts, New Hampshire and Vermont. Just south of the Massachusetts State line is the village, scattered for the most part along the main street, two miles long and 160 feet wide, on the east side of the river. On either side of the street is a double row of elms and maples, which have grown old with the village until they bend their lofty heads over the quiet roadway like the nodding guardians of some useless post. Savage neighbors are no longer near to enforce an alert sentinelship.

BIRTHPLACE OF D. L. MOODY, EAST NORTHFIELD, MASS.

Several roads cross this avenue, and all lead to scenes purely pastoral. Flanking the main street are dwellings, for the most part set well back among their lawns and fragrant gardens. These homes were built to last. They seem as substantial to-day as when they were built, although many of them are very old. The house occupied by Mr. William Alexander, for instance, has been in the hands of his family for one hundred and fifteen years. The present-day tendency to flock to the large cities has somewhat affected the younger generation of Northfield's old families, but the elms and the old houses are still there to perpetuate the atmosphere of old New England days, and better than all this the town has been so sanctified by the labors of her own best-known son that she will be remembered as the home of good works long after pompous cities have crumbled.

His Birthplace

Mr. Moody's birthplace is a plain, small farm-house, which still stands on the hillside. It looks upon one of the country roads, which winds up from the main street in an easterly direction. The building is two stories high, with green blinds, and is protected from the sun by stately trees. There is one tree, of especial majesty, under which Mr. Moody is said to have planned some of his greatest sermons.

The home in which Mr. Moody and his family were domiciled after his work had so broadened as to make necessary a larger house than the homestead, stands near the north end of the town, and is not far from his mother's house. It was purchased for about $3,000. A plain, roomy building it is. From time to time, as the requirements came up, Mr. Moody had additions built to the house, until it spread out its arms with a suggestion of hospitality most inviting to the visitor. The building fronts upon the main street. Mr. Moody's study is on the first floor, only a few steps within from the entrance. The atmosphere of the house, with its simple but substantial furniture, suggests the home of a man who desires to shape his environment to make it suit his work.

The Conception of Northfield Seminary

When Mr. Moody returned to Northfield after his evangelistic tour of Great Britain, he went home to Northfield to rest. With his eyes sharpened by travel, and with his usual alert observance of the needs of those about him, he conceived a plan of making possible education for girls who were born to the unstimulating routine of farm life. The germ of Northfield Seminary lay in this conception. In 1878 Mr. Moody purchased the first sixteen acres of land toward the two hundred and seventy acres which are now owned by the Seminary. Mr. H. N. F. Marshall, of Boston, was a guest of Mr. Moody at that time, and the decision to purchase the land was arrived at with the advantage of his advice. As he and Mr. Moody came to a decision, the owner of the land walked up the street. They invited him in, asked his price for the sixteen acres, paid the money, and had the papers made out before the owner had time to recover from his surprise.

Work was begun on the building the following year. It was intended to establish this school as a high-class seminary for girls. When it was opened in 1879, twenty-five pupils entered. At first they studied and recited at Mr. Moody's home, the first dormitory not being opened until 1880. Bonar Hall, the second dormitory, was burned a few years later, but Marquand Hall was opened in 1885. Other buildings have followed. At present the school possesses seven dormitories, a library, a gymnasium, a recitation hall and an auditorium.

The buildings have been erected with a view to artistic effect as well as adequate accomodations, and add much to the beauty of the situation. From the slopes of the school grounds, one looks up the river valley to the distant green hills of Vermont and New Hampshire, while the placid river meanders through fertile fields which show rich with the fruits of the farm. Well built roads wind through the grounds; shade trees and groups of shrubbery have been set out. Moreover, the land yields practical returns as a farm under the supervision of Mr. Moody's brother. Six horses and fifty head of cattle belong to this school farm, and from ten to fourteen men are constantly employed. The school now numbers about four hundred pupils, its graduates being admitted to Wellesley, Smith and other high-grade institutions.

The Mt. Hermon School For Boys

When Mr. Moody was conducting his earliest mission work in Chicago, he laid close to his heart a plan to provide some day a school where boys could secure training in the elementary branches and the Bible. With this still in mind he purchased, in 1880, two farms of 115 acres each, with two farm-houses and barns. They were situated on what was known as Grass Hill, four miles from Northfield Seminary, and in the town of Gill. This school was incorporated as the Mt. Hermon School for Boys. The present buildings include five brick cottages, a large recitation hall, a dining hall and kitchen, Crossley Hall and Silliman Science Hall. This school uow numbers about 400 students, and here, as at the Seminary the industrial system is a prominent feature, but at Mt. Hermon nearly all of the work of the farm and house is done by the boys.

The auditorium of the Northfield Seminary was built in 1894 and was planned by Mr. Moody for the use of the summer conferences. It seats nearly 3,000 persons. A grove of white birches on a hillside back of the Seminary becomes, during the summer meetings "Camp Northfield", where young men spend their summer outing periods.

Henry Drummond describes somewhere his first astonishment at finding this little New England hamlet with a dozen of the finest educational buildings in America, and of his surprise when he stopped to think that all these buildings owed their existence to a man whose name is perhaps associated in the minds of three-fourths of his countrymen, not with education, but with the want of it.

The Character of the Town

The eastern part of the town has of late years become known as East Northfield, and has its separate Post Office and stores. New streets have been laid out and new houses have been built. Northfield, in fact, is coming to be known as a summer resort, but not of the usual type. Frivolous recreation gives way there to sane occupation and wholesome exercise. Intemperance, the use of tobacco, card playing and dancing have no place there; but the heart of nature is opened to those, who, with minds bent upon the best things, seek her reverently.

Northfield then is both a typical New England town and the result of the individual impression of one man's life. All that is best in American culture is there epitomized, and the elms and the hazy hills and the homes of by-gone generations are witnesses of the regenerating influences which can be brought into play through the devotion and singleness of purpose of one man.

CHAPTER III

His Early Life.

DWIGHT LYMAN MOODY was born in the town of Northfield, Mass., February 5, 1837. He was the sixth of seven sons who, with two daughters, made up the family of Edwin and Betsy Holton Moody. The father had acquired a little farmhouse and a few acres of stony ground on a hillside just without the limits of the town, but the whole was encumbered by mortgage. Mr. Moody worked as a stonemason when the opportunity was afforded, using his leisure time to till his farm. The burden of his responsibilities proved to heavy; reverses crushed his spirit; and, after an illness of only a few hours, he died suddenly at the age of forty-one years, when Dwight was only four years old, leaving a large family unprovided for.

A Sudden Upheaval of the Family

Young as he was, the picture impressed on the boy's mind by this sudden upheaval of the household, consequent upon his father's death, remained vivid. He did not forget the desperate feeling which must have seized the family in that crisis; nor did he ever forget the wonderful fortitude with which his mother met the situation. Only a month after the death of the father two posthumous children were born—a boy and a girl. Neighbors advised Mrs. Moody not to attempt to face the harsh conditions now confronting her. "Keep your twin babies, but bind out your other children," they urged. "It will be so long before they can be of any real service to you that their maintenance just now will be a greater burden than you should assume."

But Mrs. Moody was not the woman to be daunted by circumstances. The idea of separating from her children was not entertained. She took upon herself the task of snatching some tribute money from an unwilling soil, and of bringing up her children to wholesome manhood and womanhood—how well she succeeded is shown by the results.

One Calamity After Another

One incident of this early period proved a severe blow to the bereaved family. The oldest son, upon whom the mother was planning to place considerable dependence, ran away from home. Mr. Moody in later years related this incident and its sequel in the following words:

"I can give you a little experience of my own family. Before I was four years old the first thing I remember was the death of my father. He had been unfortunate in business and failed. Soon after his death the creditors came in and took everything. My mother was left with a large family of children. One calamity after another swept over the entire household. Twins were added to the family, and my mother was taken sick. The eldest boy was fifteen years of age, and to him my mother looked as a stay in her calamity, but all at once that boy became a wanderer. He had been reading some of the trashy novels and the belief had seized him that he had only to go away to make a fortune. Away he went. I can remember how eagerly she used to look for tidings of that boy; how she used to send us to the postoffice to see if there was a letter from him, and recollect how we used to come back with the sad news, 'No letter.' I remember how in the evenings we used to sit beside her in that New England home, and we would talk about our father; but the moment the name of that boy was mentioned she would hush us into silence. Some nights when the wind was very high, and the house, which was upon a hill, would tremble at every gust, the voice of my mother was raised in prayer for that wanderer who had treated her so unkindly. I used to think she loved him more than all of us put together, and I believe she did. On a Thanksgiving day—you know that is a family day in New England—she used to set a chair for him, thinking he would return home.

His Brother Home Again

Her family grew up and her boys left home. When I got so that I could write, I sent letters all over the country, but could find no trace of him. One day, while in Boston, the news reached me that he had returned. While in that city, I remember how I used to look for him in every store—he had a mark on his face—but I never got any trace. One day while my mother was sitting at the door, a stranger was seen coming toward the house, and when he came to the door he stopped. My mother didn't know her boy. He stood there with folded arms and great beard flowing down his breast, his tears trickling down his face. When my mother saw those tears she cried, 'Oh, it is my lost son,' and entreated him to come in. But he stood still. 'No, mother,' he said, 'I will not come in until I hear first that you have forgiven me.' Do you believe she was not willing to forgive him? Do you think she was likely to keep him standing there. She rushed to the threshold, threw her arms around him and breathed forgiveness."

The Moody family were Unitarians. Dwight had the early advantages of Christian training, attending, as soon as he was old enough, the church in the village, where the Rev. Mr. Everett was pastor. In his interest in the efforts of Mrs. Moody to earn a livelihood for her large family, Mr. Everett once took Dwigth into his family for a time, in order that he might attend school, making return for this privilege by running errands and doing chores. It may seem strange that a Unitarian training should have fostered a temperament which afterward became, in its expression, so purely evangelical. By way of explanation, it is said, that Mr. Everett was not one of those who questioned the divinity of our Saviour. Unorthodoxy had not as yet affected this church. The Bible as the Word of God, Jesus as the Son of God, the Church and its Sacraments—these were accepted beliefs of this country pastor.

Dwight also had the benefits of religious training in the home. Mrs. Moody early taught her children to learn passages of Scripture and verses of hymns. These she would recite at her frugal table, and the children would repeat them after her.

Incidents From Moody's Early Days

When Dwight was about six years old, an old rail fence one day fell upon him. He could not lift the heavy rails. Exhausted by his efforts, he had almost given up. "Then," as he afterward told the story, "I happened to think that maybe God would help me, and so I asked Him; and after that I could lift the rails,"

Another incident, which Mr. Moody has related, seems to have made so profound an impression upon his youthful mind that its influence in preparing his heart for the Gospel message cannot have been slight. He himself has related the story in these words:

"When I was a young boy—before I was a Christian—I was in a field one day with a man who was hoeing. He was weeping, and he told me a strange story, which I have never forgotten. When he left home his mother gave him this text: 'Seek first the kingdom of God.' But he paid no heed to it. He said when he got settled in life, and his ambition to get money was gratified, it

DWIGHT L. MOODY, from a photograph taken in Boston just after he left home to make his way in the world. Photographed from a picture hanging in the house of Mrs. Fitt, Mr. Moody's only daughter.

would be time enough then to seek the kingdom of God. He went from one village to another and got nothing to do. When Sunday came he went into a village church, and what was his great surprise to hear the minister give out the text, "Seek first the kingdom of God." He said the text went down to the bottom of his heart. He thought it was but his mother's prayer following him, and that some one must have written to that minister about him. He felt very uncomfortable, and when the meeting was over he could not get that sermon out of his mind.

Again "Seek First the Kingdom of God"

He went away from that town, and at the end of a week went into another church, and he heard the minister give out the same text, 'Seek first the kingdom of God.' He felt sure this time that it was the prayers of his mother, but he said calmly and deliberately, 'No, I will first get wealthy.' He said he went on and did not go into a church for a few months, but the first place of worship he went into he heard a minister preaching a sermon from the same text. He tried to drown—to stifle his feelings; tried to get the sermon out of his mind, and resolved that he would keep away from church altogether, and for a few years he did keep out of God's house. 'My mother died,' he said, 'and the text kept coming up in my mind, and I said I will try and become a Christian.' The tears rolled down his cheeks, as he said, 'I could not; no sermon ever touched me; my heart is as hard as that stone,' pointing to one in the field.' I couldn't understand what it was all about—it was fresh to me then. I went to Boston and got converted, and the first thought that came to me was about this man. When I got back I asked mother, 'Is Mr. L—— living in such a place?' 'Didn't I write to you about him?' she asked. They have taken him to an insane asylum, and to every one who goes there he points with his finger up there and tells them to seek first the kingdom of God. There was that man with his eyes dull with the loss of reason, but the text had sunk into his soul—it had burned down deep. O, may the Spirit of God burn the text into your hearts to-night, When I got home again my mother told me he was in his house, and I went to see him. I found him in a rocking chair, with that vacant, idiotic look upon him. As soon as he saw me, he pointed at me and said: 'Young man, seek first the kingdom of God.' Reason was gone but the text was there. Last month, when I was laying my brother down in his grave, I could not help thinking of that poor man who was lying so near him, and wishing that the prayer of his mother had been heard, and that he had found the kingdom of God."

It is doubtful, however, if young Moody had experienced any real religious feeling up to the time of his conversion in Boston. He was a boy like other boys—unlike the majority, too, in his imperious will, his indifference to obstacles, his boundless energy. He was as fond of mischief as the average boy. The influences of a farm-boy's life, tempered though they were by the forceful direction of a devoted mother, were not calculated to cultivate in him a taste for the finer things of life. His passionate outbursts of temper are still remembered by those who early came into contact with him. His profanity is a matter of his own record. Still, he was doubtless in this regard merely a type of his environment. The notable thing about the boy was his force; he bore in his endowment great possibilities for good or ill.

His Early Education

Perhaps only twelve terms at the district school constituted Dwight's early education. A smattering of "the three R's," a little geography, and the practice of declamation made up the sum of his learning. The truth of the matter seems to be that he did not study faithfully. It was only during his last term that he began to apply himself with diligence, too late to make up for what he had lost. His reading is described as outlandish beyond description. With his characteristic tendency to jump directly to the heart of a question, he never stopped to spell out an unfamiliar word, but mouthed his sense of it without full dependence upon his training, or made up a new word which sounded to his ear as suitable as the original.

Of his experiences as a schoolboy Mr. Moody has given the following in his sermon on " Law *versus* Grace :"

"The Law Party and the Grace Party"

"At the school I used to go to when I was a boy, we had a teacher who believed in governing by law. He used to keep a rattan in his desk, and my back tingles now [shrugging his shoulders] as I think of it. But after a while the notion got abroad among the people that a school might be governed by love, and the district was divided into what I might call the law party, and the grace party; the law party standing by the old schoolmaster, with his rattan, and the grace party wanting a teacher who could get along without punishing so much.

"After a while the grace party got the upper hand, turned out the old master, and hired a young lady to take his place. We all understood that there was to be no rattan that winter, and we looked forward to having the jolliest kind of a time. On the first morning the new teacher, whom I will call Miss Grace, opened the school with reading out of the Bible and prayer. That was a new thing, and we didn't quite know what to make of it. She told us she didn't mean to keep order by punishment, but she hoped we would all be good children, for her sake as well as our own. This made us a little ashamed of the mischief we had meant to do, and everything went on pretty well for a few days; but pretty soon I broke one of the rules, and Miss Grace said I was to stop that night after school. Now for the old rattan, said I to myself; it's coming now after all. But when the scholars were all gone she came and sat down by me, and told me how sorry she was that I, who was one of the biggest boys, and might help her so much, was setting such a bad example to others, and making it so hard for her to get along with them. She said she loved us, and wanted to help us, and if we loved her we would obey her, and then everything would go on well. There were tears in her eyes as she said this, and I didn't know what to make of it, for no teacher had ever talked that way to me before. I began to feel ashamed of myself for being so mean to any one who was so kind; and after that she didn't have any more trouble with me, nor with any of the other scholars either. She just took us out from under the Law and put us under Grace."

Departure From Home

The circumstances which led up to the departure of young Moody from home have been variously stated. He had come to the age of seventeen. In those days a boy of seventeen was supposed to be ready to enter upon the serious business of life. New ambitions were arising in Dwight's heart. Mr. Edward Kimball, who afterwards led the boy to the Lord, is perhaps as well informed of the circumstances of his life in Boston as any man now living. He gave the facts as he was familiar with them at the time of Mr. Moody's death.

"To tell the story correctly," said Mr. Kimball, "I must go back to Thanksgiving day forty-five years ago. A Thanksgiving family dinner party was assembled at the Moody home, which was on a farm a mile and a half from Northfield, Mass. At the table, among others, were Samuel and Lemuel Holton, of Boston, two uncles of the Moody children. Without any preliminary warning young Dwight, a boy of about seventeen, spoke up and said to his uncle Samuel: "Uncle, I want to come to Boston and have a place in your shoe store. Will you take me?" Despite the directness of the question, the uncle returned to Boston without giving his nephew an answer. When Mr. Holton asked advice in the matter from an older brother of Dwight, the brother told his uncle that perhaps he had better not take the boy, for in a short time Dwight would want to run his store.

Young Moody Looking For a Job

"Dwight was a headstrong young fellow who would not study at school, and who was much fonder of a practical joke than he was of his books. His expressed desire to go to Boston and get work was not a jest that the boy forgot the day after Thanksgiving. The two uncles were surprised when one day in the following spring Dwight turned up in Boston looking for a job. His uncle Samuel did not offer him a place. Dwight, when asked how he thought he could get a start, said he wanted work and he guessed he could find a position. After days of efforts, and meeting nothing but failures the boy grew discouraged with Boston, and told his uncle Lemuel he was going to New York. The uncle strongly advised Dwight not to go, but to speak to his uncle Samuel again about the matter. The boy demurred, saying his uncle Samuel knew perfectly well what he wanted. But the uncle insisted so that a second time the boy asked his uncle Samuel for a place in his store.

"'Dwight, I am afraid if you come in here you will want to run the store yourself,' said Mr. Holton. 'Now, my men here want to do their work as I want it done. If you want to come in here and do the best you can, and do it right, and if you'll ask me when you don't know how to do anything, or if I am not here, ask the bookkeeper, and if he's not here one of the salesmen or one of the boys, and if you are willing to go to church and Sunday school when you are able to go anywhere on Sundays, and if you are willing not to go anywhere at night or any other time which you would not want me or your mother to know about, why, then, if you'll promise all these things, you may come and take hold, and we'll see how we can get along. You can have till Monday to think it over.'

"'I don't want till Monday,' said Dwight; I'll promise now.' And young Moody began to work in his uncle's shoe store.

"A remark the boy's uncle made to me afterward will give an idea of the young man's lack of education at this time. The uncle said that when Dwight read his Bible out loud he couldn't make anything more out of it than he could out of the chattering of a lot of blackbirds. Many of the words were so far beyond the boy that he left them out entirely when he read, and the majority of the others he mangled fearfully.'

CHAPTER IV.

His Mother.

DEVOTION to his mother was a duty and a privilege second only to devotion to his God, in the mind of Mr. Moody.

When at home in Northfield, he never failed to look in upon his mother in her cottage early every morning, to give her a hearty greeting, and to see that she was provided with every comfort and many luxuries.

When away, no matter how many times a day he preached, nor how many informal meetings he personally conducted, a letter was posted to his mother at frequent intervals in which she was told at length of the success of the meetings.

A Picture Never to be Forgotten

During the last years of her life, when failing health prevented her from attending public worship, the devoted son never forgot the aged mother, and he often arranged for her to hear the noted speakers and singers of the conferences.

There is one picture associated with Northfield I can never forget. It had to do with one of the summer conferences. Some one had been asking about Mr. Moody's mother, and he had spoken to a few of those who gathered about him and said, "We might have a little service just at her house on the lawn, for she is not able to be out;" and so a number of distinguished Christian workers gathered just outside her window, sang the hymn she loved, prayed God's special blessing upon her and her distinguished son, and then one after the other spoke some word of appreciation of their visit to Northfield. I was standing just by Mr. Moody's side, and I heard him say to one of his friends, "I always thought she had such a beautiful face," and as he looked at her the tears started in his own eyes, rolled down his cheeks, and he said with much emotion to a distinguished English Christian standing by his side, "I think she has been the best mother in the world."

His Mother's Blessing

Once again when many young men were gathered from all over the eastern part of our country in the World's Students' Conference, Mr. Moody said:

"You know my mother is an old lady. She is too feeble to attend these meetings. She is deeply interested in this work, and she has prayed earnestly for its success. I want her to hear some of you speak and sing. We are going up the mountain this afternoon to pray for the baptism of the Holy Spirit. Meet me at my house at three o'clock. We will have a little service there, and then I want you to go on to my mother's home, and I want some of you to speak, and we will all sing.

"I want you to receive my mother's blessing before we go to the mountains to pray, for next to the blessing of God I place that of my mother."

The three hundred anxious pilgrims who gathered on Mr. Moody's spacious lawn that afternoon, and who, after a brief service of song and prayer, journeyed on to the mother's cottage and later to the mountain top, presented a picture never to be forgotten by the members of that company.

Much that is here written is his own words concerning her.

"I have an old mother away down in the Connecticut Mountains," Mr. Moody used to say, "and I have been in the habit of

D. L. MOODY'S MOTHER. Photograph taken on her 90th birthday.

D. L. MOODY'S GRANDMOTHER. Photograph made in 1856.

going to see her every year for twenty years. Suppose I go there and say, 'Mother, you were very kind to me when I was young—you were very good to me; when father died you worked hard for us all to keep us together, and so I have come to see you, because it is my duty.' Then she would say to me, 'Well, my son, if you only come to see me, because it is your duty, you need not come again.' And that is the way with a great many servants of God. They work for Him, because it is their duty—not for love. Let us abolish this word *duty*, and feel that it is only a privilege to work for God, and let us try to remember that what is done merely from a sense of duty is not acceptable to God."

And so it was. Year after year, in the very heat of those spiritual campaigns which brought him prominently before the people of the two continents, Mr. Moody would slip away regularly to the spot where, amid the serene surroundings of the Northfield hills, his mother sat with her thoughts upon him and his work, praising God who had permitted her boy to become the instrument of so much blessing.

Her Puritan Ancestry

Betsey Holton, the mother of Dwight L. Moody, was a descendant in the fifth generation of William Holton, one of the first settlers of Northfield. In fact, this ancestor was one of that committee of the General Council of Massachusetts which laid out the plantation of Northfield, after it had been purchased from the Indians in 1673. The marriage of Betsey Holton to Edwin Moody united two strains of old Puritan blood. Doubtless this lineage accounts in no slight degree for the restless energy and dogged earnestness of the son, Dwight.

"I always thought that Dwight would be one thing or the other," the dear old woman once remarked. Where others had failed to see, she had early recognized the hardiness of the boy's character,

—a hardiness which she must have seen through its very kinship with her own. For her schooling had not been easy. Left a widow with nine children, a small house, and an acre or so of heavily mortgaged land, she had taken upon her womanly shoulders the full responsibility of bringing up her family. Tilling the ground, and doing odd jobs for the neighbors, she continued to scrape together enough to keep her children fed and clothed, although the margin between plenty and want was frequently so slim as to bar out comfort. There were times when no food seemed forthcoming; but a Providence whose care extends even to the sparrows did not permit the burden to become too heavy for this widowed mother, although her resources were often taxed to the utmost.

Young Moody at the Village School

Every day she taught the children a little Bible lesson, and on Sundays accompanied them to the Unitarian Sunday school. They were sent, too, to the village school. Dwight was as loth as the average young boy to endure the discipline of the school-room. It is not hard to picture him "with shining morning face, creeping like snail unwillingly to school." But the wise mother knew. Seeds were being scattered in the fertile heart and mind of the boy; and if they did not seem to sprout at once, perhaps it was for the very reason that they had not been sown in a shallow soil.

The Rev. Dr. Theodore Cuyler, when he first met Mrs. Moody, turned to her son, and said, "I see now where you got your vim and your hard sense!" Others remarked the same resemblance of the son to his mother. I speak of this merely to make it evident how much he owed her.

However completely she came into sympathy with her son's work in later years, at the outset of his labors his mother did not give him her sanction. She herself was a member of a nonevangelical church. For a long time she did not even hear her son preach. How he finally not only convinced her of his fitness for his work, but also became the means of leading her into the higher life has been related by a close friend of the family in the following words:

His Mother's Conversion

"In 1875 he returned to his home in Northfield to preach, shortly after coming back to America from one or his great London successes. The family still lived on the old farm, and still drove to town to Sunday meeting in the old farm wagon, just as they used to do in the days gone by. Most of the members of the family were going to drive to town that morning to hear Dwight preach. The mother startled a daughter by saying to her:

"'I don't suppose there would be room in the wagon for me this morning, would there?'

"No one had ever thought of the mother unbending and going to hear her son.

"'Of course there will be room, mother,' said the daughter.

"And the mother was taken down to the church with the rest. Mr. Moody preached from the fifty-first Psalm, and preached with a fervor that was probably inspired by the presence of his mother. When those who wished prayer were asked to arise, old Mrs. Moody stood up.

"The son was completely overcome, and, turning to B. F. Jacobs, now of Chicago, said with emotion, 'You pray, Jacobs, I can't.'"

When he returned to Northfield after some evangelical tour, Mr. Moody would invariably drive directly to see his mother, to receive her welcome, even before joining his immediate family. Sitting in her sunny room the kindly, keen, old lady would give to her son kernels of sound wisdom with the blessing of her approval.

She was permitted to remain in this world until her ninety-first year. When at the last she began to sink, it was not thought by those about her that there was any immediate danger, and Mr. Moody, who was at the time conducting services in a distant city, was not informed as to the state of her health. But toward the close of a week of meetings the evangelist grew restless. He felt a strange intuition that his presence was needed at home, and, for no other reason, he canceled his engagement and started for Northfield. He arrived in time to receive her blessing.

At his mother's funeral, acting upon an impulse, Mr. Moody delivered a touching tribute to her memory. Mrs. William R. Moody had concluded her song "Crossing the Bar," when the evangelist rose from his place with the family, and, bearing in his hands the old family Bible, and a worn book of devotions, came forward. Standing by the body of his mother, he said:

His Tribute to His Mother

"It is not the custom, perhaps, for a son to take part in such an occasion. If I can control myself I would like to say a few words. It is a great honor to be the son of such a mother. I do not know where to begin; I could not praise her enough. In the first place my mother was a very wise woman. In one sense she was wiser than Solomon; she knew how to bring up her children. She had nine children and they all loved their home. She won their hearts, their affections, she could do anything with them.

"Whenever I wanted real sound counsel I used to go to my mother. I have traveled a good deal and seen a good many mothers, but I never saw one who had such tact as she had. She so bound her children to her that it was a great calamity to have to leave home. I had two brothers that lived in Kansas and died there. Their great longing was to get back to their mother. My brother who died in Kansas a short time ago had been looking over the Greenfield papers for some time to see if he could not buy a farm in this locality. He had a good farm there, but he was never satisfied; he wanted to get back to mother. That is the way she won them to herself. I have heard something within the last forty-eight hours that nearly broke my heart. I merely mention it to show what a character she was. My eldest sister, her oldest daughter, told me that the first year after my father died she wept herself to sleep every night. Yet, she was always bright and cheerful in the presence of her children, and they never knew anything about it. Her sorrows drove her to Him, and in her own room, after we were asleep, I would wake up and hear her praying, and sometimes I would hear her weeping. She would be sure her children were all asleep before she would pour out her tears.

It is a Great Thing to Have Such a Mother

"And there was another thing remarkable about my mother. If she loved one child more than another, no one ever found it out. Isaiah, he was her first boy; she could not get along without Isaiah. And Cornelia, she was her first girl; she could not get along without Cornelia, for she had to take care of the twins. And George, she couldn't live without George. What could she ever have done without George? He staid right by her through thick and thin. She couldn't live without George. And Edwin, he bore the name of her husband. And Dwight, I don't know what she thought of him. And Luther, he was the dearest of all, because he had to go away to live. He was always homesick to get back to mother. And Warren, he was the youngest when father died; it seemed as if he was dearer than all the rest. And Sam and Lizzie, the twins, they were the light of her great sorrow.

She never complained of her children. It is a great thing to have such a mother, and I feel like standing up here to-day to praise her. And just here I want to say before I forget it, you don't know how she appreciated the kindness which was shown her in those days of early struggle. Sometimes I would come home and say, such a man did so and so, and she would say, 'Don't say that, Dwight; he was kind to me.'

"The Biggest Load of Wood I Ever Saw"

"My father died a bankrupt, and the creditors came and swept everything we had. They took everything, even the kindling wood; and there came on a snowstorm, and the next morning mother said we would have to stay in bed until school-time, because there was no wood to make a fire. Then, all at once, I heard some one chopping wood, and it was my Uncle Sam. I tell you I have always had a warm heart for that uncle for that act. And that night there came the biggest load of wood I ever saw in my life. It took two yoke of oxen to draw it. It was that uncle that brought it. That act followed me all through life, and a good many acts, in fact. Mr. Everett, the pastor of the Unitarian Church, I remember how kind he was in those days. I want to testify to-day how my mother appreciated that.

"I remember the first thing I did to earn money was to turn the neighbor's cows up on Strowbridge Mountain. I got a cent a week for it. I never thought of spending it on myself. It was to go to mother. It went into the common treasury. And I remember when George got work we asked who was going to milk the cows. Mother said she would milk. She also made our clothes, and wove the cloth, and spun the yarn, and darned our stockings; and there was never any complaining.

"I thought so much of my mother I cannot say half enough. That dear face! There was no sweeter face on earth. Fifty years I have been coming back and was always glad to get back. When I got within fifty miles of home I always grew restless and walked up and down the car. It seemed to me as if the train would never get to Northfield. For sixty-eight years she has lived on that hill, and when I came back after dark, I always looked to see the light in mother's window.

In Time to Receive Her Blessing

"When I got home last Sunday night—I was going to take the four o'clock train from New York and get here at twelve; I had some business to do; but I suppose it was the good Lord that sent me; I took the twelve o'clock train and got here at five—I went in to my mother. I was so glad I got back in time to be recognized. I said, 'Mother, do you know me?' She said, 'I guess I do.' I like that word, that Yankee word 'guess.' The children were all with her when she was taking her departure. At last I called, 'Mother, mother.' No answer. She had fallen asleep; but I shall call her again by-and-by. Friends, it is not a time of mourning. I want you to understand we do not mourn. We are proud that we had such a mother. We have a wonderful legacy left us.

"One day mother sent for me. I went to see what she wanted, and she said she wanted to divide her things. I said, 'Well, mother, we don't want anything you've got; we want you. We have got you, and that's all we want.' 'Yes, but I want to do something.' I said to her, 'Then write out what you want, and I will carry it out.' That didn't satisfy her. Finally she said, 'Dwight, I want them all to have something.' That was my mother, and that was the way she bound us to her.

"Now, I have brought the old Bible, the family Bible, for it all came from that book. That is about the only book we had in the house when father died, and out of the book she taught us. And if my mother has been a blessing to this world, it is because she drank at this fountain. I have read twice at family worship, and will read here a few verses which she has marked.

Verses She Marked

"'Who can find a virtuous woman? for her price is far above rubies. The heart of her husband doth safely trust in her.'

"She has been a widow for fifty-four years, and yet she loved her husband the day she died as much as she ever did. I never heard one word, and she never taught her children to do anything but just reverence our father. She loved him right up to the last.

"'She seeketh wool and flax, and worketh willingly with her hands.'

"That is my mother.

"'She considereth a field and buyeth it; with the fruit of her hands she planteth a vineyard. She girdeth her loins with strength and strengtheneth her arms. She perceiveth that her merchandise is good, her candle goeth not out by night.'

"Widow Moody's light had burned on that hill for fifty-four years, in that one room. We built a room for her, where she could be more comfortable, but she was not often there. There was just one room where she wanted to be. Her children were born there, her first sorrow came there, and that was where God had met her. That is the place she liked to stay, where her children liked to meet her, where she worked and toiled and wept.

"'She stretcheth out her hands to the poor; yea, she reacheth forth her hands to the needy.'

"Now, there is one thing about my mother, she never turned away any poor from her home. There was one time we got down

THE MOODY FAMILY, showing the mother, brothers and sisters of the great evangelist. Photographed from a picture hanging in Mr Moody's house Dec. 1899.

to less than a loaf of bread. Some one came along hungry, and she says, 'Now, children, shall I cut your slices a little thinner and give some to this person?' And we all voted for her to do it. That is the way she taught us.

"'She is not afraid of the snow for her household; for all her household are clothed with scarlet.'

"She would let the neighbors' boys in all over the house, and track in snow; and when there was going to be a party she would say, 'Who will stay with me? I will be all alone; why don't you ask them to come here?' In that way she kept them all at home, and knew where her children were. The door was never locked at night until she knew they were all in bed, safe and secure. Nothing was too hard for her if she could only spare her children.

I Honor Her for the Punishment I Got

"The seven boys were like Hannibal, whose mother took him to the altar and made him swear vengeance on Rome. She took us to the altar and made us swear vengeance on whiskey, and everything that was an enemy to the human family; and we have been fighting it ever since and will to the end of our days.

"My mother used to punish me. I honor her for that. I do not object to punishment. She used to send me out to get a stick. It would take a long time to get it, and then I used to get a dead stick if I could. She would try it and, if it would break easily, then I had to go and get another. She was not in a hurry and did not tell me to hurry, because she knew all the time that I was being punished. I would go out and be gone a long time. When I came in, she would tell me to take off my coat, and then she would put the birch on; and I remember once I said, 'That doesn't hurt.' She put it on all the harder, and I never said that the second time. And once in awhile she would take me and she would say, 'You know I would rather put this on myself than to put it on you.' I would look up and see tears in her eyes. That was enough for me.

"What more can I say? You have lived with her and you know her. I want to give you one verse, her creed. Her creed was very short. Do you know what it was? I will tell you what it was. When everything went against her, this was her stay, 'My trust is in God. My trust is in God.' And when the neighbors would come in and tell her to bind out her children, she would say, 'Not as long as I have these two hands.' 'Well,' they would say, 'you know one woman cannot bring up seven boys; they will turn up in jail, or with a rope around their necks.' She toiled on, and none of us went to jail, and none of us has had a rope around his neck. And if every one had a mother like that mother, if the world was mothered by that kind of mothers, there would be no use for jails.

"Here is a book (a little book of devotions); this and the Bible were about all the books she had in those days; and every morning she would stand us up and read out of this book. All through the book I find things marked.

"Every Saturday night—we used to begin to observe the Sabbath at sundown Saturday night, and at sundown Sunday night we would run out and throw up our caps and let off our jubilant spirits—this is what she would give us Saturday night, and it has gone with me through life. Not all of it, I could not remember it all:

> 'How pleasant it is on Saturday night
> When I've tried all the week to be good.'

"And on Sunday she always started us off to Sunday school. It was not a debatable question whether we should go or not. All the family attended.

"I do not know, of course, we do not know, whether the departed ones are conscious of what is going on on earth. If I knew that she was I would send a message that we are coming after her. If I could, I believe I would send a message after her, not only for the family, and the town, but for the Seminary. She was always so much interested in the young ladies of the Seminary. She seemed to be as young as any of them, and entered into the joys of the young people just as much as any one. I want to say to the young ladies of the Seminary, who acted as maids of honor to escort my mother down to the church this morning, that I want you to trust my mother's Saviour.

"I want to say to the young men of Mt. Hermon, you are going to have a great honor to escort mother to her last resting-place. Her prayers for you ascended daily to the throne of grace. Now, I am going to give you the best I have; I am going to do the best I can; I am going to lay her away with her face toward Hermon.

"She Was True as Sunlight"

"I think she is one of the noblest characters this world has ever seen. She was true as sunlight; I never knew that woman to deceive me.

"I want to thank Dr. Scofield for the comforting words he has brought us to-day. It is a day of rejoicing, not of regret. She went without pain, without a struggle, just like a person going to sleep. And now we are to lay her body away to await His coming in resurrection power. When I see her in the morning she is to have a glorious body. The body Moses had on the Mount of Transfiguration was a better body than God buried on Pisgah. When we see Elijah he will have a glorious body. That dear mother, when I see her again, is going to have a glorified body. [Looking at her face] God bless you, mother; we love you still. Death has only increased our love. Good-bye for a little while, mother. Let us pray."

CHAPTER V.

His Conversion.

DWIGHT L. MOODY was not the boy to forget his compact with his uncle. He went to church every Sunday—because he had promised to go,—attending the Mount Vernon Congregational Church, of which the Rev. Dr. E. N. Kirk was pastor.

Dr. Kirk was an excellent preacher, but young Moody was at a stage where all sermons sounded alike to him. Frequently he would fall asleep during service, at least until an occasion when he was suddenly awakened from his complete repose by a stern-faced deacon, who, as he roused the lad from his slumbers, pointed to Dr. Kirk, who was preaching—as much as to say, "Keep your eyes on him!" Thereafter Dwight remained awake. Moreover, for lack of something else to do, he began to listen to the sermons. "For the first time in my life," he said in later days, "I felt as if the preacher were preaching altogether at me."

His First Acquaintance with Mr. E. D. Kimball

One Sunday the young man appeared in the Sunday school of Mount Vernon Church. The superintendent, Mr. Palmer, to whom he gave his name, took him to the class taught by Mr. Edward D. Kimball, and he took his seat among the other boys. Says Mr. Kimball, "I handed him a closed Bible and told him the lesson was in John. The boy took the book and began running over the leaves with his finger away at the first of the volume looking for John. Out of the corners of their eyes the boys saw what he was doing and, detecting his ignorance glanced slyly and knowingly at one another, but not rudely. I gave the boys just one hasty glance of reproof. That was enough—their equanimity was restored immediately. I quietly handed Moody my own book, open at the right place, and took his. I did not suppose the boy could possibly have noticed the glances exchanged between the other boys over his ignorance, but it seems from remarks in later years that he did, and he said in reference to my little act in exchanging books that he would stick by the fellow who had stood by him and had done him a turn like that."

This Sunday school teacher was not one of the ordinary type. Mere literal instruction on Sunday did not satisfy his ideal of the teacher's duty. He knew his boys, and, if he knew them, it was because he studied them, because he became acquainted with their occupations and aims, visiting them during the week. It was his custom, moreover, to find opportunity to give to his boys an opportunity to use his experience in seeking the better things of the Spirit. The day came when he resolved to speak to young Moody about Christ, and about his soul.

Just Ready for the Light

"I started down town to Holton's shoe store," says Mr. Kimball. "When I was nearly there, I began to wonder whether I ought to go just then, during business hours. And I thought maybe my mission might embarass the boy, that when I went away the other clerks might ask who I was, and when they learned might taunt Moody and ask if I was trying to make a good boy out of him. While I was pondering over it all, I passed the store without noticing it. Then when I found I had gone by the door, I determined to make a dash for it and have it over at once. I found Moody in the back part of the store wrapping up shoes in paper and putting them on shelves. I went up to him and put my hand on his shoulder, and as I leaned over I placed my foot upon a shoe box. Then I made my plea, and I feel that it was really a very weak one. I don't know just what words I used, nor could Mr. Moody tell. I simply told him of Christ's love for him and the love Christ wanted in return. That was all there was of it. I think Mr. Moody said afterward that there were tears in my eyes. It seemed that the young man was just ready for the light that then broke upon him, for there at once in the back of that shoe store in Boston the future great evangelist gave himself and his life to Christ."

Many years afterward Mr. Moody himself told the story of that day. "When I was in Boston," he said, "I used to attend a Sunday school class, and one day I recollect my teacher came around behind the counter of the shop I was at work in, and put his hand upon my shoulder, and talked to me about Christ and my soul. I had not felt that I had a soul till then. I said to myself: 'This is a very strange thing. Here is a man who never saw me till lately, and he is weeping over my sins, and I never shed a tear about them.' But I understand it now, and know what it is to have a passion for men's souls and weep over their sins. I don't remember what he said, but I can feel the power of that man's hand on my shoulder to-night. It was not long after that I was brought into the Kingdom of God."

Applies for Admission into the Church.

One of his first steps after his conversion was to apply for admission into the Mount Vernon Church.

It is frequently stated that after his application for membership in the Mount Vernon Church, he was looked upon so unfavorably as a candidate that he was kept waiting for a year before he was granted admission. It has also been said, that even after his acceptance by the church his remarks in the church meetings were so far from edifying that his pastor was obliged to suggest to him, that he could serve the Lord much more acceptably by keeping silence.

While there is a foundation of truth in these statements, they must not be taken too literally. Mr. Moody was undoubtedly at that time ignorant of many of the most important reasons of his profession; but Dr. Kirk's church was a revival church, and his spirit was not such as to deny the opportunities of grace to any one who deserved them. The Rev. Dr. James M. Buckley, editor of the *Christian Advocate*, has written quite exhaustively on this matter. He has said:

"Those sympathizing with his [Dr. Kirk's] peculiar work, gathered about him. Among them were such men as Julius Palmer, the brother of Dr. Ray Palmer, the author of 'My Faith Looks Up to Thee'; he was one of the deacons, and all the rest had the same sympathies. Mr. Kimball was not only Mr. Moody's Sunday school teacher, and, as Mr. Moody expressly informed us, the means of his conversion, but was also one of the examining committee. But the Mount Vernon Church did not receive a person who could not furnish evidence that he was converted, even if he was perfectly orthodox in doctrine.

True Evidence.

"About the time Mr. Moody was converted, a young man came from Scotland with a letter from a Presbyterian church. He could repeat the Shorter Catechism, answer all doctrinal questions glibly, but when he was asked of his position before God as a sinner and his conscious relation to Christ as a Saviour, he knew nothing of it and made no reply, except that 'such questions were never asked him before'. He confessed that he had simply 'joined' because he was advised and expected to do so. This young man was advised to wait, and brethren were appointed to try to arouse in him a consciousness of his need of a Saviour and of a work of grace, and to point him to the Lamb of God. About the same time, a young woman applied who was wholly in the dark on 'doctrines'; tender, tearful, hesitating, distrustful of herself, she could not tell why she thought herself a Christian, but could only say that she loved Christ and the prayer meeting. One of the committee said, 'Do you love God's people because they are His?' Her face brightened, and she said, 'O, sir, is that an evidence?' 'Yes.' 'Then I am sure I have that if I have no other, for I love to be with Christians anywhere.' She was promptly received.

His First Examination

"When Mr. Moody appeared for examination, he was eighteen years old. He had only been in the Sunday school class a few weeks; he had no idea and could not tell what it was to be a Christian; even when aided by his teacher, whom he loved, he could not state what Christ had done for him. The chief question put to him was this: 'Mr. Moody, what has Christ done for us all —for you—which entitles Him to our love?' The longest answer he gave in the examination was this: 'I do not know. I think Christ has done a great deal for us, but I do not think of anything particular as I know of.'

"Under these circumstances, as he was a stranger to all the members of the committee, and less than a month had elapsed since he began to give any serious thought to the salvation of his soul, they deferred recommending him for admission to the church. But two of the examining committee were specially designated to watch over him with kindness, and teach him 'the way of God more perfectly'.

MR. MOODY PREACHING FROM HIS MISSIONARY PONY TO CHILDREN IN THE SLUMS.

"When he met the committee again no merely doctrinal questions were asked of him; but as his sincerity and earnestness were undoubted and he appeared to have more light, it was decided to propound him for admission. About eight years after this, and when Mr. Moody had become prominent as an evangelist, he expressed his gratitude to one of the officers of the church for the course pursued, and said his conviction was that its influence was favorable to his growth in grace. He also said he was afraid that pastors and church officers generally were falling into the error of hurrying new converts into a profession of religion. To a person of our acquaintance Dr. Kirk himself referred with the deepest grief to these imputations upon the Church, and declared them to be without foundation in truth; as well he might, for if there ever existed a man in New England who was free from the spirit of 'staid and stiff New England orthodoxy', it was Dr. Kirk.

"As for the suggestion to say but little in prayer meeting, we have little doubt that some one suggested that, for Mr. Moody has told us of his utter ignorance of the evangelical system. He was converted, he 'wished to do his duty', he said, 'whatever came to his lips', knowing nothing about its consistency or inconsistency; but he acted on John Wesley's rule, 'Do every religious duty as you can until you can do it as you would.'"

Mr. Moody's Life in Boston

One of those who knew Mr. Moody at the time of his conversion was Mr. Charles B. Botsford, of Boston. Shortly after the death of Mr. Moody, Mr. Botsford related what he knew of the life of Moody in Boston.

"I distinctly recall my first interview with Mr. Moody, early in 1856," said Mr. Botsford. "It was at the close of one of the Monday evening religious meetings of the Mt. Vernon Association of Young Men, formed several years before by Dr. Edward N. Kirk, for the benefit of young men of his church and congregation. Antedating the Y. M. C. A. by several years, it continued a vigorous life for several decades, and proved of great value.

"A literary meeting alternated with a devotional meeting. It was at this, his first attendance, at one of the latter, that, in a broken and trembling way, he earnestly stated his purpose to turn over a new leaf and lead a Christian life. When the meeting was over I took him by the hand and conducted him for the first time to the rooms of the Y. M. C. A., in the old Tremont Temple, to attend, as was my custom, the 9 o'clock prayer and conference meeting. Moody spoke, but much more zealously than grammatically, and he continued to be an active participant in the meetings from week to week.

"Let the Leaven Work"

"After a time, one of the most cultured members complained to Mr. Moody's uncle, a shoe dealer on Tremont Row, between Brattle and Hanover streets, that his nephew was altogether too zealous and conspicuous in the Y. M. C. A. meetings, saying that he wished in some way to have the zealot restrained. When consulted about the matter I said: 'No, let the leaven work!' The world knows what Mr. Moody has since done, in, by and for Y. M. C. A.'s, to say nothing of his other work.

"In the meantime I had taken Moody to a Sunday morning devotional meeting, that I was accustomed to attend, in the vestry of Dr. Neal's [Baptist] church, where the Boston University now stands. At that meeting, also, with its strong sectarian atmosphere, Moody spoke, and so stumbled in absolute disregard of the Pilgrim's English, that, in embarrassment, I bowed my head on the rail of the seat before me. He continued there, also.

"It was from this church, later, that a good sister, more zealous to steady and guard the ark of the Lord than to encourage unlearned young men to become leaders in Israel, went to Mr. Holton and said: 'If you have any interest in or regard for your nephew, you had better admonish him not to talk so much, for he is making a fool of himself.' But still the leaven worked.

"May 4, 1856, Mr. Moody united with the Mt. Vernon Church, where he was a member of Mr. Kimball's class in the Sunday school. He was not a constant attendant of the mid-week devotional meetings of the church, for, as he expressed it, he did not 'have liberty' there in his utterances, and, naturally enough, perhaps, for the atmosphere of the meetings was strongly intellectual and positively spiritual, with such leaders as Deacons Palmer, Kimball, Pinkerton and Cushing, with Dr. Kirk, at the close, to deepen and seal the impression."

A Changed Life

Concerning his relations to the Mount Vernon Church, Mr. Moody afterward said: "When I first became a Christian, I tried to join the church, but they wouldn't have me, because they didn't believe I was really converted."

A number of years afterward, Dr. Kirk was attending the anniversary of the American Board of Commissioners for Foreign Missions, which was held that year in Chicago. He was entertained by Mr. Moody, the man who as a boy had come into the light, in some measure, under his influence, and he preached on Sunday in the pulpit of his former parishioner. When he returned to Boston Dr. Kirk called upon Mr. Moody's uncle, Mr. Holton, and said: "I told our people last evening that we had every reason to be ashamed of ourselves. That young Moody, whom we thought did not know enough to belong to our church and Sunday school, is to-day exerting a wider influence for the Master than any other man in the great Northwest."

Speaking of his experience in passing from the life of sin to the life of religion, Mr. Moody once said: "I used to have a terrible habit of swearing. Whenever I would get mad, out would come the oaths; but after I gave my heart to Christ, He took the oaths away, so that I did not have the least disposition to take God's name in vain."

At another time, when waited upon by a journalist, who asked him for a sketch of his life, Mr. Moody said: "I was born in the flesh in 1837; I was born in the Spirit in 1856. What is born of the flesh may die; that which is born of the Spirit will live forever."

How Moody Revenged Himself Upon the Deacon

The Rev. Dr. Savage, of Chicago, used to tell of the way in which Mr. Moody revenged himself upon one of the deacons who had been instrumental in keeping him waiting for admission to the church. Mr. Moody's action was, of course, good-natured, for he not only bore no malice, but, on the other hand, was thankful for the wisdom which had required of him some sane understanding of his own state before he was allowed full fellowship with God's people. The earnest inquirer finds only a stimulus to further search when his own unfitness is made clear to him.

To return to the story. It was during the London campaign, and in the midst of one of the great meetings in Exeter Hall. Mr. Moody, whose sharp eyes never missed a detail in the great audiences which he faced, saw, away back under a gallery, his old friend, the deacon. The good man was traveling at the time, and had come to the meeting largely out of curiosity. Mr. Moody said nothing until toward the close of the service. Then he suddenly exclaimed: "I see in the house an eminent Christian gentleman from Boston. Deacon P., come right up to the platform; the people are anxious to hear you."

The deacon was far from eager to accept this hearty invitation, but he found that there was no alternative. So, mounting the platform, he began to speak. He told of having been acquainted with Mr. Moody during the evangelist's early life—of the fact that they had been members of the same church. Here Mr. Moody suddenly interrupted: "Yes, Deacon, and you kept me out of that church for six months, because you thought I did not know enough to join it." The deacon, at last succeeding in making himself heard above the roar of laughter which greeted Mr. Moody's sally, retorted that it was a privilege to any church to receive Mr. Moody at all, even though with considerable trepidation, and after long endeavor to know him thoroughly.

How he Repays His Old Sunday School Teacher

A number of years after his own conversion Mr. Moody found an opportunity to repay his old Sunday school teacher in kind for the help which Mr. Kimball had given to him. After a service in Boston a young man came to Mr. Moody and introduced himself as a son of Mr. Kimball. "I'm glad to meet you," said Mr. Moody. "Are you a Christian?" The young man admitted that he was not, and Mr. Moody inquired of him as to his age. "I am seventeen," was the reply. "That was just my age, when your father led me to the Lord," said Mr. Moody, "and now I want to repay him by leading his son to Christ."

The coincidence in age made an impression on the young man. After a brief conversation, he promised to surrender his heart to the Saviour, and a short time afterward Mr. Moody received a letter from him, stating that he had found what he had sought.

After his reception into the Mount Vernon Church, Mr. Moody remained in Boston for about five months. The restraint of his conservative surroundings lay heavy upon him. He yearned for freedom—freedom to think, freedom to speak, freedom to work. He must have had some consciousness of the great intuitions, the great feelings, which were struggling in him to burst forth into bloom, and he must have realized that the soil of staid Boston was not stimulating to such a growth. He had come into a new life; his forceful nature was not the kind to wait for circumstances to develop it. He required broad opportunity.

He Seeks His Future in the West

His unrest finally decided him definitely to seek a future in the West. His mother, it is said, did not approve of the move, dreading, as do all good mothers, the change which would take her son farther from her, and possibly fearing the dangers of a new environment which might not prove wholesome. Any dread which she may have felt was afterward proved to have been ill-founded.

Securing a letter from his uncle, Mr. Moody set out for Chicago in September, 1856, and entered the Western Metropolis with small store of earthly goods, but with a large fund of buoyant hope and energy, and a devoted purpose to serve his Divine Master.

CHAPTER VI.

Sunday School Work.

WHEN young Moody arrived in Chicago, he presented a letter which his uncle had given him to Mr. Wiswall, a shoe dealer on Lake Street. The boy was not altogether a prepossessing candidate for a position. He was boisterous and uncouth, and it was with many misgivings that Mr. Wiswall took him into his store. His employer's decision, however, was fully justified by the young man's work. It was not long before young Moody had the reputation of being the best salesman in the employ of the firm. He especially delighted to take in hand customers who were unusually difficult to deal with, and, while he never overstepped the line between honesty and deceit in his business dealings, when it came to a contest of wits he was almost invariably victorious.

GOOD PREPARATION FOR FUTURE WORK

It was not long before the growth of Mr. Wiswall's business led him to open a jobbing department. Mr. Moody was promoted to a situation in the new department, and in this wider opportunity for the exercise of his business faculties, he continued to win approval as a valuable assistant. His work took him to the railroad stations, hotels and other business places in search of customers, and doubtless did much toward widening his acquaintance, and adding to his experience in dealing with men. The acquirement of practical knowledge of the best way to approach men, was a wonderful preparation for the great work of his later years.

A number of Mr. Wiswall's clerks slept in rooms in the store building, an arrangement which naturally led to a fraternal intercourse. It is said that in the evenings these young men made it a habit to enter into debates upon the live questions of the day—and sometimes even questions which were not living issues. Politics, theology, business, all supplied topics to these young orators, and frequently discussions became very enthusiastic. The slavery question was often mooted. My Moody was, as might be expected from his vehement nature, an earnest participant in these debates. Unembarrassed by the limitations placed upon him by lack of education, he plunged boldly into whatever subject was under discussion, and generally made his point. In theology the main subject of debate was the old, old question, foreordination *versus* free will. Mr. Moody had developed strong Calvinistic tendencies, and he found a worthy opponent in one of his fellow clerks who, by bringing up, was a Methodist. The question of amusements was also taken up. Mr. Moody was strongly averse to any frivolous form of amusement, or any amusement which seemed to him frivolous. The story is told that he came into the store one night from some religious meeting, and found two of the clerks engaged in a game of checkers. He dashed the checker board to the ground; then, before any one could protest, dropped upon his knees and began to pray. It must not be thought, however, that he was entirely averse to healthful sports. On the contrary, rough games and practical jokes were a keen delight to him.

Recruiting for the Church

Shortly after his arrival in Chicago, Mr. Moody united by letter with the Plymouth Congregational Church, of which Dr. J. E. Roy was at that time pastor. It was a hospitable church, and Mr. Moody was not slow to find an opportunity to exercise his

MR. MOODY'S FIRST SUNDAY-SCHOOL CLASS IN CHICAGO. The picture shows Mr. Moody when quite a young man, wearing full beard and cap, to his left is his friend and Sunday-school superintendent, Mr. J. V. Farwell; in front are the rough boys whom he had picked up from the streets of Chicago to form his first Bible Class. Photographed by our own photographer from picture hanging in Mr. Moody's house.

desire to do practical Christian work. He rented five pews and kept them filled with young men at every service. He also went out and hunted up boys and girls for the Sunday school. The statement has been made that he asked for a class in the Sunday school but was refused. This is doubtful, for Mr. Moody himself recognized and declared at that time that he could not teach. He, however, took part in the prayer meetings, and in his work as a recruiting officer for the church of Christ, began to ignore denominational lines.

Recruiting for Sunday Schools

It seemed as if no church could give him enough to do; therefore he began to attend a Sunday morning class in the First Methodist Church, and to work with its Mission Band, which was composed of a number of devoted young men, who every Sunday morning used to visit various public places and invite strangers to attend church services. It will be seen that Mr. Moody's Christian work was purely practical. This was a characteristic determined by his temperament. Theorizing had no place in his energetic mind, but his whole heart was bent to secure the best results from the means at hand, and when means were lacking, to find them. We are struck with his method of making use of every opportunity, however slight. He never ignored small things; he felt it as incumbent upon him to help the clerk who worked beside him in the store, and the stranger whom he met casually upon the street, as to endeavor to sway large audiences from the rostrum. As a matter of fact, it is doubtful if, in these humble beginnings of his efforts, he had any realization of the great work that lay in store for him. He simply saw men and children sinking in the moral lazaretto of a great city. and stretched out his hand to help them.

A scientific study of the principles of education has impressed upon our minds the necessity of dealing with children, if we desire to effect any permanent change in the mental or moral condition of the world; for the children of to-day are the fathers and the mothers of the next generation. Without theorizing, Mr. Moody must have had an understanding of this principle. It was not long after he came to Chicago that he began to work among the children. His success in recruiting for the Sunday schools was wonderful. On one occasion he found a little mission Sunday school on the North side, and offered to take a class. The superintendent pointed out that they already had almost as many teachers as pupils, but added that, if Mr. Moody would get his own pupils, he would be at liberty to conduct a class. The next Sunday Mr. Moody appeared with eighteen ragamuffins. They were dirty, unkempt, many of them barefoot, but as the young teacher said, "each had a soul to save."

His Sunday School on "The Sands"

Mr. Moody's missionary explorations led him into the most evil parts of the city. His face became familiar in the worst saloon districts, among the sailors' boarding houses, and on the docks. It was on one of these excursions that he fell in with Mr. J. B. Stillson, a business man who was employing his spare time in the same missionary work. The two men cast in their lot together, and, according to one historian, during a single summer helped to recruit twenty mission Sunday schools.

Mr. Moody recognized that the average mission school was not calculated to reach the lowest *strata* of society. There was too large a requirement of order, too little allowance for the homes from which the pupils had come. Accordingly, he decided to begin a mission school of his own. On the north side of the Chicago River was a district called "The Sands", sometimes also known as "Little Hell". To-day, some of the finest residences of Chicago stand there where, in the early fifties and sixties, crime and debauchery reigned supreme. It was to this home of vice Mr. Moody went to begin his work. He found a deserted shanty which had formerly been a saloon, and hiring this ramshackle place, started out to drum up children to fill it. At first he found it hard to get at the young street Arabs; then he filled his pockets with maple sugar, and, judiciously distributing it among those who promised to come, soon had his little room overflowing with barbarians. One who visited the school in those days has described his experiences. "When I came to the little old shanty and entered the door," he said, "the first thing I saw by the light of the few candles, was a man standing up, holding in his arms a negro boy, to whom he was trying to read the story of the Prodigal Son. A great many words the reader could not make out and was obliged to skip. My thought was, If the Lord can ever use such an instrument as that for His honor and glory it will astonish me! When the meeting was over, Mr Moody said to me, 'I have got only one talent. I have no education, but I love the Lord Jesus Christ, and I want to do something for Him.' I have watched him since, and have come to know him thoroughly, and for consistent walk and conversation I have never met a man equal to him."

Muscular Christianity

There was probably never another school just like this school on "The Sands" to which young Moody devoted his spare time. Speaking from the steps of the hall entrance, the evangelist could make his voice heard in the doors of two hundred saloons. At first he had no seats for his school, and for some time none of the other usual requisites; no blackboard, no library, no maps; but it was a live school—in fact, it was about as much as the teachers could do to keep the turbulent membership sufficiently quiet to sing a little and hear a little talking. Mr. Moody was helped here by his friend Mr. Stillson. As a cardinal doctrine they held that the worse a boy was the more necessity there was to keep him in the school. There is a story of one young rough who defied for a long time all efforts to tame him, and whose riotous behavior endangered the existence of the school. Having meditated and prayed over the matter all the week, Mr. Moody came to the school on Sunday persuaded that there was but one remedy that would reach this case, and that was a good thrashing. Coming up behind the young rowdy, he seized him and pushed him through the open door of a little anteroom, then, locking the door, proceeded to business. The excitement in the schoolroom was drawn off by singing until the two reappeared after a somewhat prolonged and noisy recess in the anteroom. Both were evidently well warmed up, but the humble bearing of the offending boy made manifest the result of the battle. "It was hard work," remarked Mr. Moody, "but I guess we have saved him." This proved to be true; and, moreover, this exhibition of muscular Christianity served as a strong claim on the admiration of the school; Mr. Moody had demonstrated his ability to keep order, and thereafter found many helpers. One day an old pupil, coming up the aisle, noticed a new recruit with his cap on. He snatched it off, and with one blow sent the offender to the floor. "I'll teach you to keep your cap on in this school," was the explanation of the young protector as he passed to his own seat with the air of one ready to do his duty.

The North Market Mission

After a while the little shanty became too small for Mr. Moody's purpose, and, with the permission of Mayor Haines, the school was removed to a large hall over the North Market. This hall was generally used on Saturday evenings for dancing, and it often took the whole Sunday morning for Mr. Moody to clean it up so that it would be in condition for his use in the afternoon. There were no chairs, so Mr. Moody set out to secure money to buy them. He went to several rich men, among others to Mr. J. V. Farwell, a prominent merchant. After receiving a contribution, he asked Mr. Farwell what he was doing in a personal way for the unsaved, and invited him to attend the mission. The next Sunday Mr. Farwell appeared at the North Market School. The scene, to his imagination, defied all description. Ragamuffins were darting hither and thither, crying their street cries, and entering upon all sorts of mischief, but from this state of confusion Scripture readings, songs, and speeches occasionally rescued them. Mr. Farwell made a speech, and at the close, to his great consternation, was nominated by Mr. Moody superintendent of the school. The election was carried by acclamation before he had time to object. This office, so suddenly pressed upon him, was filled by Mr. Farwell for more than six years.

A Plan That Worked to a Charm

It was not easy to find suitable teachers for the classes which made up such a school, and it was not always easy to get rid of unsuitable teachers, but a plan was hit upon that worked to a charm. As no teacher could do such pupils good unless he could interest them, a rule was made, giving the pupil the privilege, under certain limitations, of leaving his class when he chose and going into another one. The result was that the superintendent was relieved from the unpleasant task of taking a dull teacher's class away from him, for the class, one by one, quickly took itself away.

Mr. Moody put a vast amount of work into the school. His evenings and Sundays were spent in skirmishing about "The Sands", looking after old pupils or hunting up new ones. Along with the Gospel he gave a great deal of relief for the sick, the unemployed, and the unfortunate. He was the almoner not only of his own charity, but also of the gifts of the many friends who became interested in his work. His old employer has stated that as many as twenty children used to come into the store at one time to be gratuitously fitted with new shoes.

As the school became popular, interest and curiosity brought many visitors, and it became easier to find teachers for the seventy or eighty classes. The attendance at the school increased in the most astonishing fashion. In three months there were 200 pupils; in six months 350, and within a year the average attendance was about 650, with an occasional crowd of nearly 1,000. The city missionary made objection to the wide range from which Mr. Moody was now drawing his recruits, on the plea that he was infringing on the work of other missions, but the work of the North Market School continued. No uniform lesson leaf was used in the school, but each teacher and pupil was supplied with a copy of the New Testament, and from this drew information and inspiration.

President Lincoln's Visit

A notable event in the history of the school was the visit of President-elect Lincoln, who came one Sunday at the request of Mr. Farwell. When the carriage went to the house where Mr. Lincoln was visiting, he left an unfinished dinner in order to keep his appointment, and was hurried northward to the unsavory district in which the North Market was situated. The President-elect was perhaps not accustomed to talk to Sunday schools; at any rate he requested that he should not be asked to make a speech; but when he was introduced to the spirited aggregation in the North Market Hall, the enthusiasm was so great that he yielded and spoke. His words were for right thinking and right acting. When a few months later this man issued a call for 75,000 volunteers, about sixty of the boys who had heard him that day in the North Market Hall answered. To them the words of the man who had told them of duty still rang through the words of the head of the State.

Conversions and transformations were continually occurring as a result of the work of Mr. Moody's school. More are related than can possibly be mentioned here.

Many Times in Danger of His Life

It must not be supposed that in his peregrinations among the lowly and the wretched, Mr. Moody always met with a welcome reception. There were many times when he stood in danger of his life. On such occasions he made it a principle to run away just as fast as he could, and he generally escaped because he could run faster than those who pursued him. One Sunday morning he was visiting some Roman Catholic family, with the purpose of bringing the children to the school, when a powerful man sprang at him with a club. The man had sworn to kill him, but a hard run saved the life of the young evangelist. Even after this attack he did not desist in his visit to this house, but continued again and again, until his tact and patience disarmed his adversary.

On another occasion, one Saturday evening he found in a house a jug of whiskey, which had been stored there for a carouse the following day. After a rousing temperance lecture, Mr. Moody persuaded the women of the house to permit him to pour the whiskey into the street. This he did before departing. Early the next morning he came back to fetch the children of the place to Sunday school. The men were lying in wait for him to thrash him. It was impossible to get away, for he was surrounded on all sides, but before they could touch him, Mr. Moody said, "See here, men, if you are going to whip me, you might at least give me time to say my prayers." The request was unusual; perhaps it was for that very reason that it was acceeded to. Mr. Moody dropped upon his knees and prayed such a prayer as those rough men had never heard before. Gradually they became interested and then softened, and when he had finished they gave him their hands, and a few minutes later Mr. Moody left the house for his school, followed by the children he had come to find.

He Knew His Work Thoroughly

Mr. Moody was not only busily engaged in Chicago, but early in his missionary life he was called to speak in small Sunday school conventions chiefly because he had already gained the reputation of reaching the masses of poor children in the cities. He knew this work thoroughly, and in his own way he could tell about it, not only to the instruction but often to the amusement as well of his audience. At one time he was invited to a place in Illinois and was accompanied by a Christian Association secretary; they two were advertised to speak. The secretary, in speaking of it afterwards said, "If ever two poor fellows were frightened, it was Moody and I." They reached their destination about two o'clock in the morning, too early to sit up and too late to go to bed, but they determined that they would spend all the time that was given them in prayer. During the rest of the night they sought God for power and guidance. Before the hour came when they were to speak, Mr. Moody secured the use of a public-school room which was quite near the place of the larger meeting. When asked what he wanted to do with it, he said, "I want it for an inquiry meeting." Both these young men were to speak, and each agreed that while the other spoke he would pray for him. When Mr. Moody was announced he seemed like one inspired. He pictured to them their need of Christ to help them as Sunday school teachers; told them it was an awful sin to do their work in a careless manner, and after an address of an hour called upon all who wanted to meet him, and to know Christ, to come with him to the school-room next door, where great numbers were helped. This was the beginning of a widespread spirit of revival, but it was also the beginning of a new life for Mr. Moody. From 1858 to 1865, Mr. Moody, Mr. Jacobs and Major Whittle, who were closely identified in conventions held in different parts of the country, became deeply impressed with the need of more of the presence of the Holy Spirit. The annual convention was to meet in Springfield, and these three workers were deeply concerned that it should be the best convention in the history of the State. They reached Springfield before the association convened, and held revival meetings as a prelude to what was to follow afterward. Seventy persons were converted. This became the Revival Conference. The next year the Sunday school workers met in the city of Decatur, and a record was brought up of ten thousand persons brought to Christ in a year. From this time on Mr. Moody was constantly invited to other States, and from Maine to Texas, from Montreal to San Francisco, from St. Paul to New Orleans, he went year after year, preaching and praying, rousing the Christian Associations into activity, inspiring the pastors to labor for revivals, helping the Sunday school teachers to reach their scholars for Christ; and in all his work as an evangelist throughout the world, deeper impressions were never made than in the first days of his active work as a Sunday school teacher and leader

CHAPTER VII.

The Young Men's Christian Association and the Chicago Avenue Church

MR. MOODY had not been long identified with active Christian work in Chicago, before he saw an opportunity for service in connection with the Young Men's Christian Association. This organization had been established in Chicago as a result of the great revival of 1857–8, but after a few years the interest in the daily noon prayer meeting began to wane. To increase this interest impressed Mr. Moody as his duty. His abilities were soon recognized by those in charge of the work, and he was appointed chairman of the Visiting Committee to the sick and to strangers. His work in behalf of the noon meetings was blessed moreover with large results.

Result of His First Years Work

He had found the Association made up of conservative men of middle or advanced years, but his advent among them was, as an officer of the Association has said, "like a stiff northwest breeze," and under his influence the institution became free and popular, and its influence was extensively widened. His abilities were especially eminent in raising money, but of the thousands of dollars he secured he would take nothing for himself. Among other schemes devised by him was one which federated the mission schools of the city under the Association, and brought them under the care of the stronger churches. The report of the first year of the work of his committee on visitation gives the number of families visited as 554, and the amount of money used for charitable purposes as $2,350.

Meanwhile, the growing strength of the North Market Mission taxed the ingenuity of the young superintendent to provide room for its expansion. He set himself to work to secure a suitable edifice, and, collecting personally about $20,000, saw a neat chapel rise in Illinois Street, not far from the old North Market Hall. This was in 1863. Mr. Moody had ever aimed, as the converts of the Mission grew in number, to recommend them to regular church homes, but an increasing unwillingness on the part of the converts to leave the influences of his personal presence seemed to necessitate the organization of a regular church to be made up of the converts of the Mission.

The Illinois Street Church

"The Illinois Street Church" was therefore organized under Congregational auspices. Members were baptized and received into the church by regular pastors of other Congregational churches, but the communion service was conducted by Mr. Moody without reference to established forms. He was the pastor of the church, although he never received ordination. For this reason, probably, the church, although organized by Congregationalists, was not reckoned a Congregational Church. Its discipline and confession of faith were made up with the end that no true lover of the Lord should be kept from the fellowship of this Christian band by any non-essential of doctrine or observance.

The membership of this church in the beginning was unique. Almost every communicant had been rescued from degradation by the work of the Mission. And it was a *working* congregation. Labor was so divided that every member had something to do, and every night saw some service in the chapel. The meetings seemed to be a continuous revival. Boundless energy and great physical strength, with the constant dwelling of God's spirit in him, alone enabled Mr. Moody to bear up under the great strain. At times he would find himself completely exhausted and almost ready to give up, but a few hours of rest or a slight change of occupation generally sufficed to put him very quickly on his feet again.

Two Hundred Calls in a Day

The story is told of how he made two hundred calls on New Year's Day. "At an early hour the omnibus which was to take him and several of his leading men was at the door, and, with a carefully prepared list of residences, they began the day's labor. The list included a large proportion of families living in garrets and the upper stories of high tenements. On reaching the home of a family belonging to his congregation he would spring out of the 'bus, leap up the stairways, rush into the room, and pay his respects as follows:

"'I am Moody; this is Deacon De Golyer; this is Deacon Thane; this is Brother Hitchcock. Are you well? Do you all come to church and Sunday-school? Have you all the coal you need for the winter? Let us pray?' And down we would all go upon our knees, while Mr. Moody offered from fifteen to twenty words of earnest, tender, sympathetic supplication.

"Then springing to his feet, he would dash on his hat, dart through the doorway and down the stairs, throwing a hearty 'good-bye' behind him, leap into the 'bus, and off to the next place on his list; the entire exercise occupying about one minute and a half.

"Before long the horses were tired out, for Mr. Moody insisted on their going on a run from one house to another; so the omnibus was abandoned, and the party proceeded on foot. One after another of his companions became exhausted with running upstairs and downstairs, and across the streets, and kneeling on bare floors, and getting up in a hurry; until, reluctantly, but of necessity, they were obliged to relinquish the attempt, and the tireless pastor was left to make the last of the two hundred calls alone. He returned home in the highest spirits to laugh at his exhausted companions for deserting him."

The next year Mr. Moody went on foot through another such day—reminding his friends that on the previous New Year they had often felt obliged to leave the 'bus before reaching a house, lest the sight of the vehicle should hurt the poor they visited, as an apparent waste of money.

Elected President of the Y. M. C. A.

The increase of the work of the Young Men's Christian Association during the Civil War called for increased accommodations. Mr. Moody's success with his Mission, and his well-known energy and boldness, led to the proposal that he be elected president of the Association. His lack of learning and his bluntness caused considerable opposition to his election, but he received a small majority. A building committee was immediately organized. Mr. Moody's plan was to organize a stock company, with twelve trustees, who should erect and hold the building in trust. The stock was to bear six *per cent*. interest, from the completion of the building, and the interest on the stock was to be paid out of the rentals of such portions of the building as were not needed for the use of the Association, and also from the rent of the great Hall. The excess of the rentals over the interest was to be used to buy up the stock, at par, in behalf of the Association. Mr. Moody succeeded in placing the stock to the value of $101,000.

The new building was erected in Madison Street, between Clark and La Salle Streets. The large hall had a seating capacity of three thousand. There were in the building a large room for the noon prayer meetings, a library, offices, etc. The hall was dedicated September 29, 1867. The report of the treasurer, Mr. John V. Farwell, on that occasion, showed that the entire cost of land, building, etc., was $199,000. Stock had been subscribed to the amount of $135,000; $50,000 had been loaned on mortgages. The remaining indebtedness was at once cleared up by subscriptions.

Dedication of the New Building

Among the speakers at the dedicatory service was Mr. George H. Stuart, president of the United States Christian Commission. His address sketched the history of the Association, and described the possibilities that were open to its efforts. The effect of his speech was marvelous. It seemed as if the words of this great Christian man had loosened the heart-strings of every individual in the large audience. The hall was still unnamed, but on Mr. Moody's nomination it was christened "Farwell Hall," in honor of Mr. John V. Farwell.

Under the management of Mr. Moody, Farwell Hall became very popular. The daily noon prayer meeting was so well attended that occasionally the one thousand seats in the prayer room were not sufficient to hold the people, and it was necessary to adjourn to the large hall. Monday evening a special meeting was held for strangers. Every noon Mr. Moody would go to the street in front of the hall a few minutes before the meeting, and endeavor to send within as many of the passers-by as he could approach. Then, as the clock struck twelve, he would hurry up the stairs and take his usual seat, near the leader, where, if the meeting seemed to drag or to require a stimulus, he would take it in hand and do everything necessary to animate it.

Mr. Moody began to be known in Young Men's Christian Association work throughout the United States and Canada, and his services were in frequent demand for conventions and revival services.

Four months after its dedication, Farwell Hall was burned, in January, 1868. Mr. Moody did not lag when this catastrophe overtook the enterprise in which he was bound up. Subscriptions were opened immediately, and most of the original stockholders came to the front with renewed support. On the old foundations a new Farwell Hall was erected. It was dedicated in 1869, to an only too brief period of noble service for the Master.

A Great Religious Centre

Mr. Moody continued president of the Association for four years. He then declined re-election, but consented to act as vice-president, with Mr. J. V. Farwell in the chair. The Sunday evening meetings in the new hall were wonderful. Mr. Moody would there preach the same discourse he had delivered to his congregation in Illinois Street in the morning. Such throngs attended these evening meetings that they came to compose, with one exception, the largest protestant congregation in Chicago. The sermon was followed by an inquiry meeting.

Farwell Hall soon became a great religious centre. That its success as an institution was due in large degree to Mr. Moody cannot be doubted. His energy made possible the erection of the first structure; his perseverance called forth the second, phœnix-like, from the ashes of the first; his devotion filled the prayer meetings; his faith led hundreds to a changed life; and his directness, his singleness of purpose, prevented any deviation of the work from the paths of Christian helpfulness. The second Farwell Hall went down in the great fire of 1871, but its work still lived.

Mr. Moody used to give an incident of his last service in Farwell Hall on the night of the great fire. He said:

Incident of His Last Service in Farwell Hall

"The last time I preached upon this question was in Farwell Hall. I had been for five nights preaching on the life of Christ. I took Him from the cradle and followed Him up to the judgment hall, and on that occasion I consider I made as great a blunder as ever I made in my life. If I could recall my act I would give this right hand. It was upon that memorable night in October, and the Court House bell was sounding an alarm of fire, but I paid no attention to it. You know we were accustomed to hear the fire-bell often, and it didn't disturb us much when it sounded. I finished the sermon upon 'What shall I do with Jesus?' And I said to the audience, 'Now I want you to take the question with you and think over it, and next Sunday I want you to come back and tell me what you are going to do with it.' What a mistake! It seems now as if Satan was in my mind when I said this. Since then I have never dared to give an audience a week to think on their salvation. If they were lost, they might rise up in judgment against me, 'Now is the accepted time.' We went down stairs to the other meeting, and I remember when Mr. Sankey was singing, and how his voice rang when he came to that pleading verse:

> "'To-day the Saviour calls;
> For refuge fly.
> The storm of justice falls,
> And death is nigh.'

After the meeting we went home. I remember going down La Salle street with a young man who is probably in the hall to-night, and saw the glare of flames. I said to the young man, 'This means ruin to Chicago.' About one o'clock Farwell Hall went; soon the church in which I had preached went down, and everything was scattered. I never saw that audience again. My friends, we don't know what may happen to-morrow, but there is one thing I do know, and that is, if you take the gift, you are saved. If you have eternal life, you need not fear fire, death, or sickness. Let disease or death come, you can shout triumphantly over the grave, if you have Christ. My friends, what are you going to do with Him to-night? Will you decide now?"

The North Side Tabernacle

The Illinois Street Church was also burned in the great fire, and Mr. Moody at once began the work of feeding and sheltering the homeless. Complaints were made of his too bountiful distribution, for he would refuse no one who asked. He therefore withdrew from the relief work, and went East, to hold revival meetings and to raise money toward rebuilding his church. With the large assistance of Mr. George H. Stuart and Mr. John Wanamaker, of Philadelphia, he obtained three thousand dollars for the erection of a rough struture in the burned district, not far from the ruins of the old church. This " North Side Tabernacle," as it was called, covered a plot of ground one hundred and nine feet long and seventy-five feet wide. All around it were the ruins. There was some doubt whether the situation of the Tabernacle would permit a large attendance, but on the day of dedication more than one thousand children came together.

The meetings in the Tabernacle were distinguished by a remarkable revival. During the year following the fire eight services were held every Sunday. A wide relief work was also instituted by the indefatigable pastor. Mr. Moody had returned from the eastern tour refreshed spiritually, and blessed by a large access of power. He has told us how, while he was in New York City on that memorable journey, God revealed Himself especially to his servant. This baptism of the Divine Love vivified his later work and made it tell with the unconverted as never before. And so, in the Tabernacle among the ashes, sprang up a wonderful manifestation of God's presence, and hundreds were led to Christ.

Development of the Chicago Avenue Church

The new church, which afterward came to be known as "The Chicago Avenue Church", was partly erected in 1873. From that time it was used by the congregation, a temporary roof being built over the first floor, but not until 1876 was it completed, freed of debt, and dedicated. Up to this time the preaching and pastoral work was done chiefly by Mr. Moody and Mr. Watts De Golyer. Since then the Rev. W. J. Erdman, the Rev. Charles H. Norton, the Rev. G. C. Needham, President Blanchard, the Rev. Charles F. Goss and the Rev. F. B Hyde have occupied the pulpit and acted as pastors. The present pastor is the Rev. Dr. R. A. Torrey. The church has always maintained its early character as an undenominational, evangelical and aggressive congregation. The sittings and other privileges are all free, and the motto selected at the organization of the church, and still inscribed over the main entrance, is "Welcome to this House of God are strangers and the poor." It has always been dependent upon the offerings of the people for its support, and the expenses are met through the systematic weekly giving of the congregation.

CHAPTER VIII.

Giving Up Business.

IT is not hard to appreciate the straits to which Mr. Moody was subjected by the conflicting claims of his business and his mission work. Only a man of boundless energy and fine physique could have accomplished what he was accomplishing. His business received its full share of his attention as formerly, but in his every spare moment his mind was occupied by plans for the work at North Market Hall, while every evening and every Sunday he gave himself up wholly to his labors for the Master.

Moody as a Commercial Traveler

Meanwhile he had not remained with Mr. Wiswall. After two years with his first friend, he entered the establishment of Mr. C. N. Henderson, who had become acquainted with him at the Mission, and had taken interest in the young man and his work. This new connection forced upon him the work of a commercial traveler. His evenings could no longer be given to mission work at home, for the greater part of his time was spent out of the city. However, no matter how far his travels might have taken him during the week, he never failed to return on Saturday night, that he might be at North Market Hall on Sunday. It will be readily understood that inasmuch as his business arrangements provided for his return to the city only one Sunday out of four, the expenses of his weekly trips would have been a serious drain upon his slender financial resources. But the superintendent of the Chicago,

Burlington and Quincy Railroad, a man of generous impulses, who felt deeply interested in the North Side Sunday school, finding that Mr. Moody's presence was essential to the Sunday work, provided him with a free pass over the railroad lines under his control, to bring him home three Sundays out of the four.

Mr. Moody had not held his position very long before Mr. Henderson died. In the changes which the removal of this good man entailed in the house, Mr. Moody severed his connection with the firm and removed to the establishment of Messrs. Buel, Hill, & Granger, with whom he remained for about one year. More and more was his heart wrapped up in his practical Christian work; business meant less and less to him. Finally he made his decision and gave up secular business entirely that he might devote his whole strength and time to practical work for the Lord.

"God Will Provide"

This was no sudden decision, no lightning conviction of a great duty. On the contrary, the step was decided upon only after mature deliberation and a thorough test of his fitness for his chosen work. His first ambition had been to become a great merchant; now this was thrown aside, and when at last he bade good-bye to business, he said to one of his friends, "I have decided to give to God all my time". "But how are you going to live?" asked his friend. Mr. Moody replied, "God will provide for me, if he wishes me to keep on, and I shall keep on until I am obliged to stop."

There was no unpleasantness in his severance of the old business connections. All his former employers spoke in the highest terms of Mr. Moody and of his work with them. Said Mr. Hill, a member of the last firm for whom he worked, "One day not long after he left our house I ran across him, and I asked him, 'Moody, what are you doing?' 'I am at work for Jesus Christ,' was the reply. At first his answer shocked me a little, but after I had thought it over I decided that it was a fair statement of the facts in the case. It was true; that was just what he was doing, and his work for the Lord was as vigorous, as practical, as it had always been for other employers." Mr. Hill added that Mr. Moody had left the employ of his firm in the pleasantest circumstances, having retained his Christian character unblemished. All of his old employers, as a matter of fact, not only bade him God speed when he left them, but kept some track of his future course, with the conviction, even in those early days, that he would succeed in accomplishing great things.

Free to Devote His Time to His Mission

It had not been difficult for Mr. Moody, during his years of business life, to lay up a considerable sum of money out of his salary, for his living expenses were very light and his frugality a matter of record; but a great part of what he earned went into his mission work. Before leaving the world of business he set aside a certain sum. Part of this money he invested, but he saved out $1,000 to pay his first year's expenses. He was now happy. Free to devote his time to his loved Mission, and to the Y. M. C. A. work, which was becoming almost equally dear to him, and conscious of the fact that he had in his pocket money to enable him to accomplish many of his plans, he set out with a light heart on his new life. And yet, it was not a new life, it was simply a ripening of those seeds which had been sown back there in his uncle's store in Boston when he first gave his heart to the Lord.

One of the first things he did was to invest part of his thousand dollars in a small pony. With the help of this animal he was able to extend his missionary excursions over a much wider area, and to accomplish much more than theretofore. The sight of Mr. Moody on his pony became a familiar one in the poor districts of

Chicago. It is said that often after a Sunday morning hunt for Sunday school recruits, he would be seen emerging from some squalid street, surrounded by children, some of whom had clambered upon the pony with him, while others hung to the bridle reins or marched behind in procession on their way to the Sunday school.

His Means Exhausted

Meanwhile the thousand dollars quickly vanished. It did not prove enough to meet half the demands which the mission work and various other deeds of charity brought upon Mr. Moody. Then the rest of his small fortune disappeared, and he found himself reduced to the proverbial water and a crust. One of the few books which he had read was the life of George Müller, whose work of faith in England had impressed him so deeply that he determined to follow that good man's principle and trust in the Lord even for his sustenance. When the growth of the Y. M. C. A. noon prayer meetings necessitated their removal to a large backroom in the First Methodist Church block, Mr. Moody betook himself there, and, though at length brought to the necessity of sleeping on the benches of the prayer room and living on crackers and cheese, he kept on with his work, not even making his condition known to his friends, who would have been glad to help him. All this time he was collecting considerable sums for charitable purposes, but not one cent did he devote to himself. He had determined to give his faith a thorough test. At times he must have felt some faltering, but at those times the Lord always gave him some reassurance.

After a time some of his friends began to wonder how he was living, and were greatly astonished at the result of the investigations. Discovering his poverty, they insisted upon supplying him with the necessities of life. From this time on, trust in God always brought Mr. Moody an answer to his needs. This does not mean that he was never tried, but simply that, taking everything into consideration, he was supplied comfortably, and sometimes even bountifully. People who knew him came to esteem it a privilege to help him.

It is of interest here to give Mr. Moody's own narrative of the incident which finally influenced his decision to leave business for Christian work.

Moody's Own Narrative

"I had never lost sight of Jesus Christ since the first night I met Him in the store in Boston. But for years I was only a nominal Christian, really believing that I could not work for God. No one had ever asked me to do anything.

"I went to Chicago, I hired five pews in a church, and used to go out on the street and pick up young men and fill these pews. I never spoke to those young men about their souls; that was the work of the elders, I thought. After working for some time like that, I started a mission Sabbath school. I thought numbers were everything, and so I worked for numbers. When the attendance ran below one thousand, it troubled me; and when it ran to twelve or fifteen hundred, I was elated. Still none were converted; there was no harvest. Then God opened my eyes.

"There was a class of young ladies in the school, who were, without exception, the most frivolous set of girls I ever met. One Sunday the teacher was ill, and I took that class. They laughed in my face, and I felt like opening the door and telling them all to get out and never come back. That week the teacher of the class came into the place where I worked. He was pale, and looked very ill. 'What is the trouble?' I asked. 'I have had another hemorrhage of my lungs. The doctor says I cannot live on Lake

Michigan, so I am going to New York State. I suppose I am going home to die.'

"He seemed greatly troubled, and when I asked him the reason, he replied: 'Well, I have never led any of my class to Christ. I really believe I have done the girls more harm than good.' I had never heard any one talk like that before, and it set me thinking. After a while I said: 'Suppose you go and tell them how you feel. I will go with you in a carriage, if you want to go.'

They Sought Salvation

"He consented, and we started out together. It was one of the best journeys I ever had on earth. We went to the house of one of the girls, called for her, and the teacher talked to her about her soul. There was no laughing then! Tears stood in her eyes before long. After he had explained the way of life, he suggested that we have prayer. He asked me to pray. True, I had never done such a thing in my life as to pray God to convert a young lady there and then. But we prayed, and God answered our prayer. We went to other houses. He would go upstairs, and be all out of breath, and he would tell the girls what he had come for. It wasn't long before they broke down, and sought salvation.

"When his strength gave out, I took him back to his lodgings. The next day we went out again. At the end of ten days he came to the store with his face literally shining. 'Mr. Moody,' he said, 'the last one of my class has yielded herself to Christ.' I tell you we had a time of rejoicing. He had to leave the next night, so I called his class together that night for a prayer meeting, and there God kindled a fire in my soul that has never gone out. The height of my ambition had been to be a successful merchant, and, if I had known that meeting was going to take that ambition out of me, I might not have gone. But how many times I have thanked God

D. L. MOODY AT THE AGE OF 35, from a steel engraving.

since for that meeting! The dying teacher sat in the midst of his class, and talked with them, and read the fourteenth chapter of John. We tried to sing 'Blest be the tie that binds,' after which we knelt down to prayer. I was just rising from my knees, when one of the class began to pray for her dying teacher. Another prayed, and another, and before we rose, the whole class had prayed. As I went out I said to myself: 'O, God, let me die rather than lose the blessing I have received to-night!'

"The next morning I went to the depot to say good-bye to that teacher. Just before the train started, one of the class came, and before long, without any prearrangement, they were all there. What a meeting that was! We tried to sing, but we broke down. The last we saw of that dying teacher, he was standing on the platform of the car, his finger pointing upward, telling that class to meet him in Heaven. I didn't know what this was going to cost me. I was disqualified for business; it had become distasteful to me. I had got a taste of another world, and cared no more for making money. For some days after, the greatest struggle of my life took place. Should I give up business and give myself to Christian work, or should I not? I have never regretted my choice. O, the luxury of leading some one out of the darkness of this world into the glorious light and liberty of the Gospel!"

Mr. Moody's Marriage

It is time to speak of Mr. Moody's marriage. There was a lady who for some years had been a helper in his Mission. His first acquaintance with her dated from that little North Side Mission Sunday school in which he was offered a class on condition that he provide his own pupils. The interest of Mr. Moody for this young lady, whose name was Miss Emma C. Revell, grew deeper and deeper, and meanwhile her interest in him developed.

It would hardly be thought by the average man of affairs, that marriage was a safe step for a man who had thrown up all business and had entered upon unsalaried mission work. But Mr. Moody was living the life of trust, and the faith of Miss Revell was not less strong. They were married August 28, 1862.

They made their first home in a small cottage. A hospitable home it was, and a cheery one, and yet the little household was sometimes in great straits. Even after his marriage, Mr. Moody continued to refuse all offers of a salary. Often the family was in sight of want, but the Lord never permitted real distress. A number of instances are related of the ways in which his trust in God was honored.

A Remarkable and Surprising Gift

A remarkable way in which the Lord remembered Mr. Moody, was by the gift of a new and completely furnished home. An old friend had erected a row of fine houses, one of which he privately set aside for Mr. Moody, free of rent, on the understanding that the evangelist's other friends would furnish it. The enterprise was taken up with enthusiasm, all unknown to Mr. Moody and his wife, and the house was fitted up comfortably. Early on a New Year's morning Mr. Moody and his family were captured and driven to the house. When they entered they were surprised to find it full of acquaintances and friends. Their surprise was turned to gratitude and joy when a spokesman of the company handed to Mr. Moody a lease of the house and the free gift of all it contained This home was not long left to them, for the great Chicago fire carried it away.

No Life of Mr. Moody would be complete without further reference to his wife, who has been his constant companion in all his sorrows and his joys. She is of a retiring disposition, and yet in that day of rewards when D. L. Moody is crowned, it is the opinion of his many friends who know whereof they speak, that Mrs. Moody will have no small share of reward.

Mr. Ira D. Sankey has said, "Amid all that has been said about what has made Mr. Moody so great a man, I want to say that one of the greatest influences of his life came from his wife. She has been the break upon an impetuous nature, and she more than any other living person is responsible for his success."

His Wife and Her Influence

She has been more than interested in his work from the beginning. In connection with his Sunday school work in Chicago, the following incident is told : " A stranger who was visiting the Sunday school in Chicago, noticed a lady teaching a class of about forty middle-aged men, in the gallery. Looking at her and then at the class, he said to Mr. Moody, 'Is not that lady altogether too young to teach such a class of men ? She seems to me very youthful for such a position.' Mr. Moody replied, 'She gets along very well, and seems to succeed in her teaching.' The stranger did not appear to be altogether satisfied. He walked about the school, evidently in an anxious state of mind. In a few moments he approached the superintendent again, and, with becoming gravity, said, 'Mr. Moody, I can not but feel that that lady must be altogether too young to instruct such a large company of men. Will you, sir, please to inform me who she is ?' 'Certainly,' replied Mr. Moody, 'that is my wife.' The stranger made no more inquiries, and nothing occurred to indicate the state of his mind during the remainder of his visit "

One of the members of his family has said, "No man ever paid greater homage to his wife than Mr. Moody. I never met with a happier couple. In every way he deferred to her. She answered all his voluminous correspondence. She was the person to whom he always spoke of his plans and his work. No trouble was too great for him, if he could save her any bother or every-day, ordinary little troubles."

Mrs. Moody has done some remarkable work in the inquiry meetings held in different parts of the country. One of my dear friends is Mr. E. P. Brown, for a long time the editor of the *Ram's Horn*. I knew him in the days of his infidelity. A more bitter infidel I have never known in my life. He has told me how one night he entered the Chicago Avenue Church that he might criticise Moody in his article which he was writing for his infidel paper. Mr. Moody's sermon was on the father of the prodigal, and looking squarely into the face of my friend, he said, " My friend, the father of the prodigal is the picture of God, and as the father of the prodigal is waiting for his son, so God is waiting for you."

"I Would Like to Know Him"

E. P. Brown was startled. He has since said: "I heard the theologians talk about God, and I hated Him, but I had a father and I knew what his love was, and I found myself saying, If this is the true picture of God then I would like to know Him." When the invitation was given for the inquiry meeting, E. P. Brown accepted it, and it was Mrs. Moody who gave him help which finally led him out of his darkness of unbelief and led him into the glorious light and liberty in which he now stands as a son of God.

This is but one instance. Hundreds of others might be repeated. We can quite understand, therefore, how it is that from the very day when D. L. Moody determined to give up his business to the last moment of his life when he said good-bye to his beloved wife, she was more helpful and inspiring to him than any other person in the world.

Mr. Moody's family consists of three children.

William Revell Moody, his eldest child, has ever been the constant companion of his father, who relied upon him. If a father's mantle may fall upon his son's shoulders, William R. Moody in his father's purpose and plan, ought to lead in the carrying on of his great work. He is a graduate of Yale and is a consecrated Christian man with a great desire to do everything his father could wish. He is happily married to the eldest daughter of Major D. W. Whittle. It was with great pleasure that the Christian world knew that in this way these two families so greatly used of God were so happily to be brought into closer and more sacred relations. Mrs. W. R. Moody is the author of the hymn "*Moment by Moment*", and has been very useful in Christian service both at home and abroad.

Mr. Moody's Family

Emma Moody Fitt, Mr. Moody's second child, was as near to him as a daughter can be to her father. The most intense affection made them one in their interests and work. She is the wife of Mr. A. P. Fitt, for some time Mr. Moody's private secretary, and latterly his valued helper in every way. I have heard Mr. Moody say again and again, "I do not know how I should get along, if it were not for Fitt." He has been the superintendent and prime mover in the colportage work in Chicago, and Mr. Moody's work in general owes much to his faithful, untiring and affectionate interest.

Paul, the second son and youngest child, is a member of the Junior Class at Yale College. An earnest, active Christian young man, he is making his life tell for Christ among the students and giving great promise of future usefulness in the world. Very many people look to him in future days largely to carry on his father's public work.

CHAPTER IX.

Moody and Sankey.

AN international convention of the Young Men's Christian Association was held at Indianapolis in June, 1870. Mr. Moody attended. During the convention an early morning prayer-meeting was conducted in a church adjoining the hall where the convention was held. Mr. Moody led this meeting.

Ira D. Sankey, who at that time was Assistant Collector of Revenue in New Castle, Pa., but whose interest in religious work had made him an active worker in the field, had come to Indianapolis to attend the convention. He had heard of Mr. Moody, but had never seen him, and learning that the Chicago preacher was to lead this morning meeting, he yielded to a strong impulse and attended

Mr. Sankey's First Singing at a Moody Meeting

When Mr. Sankey entered, the singing was being led by a man who was dragging through a long metre hymn in the slow old-fashioned way. Mr. Sankey was scarcely seated when some one touched his elbow, and turning around, he discovered that he was sitting beside the Rev. Robert McMillen, with whom he happened to be well acquainted. Mr. McMillen whispered to Mr. Sankey that nobody present seemed able to put any life into the singing, adding, "When that man who is praying gets through, I wish you would start up something."

Without waiting for any further invitation, Mr. Sankey arose and sang with wonderful feeling,

"There is a fountain filled with blood,
Drawn from Immanuel's veins,
And sinners plunged beneath that flood,
Lose all their guilty stains."

The power and fervor of the singer's voice was such that the congregation forgot to join in the chorus, and Mr. Sankey finished the hymn by himself.

The effect of this song was not missed by Mr. Moody. At the close of the service, when Mr. McMillen brought Mr. Sankey forward, Mr. Moody stepped to one side and took the singer by the hand. "Where do you come from?" he asked. "Pennsylvania," replied Mr. Sankey. "Are you married or single?" "Married; I have a wife and one child." "What business are you in?" "I am a government official connected with the Internal Revenue service," answered Mr. Sankey, not realizing what motive was subjecting him to such cross-examination.

A Sudden Proposition

"Well," said Mr. Moody, decidedly, "you will have to give that up; I have been looking for you for eight years." Mr. Sankey stood amazed and was at a loss to understand just what Mr. Moody meant by telling him that he would have to give up a comfortable position, and he was so taken aback for a few seconds that he could scarcely reply. At last, however, recovering from his astonishment, he asked the evangelist what he meant. Mr. Moody promptly explained. "You will have to give up your government position and come with me. You are just the man I have been looking for, for a long time. I want you to come with me; you can do the singing, and I will do the talking."

The proposition did not sound particularly attractive to Mr. Sankey, and he told Mr. Moody, that he did not feel he could accept it and begged for time in which to consider the matter.

Mr. Moody asked him if he would join him in prayer in regard to it, and the singer replied that he would most gladly do so. Says Mr. Sankey, "I presume I prayed one way and he prayed another; however, it took him only six months to pray me out of business." It was true that Mr. Moody was praying that Mr. Sankey would see his way clear to do as he had asked, while Mr. Sankey was arguing with himself against the proposition. This first meeting between the two men was on Sunday. All that day and night Mr. Sankey thought over Mr. Moody's words, but the next morning found him still inclined to stick to the government position with its assured salary.

A Street Service

Just at a moment when he was in considerable doubt as to the suitable course, a card was brought him which on examination proved to be from Mr. Moody. It requested him to meet Mr. Moody at a certain street corner that evening at six o'clock. Mr. Sankey did not know what he was wanted for, but he accepted the invitation, and, accompanied by a few friends, met the appointment promptly. In a few minutes Mr. Moody appeared, and without stopping to speak, walked into a store on the corner and asked permission to use a dry-goods box. The permission granted, the evangelist rolled a large box out to the edge of the sidewalk, and then calling Mr. Sankey aside asked him to climb up and sing something. Mr. Sankey complied. A crowd began to collect, and Mr. Moody getting upon the box began to preach. Mr. Sankey says of that sermon, "He preached that evening as I had never heard any man preach before." The hearers, most of them workingmen on their way home from the mills and factories, were electrified. They hung on every word, apparently forgetting that they were tired and hungry, and when Mr. Moody closed, which he was

GROUP OF MR. MOODY'S FRIENDS showing Ira D. Sankey in the centre, and Tamil David, the native preacher from India at his extreme left.

forced to do by the density of the crowd, he announced that he would hold another meeting at the Academy of Music, and invited the crowd to accompany him there. Arm in arm with Mr. Moody, Mr. Sankey marched down the street singing hymn after hymn as he went, the crowd following closely at their heels. Mr. Sankey has since declared that this was his first experience in Salvation Army methods. The meeting in the Academy of Music was necessarily brief because the convention was soon to come together, oddly enough to discuss the question, "How shall we reach the masses?" and as the delegates came in Mr. Moody, with a short prayer dismissed the meeting.

Mr. Sankey Joins Forces With Mr. Moody

Although deeply affected by the power of Mr. Moody's inspiring message, Mr. Sankey was still undecided. He went home to talk the matter over with his wife, and to her the proposed partnership seemed, at that time, an unwarranted and injudicious step, but after several months, the influence of Mr. Moody's invitation still working in him, he went by request to Chicago and spent a week with Mr. Moody. For several days they worked together in church, in Sunday school, in saloons and drinking dens, joining their gifts of speaking and singing to bring light to the discouraged and the sinful. When the week was over, Mr. Sankey had decided. He sent his resignation to Hugh McCulloch, who at that time was Secretary of the Treasury; another veteran of the War was given his place in the Internal Revenue Service, and Mr. Sankey joined forces with Mr. Moody.

This was about six months before the great Chicago fire. When that tidal wave of flame overwhelmed that part of Chicago where Mr. Moody's work was especially located, and destroyed his church and his home, the evangelist's plans were for a time completely disarranged, and he went for a tour in the

Eastern States, while Mr. Sankey returned to his home in Pennsylvania. But when the new tabernacle sprang from the ashes of the old, the two brethren once more began their labors, taking up their lodgings in anterooms of the great rough building, and throwing themselves heart and soul into the effort to bring the unfortunate people to Christ. This work in the rough chapel among the ruins was signalized by a great revival. While Mr. Moody was on his second visit to Great Britain in 1872, Mr. Sankey took charge of the meetings. Mr. Moody had gone more especially to attend the Mildmay Conference in London. When he returned, he found that Mr. Sankey had received an especial baptism of the Holy Spirit, and that the blessings of his work had been increased a thousand fold by the responsibilities which had been left with him.

Mr. Sankey Follows Mr. Moody to England

It was about this time, possibly under the influence of this second trip to England, that Mr. Moody decided upon that third tour which was to bring to Great Britain a spiritual regeneration such as had not been known since the days of John Wesley. Mr. Moody said to his co-worker, "You have often proposed that we make an evangelizing journey together; now let us go to England."

Again Mr. Sankey found himself in some doubt as to his proper decision. It happened that he was then considering an offer from Mr. Phillips to go to the Pacific Coast and give a series of "Evenings of Song." Fortunately he again decided to follow Mr. Moody. Possibly he was influenced in his decision by a realization that if he went with Mr. Phillips he would be associated with a man whose gifts were similar to his own, a condition which might lead to difficulties, while if he went with Mr. Moody he would have his own work to do entirely separate from the work of

Mr. Moody, although complementary to it. So attended by his little family, he trustfully set forth with Mr. Moody and his family, June 7, 1873, on a journey of four thousand miles.

The joyful, prayerful singing of the Gospel hymns by Mr. Sankey was a revelation of unexpected truth and grace to the people of the British Isles. In Scotland especially, the masses were moved by him. With an indescribable impulse, the cautious, distrustful followers of John Knox, worshippers who for generations had been accustomed to reject as uninspired all other services of praise than their own rude version of the Psalms, now listened with delight to the music which fell like a blessing from the lips of the most gifted Christian singer of the time.

Sankey's Singing in Edinburgh

One of his hearers has thus described the impression made by Mr. Sankey's singing in Edinburgh. "Mr. Sankey sings with the conviction that souls are receiving Jesus between one note and the next. The stillness is overawing; some of the lines are more spoken than sung. The hymns are equally used for awakening, none more than 'Jesus of Nazareth Passeth By'. When you hear the 'Ninety and Nine' sung, you know of a truth that down in this corner, up in that gallery, behind that pillar which hides the singer's face from the listener, the hand of Jesus has been finding this and that and yonder lost one to place them in His fold. A certain class of hearers come to the services solely to hear Mr. Sankey, and the song draws the Lord's net around them. We asked Mr. Sankey one day what he was to sing. He said, 'I'll not know till I hear how Mr. Moody is closing.' Again we were driving to the Canongate Parish Church one winter night, and Mr. Sankey said to the young minister who had come for him, 'I am thinking of singing 'I am so Glad' to-night. 'O!' said the young man, 'please rather sing 'Jesus of Nazareth.' An old man told me to-day that he had been awakened by it the last night you were down. He said, 'It just went through me like an electric shock.' A gentleman in Edinburgh was in distress of soul, and happened to linger in a pew after the noon meeting. The choir had remained to practice and began, 'Free from the Law, O, Happy Condition.' Quickly the Spirit of God carried the truth home to the awakened conscience, and he was at last in the finished work of Jesus."

Sankey's Favorite Hymn

Mr. Sankey's hymns were gathered from a hundred sources. A great many of them are to-day known by every child in the land and are remembered by many other persons as means of grace in their own conversions. Of all his songs the favorite was, " The Ninety and Nine". This beautiful hymn has an interesting little history.

While Mr. Moody and Mr. Sankey were in the Highlands of Scotland they were subjected to some criticisms because Mr. Sankey's music was so much of a deviation from the established music of the Scotch churches. Anxious not to offend the prejudices of any in the multitudes whom they were meeting, Mr. Sankey cast about him for a song which might satisfy not only the hearts, but the ears as well of the rough shepherds of the Highlands. One day in the corner of a newspaper he found the words of "The Ninety and Nine". They had originally been printed in *The Christian*, of Boston, Mass., and were reprinted in England in *The Rock*. The melody came to him like an inspiration. The first time he sang it, it was not even written out. It is natural that a song like this should have appealed to the shepherds of Scotland, to whom its sentiment came with an especially pleasing force. It became their favorite among Mr. Sankey's songs, and when he went to Ireland and England it was called for more, and appreciated more, than any other song in his collection.

It was also said of the results of Mr. Sankey's singing, "The wave of sacred song has spread over Ireland and is now sweeping through England, but indeed it is not being confined to the United Kingdom alone. Far away on the shores of India, and in many other lands, these sweet songs of the Saviour's love are being sung."

"He Sang the Gospel"

It was not alone the novelty of his method that aroused interest in Mr. Sankey's songs to such a high degree. He possessed a voice of unusual purity and strength, and even when facing a great congregation of seventeen or eighteen thousand people, could make every word which he uttered so distinct that it was heard on the very outskirts of the throng. His vocal method has been criticised, undoubtedly with justice, but it can be said that, whether his method was correct or incorrect artistically, it was at least effective. Patti at her best could not move hearers with her singing in the way that Mr. Sankey won the hearts of his audiences. He literally, as he himself proclaimed, "sang the Gospel".

This phrase, novel as it was, was criticised by many staid conservatives in the matter of religion, but its truth cannot be questioned. If it were not true how could it have been that so many should have been led to Christ through the influence of that marvelous singing. An English journal has told of a little girl only ten years old who had listened with delight to Mr. Sankey's singing. "O!" she said, "How I love those dear hymns! When I am gone, mother, will you ask the girls of the school to sing the hymn.

'Ring the bells of Heaven!
There is joy to-day,
For a soul returning from the wild;
See the Father meets him out upon the way,
Welcoming his weary, wandering child.'"

The night before her death, she said, "Dear father and mother, I hope I shall meet you in Heaven. You cannot think how bright and happy I feel," and half an hour before her departure she exclaimed, "O! mother, listen to the bells of Heaven, they are ringing so beautifully." She closed her eyes awhile, but presently she cried again, "Hearken to the harps, they are most splendid; O! I wish you could hear them," and then, "O! mother, I see the Lord Jesus and the angels. O, if you could see them too! He is sending one to fetch me!" About five minutes before her last breath she said, "Lift me up from the pillow; high, high up! O! I wish you could lift me right up into Heaven!" Then doubtless conscious that the parting moment was at hand, "Put me down again, quick," and calmly, joyously, brightly, with her eyes upward, as if gazing upon some vision of surpassing beauty, she peacefully breathed forth her spirit into the arms of the ministering angels whom Jesus had sent for her. How can we measure what the voice of the singer had done for that little girl.

A Novelty in Religious Work

An innovation in Mr. Sankey's singing was the use of the parlor organ to accompany himself. Wherever he went this little instrument was placed upon the platform for his use, and it is doubtful if he could have found anything more effective for his accompaniment. Criticised it was, for, like "singing the Gospel," it was a novelty in religious work and, therefore, was frowned upon by those who felt that established methods should never be violated. It was even charged that he had been sent to England by a firm of organ makers who paid him a large salary on the condition that he use their organs in his services. This charge was denied both by the organ makers and by Mr. Sankey, and it does not seem likely that a man, who by agreement with Mr. Moody, turned over a fortune in royalties on books of song to charitable and religious purposes, would stoop to accept such an unworthy tribute.

At a children's meeting in Edinburgh in 1874, M. Sankey related the following incident: " I want to speak a word about singing, not only to the little folks, but also to grown people. During the winter after the great Chicago fire, when the place was built up with little frame houses for the poor people to stay in, a mother sent for me one day to come to see her little child, who was one of our Sunday school pupils. I remembered the little girl very well, having often seen her in our meetings, and was glad to go.

A Little Girl's Testimony

She was lying in one of the poor little huts, all the property of the family having been destroyed by the fire. I ascertained that she was beyond all hopes of recovery, and that they were waiting for the little one to pass away. 'How is it with you to-day?' I asked. With a beautiful smile on her face, she said, 'It is all well with me to-day. I wish you would speak to my father and mother.' 'But,' said I, 'are you a Christian?' 'Yes.' 'When did you become one?' 'Do you remember last Thursday in the Tabernacle when we had that little singing meeting, and you sang, 'Jesus Loves Even Me?' 'Yes.' 'It was last Thursday I believed on the Lord Jesus, and now I am going to be with Him to-day.' That testimony from that little girl in that neglected quarter of Chicago has done more to stimulate me and to bring me to this country than all that the papers or any persons might say. I remember the joy I felt when I looked upon that beautiful child face. She went up to Heaven, and no doubt said that she learned upon earth that Jesus loved her, from that little hymn. If you want to enjoy a blessing, go to the couches of the bedridden and dying ones, and sing to them of Jesus, for they cannot enjoy these meetings as you do, and you will get a great blessing to your own soul."

A story is told of a young Highlander who had lived far from the Lord for so long that his pastor had come to believe that the truth could not touch him, but one day he was found deeply awakened. When asked what had brought about this change in his feelings he said that it was the result of hearing his little sister sing.

"When He cometh, when He cometh
To make up His Jewels."

During the great revival in Scotland, a certain writer said, "Perhaps not a week has passed during the last year in which we have not had evidence that the Lord had directly used a line of one of these hymns in the salvation of some soul."

Wonderful Spiritual Returns

Mr. Moody's preaching, Mr. Sankey's singing—how indissoulbly these two are associated in the minds of millions of people! And how wonderful were the spiritual returns that this partnership brought! Often Mr. Moody's words would bring a sinner to the point of conviction, and then the tender pathos of Mr. Sankey's singing would let a great flood of blessing into that sinner's soul, and the softening influences would work until he would cry out in his joy, "I am saved!" And, on the other hand, when a meeting had just begun, and away back in the farthest corners men were sitting who had come in a scoffing mood, or out of curiosity, to hear the evangelists, the preliminary song of Mr. Sankey would rouse the attention of those persons, and they would try to get nearer the platform, and by the time Mr. Moody was ready to speak, they would have forgotten why they had come, in their eagerness to hear the preacher's message.

Mr. Sankey's singing was as direct in its appeal to the individual as Mr. Moody's speaking. Their was no sentimental

MR. MOODY PREACHING IN THE GREAT OPERA HOUSE, HAYMARKET, LONDON.

clap-trap about either, in spite of the charge which we have frequently heard to that effect against the "Gospel hymns". Music, of all the arts, is now in the highest development. John Addington Symonds in his story of the Renaissance tells us that the form of art in which any given generation finds the most perfect expression for its ideals of beauty depends upon the nature of the religious feeling of that generation, Thus, the mysticism of the mediæval Church was typified in the symbolism, the lofty aspiration of Gothic architecture; the rich formalism, the sensuous comprehensiveness of the Church of Rome in the sixteenth and seventeenth centuries established the ideals and led to the feelings which were spread in glowing colors upon the canvasses of the greatest painters the world has ever known; while, in present times, the development of religious life to a plane of lofty hope, brotherly love, and a consciousness of salvation has found its highest expression in music.

A Blessed Partnership

Music comes from the heart in a way that words cannot; there are times when its appeal is resistless, and so, for nearly thirty years, to the sound sense of Mr. Moody's words, illumined as they were by the reflection of a great heart, was added the appeal of Mr. Sankey's song. Surely this partnership was blessed beyond our comprehension.

It has been wonderful the way Mr. Sankey's song has been carried beyond the mere locality of utterance. An illustration of the way in which it heralded and accompanied the Gospel message as sent out from the words of his brother evangelist is found in the letter of a traveler who was going from England to France in 1875. "It has been perfectly delightful," he says "to find traces of the work everywhere. While waiting at ―― I heard a porter filling the whole station with the 'Sweet Bye and Bye.' As he came up to my carriage, I was struck with his bright, cheery face and spoke to him. The man's face glowed when he talked of Mr. Moody and Mr. Sankey. * * * Sunday afternoon at ———, I was alone in the reading room and began to sing to myself one of 'the hymns'. Presently the door creaked, and on looking up I saw that a whole bevy of maids had gathered and were listening attentively. It was so unlike what foreign servants would do, I felt sure that they must be English, and I knew that if I moved they would run away, so I sang on as if I had not seen them. Then an old gentleman came in, and on my stopping, said, 'O! don't stop, but please sing 'The Home Over There'. He went on to tell that he had been sitting gloomily in his room when he heard a Sankey hymn. How one is taught every day that one's 'times' are not in one's own hands! I wanted to sing for my own selfish gratification; but I was shamed by being shown how it might be used, for others came in after, and a band of us sang 'Hold the Fort', a specially necessary command it seems when traveling abroad."

CHAPTER X.

Evangelistic Work in England, Ireland and Scotland.

WHEN Mr. Moody arrived at Liverpool, June 27, 1873, he set foot upon English soil for the third time. His former trips had been brief; now he had come with a determination "to win ten thousand souls for Christ." The first word received on landing was disappointing. He learned that the two friends who had invited him to England, the Rev. Mr. Pennefather, rector of the Mildmay Park Church, in London, and Mr. Cuthbert Bainbridge, an eminent Wesleyan layman, had recently died. A third invitation had been given by Mr. George Bennett, Secretary of the Young Men's Christian Association in York.

The Outlook Not Encouraging

Mr. Moody telegraphed to Mr. Bennett announcing his arrival and readiness to begin work, but the reply stated that there was so little religious warmth in York that it would take at least a month to get ready for the meetings. Mr. Moody, however, was not afraid of the prevalent spiritual frost. He telegraphed to his friend, "I will be in York to-night," and at 10 o'clock in the evening arrived in that city, unheralded and unknown.

The outlook was not encouraging, but Mr. Moody sent for Mr. Sankey, who had gone from Liverpool to Manchester, and the meetings began at once. Only eight persons attended the first meeting. The other meetings on this first Sunday betrayed a somewhat wider interest, but during the following week the congregations were very small indeed. The second week was marked by some improvement, and before the month was over, in spite of the coldness manifested by the ministers of the place, the work had made a considerable impression. The inquiry meetings were an innovation in English services, but they grew in favor and became more and more an important instrument of spiritual success. The number of converts at York was in the neighborhood of two hundred. The work closed with an all-day meeting, beginning with an hour for conversation and prayer and continued with an hour for praise, a promise meeting, a witness meeting, a Bible lecture by Mr. Moody, and finally a communion service. The meetings were chiefly held in chapels, the evangelist preferring not to go to public halls for fear of seeming to neglect the regularly established forms of worship.

Sunderland

After attending some of Mr. Moody's meetings at York, the Rev. Arthur Rees, a liberal Baptist clergyman of Sunderland, invited the American evangelists to come and help him in his work. Accordingly Mr. Moody and Mr. Sankey began meetings in Mr. Rees' chapel, Sunday, July 27th. Here, as at York, coldness had to be delt with, and moreover the evangelists had been heralded from the scene of their first labors by criticism rather than by praise. Still from the first large congregations attended the meetings, although there is little doubt that the early motive of attendance was curiosity.

Gradually the people of Sunderland awoke. In order to avoid the appearance of sectarianism, Mr. Moody had the meetings removed to the Victoria Hall, though overflow meetings were generally conducted in various chapels.

Even after the power of the Spirit took hold of the people of Sunderland, ministerial criticism of the evangelists' course increased, but Mr. Moody was not without friends. None of the attacks troubled him so long as the Holy Spirit was manifested in the meetings and people were being converted. At the close of the month the results were not what he had hoped for, but it is interesting to note that long after the evangelists had left, and when news of the great work of God through them in Scotland came back to Sunderland, the city was stirred profoundly, and moved to genuine revival power.

Newcastle

By invitation of the Rev. David Lowe, Mr. Moody went from Sunderland to Newcastle-upon-Tyne, spending a few days in Jarrow on the way. He was greeted at Newcastle by Mr. Thomas Bainbridge, a brother of one of the friends who had invited him to England.

At Newcastle the fire was kindled which was to mightily move Great Britain. Ministerial opposition was overcome, five of the principal chapels of the town being offered for the services. Mr. Moody accepted the use of the Rye Hill Baptist Chapel, a large edifice, and within a fortnight crowds were turned away for want of room. All the neighboring towns and villages felt the spiritual impulse, and in response to requests hundreds of meetings were held outside the city by multiplying assistants of the evangelist.

Mr. Moody, in order to prevent the exclusion of the unconverted by the crowds of Christians who attended the meetings, now began to divide his congregations into classes, giving tickets of admission to the various services. Meetings for merchants were held in the Assembly Hall; meetings for mechanics were held at the Tyne Theatre, and in each instance the size of the crowds usually necessitated three or four overflow meetings.

The name and residence of every inquirer was made a matter of record, and in order that assistants in the inquiry room should be more fitted to the purpose, tickets were issued to clergymen and other men of practical experience in Christian work, that they might help in the great work of leading souls to Christ. At first most of the conversions were among the educated classes, but afterward the work became more general. The noon prayer meetings which had been commenced previous to the arrival of Mr. Moody, by way of preparation, had grown to remarkable proportions, while Mr. Moody's afternoon Bible readings drew even from the ranks of busy merchants and professional men. Two whole-day meetings or conferences were held. During the last week of the meetings, the Jubilee Singers began their connection with the work.

As a result of this month's work, hundreds of converts were received into the churches, and the whole North of England was aroused. Scores of Christian workers were sent out to carry the good tidings to the remoter districts, and the stimulus to the various churches proved unprecedented. Mr. Moody and Mr. Sankey now moved toward Scotland, holding on the way brief, though successful, series of meetings in a number of small cities.

Edinburgh.

To understand the influence of the labors of Mr. Moody and Mr. Sankey in Scotland, it is important to know something of the rise and progress of her Christian character. This takes us back to the Reformation, to the Christian organization of John Knox. In all subsequent struggles Scotland realized that the work of the Reformers had had much to do in fostering the zeal and spiritual independence for which her people were ever distinguished.

EVANGELISTIC WORK IN ENGLAND, ETC.

Down to the close of the last century the light of the Reformation shone clearly, but an eclipse came, and it was not until the appearance of the brothers James and Robert Haldane that the sun again burst forth. These men, with Mr. Simeon, an evangelical clergyman of Cambridge, were Scotland's first great evangelists. In ten years they established more than one hundred independent churches, providing also for the training of ministers. The next era was the disruption of the Church of Scotland in 1843. This, strangely enough, proved to be the beginning of Christian union, for non-conformist brethren offered to the ministers who had given up their livings and entered the Free Church of Scotland the use of their churches for half of every Sunday. Thenceforward there was one body in Christian work.

Mr. Moody's meetings commenced late in November in the Free Church Assembly Hall. From the first no place in Edinburgh could contain the crowds. Three or four of the largest halls and churches were constantly in use, and even then it was necessary to come to the place of meeting an hour or two before the appointed time in order to be sure of admittance. The converts were numbered by thousands. The awakening among the nominal church members could hardly be described. As an example of the thoroughness of the work it is stated that at one meeting, composed of sixty-six young men, sixty were converted before they left the place.

The watch-night meeting, which closed the year 1873, was perhaps the most remarkable service that had ever been held in Edinburgh. For five full hours a great audience, many of them obliged to stand, praised God and gave their testimony to the work of His saving grace in them. The Christian Conference on January 4th was attended by about 150 ministers; such a meeting had never been seen in Edinburgh before. The farewell meeting was held in the fields on the slope of Arthur's Seat, there being no building which could accommodate the multitudes who wished to join in the last service of their brethren from America. As a result of the work in Edinburgh fully 3,000 persons were received into the churches.

The Work in Scotland Continued.

From Edinburgh Mr. Moody went to Dundee, January 21st, and for several weeks the visitations with which the Holy Spirit had blessed other cities came to this old stronghold of Scottish faith.

The meetings began at Glasgow on February 8th. Three thousand Sunday-school teachers surrounded the evangelists in the City Hall at the first meeting. An hour before the time for the services such a crowd had assembled that four large churches in the neighborhood were filled by the overflow. Mr. Moody had been in Glasgow in 1872, when he had attracted no attention; now from the start the revival work exhibited a power almost unparalleled. The Glasgow noon prayer meeting had been commenced during the week of prayer for Scotland, which was held in Edinburgh a month before the evangelists went to Glasgow. This preparation was not in vain.

At first, church-going people were affected. Then the hand of God touched the great masses of the population who were without the fold. Meetings were held in the streets and squares of the city; fathers and mothers met to pray for the conversion of their children; children's meetings were also held. The great conference of Christian workers at the Kibble Crystal Palace in the Botanic Gardens, April 16, renewed the vigor of all departments of home missionary work in Scotland.

DWIGHT L. MOODY—Photograph from the painting presented to him by his English friends in 1884. This photograph was made by our photographer at the home of Mr. Moody, at Northfield, the day following the funeral, December 27, 1899.

The last meetings were the greatest of all. Going to the evening service the carriage of Mr. Moody was almost blocked by the dense throngs which surrounded the Crystal Palace, and, seeing the multitudes, the evangelist determined to preach from the carriage, as there were more without the building than within. Those inside the palace, learning of the change of program, immediately joined the throng outside, and the service which followed was one of wonderful effect. At the close of the discourse, Mr. Moody invited inquirers to meet him at the palace, and this great audience hall was filled. Large numbers gave themselves to Christ. It was at Glasgow that Henry Drummond was drawn to this great evangelistic movement.

While in Glasgow the evangelists made several brief excursions to neighboring cities.

The Tour in the North.

About the middle of May, Mr. Moody and Mr. Sankey, after a three days' visit to Edinburgh, went northward through Scotland, stopping in Perth, Montrose, Aberdeen, Inverness, and in some other towns. To the very end of Scotland, to John'-o'-Groat's house, the evangelists went, meeting crowds of people at every stopping place, and holding service after service, generally in the open air. At Aberdeen 12,000 to 20,000 people attended the outdoor services; at Inverness the meetings were held at the time of the annual wool fair, and many were reached who had been spending their lives beyond the reach of the churches. On returning from the north, farewell meetings were held in some of the places where the evangelists had labored.

The Evangelists go to Ireland

Mr. Moody and Mr. Sankey had received invitations from many different quarters, and they now decided prayerfully that the greatest opportunity before them lay in Ireland. Accordingly they bade good-bye to Scotland, and on September 6th, held the first meeting in Belfast, at Dougal Square Chapel. The second meeting was held in a larger church, while the evening meeting was adjourned to a still larger place of worship, with seating capacity for about two thousand persons, which was only about one-quarter of those who tried to gain admission. In fact, in Ireland the attendance upon the meetings was but a repetition of the crowded following which had sought to come under the spell of the American workers in Scotland. On Monday a noon prayer meeting was commenced, and that, too, had to be adjourned to a larger building. It became necessary here, as in Scotland, to divide the audiences, so that men's meetings, women's meetings etc., etc., were held. There were several great open air meetings. On one occasion two hundred young men gave themselves to Christ.

The evangelists had been invited to Londonderry by a committee of the Young Men's Christian Association, and there they went for four days, beginning October 11th, holding a number of notable meetings, and returning to Belfast on the 15th, to hold their farewell services there. The final inquiry meeting at Belfast was attended by about 2,400 persons, admitted by ticket; 2,150 converts' tickets were given before the close of the evening service.

Dublin.

The difficulty of finding a place large enough for the meetings had led Mr. Moody to name to the brethren at Dublin, as a condition of his coming, the engagement of the Exhibition Palace. This condition was met; the Palace was engaged, and on October 24th, Mr. Moody and Mr. Sankey arrived in the Irish capital.

There were in Dublin only about 40,000 Protestants, out of a population of 250,000, but the denominational line was frequently crossed by the work of the evangelists. Indeed, so deep was the encroachment of the revival upon the Roman Catholic population, that Cardinal Cullen felt himself called upon to interdict the attendance of his flock upon the Protestant meetings. In spite of this, many Roman Catholics were converted. Mr. Moody was unable to see why the line between Roman Catholicism and Protestantism should be observed in his work any more than the lines between different Protestant denominations. The fact that a man had a soul to save was a sufficient call to enlist his energies.

At Dublin, the Bible readings were, perhaps, valued more than any other of the services. One unique meeting was held for the soldiers of the garrison of Curragh, who attended in large numbers and were won by the stories and the earnest logic of the speaker. An organized society of Atheists tried their hand at opposing Mr. Moody by introducing their members into the inquiry meetings, but the scheme was discovered, and the intruders were not allowed to enter into debate or useless conversation.

The thoroughness with which the hearts of the Irish people were touched was evidenced by their liberality in providing funds to meet the expenses of the meetings. £1,500 were required, and 5,000 or 6,000 of the leading citizens of Dublin were invited by circular to contribute. There were only two instances of personal solicitation, but the money came in so rapidly that it was difficult to keep track of it. Mr. Moody and Mr. Sankey did not work for pay; they took whatever the Committees on Finance in the various cities where they were conducting services regarded as a suitable remuneration,—this in spite of the inevitable criticism made by opponents of the movement that the evangelists were "in the business for the money they could get out of it".

Dublin was merely the center of the revival interest. All over Ireland the spell was so powerful, that the mere announcement in a village that some man who had been to the Dublin services would tell what he had seen there, was sufficient to draw a great crowd. The meetings closed on November 29th, after a conference of three days, which was attended by about 800 ministers. The meeting for converts on the second day of the conference called together about 2,000 persons. When their labors ended, Mr. Moody and Mr. Sankey went once more to England, this time not unheralded.

In Ireland, as in Scotland, the spirit which they had aroused continued to manifest itself in many increasing results.

The Evangelists Return to England

The first meetings of the new campaign in England, were held at Manchester. Within a week it was said, "Manchester is now on fire." The services here were not marked so much by that joyful spirit which had characterized the evangelism of Scotland and Ireland, as by a solemn earnestness, and the influence of the meetings proper was extended in a great many practical ways throughout the city and its environs.

An important result in Manchester was the impulse given by Mr. Moody to the Young Men's Christian Association movement. He held one meeting after which a large collection was given toward a new building for the Association, and this sum proved the nucleus of more than £30,000 which was ultimately raised for the purpose. Nearly 500 names were added to the roll of active members of the Association.

Sheffield and Birmingham

Meetings were held in Sheffield, beginning on the night of December 31, 1874. It was not easy to arouse the unimpressible metal workers of Sheffield, and at first considerable disappointment was felt in the results of the services, but it was not long before the power of the evangelists' message became manifest.

Leaving Sheffield thoroughly awakened, Mr. Moody and Mr. Sankey went to Birmingham where their meetings began on January 17th, being held in the great Town Hall with its seating capacity for 5,000 persons. In the evening the services were held in Bingley Hall, a great enclosed area which was customarily engaged for the annual cattle show. In spite of its accommodations for 10,000 or 12,000 persons, the immense building was thronged every evening, an hour before the time of service. The conference with which the Birmingham meetings closed was attended by ministers from all parts of Great Britain. After the departure of the "brethren from America", the work of grace continued just as it had in every city which they had visited.

LIVERPOOL.

Mr. Moody came to Liverpool as an old friend. As the city contained no hall large enough for his purposes, an immense temporary structure, called the Victoria Hall, had been erected. It held about 10,000 persons, and the expense of building it was met by voluntary contributions, no direct solicitation being made. This was the first hall erected during the campaign especially for revival services. At the first meeting two-thirds of the congregation were young men. The noon prayer meeting was sometimes attended by 5,000 or 6,000 persons. Eighteen services were held each week in the Victoria Hall, and the Gospel was also carried into the streets and byways, and missionary services were held in warerooms and in stables, as well as in the open.

It was during one of the Liverpool meetings, that Mr. Moody gave a remarkable exhibition of his organizing abilities. A great meeting was being held and the theme for discussion was,

"How to reach the Masses". One of the speakers expressed the opinion that the chief want of the masses in Liverpool was the institution of cheap houses of refreshment to counteract the saloons. When he had finished, Mr. Moody asked him to continue speaking for ten minutes longer, and no sooner was this time up when Mr. Moody sprang to his feet and announced that a company had been formed to carry out the objects the speaker had advocated; that various gentlemen had taken 1,000 shares of £1 each, and that the subscription lists would be open until the end of the meeting. The capital was gathered before adjournment, and the company was soon floated, being known as " The British Workmen Company, Limited". It has not only worked a revolution in Liverpool, but has paid a handsome dividend as well.

During the month at Liverpool, the number of persons converted, or awakened, ran into the thousands. The inquiry rooms were invariably crowded.

The London Revival.

"If I come to London," Mr. Moody had said, "you will need to raise £5,000 for expenses of halls, advertising, etc." "We have £10,000 already," was the reply. This shows the spirit in which the efforts of Mr. Moody and Mr. Sankey in the Metropolis of the world were anticipated. The work of preparation had been carried on by able committees. Preliminary daily prayer meetings were crowded,

It was decided to attack the city in the four quarters. The meetings began in the north and were held in the great Agricultural Hall. The congregations in this immense structure averaged during the first week about 18,000 persons, but it was impossible to make so large a number hear the preaching, and the size was reduced, by means of temporary partitions, to the capacity of about

14,000, and even then it was constantly overcrowded. The inquiry meetings were held in St. Mary's Hall, but so great was the curious crowd, which blocked the adjacent streets, that it was found advisable to remove these meetings to one of the galleries of the Agricultural Hall itself.

The services were managed by a committee, with the assistance of seventy or eighty ushers. Interest increased weekly. Sometimes 400 or 500 persons at one time would be conversing in the inquirers' galleries about the salvation of their souls. As in other places, the work began with the better classes, and was afterward extended to the slums.

The campaign in the East End, which began five weeks after the meetings in the North End, centered in Bow Road Hall, built especially for the services, and designed to hold an audience of 10,000 persons. Overflow meetings were held in a large tent near the building.

In the West End the services were held in the Royal Opera House, where many thousands thronged the three or four different meetings which were held each day. For several weeks Mr. Moody divided his attention between the Opera House and the Bow Road Hall.

It was at this time that the controversy arose regarding the meetings at Eton. The patrons of the famous college which is situated in that little town, did not wish their sons subjected to irregular religious influence, and the matter was even taken up by the House of Lords. The evangelists had been invited by a large majority of the students in the college, but pressure in high quarters made it inadvisable to accept the invitation in its full intent. A meeting was held in the private grounds of a gentleman at Eton, and there Mr. Moody preached to about two hundred of the college boys, and two or three times as many citizens of the town.

In conducting the meetings in South London, a new hall, erected for them near Camberwell Green, was occupied by the evangelists. This structure seated about 8,000 persons. Here the chief interest centered in the inquiry room, where the spirit was as earnest and as deep as it had been in the other quarters of the city. When Mr. Moody and Mr. Sankey discontinued services in one of the four quarters of the city, the meetings were continued by others, and the fire which God had permitted the two evangelists to kindle was not suffered to die out. The final service was held July 12th, the evangelists having conducted 285 meetings in London, and having addressed fully 2,500,000 persons. Mr. Moody and Mr. Sankey hastily withdrew at the conclusion of this last service, rather than face the ordeal of parting with so many dear friends. This was ever Mr. Moody's custom.

The last meeting in England was held in Liverpool, and on October 6th, attended by many loving prayers, Mr. Moody and Mr. Sankey set sail toward the West, arriving in New York eight days later.

Can We Measure the Results?

Lecky, the historian, calmly and dispassionately asserts that the evangelistic labors of John Wesley and his co-workers, by lifting the moral tone of the common people, saved England from a revolution. Mr. Moody may not have served as an instrument for the accomplishment of so deep an economic purpose, but it is certain that the regenerating springs of spiritual life, which God used him to draw from the rock of indifference, refreshed and revived a people fast tending to religious numbness. And nothing is so dangerous as this apathetic numbness; it has done more to hinder the progress of salvation than all the active forces of the devil put together.

FREE ASSEMBLY HALL, EDINBURGH. AWAITING THE TIME OF MR. MOODY'S MEETINGS.

I am not prepared to deny that many who were awakened or converted during Mr. Moody's labors in Great Britain went back to their former walks soon after the immediate presence of the evangelists ceased to be felt; nor will I deny that much of the work inspired by his efforts crystallized into conventional and narrow forms; but I believe from the bottom of my heart that the movement blessed Britain as she had not before been blessed for one hundred years, and I know that tens of thousands of persons became better men and women for the effect of Mr. Moody's words upon them. Through this man God led men to read their Bibles, to live honestly, to rid themselves of besetting sins, and to place their faith in Christ as a personal Saviour.

CHAPTER XI.

Evangelistic Work in the United States.

ON his return from Great Britain, Mr. Moody went to Northfield, there to spend some little time resting at his old home and enjoying the companionship of his relatives. It will be readily understood that although he had gone from the United States two years before known to very few, the wonderful results of his labors in Great Britain had made his name a household word, and his fellow-countrymen awaited his active work in this country not only with curiosity (which it must be admitted was felt by a large body of unbelievers and indifferent ones) but also, many of them, with a deep conviction that the Lord had raised him up to lead the people in a great religious awakening.

Gospel Campaign in Brooklyn

The Gospel campaign in the United States began at Brooklyn, on Sunday, October 24, 1875. The skating rink on Clarmont Avenue, with its seating capacity of six thousand, was secured for the use of the services. Preliminary work had been conducted in Brooklyn according to the system which Mr. Moody invariably insisted upon, so that when he took up the work in person, almost everything was already in full swing. A chorus of two hundred and fifty voices had been organized to lead the music. Interest accumulated with the progress of the services, and the size of the audiences uniformly increased. Nothing in secular affairs seemed capable of drawing off the public attention, not even an exciting election, with its public meetings and torchlight processions. The very first meetings brought together enormous crowds. These audiences, it was surmised, might have been attracted by curiosity; but the novelty soon wore off, and yet the weekday meetings at 8 A.M. and 7.30 P.M., overflowed and had to be accommodated in neighboring churches. The "overflow" meetings continued as a feature of the work until the last. In the second week, a woman's prayer meeting followed the morning service, and a Bible reading was held in the afternoon, beside the regular evening meeting. These additional gatherings were almost as largely attended as the others. To all of these was added a young men's meeting held at night after the evening service to accommodate the clerks and other persons detained by business during the earlier hours, and inquiry meetings were also held in the adjoining churches. Still there was no falling off in the crowds who could not find even standing room.

Different Appearance of the Audiences

It is difficult to estimate the numbers who attended during the meetings. Counting in the overflow meetings the audiences must have included, especially toward the last, from fifteen thousand to twenty thousand per day. Perhaps a higher estimate would be nearer the fact. As in Great Britain, different expedients were employed to change the class attendance,—expedients which would have been fatal to a less absorbing interest. To many of the meetings in the Rink church-goers were not invited; indeed they were asked to stay away, and admission was procurable only on the statement that a ticket was to be used by some unconverted person. The different appearance of the audiences on successive nights was fair evidence that they were not composed of the same people.

The effect of the Brooklyn meetings was an awakening rather than a great conversion of non-church-goers, and prepared the churches for greater activity. As in England, the first work of the evangelists fell somewhat short of that which was to follow. No attempt was made to record the number of conversions, although they were by no means few. A feature of the work was the hearty and undivided support of the churches; at one prayer meeting nearly one hundred ministers were present.

During these meetings Mr. Moody sounded he keynote of his theory, if such it may be called, of bringing about a great religious awakening. He said to Henry Ward Beecher, "There is no use attempting to make a deep and lasting effect on masses of people, but every effort should be put forth on the individual."

The meetings closed November 19th. At the final service the building was crowded almost beyond its limit, while the streets were filled with thousands of persons who were disappointed in their endeavor to get in.

Campaign in Philadelphia

From Brooklyn Mr. Moody and Mr. Sankey went to Philadelphia and began their meetings in the old Pennsylvania Railroad depot at Thirteenth and Market Streets, now occupied by Mr. John Wanamaker as a great mercantile establishment.

The depot was situated in a dull and uninviting neighborhood, comparatively deserted by night, and not very well lighted, and when the suggestion was made that the property might be temporarily renovated for an auditorium until the railroad company should find a purchaser for it, there was considerable derision; but President Scott, of the Pennsylvania Railroad, had a hearty and large way of doing things, and he told the men who were giving their interest to the proposed meetings, that they could have the use of the property at the rate of one dollar per year, provided they were ready to get out at a month's notice when the company should effect a sale. It happened, however, that just about this time a Philadelphia merchant, Mr. Wanamaker, was laying plans to develop his business on a broader scale. He made the Pennsylvania Railroad Company an offer for the old depot, and became its purchaser; but, before proceeding to occupy it, he consented that the interior should be reconstructed temporarily for the revival services, of which he had been one of the chief projectors.

Preparatory Arrangements

About forty thousand dollars was spent in reconstruction and equipment of the building. Chairs were provided for about ten thousand persons, which leaves out of count the space upon the platform occupied by a chorus of six hundred singers. The expenses were met by voluntary contributions. Three hundred Christians were chosen to act as ushers while a like number of workers were selected to serve in the three inquiry rooms. The original intention had been to engage the Academy of Music, but this was overruled in favor of the depot, largely because of the suggestion that the novelty of such an auditorium would alone draw thousands of people.

The first day it rained; moreover the burning of Market Street bridge, the night before, had stopped the streetcars running on the chief thoroughfare to the place of meeting. Still the great improvised tabernacle was filled by an audience of 10,000. In Philadelphia, as elsewhere, Mr. Moody began by seeking to arouse the Christians to a sense of their responsibility. On one occasion, he spoke of the "dumb people in the churches who had said nothing for Christ for ten or fifteen years", and of the "dwarfs who had not grown since they were converted". On the second evening, a young men's meeting was conducted in Arch Street

Methodist Church, by Mr. John Wanamaker. With a few exceptions the clergy of the city took hearty interest in all the services. Many of them, whose acquaintance with Mr. Moody's methods was based entirely upon vague report, had looked forward with dread of sensational methods, but the quiet yet thorough way in which Mr. Moody entered upon his work brought to these doubters a feeling of gratified disappointment. On November 26th, the morning prayer meeting had an attendance of 8,000. A Methodist minister said, "If we had a hundred Moodys and Sankeys in the country all the Protestant sects would unite within ten years."

Variety of Subjects Discussed

The last evening service of the eighth week was attended by more than 13,000, while many thousands were turned away. The regular meetings ended January 16th. However, a convention for clergymen and Christian laymen was held January 19th and 20th; these developed more especially into services of praise. At the first meeting of the convention about 1,000 ministers and lay delegates were present. Mr. Moody spoke first on "Evangelistic Services". This was followed by "How to Conduct Prayer meetings"; "In-"Inquiry Meetings—Their Importance and Conduct", and "The Training of Young Converts and Lay Workers". On the following day the subjects discussed were, "How Should the Music be Conducted in the Lord's Work?" "How to Expound and Illustrate the Scriptures"; "How to Get Hold of Non-Church-Goers"; and "Our Young Men—What More can We Do for Them?" In the evening, Mr. Moody spoke on "Daniel". I mention these subjects to give an idea of the variety of thought which made the convention so helpful. Mr. Moody said that in all his experience thus far he had never seen such services as these in Philadelphia. For fifty miles around the city the country sent recruits, and the total attendance during the nine weeks was estimated at about 900,000. As a thank-offering a large sum was raised, amounting to about $127,000. The total expenses of the meetings were in the neighborhood of $30,000. After the evangelists had departed chairs and other articles which had been in use at the depot were sold at auction; the chair in which Mr. Moody had sat brough $55, as did also M. Sankey's chair. The principal employment of the great thank-offering collection was to help the Philadelphia Young Men's Christian Association complete its new building in time for the Centennial Exposition, which began the same year.

The meetings in Philadelphia established Mr. Moody's leadership of the Lord's active army in the United States. His clarion note had no uncertain sound.

The Great Campaign in New York

After leaving Philadelphia Mr. Moody took his family to Florida and rested for a time before entering on the great campaign in New York. But preparations in the metropolis were busily going on. Gilmore's Concert Garden, which had formerly been known as Barnum's Hippodrome, was rented for the services, $1,300 being paid weekly for its use.

The meetings in the Hippodrome began February 7, 1876, at 8 P. M. More than $15,000 had been expended on the building to make it completely serviceable. The crowds were handled by 500 ushers; a choir of 1,200 singers was placed under the order of Mr. Sankey; several hundred Christian workers gave their services to the inquiry rooms for inquiry work. There were, for work with the unconverted, each day two general directors and sixteen Christian leaders; each leader had twelve to fourteen helpers, so that in each of the seven inquiry rooms there were usually two leaders and twenty to thirty helpers. At the first meeting 7,000 persons were present in the main hall, and 4,000 others attending the overflow meeting, while several thousand were left in the streets. The service was fittingly opened with silent prayer. What that moment inaugurated for New York can never be estimated.

During the first week of services the aim was to arouse professed Christians to a higher sense of their responsibilities. The noon prayer meeting began on the second day, and at the prayer meeting after the evening service that same day almost all of the great audience who had listened to Mr. Moody's sermon on faith, remained. More than two hundred Christians who wished their faith quickened arose in response to Mr. Moody's question, and fifty unconverted persons asked for prayer. On the fourth day there were five distinct meetings, the aggregate attendance being about 20,000. But Sunday was naturally marked by the greatest crowds. On the first Sunday more than 25,000 persons attended the meetings. There were on that day two exclusive services, one for men and one for women. At the afternoon meeting for women, on Sunday, February 21st, 10,000 were present. At the evening meeting on that day such numbers arose for prayer that Mr. Moody said, "There are so many I can't count them; truly, God is in this house."

Glorious Enthusiasm for the Lord

The last two days of the Hippodrome meetings, April 18th and 19th, were devoted to the Christian Convention with which Mr. Moody's meetings generally ended. As a thank-offering the sum of $135,000 was raised. The last meeting for converts was attended by between three and four thousand persons who were able to testify to their conversion.

Both in extent of time and in the results accomplished the campaign in the New York Hippodrome was perhaps the most important ever conducted by Mr. Moody. In moving New York

THE OLD PENNSYLVANIA RAILROAD DEPOT, 13th and Market streets, Philadelphia. Used by Moody and Sankey for their great revival meetings in the Fall of 1875, now the site of Wanamaker's Department Store.

God moved the country, and the voice of the evangelists was heard throughout the land. There was so little of the sensational about the meetings that a narrative concerning them may seem monotonous, for the reason that one service so much resembled the others. In each was manifested intense earnestness for souls, and glorious enthusiasm in the work of the Lord.

It is not necessary to tell of all the great series of meetings which Mr. Moody conducted. After leaving New York he went by way of Augusta, Ga., Nashville, Tenn., Louisville, Ky., St. Louis, Mo., and Kansas City, Mo., to Chicago, and in all these cities his labors were blessed with great results. His greatest meetings in Chicago, however, were not held until October, 1876, a date from which they continued for some time. The campaign in Boston began in the last of January, 1877. The Boston meetings, like those in other cities, were a wonderful demonstration of God's power. The assistance of the late Dr. A. J. Gordon and Miss Frances E. Willard was especially helpful. Interest was so great that a daily paper, *The Tabernacle*, was published to further the work. Every home in Boston was visited by Christian workers.

In Baltimore 1878

From this time Mr. Moody's activity seldom ceased. One tour was followed by another, and hardly a city or town of any great importance in this country has failed to receive through his help a renewal of interest in spiritual affairs. The meetings in Baltimore in 1878 were marked by such notable results that I feel that possibly an account of them will most fittingly close this chapter concerning Mr. Moody's evangelistic work in the United States. After all there is space to do little more than indicate the general nature of his services to the Lord.

In the month of October, 1878 the services began in Baltimore. Mr. Moody had received a pressing invitation to visit Cleveland, but before he would give his answer he felt led to visit Baltimore. On his arrival he called into counsel some of the leading laymen of the city, and after talking the matter over with them, he was confident that God wanted him in that city. It was no half-hearted service, and, when he came to do his work, he brought to bear upon the city where he labored all his own personal influence, and the blessing also of his presence of his family. So, temporarily he removed from Northfield and came to dwell in Baltimore. A committee of laymen was selected to have charge of this work. The committee was as follows: Dr. James Carey Thomas, Dr. P. C. Williams, Gen. John S. Berry, Mr. G. S. Griffith, Mr. Henry Taylor, Mr. George W. Corner, and Mr. A. M. Carter.

EVERY EVANGELICAL DENOMINATION REPRESENTED

The following notice one day appeared in the daily papers: "D. L. Moody will conduct meetings for Christians at the Mount Vernon Place M. E. Church, Tuesday, Wednesday, Thursday and Friday of this week, at 4 P. M. Subject: "The Holy Spirit." The meetings in this church were simply preparatory to the great work which was yet to follow. Every evangelical denomination in the city was represented.

Special meetings for men were held in the Associate Reformed Church, and noonday meetings were held in the Maryland Institute. There were some notable experiences in these meetings. Several gamblers were seated in one of their accustomed haunts one evening when it was suggested as a joke that they go to hear Moody. The proposition was agreed to. The meetings were being held at that time in St. Paul's M. E. Church, South. At the close of the meeting M. Moody started towards the gamblers; they immediately arose to leave the building. He called out to them, "Don't go, men; I want to see you," but they kept on going. Following after them he called out, "Come back, young men, come back;" but they refused and left. A few days after this, one of them, who belonged to a prominent family in the city, was taken very sick, and as he lay upon his bed entirely helpless, was asked by one of Mr. Moody's workers, if he would not come to Christ. He made this promise: "If God will only allow me to leave this room I will become a Christian." He finally recovered, and one of the first things he did was to go to the meetings which were being held in the Associate Reformed Church. At the close of the preaching when the inquiry meeting was announced, Mr. Moody started down the east side aisle where this man was sitting. As he approached him he said, "I am glad to see you, I have been looking for you several weeks." "Why, you don't know me, Mr. Moody," said the man. "Yes I do," he answered, "you are one of those gamblers I saw out at Dr. Cox's church." The man fulfilled his promise to God by accepting Christ for his Saviour; gave a wonderful testimony of His saving power, and was instrumental in the conversion of many others who had been gamblers like himself.

"He Could Not Burn the Impression"

One great feature of Mr. Moody's work had always been the singing, the wisdom of which may be seen in the following: While he was holding services in the Monument Street M. E. Church, a man addicted to drink and with no thought of God attended one of the meetings. He was much impressed with the singing, particularly with one hymn, "Come, O, Come to Me." He heard the announcement for the day meetings, and he determined to attend. As he entered the church Mr. Bliss was singing the hymn above mentioned. The man bought a hymn book that he might read the hymn for himself, and testified that he had no peace. Finally he burned the book, but he could not burn the impression that had been made by the Spirit. He then drank the harder, but could not drown the impression. Time passed on; one night he wandered into the Methodist Church, and as he did so he heard them singing again, "Come, O, Come to Me," and there that night he obeyed the call and accepted Christ. The hymn was number eighty-eight (88) in Gospel Hymns, No. 3. Mr. Moody always spoke of him after that as No. 88.

During the meetings at Broadway M. E. Church, a pickpocket entered the meeting for the purpose of relieving some one of his gold watch, which he was not long in doing; after procuring his prize, he started to leave the church but was unable to do so, for those who were in had to remain, and those who were out could not get in; he was therefore led to listen, was much impressed with the sermon, and stayed for the inquiry meeting, where he accepted Christ as his personal Saviour. The next day the door bell of the parsonage was rung, and when the servant answered, she found no one, but tied to the knob of the door was a package. This when opened was found to contain a gold watch and chain, and with it a note stating the facts, and asking that it be returned to the owner, which was done. The repentant thief gave his name and address, but asked that he might be forgiven, as God had forgiven him.

"Do You Want This Saviour"

Dr. Leyburn's church (Associate Reformed), where the meetings, for men only, were held at 4 P. M. was the scene of many new births. One day a man who had lost all through drink and who had brought his family to the verge of starvation, was asked by an unsaved man to go to hear Mr. Moody. At first he ridiculed the idea, but finally said, "Can a fellow get warm there?" (his feet being out of his shoes). On being assured that he could, he went. He was ushered to the third seat from the front. Mr. Moody took for his text Matt. 1:21, "Thou shalt call his name Jesus for he shall save his people from their sins." The man said to himself, "That is what I need, some one to save me from my sins; I have been trying to save myself, and have made a miserable failure." When Mr. Moody had finished his talk, he looked straight at the man, and said, "Do you want this Saviour?" He answered, "I do." Turning to one of the workers, Mr. Moody said, "Go talk to that man." In a little while the worker said, "Would you like me to pray with you?" The man replied, "That is just what I have been wanting you to do ever since you have been here." The worker prayed, and a familiar expression with that man afterward was, "I left my sins in the third pew of Dr. Leyburn's church." He became a great worker for Christ, and is now a preacher of the Gospel.

"What Think Ye of Christ"

In this same church a physician who was an infidel, attended the services, simply through curiosity. Mr. Moody's text was, "What think ye of Christ?" The next day he attended again, and Mr. Moody spoke on "Walking with God". He began an investigation to find if such a person did really live. This must be done outside the Word of God as he did not claim to believe in the Bible. The result of his investigation was the acceptance of the Christ of God and Bible. Since that time he has been an active Christian worker.

Perhaps no meetings were more interesting than those held in the Maryland Institute at noon. At the door taking tickets was a man who, but a few months before, was running a beer saloon in East Baltimore. On entering, one who knew him said, "Why, Tom, what are you doing here?" His reply was, "O, I have given up that business and accepted Jesus Christ as my Saviour, and now I am a doorkeeper in the house of my God."

On the 26th of March, 1879, Detective Tod B. Hall, of the Baltimore City Detective Force, entered the Institute looking for a man with whom he had business, who, he was told, was in the meeting. He was persuaded to remain and was ushered to a front seat. He was much impressed with Mr. Moody's earnestness and simplicity. The text was John III: 14, 15. "As Moses lifted up the serpent in the wilderness, etc." When he had finished his sermon, Mr. Moody asked that all Christians rise, and many arose. Then he said, "All those who believe that by putting into practice what I have said they will receive the benefits of a saved life, please rise."

THE DETECTIVE WAS ONE OF THE FIRST TO RISE

He then and there believed on the Lord Jesus Christ, and received Him as his personal Saviour. Passing out from the seats into the aisle he was met by many who knew him, and to all he said, "It is settled I am determined to live a different life the balance of my days." He entered the Institute to find a man, and found *The Man* Christ Jesus. His first act was to go to the City Hall, and into the office where the detectives were at that hour of the day. He told them what he had done, and how he proposed by God's help to live, and then said, "Now, boys, all I ask is, don't ridicule me, but give me your sympathy." He then and there started for his home, and when he arrived he found a strange lady in the house, and the devil suggested, "Don't say anything until this strange lady is gone." In his own language, "I saw it was a trick of the devil," and walking to the center of the room he said. "Annie, I left you this morning not worthy the name of a husband, **not worthy** the name of father to our children, but a little while ago, at the Maryland Institute, I determined to live a different life; let us kneel down and ask God to help me be a better man." They did so, that being the first prayer ever offered by him in his home; when he arose his wife said, "Tod, if you have made up your mind to be a Christian I will be one too;" and they both took their stand for Christ the same day. And no one who visited that home after that day, would doubt that Christ had an abiding place there. In July, 1896, his wife took her departure to be with Christ; as she bade him good-bye she said, "Tod, I'll wait and watch for you, and give you a royal welcome when you come."

HE LED SCORES OF MEN TO CHRIST

I know of very few men who have been more wonderfully blessed in their Christian experience than Tod B. Hall. I have seen him in my own church, and in other places, literally lead scores of men to Christ.

In the same place one day, as Mr. Moody was working in the after-meeting, he came to a man in the centre aisle and said, "Are you a Christian?" To this question the man replied, "Yes sir. I am glad to say, Mr. Moody, I am." Passing on, he came to one who was not a Christian. He suddenly turned to one of the ushers and said, "Tell that man to come here" (referring to the one who was glad he was a Christian). As he approached, Mr. Moody said, "Sit down there and talk to this man." Whereupon the man replied, "You will have to excuse me, Mr. Moody; that is something I never do." Mr. Moody turned to him quickly and said, "Either sit down and talk to that man, or else sit down and let some one talk to you."

On Friday evening, May 16th, Mr. Moody preached his last public sermon in the Mount Vernon Church, where nearly eight months before he had begun the meetings. On the evening of

May 26th, after the usual meeting of the converts in the Y. M. C. A. rooms, conducted by E. W. Bliss it was proposed that the entire company go in a body to Mr. Moody's house on Lanvale street. He was to leave the next day, and all wanted to show their love in this simply way. On reaching his house they sang, "He will hide us". Mr. Moody appeared and spoke loving words in saying good-bye. One of the company then sang, "There's a land that is fairer than day". Mr. Moody then offered a fervent prayer and said good-bye. The next day he left for his home in Northfield.

CHAPTER XII.

Mr. Moody In Two Wars.

WHEN the Civil War broke out Mr. Moody was one of the busiest men in Chicago. The Young Men's Christian Association work and his Mission were occupying his time fully, but he and his associates were not slow to see the great opportunity which the army camps afforded to reach throngs of men who were not easy to approach under normal conditions. Not long after the commencement of hostilities there came into being two great organizations, the Sanitary Commission and the Christian Commission—the one to look after the physical welfare, the other to look after the spiritual welfare of the soldiers.

THE SANITARY AND CHRISTIAN COMMISSIONS.

The Sanitary Commission was the result of the federation of the so-called "Soldiers' Aid Societies", which had individually already accomplished much good. At the outset the Government had not approved of these societies, fearing the effect of their operation upon the discipline of the troops, but, as their value became more apparent, and after they had been consolidated in one general organization, the field widened until the Sanitary Commission ranged in importance along with the Government Medical Bureau.

The Christian Commission was projected by a convention, held in Norfolk, Va., November 16, 1861, and Mr. George H. Stuart, of Philadelphia, was elected president. Like the Sanitary

Commission it was recognized and countenanced by the Government. Says one writer: "The Commissions aided the surgeon, helped the chaplain, followed the armies in their marches, went into the trenches and along the picket-lines. Wherever there was a sick, a wounded, a dying man, an agent of the Christian Commission was near by." As often as possible the workers gave Christian burial to the dead, and marked the graves so that later they could be identified by the relatives or friends. Religious services were conducted in camp or in the field; religious literature was distributed widely; in short, every means was employed to turn to the call of their Divine Master the attention of thousands of men who had answered their country's call.

Mr. Moody's Zeal

The Chicago Young Men's Christian Association was one of many whose individual efforts in behalf of the soldiers led to the convention which formed the Christian Commission. The devotional committee, of which Mr. Moody was chairman, began to work immediately after the second call for volunteers, when the great rendezvous of Camp Douglas was established near the southern limits of Chicago. The committee was on the ground at the arrival of the first regiment, and began prayer meetings at once. Religious literature was given out among the soldiers, and Sunday services were established where they could easily be attended by the soldiers. The work spread so rapidly that the committee was obliged to send out a call for assistants. One hundred and fifty men, clerical and lay, responded, and eight or ten meetings were held every evening in the different camps.

During the war the Association held more than 1,500 services in or near Chicago. The Association Chapel, built at Camp Douglas in October, 1861, was the first camp chapel erected.

Soldiers who were converted at Camp Douglas went to the front, and presently a call came to Chicago to send Christian workers to the Union lines. Mr. Moody answered this invitation in person, being the first regular army delegate from Chicago. His earliest work in the field was with the troops near Fort Donelson.

Mr. Moody's idea of the best treatment for dying soldiers was to carry to them the glad tidings of salvation and to point out to them the open gates of Heaven. He maintained that the administration of physical comforts was comparatively an unimportant matter. When death is a question of only a few hours and he whom the dark angel is claiming is far from the path of righteousness, who will care to hear of temporal things while some friend stands ready, to lead him back to the way of truth?

Experiences From the War

As long as the War continued Mr. Moody went back and forth between Chicago and the various camps and battlefields. How his experience was widened, how his faith was strengthened by the visions of grace which God permitted him to see! The triumphant deaths which he and his fellow laborers witnessed are almost beyond enumeration. Many were the assurances of salvation which came to their ears from dying lips, and they saw hundreds of ashy faces lighted up with a "light that never was, on sea or land". It was practical work, this. Often there was time only for a few words of prayer, or a brief exhortation But God's blessing came with the asking.

From the many stories which I have heard Mr. Moody tell of his experiences during the terrible years of the war, I have selected the following:

"I was in a hospital at Murfreesboro, and one night after midnight I was woke up and told that there was a man in one of the wards who wanted to see me. I went to him, and he called me 'chaplain'—I wasn't a chaplain—and he said he wanted me to help him die. And I said, 'I'd take you right up in my arms and carry you into the Kingdom of God if I could; but I can't do it; I can't help you to die.' And he said, 'Who can?' I said, 'The Lord Jesus Christ can—He came for that purpose.' He shook his head and said, 'He can't save me; I have sinned all my life.' And I said, 'But He came to save sinners.' I thought of his mother in the North, and I knew that she was anxious that he should die right, and I thought I'd stay with him. I prayed two or three times, and repeated all the promises I could, and I knew that in a few hours he would be gone. I said I wanted to read him a conversation that Christ had with a man who was anxious about his soul. I turned to the third chapter of John. His eyes were riveted on me, and when I came to the 14th and 15th verses, he caught up the words, 'As Moses lifted up the serpent in the wilderness, even so must the Son of Man be lifted up; that whosoever believeth on Him should not perish, but have eternal life.' He stopped me and said, 'Is that there?' I said, 'Yes,' and he asked me to read it again, and I did so. He leaned his elbows on the cot and clasped his hands together and said, 'That's good; won't you read it again?'

He Entered the Kingdom of God

"I read it the third time, and then went on with the rest of the chapter. When I finished, his eyes were closed, his hands were folded, and there was a smile on his face. O! how it was lit up! What a change had come over it! I saw his lips quivering, and I leaned over him and heard, in a faint whisper, 'As Moses lifted up the serpent in the wilderness, so must the Son of Man be lifted up, that whosoever believeth on Him should not perish, but have eternal life.' He opened his eyes and said, 'That's enough; don't read any more.' He lingered a few hours, and then pillowed his head on those two verses and went up in one of Christ's chariots and took his seat in the Kingdom of Cod.

"You may spurn God's remedy and perish; but I tell you God don't want you to perish. He says, 'As I live I have no pleasure in the death of the wicked.' 'Turn ye, turn ye, for why will ye die?'"

A CHRISTIAN SOLDIER

"After the terrible battle of Pittsburg Landing, we were taking the wounded down the Tennessee River to a hospital. I said to some of the Christian Commission, 'We must not let a man die on the boat without telling him of Christ and Heaven.' You know the cry of a wounded man is 'Water! water!' As we passed along from one to another, giving them water, we tried to tell them of the water of life, of which, if they would drink, they would never die. I came to one man who had about as fine a face as I ever saw. I spoke to him, but he did not answer. I went to the doctor, and said: 'Doctor, do you think that man will recover?' 'No; he lost so much blood before we got him off the field that he fainted while we were amputating his leg. He will never recover.' I said: 'I can't find out his name, and it seems a pity to let him die without knowing who he is. Don't you think we can bring him to?' 'You may give him a little brandy and water,' said the doctor; 'that will revive him if anything will.'

"TELL MY MOTHER I DIED TRUSTING IN JESUS"

"I sat down beside him, and gave him brandy and water every now and then. While I was waiting I said to a man near by: 'Do you know this man?' 'O yes, that is my chum.' 'Has he a father and mother living?' 'He has a widowed mother.' 'Has he any brothers or sisters?' 'Two sisters; but he is the only son.' 'What is his name?' 'William Clarke.' I said to myself that I could not let him die without getting a message for that mother. Presently he opened his eyes, and I said: 'William, do you know where you are?' He looked around a little dazed, and then said: 'O, yes; I am on my way home to mother.' 'Yes, you are on your way home,' I said; 'but the doctor says you won't reach your earthly home. I thought I'd like to ask you if you had any message for your mother.' His face lighted up with an unearthly glow, as he said: 'O, yes; tell my mother that I died trusting in Jesus.' It was one of the sweetest things I ever heard in my life! Presently, I said: 'Anything else, William?' With a beautiful smile he said, 'Tell my mother and sisters to be sure and meet me in Heaven;' and he closed his eyes. He was soon unconscious again, and in a few hours his soul took its flight to join his Lord and Master.

The Prison Doors Opened

"It was my privilege to go to Richmond with General Grant's army. Now just let us picture a scene. There are a thousand poor captives, and they are lawful captives, prisoners in Libby Prison. Talk to some of them that have been there for months, and hear them tell their story. I have wept for hours to hear them tell how they suffered, how they could not hear from their homes and their loved ones for long intervals, and how sometimes they would get messages that their loved ones were dying, and they could not get home to be with them in their dying hours. Let us, for illustration, picture a scene. One beautiful day in spring they are there in the prison. All news has been kept from them. They have not heard what has been going on around Richmond, and I can imagine one says one day, 'Ah, boys, listen! I hear a band of music, and it sounds as if they were playing the old battle-cry of the Republic. It sounds as if they were playing the 'The Star

Spangled Banner! Long may it wave o'er the land of the free and the home of the brave!' And the hearts of the poor fellows begin to leap for joy. 'I believe Richmond is taken. I believe they are coming to deliver us;' and every man in that prison is full of joy, and by and by the sound comes nearer and they see it is so. It is the Union army! Next the doors of the prison are unlocked; they fly wide open, and those thousands of men are set free. Wasn't that good news to them? Could there have been any better news? They are out of prison, out of bondage, delivered. Christ came to proclaim liberty to the captive."

Reminiscences of a Veteran

A veteran of the war tells the following story, which, while its importance is slight, gives an idea of the interest aroused by Mr. Moody's work.

"The death of Mr. Moody calls to my mind the first time I ever saw or heard of him. It was at Murfreesboro, Tenn., in the spring of 1862, when General Rosecrans was preparing his army for an advance on Tullahoma. Moody came there under the auspices of the Christian Commission. His preaching resulted in quite a revival in a number of regiments and brigades, and caused considerable excitement and great interest. General Alexander McDowell McCook, who commanded one of the corps, became much interested in the work. There was something of a rivalry between a number of regiments as to which furnished the most recruits to Moody's Christian army. They told a story on Colonel Fred Kneffler, of an Indiana regiment, who was an enthusiastic admirer and defender of his regiment and did not propose to allow it to play second to any regiment in the army of the Cumberland.

"One day an officer of another regiment came over and related in the hearing of Colonel Kneffler that the evening before some **twenty converts** had been baptized. This made the number exceed the converts of Colonel Fred's regiment by some twelve or fifteen. The Colonel immediately summoned his adjutant and in his extremely German brogue—made more broken by the excitement under which he labored—ordered him to detail fifteen men and have them baptized without delay."

The Revival at Camp Douglas

Mr. Moody was at Shiloh, at Murfreesboro, with the army at Cleveland and Chattanooga; he was one of the first to enter Richmond with Grant's army, devoting himself there to the soldiers of both armies without discrimination. But the greatest Christian work with which he was connected during the war was the revival among the Confederate prisoners at Camp Douglas. This camp, originally used for the instruction of Union recruits, was transformed into a prison at the time when about 10,000 rebel captives were sent there after the taking of Fort Donelson. The burden of the souls of these men lay heavy on Mr. Moody's heart. One day he secured a permit to visit them, and gave it to the secretary of the Young Men's Christian Association, himself accompanying him in the thought that as assistant to the other he might enter the lines without a question. The guard refused to let both the men in on one pass, Mr. Moody exhibiting in vain the can of oil which he was carrying to furnish light for the service. But the officer of the day, who overheard the conversation and came up to investigate, recognized Mr. Moody and took him to headquarters, where through the exercise of his official influence the young missionary was given a pass to go in and hold meetings for the prisoners whenever he might choose.

A few minutes later Mr. Moody and his friend, Mr. Hawley, began their first meeting for the prisoners. Deep interest was manifested from the start. Meetings were held in the prison camp thereafter every afternoon and evening. Great numbers were soundly converted, and they were organized into a Young Men's Christian Association. As large an opportunity as possible was given them for Christian culture. In this revival work a great many Christian ministers and laymen assisted.

What He Did for the Prisoners

The report of the Army Committee for the year 1865 shows a distribution of 1,537 Bibles, 20,565 Testaments, 1,000 prayer books, 2,025 hymn books, 24,896 other religious books, 127,545 religious newspapers, and 43,450 pages of tracts, besides 28,400 literary papers and magazines. The Camp Douglas chapel was erected at a cost of $2,300, and a soldiers' library and reading room were furnished by the Association, in a building erected by the Christian Commission. This was all in addition to the regular home work.

An employment bureau was established this year, chiefly for the benefit of the many wounded soldiers who were continually applying to the Association for assistance. Situations were found for 1,435 men, 124 boys, and 718 girls, besides transient employment for many persons who were unable to get out to service.

All this work was due in large part to the consecrated zeal of Mr. Moody. He never would be limited to a certain line of opportunity, but always took advantage of every chance to do something for his Master. His work during the Civil War exemplified all those qualifications of his which shone through his later and more extended efforts, and it was for him, moreover, practically the first recognition he received outside his own city of Chicago.

More than thirty years passed by before the United States again found itself in arms. Like the Civil War, the War with Spain was undertaken for the relief of an oppressed people. The opportunity for a Christian campaign in the army camps was as great in 1898 as in 1861, perhaps greater, and the organized forces of Christian workers were much more efficient at the outset in the later year. This increased efficiency in Christian organization, who shall say in how much it was due to Mr. Moody's service during the long interval?

IN THE WAR WITH SPAIN

April 25, 1898, three days after the President's first call for volunteers, the International Committee of the Young Men's Christian Association met in New York City to discuss the situation, and decided to undertake immediately a work among the soldiers and sailors. The organization had the machinery necessary for the undertaking. In nearly 700 cities throughout the country there were local associations; these in the several states were united in state organizations, with state committees and state secretaries, and were finally all bound together in an international organization, with its international committee, sub-committees and Secretaries. Accordingly, in order to promote united effort and to secure effective co-operation, the international committee appointed a sub-committee to organize and supervise the work, its official title being "The Army and Navy Christian Commission of the International Committee of Young Men's Christian Associations." The work of the Commission was divided into three departments: the Executive, for general supervision, with Colonel John J. McCook as chairman; the General work, for the direction of the social, physical and regular religious effort, including the Bible classes, with C. W. McAlpin as chairman; and the Evangelistic department, for the promotion of evangelistic effort in the different camps, with D. L. Moody as chairman.

The Evangelistic department through Mr. Moody kept a force of clergymen and evangelists in the field, co-operating with the regular religious work carried on in the tents. A careful and conservative estimate shows over 8,000 soldiers who publicly professed to accept Christ in all the meetings during the summer, while the number of those stimulated in their Christian lives cannot be estimated. An interesting fact in this connection is that the regiments that suffered most in the battles around Santiago were, with few exceptions, the regiments that, when in Tampa, were encamped around the great canvas-covered tabernacle where were held nightly services, some of which were attended by more than 2,500 soldiers, and where many of these men became Christians. One of these companies went into the battle with seventy-six men, and the next day, at roll call, only seventeen answered.

The work was established in the regiments of colored troops at the various camps, with colored young men of influence and ability in charge. This received the approbation of all students of the race problem. A prominent colored minister, after watching it carefully, termed it the "most practical and most helpful work I have ever seen carried on among the colored people."

Visitation of the Sick

In all the camps visitation of the sick was carried on, both the camp secretaries and visiting evangelists taking part in this service.

The following is one of many incidents: A new ward being opened one day was at once filled with sixty-six invalid soldiers. Going through the wards a worker came in contact with a sick boy from a Pennsylvania regiment, and stopping to talk to him, found the boy ready for the Gospel message. The boy said he came from a Christian home and had a brother in the missionary field, but that he had been a bad boy and had given his family much trouble. After talking with him a while, he said to the secretary, "Do you mean to say that I can be saved now and here?" The secretary assured him that such was the case, and opened to him the simple way of salvation. Before the secretary left, the boy joined him in prayer, praying for himself, and when he was leaving he said, " Now, remember, chaplain, I have accepted Jesus Christ as my personal Saviour, and in so doing you tell me I am saved." He exacted a promise from the secretary that he would return during the evening, and when he returned the boy greeted him cheerfully, and said, " I am a very sick boy, but remember, whatever comes, I tell you now that I have accepted Jesus Christ and am trusting Him as my Saviour." The next morning, as the secretary made his rounds, the soldier boy had gone to his long home.

On Sea and Land

The Commission followed closely in the wake of the Army of invasion, and pressed its work among the soldiers around Santiago de Cuba. It followed General Miles' army to Porto Rico, and with the third expedition to the Philippines workers and equipment were sent to render similar service.

The Navy Department at Washington supported the plan cordially, although from the nature of the case it was not easy to accomplish work on the ships. It was decided to place a representative of the Commission on each ship that had no regular chaplain, but the war was over so quickly that only one vessel was thus supplied. An idea of the feasibility of the work, however, is shown in the following incident from the one worker's report:

" At first, as I started to go over the ship with other things, I would fill my side pockets with copies of the New Testament, and give a copy away now and then, after a special personal talk with an open-hearted sailor or marine. As a matter of fact, I thought there would be no general eagerness for the books, and so great tact should be exercised in giving them out. I said to myself the first day, 'These 300 Testaments will last through my entire service,' but I was utterly mistaken. One day a marine said, 'What are those little books in your pockets?' I replied, 'Testaments.' Then he quickly said, 'Will you give me one?' I gave him one, and by that time there was about me quite a crowd of men who were off duty (I was below in their quarters), and they all wanted the books. From that time I gave away fifty books a day until they were all gone. One night I heard some one at my window. I sprang up, thinking it was a marine after a drink of ice-water; but, to my surprise, a sailor was standing there in the dark, like Nicodemus. He said, with some hesitation, 'Chaplain, I am after one of those little Bibles.'"

All this evangelistic work was directed by Mr. Moody from Northfield. His health made it inadvisable for him to go to the front during the summer heat, so he planned to take the field in person in the autumn. But when the autumn came the war was over, and his presence was no longer necessary. To him, however, belongs the credit of organization.

The Army and Navy Y. M. C. A.

At the beginning of the war, the International Committee undertook the task to which it had been manifestly called, with but little, if any, thought of the far-reaching possibilities of the future. When the war closed it was evident that a door of opportunity had been opened for a permanent service to a large and important class of young men. Accepting the responsibility of the situation, the International Committee voted to make the work, so auspiciously begun, a permanent feature of its plan and effort, and in September 1898, its Army and Navy Department was organized. The ninety-seven army posts in this country, and such as may be established in the new possessions, will form a field for extended effort, and already in several of these, associations have been organized. The regimental plan of organization is also being tested with good results. A comprehensive plan of work covering the entire Navy has already been inaugurated. A Naval Young Men's Christian Association has been formed.

Striking Illustrations

The following incidents illustrate the value of the evangelistic work during the war with Spain.

"I'll never surrender to Spain," said a great stalwart soldier, "but, boys, I'm going to surrender to Jesus Christ to-night." What that meant in the way of moral courage few can understand, facing as he did the jibes and sneers of his old companions.

At the close of a meeting in Camp Thomas theatre three soldiers came to an association worker and said that a man who had been converted a week before was sick, and wanted to see them. They went up to his tent, and found him suffering terribly, but rejoicing that he had accepted Christ. He said several times, "Well, I've lived right one week, anyway."

A young soldier from one of the Texas regiments was reproved gently by the camp secretary for swearing and he immediately arose and apologized, saying: "I don't know why I utter these oaths except that I am living in an atmosphere of obscenity and cursing; I never swore at home; I trust you will forgive me, sir; I did not realize that you were present."

It was at the close of the service in the Third Brigade Young Men's Christian Association tent, Camp Cuba Libre, Jacksonville, Florida. A hundred soldiers had risen for prayers, and at least fifty had come forward and given their hands in token of a surrender to Christ as a personal Saviour. The benediction had been pronounced when a bright-faced Virginia boy, nineteen years old, came to the platform and said: "Won't you pray for me, sir? I want to be a Christian here in camp." They knelt together, and others gathered around until twenty noble fellows were in the group of prayer. Nearly all confessed the Lord Jesus Christ in prayer and went down to their tents rejoicing.

"God Keep us From War"

From the activity which Mr. Moody displayed in the two wars which were fought during his working career, it might be thought that he was not averse to international conflicts. This was far from true. It was simply that when war came he saw in it, and took advantage of an opportunity to do good. Just before the commencement of the Spanish war, in a meeting at Pittsburg, he told his hearers what he thought of war.

"War, awful war!" he exclaimed. "Never has our country had more need of your prayers than at the present time. God keep us from war, if it be possible, and God keep hate of Spain out of our hearts! I have not met a man who served in the last war who wants to see another. God knows that I do not want to see the carnage and destruction that such a war would bring. God pity America and Spain. There are many mothers who will be bereaved, many homes broken up, if we have war. Have you thought of this?"

"Have you thought of this?" No; in the heat of preparation, in our eagerness to avenge a wronged people, in all the excitement of what seemed to be a Divine call to arms, many of us did not think of this. But the great, tender heart of Moody ached with the sorrow of anticipation. He knew that nations are nourished by the rain of mothers' tears; he knew that sad-faced fathers to-day, like Abraham of old, stand ready to offer up their sons on their country's altar. And with a pity—dare I say it?—a pity akin to the pity of his Master, he yearned for his people.

CHAPTER XIII.

The Spiritual Side of Northfield.

NORTHFIELD is beautiful for situation, and the words of the Psalmist in Psalm xlviii : 2, "Beautiful for situation, the joy of the whole earth, is Mount Zion," in the judgment of many people could be applied to this center of influence in the Christian world of to-day.

It is impossible to think of Northfield without thinking of Mr. Moody, and equally impossible to consider for a moment the work of D. L. Moody, without being compelled to give much consideration to his native town, the place he loved as few men love the place of their birth.

A Beautiful Place

Independent of its spiritual attractions, there are few more beautiful places; the Connecticut River, bending here and there between hill and vale, is more than interesting. The poet speaks of "rivers singing their way to the sea;" one can quite understand how this expression could be used in this connection, for we quite believe that it would be true of the Connecticut. And if the river itself could speak it would tell many a story of lives that from Northfield have sung their way on up to Heaven, and have started the melody of song in many other lives as well. It is said that Mr. Moody loved the view from his own house better than from almost any other point of observation, and well he might. Dr. Gordon once wrote of him, "Moody cannot endure the seashore; his green fields and ever shadowy hills and deep-rolling Connecticut are his paradise."

MR. MOODY IN A FAVORITE SEAT ON HIS NORTHFIELD CAMP GROUNDS. For many years Mr. Moody held a series of Bible Conferences at Northfield, which were attended by thousands of Christian workers from all over the country.

THE SPIRITUAL SIDE OF NORTHFIELD

Northfield is a typical New England town. It consists practically of one long street, on either side of which stand stately elms, their branches meeting overhead and forming an arch, which has ever increasing beauty for the lovers of the quaint old town. It has ever been a very winsome place both because of the fact that it is so far removed from the busy hum of cities as to make it restful, and also because here within the boundaries of the town so many people have seen themselves to be out of touch with God and have come to know Him in all His fulness, and thus have entered the life of blessing.

Northfield Dear to Mr. Moody

But Northfield was dear to Mr. Moody for more reasons than one, and I am quite sure that he never thought of it, that there were not more than a hundred reasons why it should be much to him. He used to say that when the train left Greenfield, which was not far away from his own home, he found himself so impatient to be with his loved ones that it was impossible to sit still, and so he would frequently walk up and down the aisle of the car until he was safely home.

The center of Northfield, to the pilgrim journeying thither from all parts of the world, was the home of Mr. Moody himself, and the visit to that home, and a vision of it, both within and without, furnished one of the best comments on his life. Here dwelt a man through whose hands millions of dollars had passed, and practically none of it, though he had the best of right to a portion of it, both legally and morally, was turned aside to give him what the world would count luxuries. Tens of thousands of homes are more beautifully and expensively furnished, but there was an air about this heart of Northfield which one detected the moment he crossed the threshold of the home—an air not of necessity associated with tapestries or pictures or paintings or furnishings ordinarily found in the homes of the rich, but which ever comes, when Christ is the unseen guest and the head of the house.

Is it Any Wonder That he Loved Northfield?

The old home was much to the Great Evangelist because it was his home. It was associated with his early struggles with poverty, with his father and mother, so dear to him, with his own immediate household, bound to him, it would seem, with ties stronger than those that ordinarily unite the members of the family; with the students whom he loved and whom it was his delight to help to gain an education. It was the scene of the beginning and the growth of the Bible Conferences, which have yearly increased in influence and power until the whole Christian world acknowledges its indebtedness to God for this fountain of blessing. There, at Mt. Hermon, the site of the boys' school, was started the Student Volunteer movement, which has been used of God to send hundreds of young men and women to foreign fields, and influenced hundreds more who now stand waiting for an opportunity to go. Is it any wonder that Mr. Moody loved Northfield? We love it too because it is associated with his triumphs. "Triumphs over the obstacles which stood in the way of his buying back his old home which had been lost by his father's failure in business. Triumphs over the discouragements that stood in the way of his giving an education to boys and girls who were poor, as he once had been; discouragements that would have defeated any other man, and at last the scene of the triumphant and victorious ending of his life and his glorious entrance into Heaven when he said, "Earth is receding, Heaven is opening, God is calling, and I must go."

Northfield is known throughout the world also because of the celebrated people whose names and words are interwoven in its latter day history. But whoever has visited Northfield in the past, or whoever may turn his face thither in the future, no name, however great it may be, can ever outshine his of whom we write. He was the gentlest, the kindest, the noblest Christian man it has ever been our good fortune to meet. One of the most familiar Northfield pictures was D. L. Moody sitting on the little porch in front of his house early in the morning hailing passers-by in whom he might have some special interest, directing this one, giving an order to another one, until he would have transacted half a day's business when others were just rising from their beds. I can hear his voice now as I write, as it sounded out one morning not later than 5.30 o'clock, when I heard him calling, "Chapman, Chapman," and, looking out of my window of Weston Hall, saw him sitting in his buggy ready for a drive, and then for an hour and a half we rode up through his favorite glen past Dr. Pierson's summer home, and the site where later Drs. Mabie and Torrey were to build.

His Great Love of Nature

His love of nature was manifest in every turn of the road. "Look at that," he would say, and before us was a beautiful picture of a running stream and bending boughs of trees, through which the morning sun was breaking. "Listen," he would exclaim again, and the whole of the forest on either side of the road seemed vocal with the song of birds. "Isn't it beautiful," he would say over and over. To take a morning ride with D. L. Moody was to see God in all nature, but most of all was to feel His presence in the remarkable personality of the man who sat beside you, impressing you by his every word and gesture with the fact that he was absolutely surrendered to God.

It always seemed to me that his favorite meal for guests was breakfast. Happy that man who had an invitation to this feast of the day, for he could then see D. L. Moody at his best in his home life, and bow with him about his family altar, forth from which streams of blessing had gone to the very ends of the earth.

Northfield is associated with certain other people whom Mr. Moody was wise enough to call to his assistance and help. First and foremost would be Major D. W. Whittle; for next to Mr. Moody, as a preaching evangelist, stands Major Whittle, a man of plain speech and solid piety, whose words have been already owned of God to the awakening of thousands of souls.

Major Whittle is a native of Vermont, is about sixty-three years of age, and when Mr. Moody first met him was a resident of Chicago, where he was converted, and united with the First Congregational Church, under the pastorate of Rev. W. W. Patton, D. D.

Major Whittle was employed in the office of Fargo & Co.'s Express until the breaking out of the war, when he enlisted a company in Chicago and joined the army as a captain of infantry.

During his army life he maintained his Christian profession, and for a long time kept up a company prayer meeting,

At the close of the war he returned with the brevet rank of major, and soon after was offered a situation as business manager of the Elgin Watch Company, with a salary of five thousand dollars a year, which he accepted.

His work as superintendent of the West Side Tabernacle Sunday School, a mission opened by the first Congregational Church, was greatly blessed, and for some time before his entrance upon the work of an evangelist his services were in considerable demand as a Bible reader and helper in revivals of religion.

At length feeling called of God to a wider field of Christian labor, he resigned his position, with its ample salary, and gave himself wholly up to Christ, trusting in Him for direction and support.

Major Whittle is laid aside at Northfield now, his very presence in the old town meaning a blessing to many. His ministry too has been a benediction to all with whom he has come in contact. I question if a more godly man lives to-day than this honored servant.

Dr. A. J. Gordon

Next in importance, possibly, would be Dr. A. J. Gordon, the honored pastor for so many years of the Clarendon Street Baptist Church in Boston. Mr. Moody relied much upon him, often did the great evangelist dwell upon his readiness to do any service, to take any place, to stand in any gap. "I cannot thank you enough," he wrote one summer, when his absence had thrown the whole charge of the Conference upon Dr. Gordon, "for your great help at Northfield. All the letters I have got from there speak in the highest terms of your generalship.

"I know of no one who could have taken your place.

"*It will now answer the question 'What is going to become of the work when I am gone?'*"

The presence of such men as these made Northfield a heavenly place in its atmosphere.

Mr. Moody never displayed greater wisdom than in his selection of men to aid him in his Conferences.

"One of the interesting features of Dr. Gordon's later ministry at Northfield was the evening baptism in the lake which has, since his death, been called after his name. These services were of great solemnity. The assembled people, the soft singing in the eventide air, the majestic baptismal formula 'Know ye not that so many of us as were baptized into Jesus Christ were baptized into his death?'

the face as it had been the face of an angel, the broken waters, and the resurrection chant at the end—these things can never be forgotten by those who stood by the water's edge."

Rev. F. B. Meyer of London

Certainly no one has ever visited Northfield who has made a deeper impression by his ministry, than the Rev. F. B. Meyer. He is now the minister of Christ Church, London, having succeeded in that historic pulpit Rev. Newman Hall, D. D., but he is known in this country, because of the fact that he has led, by the direction of the Spirit, thousands of people into the joys of the surrendered life, and Mr. Moody will doubtless hear in Heaven words of appreciation of the fact that he ever secured Mr. Meyer for his Northfield work.

Time does not permit in this connection to mention the names of MacGregor and Morgan, Andrew Murray, Dr. Webb-Peploe and hundreds of others of the real leaders in the Christian world to-day. They have counted it an honor to visit Northfield and give the very best of their thought to help carry on a movement which was manifestly of God.

There are many special incidents which have made Northfield blessed in its memory. One is related by Mr. George C. Needham, of the sainted A. J. Gordon of Clarendon Street Church.

"Dr. Gordon, unlike some Christians, believed there was something always beyond. This he ever sought to attain. Some years ago, during the first Northfield convention, he was desirous to secure what he yet needed as a saint and servant of Christ. Toward the close of those memorable ten days, spent more in prayer than in preaching, my beloved friend joined me in a midnight hour of great heart-searching and in-filling of the Spirit. He read with peculiar tenderness our Lord's intercessory prayer of John xvii. The union of the believer with Christ and the Father, as taught by our Lord in that chapter, called out fervent exclamations, while with deep pathos he continued reading. During united prayer which followed, the holy man poured his soul with a freedom and unction indescribable. I never heard him boast of any spiritual attainment reached during that midnight hour. Soul experiences were to him very sacred, and not to be rehearsed on every ordinary occasion. But I have no doubt that he received then a divine touch which further ennobled his personal life and made his ministry of ever-increasing spirituality and of ever-widening breadth of sympathy."

A Star in the Midnight Darkness

One incident connected with my own Christian experience can never be effaced from my memory. I was seated in my country home reading the accounts of the Northfield conferences, before I had ever thought of attending the same, when one sentence in an address delivered by Mr. Meyer arrested my attention. It was concerning the life of surrender, and the sentence was as follows: "If you are not willing to give up everything to God, then can you say, *I am willing to be made willing?*" It was like a star in the midnight darkness of my life and led to a definite surrender of myself in October 1892. But after that there were still some discouragements and times of depression, and standing one morning very early in front of Mr. Moody's house with the Rev. F. B. Meyer, I said to him, "Mr Meyer, what is my difficulty?" I told him of my definite surrender and pointed out to him my times of weakness and discouragement, and in a way which is peculiar to himself he made answer, "My brother, your difficulty is doubtless the same as the one I met. Have you ever tried to breathe out six times without breathing in once?" Thoughtlessly I tried to do it and then learned that one never breathes out until he breathes in, that his breathing out is in proportion to his breathing in; that he makes his effort to breathe in and none to breathe out. Taking my hand in his, my distinguished friend said, "it is just so in one's Christian life, we must be constantly breathing in of God, or we shall fail," and he turned to make his way to Mr. Moody's house for breakfast while I hastened up to my room in Weston Hall thanking God that I had had a message better to me than any sermon I had ever heard.

Such incidents as these in the lives of thousands of ministers make Northfield a place delightful to visit and Northfield meetings a benediction.

A very wealthy family, the father and mother of which had been frequent visitors at Northfield, could never induce the young ladies of their home to go with them, their idea of a Bible conference being such that they considered it a poor way to spend a vacation; but one summer, because of the description of the beauty of the scenery, they consented to go. They were seated one morning on the piazza of the Northfield Hotel with Mr. Meyer, when something in his conversation led them to say that they would hear him preach that morning. The power of God came upon one of the young ladies and she returned to her room only to fall upon her knees and definitely yield herself to God. She returned to her home to engage most actively in Christian service. Shortly after her return she was taken ill and died, and before her death she called her mother to her room to say to her that she wanted her to call to her room, before the funeral, every girl whom she had ever known intimately and socially and to tell them that in the little time she had known Christ fully she had had more joy than in all her social life put together.

This is but one incident among thousands that could be related concerning the influence of Northfield. Is it strange, therefore, that many who love it can say as the Psalmist said of Zion, "Beautiful for situation, the joy of the whole earth, is Northfield."

NORTHFIELD SEMINARY GROUNDS, From Betsy Moody's cottage.

CHAPTER XIV.

The Northfield Schools

A FAVORITE aphorism with Mr. Moody was, that "it is better to set ten men to work than to do the work of ten men", and his institutions were every one of them founded with this idea in mind. He ever had a great desire more thoroughly to equip young men and women that they might more properly do the work to which God had called them. In one sense Mr. Moody was not an educated man, for, so far as the schools were concerned, he had the scantiest equipment for his life work. This was always a source of sincere sorrow to him, and he determined that others should not meet this difficulty if he could prevent it, yet in the very widest sense he was most thoroughly educated, and it was entirely fitting that Professor Henry Drummond should speak of him as "one of the greatest educators of his day."

His Truly Marvelous Educational Work

There is really no greater proof of Mr. Moody's breadth of mind than that he should have started these different institutions. I think he is the only evangelist in this country that has ever, to any great extent, concerned himself with such matters, and since he is easily the greatest evangelist that this country has produced in modern times, it is all the more remarkable that in the very prime of his life, and at the time when he was really at the height of his success as an evangelist, he should give so much of his strength to educational causes.

If there ever has been a disposition to criticise Mr. Moody's latter day evangelistic effort, such criticism should always be made in the light of his truly marvellous educational work. Personally I do not think that he is rightly a subject for unfavorable criticism in his last efforts along evangelistic lines, for whenever I heard him, even to the very last, he always seemed to have a special anointing of God upon him. But I have heard men say that his special efforts in his last days were not to be compared with the work of his earlier ministry. However, let me repeat again, that if to his evangelistic work you add his educational interests, then each succeeding day of D. L. Moody's life was greater than the day that preceded it, and he was at the very zenith of his power when God called him home. He knew that the object of Christianity was to make men and women better in every way, and fit them, not only with all their heart but with all their mind to serve their God and their country, so he founded these institutions for the turning out of such characters.

Henry Drummond has said, "his pupils should be committed to nothing as regards a future profession. They might become ministers or missionaries, evangelists or teachers, farmers or politicians, business men or lawyers; all that he would secure would be that they should have a chance of becoming useful, educated, God-fearing men and women." But he would help them if he could to fill these positions to the glory of God.

Northfield Made His Permanent Residence

On his return to America from Great Britain, Mr. Moody went with his family to the home of his boyhood days. He decided to make Northfield his permanent place of residence, and he settled down to enjoy a period of rest before he formed new plans for work. It was a time of real preparation for the future, and the history of to-day proves that God was as truly speaking to him then as to Moses when He was alone with him on the mountain. During journeys over the hills about his native town, he met many of the farmers' daughters, bright, intelligent girls, with ambitions extending beyond the routine of the farm-house drudgery. They appealed so strongly to him that he conceived the plan of a school where such girls, possessed of moderate means, might receive a careful training in the Bible and ordinary English branches. This was the seed thought, and out of it has grown the Northfield Seminary, Mt. Hermon, and the Northfield Training School.

Purchase of Ground and Opening of the School

It has been said that this educational idea was not alone D. L. Moody's. A brother, not now living, Samuel Moody, an active, intelligent man, had long desired the establishment of a High School in his native place, and frequently talked of it. There is still another thing that should be mentioned. At this time Mr. D. L. Moody was deeply interested in the education of a young lady cousin, whom he afterward sent to Wellesley College. This cousin, Miss Fanny C. Holton, died in February, 1887, but her character, influence and helpfulness had a most important relation to the origin of the Northfield Seminary and to its entire history. In 1887, Mr. Moody held meetings in Boston, and there met Mr. H. N. F. Marshall, who was intimately connected with the founding of both schools. It was Mr. Marshall who made the first purchase of ground for the school.

In 1878, Mr. Marshall first visited Northfield, and this visit led to the above-mentioned purchase of the sixteen acres of ground nearly opposite Mr. Moody's house. In 1878 and 1879, while Mr. Moody was working in Baltimore, Mr. Marshall again joined him, and the project of the school for young ladies was further discussed. A second lot of ground was purchased adjoining the first, and on this the first recitation building was erected. In 1879, during the summer, Mr. Moody altered his own house for the accommodations of the pupils. A long wing, adjoining the house, was divided into ten rooms for the accommodation of the students. November 3, 1879, the school opened, not with eight or ten pupils, as they had dared to hope, but with twenty-five, and until the recitation hall was finished, in December, the pupils studied in Mr. Moody's own home. Miss Harriet W. Tuthill came as the first teacher and principal of the school. The price charged to every pupil then, as now, was but $100, and applications came pouring in from all parts of the country.

Three Great Ends in View

In this work of education there were three great ends which occupied Mr. Moody's thought in addition to the natural educational advantages. *The first* had to do with a better Biblical education, and his great object was to help and encourage them, and fit them in the best way for a happy and useful life, to bring them in close contact with the Fountain of Life, from which they might draw freely for all their needs. *The second* end in view was to meet the demand for trained women who would devote themselves to missionary work, either at home or abroad, but more particularly among the poor of the great cities. But *a third* object in founding the school was that the buildings which should be erected for purposes of education should be available during the summer and vacation months for another use. They could be used for gatherings of persons who delighted to study the Bible, and also to confer concerning matters touching the Kingdom of Christ. Mr. Moody lived long enough to see these three ends more than fulfilled, and great numbers of young women the country over bless God that he was ever used to inaugurate such a work in their behalf.

On the first day of April, 1880, ground was broken for East Hall, and on the first of October the building was finished. It became the home for sixty-three students. When the Hall was opened Mr. Moody said, "I would like to give this Hall a motto, and let it also be the motto of the school. Isaiah xxvii: 3: 'I, the Lord do keep it; I will water it every moment; lest *any* hurt it, I will keep it night and day.'" When this remark was made he committed the building and school, in a special prayer, to the continual service and never-failing care of God.

Constantly Increasing

The second year of the Seminary began, with East Hall well filled, and a large number of day scholars, while the third year opened with every room that was obtainable more than crowded. Not only was this building used, but while Mr. Moody was absent in Great Britain, his own house was given up entirely to the use of the school. The school has always been much like a home, and the spirit of happiness and harmony, which is the real spirit of Christ, has always prevailed.

The fourth year of the Seminary began with a new dormitory. The building was named Bonar Hall, in memory of the visit made to Northfield by Dr. Andrew Bonar. This structure was afterward destroyed by fire. The school was constantly increasing in numbers and widening its influence. In 1885, Marquand Hall was formally opened. At the same time was celebrated the eightieth birthday of Mrs, Betsey Moody, and the forty-eighth birthday of her son D. L. Moody, In 1886, the corner-stone was laid of another dormitory, holding forty-five pupils. It was finished in the summer of 1887 at a cost of $25,000, and bears the name of Weston Hall.

It was this Hall that was set apart for the use of the New York Presbytery at the last meeting of the Northfield Conference. In the spring of 1887, the Talcott Library was built, the gift of James Talcott, of New York, a trustee of the school, and the Rev. Mark Guy Pearse, of England, made an address on this occasion. But even though the buildings were constantly increasing, and were not at all small in their dimensions, each succeeding year found them filled to overflowing, until in the ninth year there were 252 boarding pupils and eighteen teachers.

Present Condition of the Seminary

In the judgment of many of his friends D. L. Moody never performed a more important service than when he gave to the world the Northfield Seminary. Other buildings than those mentioned above have been erected, until to-day the school possesses as many dormitories as any girls' school in the country. In addition it has the Skinner Gymnasium, and the new Auditorium built by Mr. Moody in 1894, to accommodate the increasing crowd at the summer conferences. The buildings all possess a wide degree of artistic beauty. The 270 acres belonging to the Seminary show good results from the time and money expended on them. The hillside, once so desolate, is covered with a beautiful turf. Well built roads wind through the grounds and from ten to twenty men are kept constantly employed. The entire production of the farm, with the exception of a few apples, are used by the farm or the school. While the price of board and tuition at the Seminary from the outset has been $100 a year, as before mentioned, yet it must not be supposed that this pays for the education of the girls. In point of fact it covers not more than one-half the running expenses of the school. The other half Mr. Moody became responsible for, and he toiled day and night, early and late, that he might make the education of these girls possible, and the schools a success.

I am very sure that no one could ever invest his money better than to help in the memorial endowment fund which is now being solicited throughout the country, that Mr. Moody's work may be perpetuated and grow in increasing usefulness.

MT. HERMON

The plan for a school where boys could have a training in elementary English branches and also the Bible, really dates back to Mr. Moody's mission work in Chicago, and he never abandoned his purpose. Four miles distant from the Young Ladies' Seminary, on the opposite side of the river, the Mt. Hermon buildings, composing the Mt. Hermon School for young men are to be found. While the plan was conceived earlier it was carried out later than that of the Northfield Seminary, but it is not to be placed second in point of influence; side by side these two institutions have come along together to positions of influence and power.

In 1880 the ground for Mt. Hermon was purchased. Through the generosity of Mr. Hiram Camp Mr. Moody was fortunately able to secure his farms, and subsequent purchases have put the boys' school in possession of more than 700 acres of ground. The price of board and tuition is the same as at the girls' school, and it was Mr. Moody's plan to have the work of the house and the farm performed by the boys themselves. For two years the school numbered not more than twenty-five boys, the ages ranging from eight to eighteen. Two farm houses served as dormitories and a small building was erected to serve as a schoolhouse. It was soon decided that better results would be obtained by admitting only older boys, and the minimum age of admission was made sixteen. In 1882 five brick cottages were built, four of which were used as dormitories, and the middle one designed to serve as a kitchen from which the meals were carried to the other buildings. Since then there have been added a three-story recitation hall, dining hall and kitchen, Crossley Hall and Silliman Science Hall.

Mt. Hermon gives a good education to boys who have been deprived of earlier advantages, and who cannot attend more expensive schools. The industrial system of Mt. Hermon tends to exclude undesirable students. In their spare time boys are allowed to do overwork, for which they are paid. Many of the students remain at Mt. Hermon throughout the year because they have no homes, or because they desire to earn money. During the vacation pupils pay three dollars a week for board. However, this is not paid in money but in work.

The Educational Plan in Mount Hermon

The educational plan in Mt. Hermon, as in all other institutions associated with Mr. Moody's name, centres around the Bible, and the results are apparent in the large number of students engaged in home and foreign missionary work.

People sneered in the beginning at the idea of an uneducated evangelist teaching the youth anything about education, but as the buildings rose one after the other their sneers soon changed to astonishment, and now one only hears words of praise for this noble work. Mr. Moody had the most supreme faith in God as touching this educational work at Northfield. He knew that God had laid it on his heart, and was persuaded that He would help him to carry it through.

I remember his telling at one time an incident which had to do with the completion of one of the buildings. They were out of money, and the work could not go on unless the money should be provided, so he made his way up to his study, wrote the

STONE HALL OR RECREATION HALL, Northfield Seminary. In this hall all conventions were held prior to the building of the new Auditorium, 1894.

strongest letter he could to a great business man, and told him that he must have several thousand dollars at once. When the letter was finished he put it on a chair before him and got down upon his knees to pray God that this letter should accomplish the object he had in mind. The letter went on its way and reached the business man in his home as he sat at the breakfast table. He read it with indifference, and then for some reason read it the second time, with a little bit of interest. For some reason he could not explain he read it the third time, and then went to his library and wrote a check for the full amount, saying in the letter which accompanied the check, "for some reason unaccountable I am unable to get away from your request, and I send you my check as you desire. I am sending it to you from my home for fear that I might change my mind when I reach my place of business."

Convincing Incidents

Incidents like this could be multiplied without number, and when one looks at Mt. Hermon, studies its great buildings, familiarizes himself with the number of lives that have come forth from the school to make the world better and brighter, and then studies the whole of Mr. Moody's plant, his first impression is one of wonder and admiration, the second a feeling of gratitude that he has an object lesson proving the truth that, if God only has His way with His own, the day of miracles is not past.

I wish I might put into this chapter an appeal to philanthropists everywhere to support the work of this man who was sent from God. I am persuaded that the blessing of God will be on one who in any way answers the appeal sent forth.

There is a third institution at Northfield which should not be overlooked. On Friday, June 1, 1888, "The Northfield" was opened to the public. It is a fine hotel, designed expressly to meet the needs of the many who annually visit Northfield, who attend the summer conferences, or as friends of the two schools. It was opened with an overflow of guests. It was at this hotel that the friends of Mr. Moody gathered on the night preceding his funeral and the evening following it, and it is in this hotel that the Moody Training School for Women meets.

THE NORTHFIELD TRAINING SCHOOL

In his work in Chicago, and in his evangelistic work throughout the world, Mr. Moody had learned to appreciate the especial influence of women in ministering to the poor. He also found that it was almost impossible to secure the right standard of women to do the work he had in mind. Sometimes their influence was marred by inexperience, more frequently by lack of training. He determined to start a training school, which city churches and mission fields could draw upon, not for highly educated missionaries, but for Christian women who could be trained especially in Bible knowledge and domestic economy.

The Northfield Hotel was an eyesore to Mr. Moody because it was empty from October to the end of March. He determined that this should not be so, and in 1890, the first term of the training school began there. Fifty-six students took up residence at once, and the next year the numbers were quite doubled. In addition to systematic Bible study, the pupils are taught such branches of domestic economy as will make them useful in their work with the poor, and they are especially instructed in preparation of foods for the sick.

It seems an incredible thing that a man without education himself, as the world speaks of him, should have been used of God to establish a work which in many ways is the wonder of all who see it, but it is an illustration of the fact, that we can do all things through Christ which strengtheneth us.

CHAPTER XV.

The Northfield Conference and the Student Volunteers.

THIS is a day in which God is using in a very remarkable way what is known as the Bible Conference. In many parts of the country there are annual summer gatherings of Christian people for the study of God's Word. The number is rapidly increasing, and the growth of some of these conferences is really remarkable. In a sense, at least, the Northfield Conference which came out of the heart and the deep study of D. L. Moody, is responsible for them all.

VARIOUS BIBLE CONFERENCES

There has been annually, until within the past two years, a gathering of earnest, active Christians at Niagara, on the Lake, and some of the most widely known Bible students in the country have gathered there to consult together concerning the things of the Kingdom. The teaching at this conference has been largely along dispensation lines, and the prominent truth presented in all their services has been the return of the Lord, while the majority of the teachers at Northfield have not only accepted, but strongly advocated the truth known as the "blessed hope". Still Mr. Moody had one characteristic which impressed itself on all his associates. He would not exalt one truth at the expense of another, and so Northfield has not been known as the place where any particular line of truth was promulgated. If any exception could be taken to this statement it would be in favor of those truths which contribute to the deepening of the spiritual life.

Another widely known Bible Conference, which is certainly in existence because of the influence of Northfield, is the Winona gathering at Winona Lake, Ind. For five years the Christians of the Middle and Western states in increasing numbers have gathered there for the same kind of work that was done at Northfield. Mr. Moody has ever contributed to the effectiveness of the Conference by sending such speakers as the Rev. G. H. C. MacGregor, the Rev. G. Campbell Morgan, the Rev. F. B. Meyer, and the Rev. J. G. Cunningham. The gathering has increased from thirty-five, the first year, to more than 1,500 at the last annual meeting. I desire personally to say that Winona owes to Mr. Moody more than it can ever repay.

The Keswick Movement

One of the most celebrated conferences abroad is that which meets in the early summer at Keswick, a town of Cumberland, England, on the south bank of the Greta, twenty-four miles from Carlisle. The first convention was held in July, 1875, and was only for the purpose of experiencing a fuller spiritual life. It has been thought by many that the Keswick movement stood for the promotion of the doctrine of "sinless perfection". This is most untrue. It does stand for the very highest type of Christian living, and in every way stands for the exaltation and manifestation of Christ in the life. There are six successive stages that ought to be indicated in connection with Keswick, for they have widely influenced the Northfield teachers, especially those from abroad. They are named in the order of their importance.

1. The definite and immediate abandonment of every known sin or hindrance to holy living.

2. The abandonment and renunciation by faith of the self-life, or the life, that centers in self-indulgence and self-dependence.

3. The immediate surrender of the will in loving and complete obedience to the will of God, separation for the purpose of consecration.

4. The infilling of the Holy Spirit, or the claiming of the believer's share in the Spirit's pentecostal gift of power for service.

5. The revelation of Christ as an indwelling presence in the believer's soul and daily life, and as his actual Master and Lord.

6. Beyond these there is always a sixth and last stage of teaching—the privileges and victories implied in this higher or deeper life, such as the rest life of faith, power over sin, passion for souls, conscious fellowship with God, growing possession of promises, and prevailing prayer and intercession.

The Pre-eminence of Northfield

The basis of all this teaching is, as is very apparent, the conviction that the average Christian life is too often grievously destitute of real spiritual power and is essentially carnal; and that it is the duty and privilege of every child of God to enter at once into newness of life, and to walk henceforth in the power of Christ's resurrection.

But Northfield is pre-eminently, in the judgment of many people, the most important gathering of Bible students in this country, if not in the world. Thousands of lives have been transformed, by the power of the Conference, and one of the most notable gatherings in its history was that of last year when the entire Presbytery of New York met and were assigned to quarters in Weston Hall, attended regularly the services, and came back literally filled with the Spirit of God, the result being that the whole city of New York has seemed to feel the touch of the power that rested upon them; and there is scarcely a Presbyterian Church in the city that has not had remarkably large additions as either a direct or indirect result of this last summer Conference.

However much Mr. Moody's friends may have to say of him in meetings in other places, it is certainly true that he was at his best in Northfield at the Conference. There was no more interested listener in all the audience than he. He was quick to notice the impression the speakers made upon the people, and while he was never what could be called a flatterer, yet when those whom he had invited to be present helped the people he was the first one to express his appreciation. As a rule he was at all the gatherings.

The Beginning of the Conferences

A description of the Northfield Conferences necessitates referring once again to the Round Top services, one of which is described in another chapter. These meetings were held in the evening, at the sunset time, and the influence upon all who gathered there was simply profound. I question if there is any work that Mr. Moody was engaged in throughout the world in which he was more interested than the Northfield Conference, a brief story of which ought to be given.

The Northfield Conferences began in 1880. Early in September the buildings of the Seminary were thronged with three hundred visitors. Among those who came was a delegation from Great Britain. The first conference continued for ten days. The spirit of the meeting was largely devotional, the doctrine of the Holy Spirit being largely dwelt upon; and the result was very impressive. There was at that time no large auditorium in which the various meetings could be conducted, so a large tent was pitched behind East Hall, and there the exercises were held. The culmination of the conference was pentecostal in its power, and the spiritual refreshing which came at that time to many believers is still manifest in whatever they do.

In October, 1881, the second convocation began, continuing through the month. The Rev. Dr. Andrew Bonar, of Glasgow, Scotland, was the principal speaker, and among the others who participated were Dr. George F. Pentecost, Dr. A. J. Gordon, Dr. James H. Brooks, Dr. E. P. Goodwin, Mr. George C. Needham, and Major Whittle, besides many others whose names have since come to be especially associated with Northfield work. There was great variety in the services. The spirit of the second conference was less devotional than the first, but was given more to doctrinal and practical study. Most of the meetings were held in East Hall, but in the afternoons the conference met in the Congregational Church of the village, and occasionally in the open air. The interest deepened throughout the month.

How They Have Grown

Shortly after this Mr. Moody went to England, and in his absence no summer conferences were held at Northfield for three years, and it was not until August, 1885, that the third convocation was held. Mr. J. E. K. Studd of Cambridge University, England, gave a fine impetus to the meeting, and Mr. John B. Gough delivered during this month one of his last addresses. Dr. A. T. Pierson and Dr. A. J. Gordon also helped to make the meetings signal in their influence.

And so, year after year, the Northfield Conferences have grown in interest and attendance. The new buildings which, from time to time, have been erected for the educational work of the Seminary have much increased the facilities of entertainment for visitors, and the new auditorium makes it possible to assemble a great throng under cover. Still there are many who think that the open-air services have been more stimulating and helpful than any of the others. The speakers have been drawn, as formerly, from the best, and it is a privilege indeed to receive through association with such men the best fruits of their own experiences. It has always seemed to me that the genius of Mr. Moody shone more in his management of the summer conferences than in any other detail of his work, and his earnestness and his devotion were ever so impressed on all the services that no one could go away from a meeting without carrying with him a blessing. Mr. Moody's educational ideals, which in their practical forms are visible to the visitor to the conferences in the noble buildings which crown the Northfield hills, were epitomized in the work of the summer conferences.

The Student Volunteers

Some time in the spring of 1886, with his customary foresight and intuition in regard to what might advance the Kingdom of Christ, Mr. Moody called to his side Mr. L. D. Wishard, then college secretary of the International Committee of the Young Men's Christian Associations of the United States and Canada. As a result of the conference between these two men, Mr. Moody invited each of the College Young Men's Christian Associations of the country to send a delegate to spend a month at Mt. Hermon in July of the same year, to study the Bible and methods of Christian work adapted to college students. This invitation was accepted by 250 students, from about ninety different college associations. The meetings continued from July 7th to August 2d. The program of each day was as follows: From eight o'clock in the morning the men considered informally for an hour some phase of College Association work. At ten o'clock all met and listened to addresses from noted speakers from abroad. Some time was also given to those who desired to ask practical questions, and these

A SERVICE AT NORTHFIELD CAMP GROUND. Rev. G. H. C. MacGregor, of London, England, faces the audience with Mr. Moody standing at his side.

were answered by Mr. Moody in his usual clear, direct manner. In these meetings, as elsewhere, Mr. Moody was able to exercise his wonderful ability to associate with himself a corps of prominent Bible scholars and teachers.

A large number of Christian students were present who had decided to devote their lives to the work in foreign missions. These naturally met together in a common fellowship, and their earnestness and devotion made from the outset a deep impression on all. Their appeals on behalf of the claims of missionary work on educated Christian young men also made a profound impression, and many students were then and there led to express a willingness and a desire to enter upon work in the foreign field.

Missionary Interest Awakened

The interest awakened was fostered by two young men, Messrs. Wilder and Foreman, who were led speedily to devote a portion of their time as students to deepening and widening this work among the students of the colleges not represented at Mt. Hermon. This in brief, then, is how the Student Volunteer movement was born; it came into being in connection with the first Christian Student Conference ever held at Mt. Hermon, where Mr. Moody's school for boys and young men is situated.

Like many another thing for which Mr. Moody opened the way, if he did not actually originate it, the Student Volunteer movement has grown almost beyond comprehension. It assumed organization in 1888, and has become a recognized factor and power in the missionary life of the Church throughout the world, as possibly no other single movement. Briefly stated, the four-fold purpose of the organization is: First, to awaken and foster among all the Christian students of the United States and Canada, intelligent and active interest in foreign missions. Second, to enroll a sufficient number of properly qualified student volunteers to meet the successive demands of the various missionary Boards of North America. Third, to help all such as pledge themselves to foreign missionary work to prepare for their life work, and to increase the co-operation of these young workers in developing the missionary life of home churches. Fourth, to lay an equal burden of responsibility on all students who are to remain as ministers and lay workers at home, that they may actively promote missionary enterprise by intelligent advocacy, gifts and prayers.

The Volunteer movement is not a missionary board. It never has sent out and never will send out a missionary, for it is simply a recruiting station. As in so many other ways, the wisdom of Mr. Moody in calling to his side such men as L. D. Wishard, C. K. Ober and John R. Mott, of the International Committee of the Young Men's Christian Association, was soon manifest in the progress of the movement, and these men have had much to do with the rapid increase of the work during these last years.

The Growth of the Work

Some conception may be gained of the prodigious strides which the organization has made when it is known that it already has made itself felt in more than 1,000 institutions of learning. Then it should be remembered that in many of these, perhaps more notably in state, professional and independent institutions, the subject of foreign missions was dealt with for the first time when the representatives of the student volunteers began to extend their efforts. It is safe to assert that where one student gave this subject careful consideration before the movement began, scores and scores have felt and thoughtfully considered the claims of the world-wide missions since and through the ministry of this work. It is said that the student attitude of many colleges, both denominational and state, has completely changed, and certain it is that no other subject has ever taken such a deep hold on the convictions of college men, or has called forth from them such unselfish devotion.

There are on the roll of the movement at this time about 4,000 students. Of this number about one-third are women and two-thirds are men. Forty-eight denominations are represented. Nearly 1,200 of the volunteers have already gone to the foreign field. The number of students who now are planning to become foreign missionaries is five times as great in the colleges of the land, and twice as great in the seminaries, as it was before this movement started. The Student Volunteers have also afforded substantial aid in assisting to raise money, for whereas the colleges formerly gave about $5,000 a year to foreign missionary work, they now give more than $40,000.

Some Indirect Effects

It must be plain to any thoughtful person that the reflex influence of this movement in the institutions of learning themselves is simply incalculable. For every student who has offered himself to go abroad, certainly one or more have been influenced to take up a more aggressive Christian life at home. Development in Bible study and in personal work for the salvation of their fellows on the part of the students, as a secondary influence of this movement is without any doubt one of the great evangelistic tendencies of the century. At least indirectly, it may be traced to Mr. Moody.

One of the most wonderful things about the Student Volunteer influence has been its effect upon the students of other lands. Ten years ago the organization for the United States and Canada was the only student movement in the world, employing the volunteer methods, but now there are student volunteers in Great Britain,

Scandinavian countries, Germany, France, Australasia, South Africa, China, India and Ceylon. All the organizations express their indebtedness to the American branch for the helpful and practical influence it exerted in the formative periods of the work. It is exceedingly significant that even the students of mission lands have joined hands with the students of Christian lands in a determined effort to preach the Gospel to all mankind.

In August, 1895, there was formed in the historic Vadstena Castle, on the shores of Lake Vettern, in Sweden, a World's Student Christian Federation. There were present official representatives from America, Great Britain, Germany, Scandinavia, and Mission lands. Mr. John R. Mott, in his "Strategic Points in the World's Conquest," says, "Never since the Wartburg sheltered the great German Reformer, while he was translating the Bible for the common people, has a mediæval castle served a purpose fraught with greater blessing to all mankind."

A Federation for the World

Since the formation of this federation it has been entered by the representatives of five other countries, India, Ceylon, South Africa, China and Japan, so that practically all the countries, having anything like a student volunteer movement, are now banded together.

The first convention of the World's Student Christian Federation was held in the United States, in July, 1897, in conjunction with the annual conference of the American and Canadian Intercollegiate Young Men's Christian Association, at Northfield. In addition to the 600 students who had come together from 136 universities and colleges, there were present students and Christian workers from twenty-five other nations or races. Special meetings were held on Round Top, the spot which is now especially consecrated to Mr. Moody's memory. Round Top is not less sacred because it is the place where more students have dedicated their lives to the extension of Christ's religion than any other place in the world. Says Mr. Mott, " Day after day at sunset, the hundreds of delegates from the ends of the earth met on this sacred mountain to lift their eyes and look far beyond the beautiful Connecticut valley and the distant green mountains upon the great harvest fields of the world, and linger and listen to burning messages from their fellow students, telling of the triumphs of Christ among their own people, and the need of more men in the regions beyond."

Prayer in Twenty-one Languages

The Federation delegates attended not only the large special meetings over which Mr. Moody presided, but also the conferences for the discussion of methods. One afternoon a pilgrimage was made to Mt. Hermon, which, as the reader will remember, is several miles from Northfield on the other side of the river The groves and hills and river banks about Mt. Hermon are sacred, for it was here that the Student Volunteer movement came into existence in 1886. Some who had attended that first wonderful meeting were present to recount the experiences of those first days of blessed surrender. Before the delegates left Mt. Hermon, Mr. Moody called them together for the consecrating of the ground that had been set apart as a site for a chapel. In a representative meeting this plot was dedicated to God's service. Then the delegates offered prayer in twenty-one different languages, and yet there was no confusion of tongues, for all were brought together in their common love of the Master.

What will be the result of this movement we can only conjecture, for it is yet in its infancy, but it is significant to note that already it has brought together Christian students in all the world as never before. It has made the various student movements acquainted with one another. It has organized six great national student movements, and has facilitated the organization of two others. The last conference of the Federation was held in Eisenach, at the foot of the famous Wartburg, in Germany, and was attended by students from twenty-four countries. Nearly 400 years ago, in the castle which still crowns that storied mountain, a monk made a consecration of his talents which blessed the world as it had not been blessed before for many centuries. When Martin Luther came down from that sacred hill he brought with him a Bible for the people. The perverseness of the generation did not lead him to dash his tablets to the ground as he descended, but instead they went out through the land and gave men almost for the first time an insight into the true teachings of our Lord. How fitting it is that on this spot, hallowed by the memory of the great reformer, the flower of the young men of to-day should pledge themselves to devote their lives to carrying to all the quarters of the globe the blessed Gospel!

CHAPTER XVI.

The Chicago Bible Institute.

THE Chicago Bible Institute is one of the great monuments which Mr. Moody has left for himself. That it was born in prayer is proved from the words of an address which Mr. Moody made at one of the last meetings of the World's Fair campaign: "Little we thought, when we prayed some three or four years ago for a Bible Institute near the church, that we should have any such opportunity to preach the Gospel to the world as we have had these last six months. We should not have been able to do the work we have done during these past months but for the Institute and the three hundred workers who had gathered there from every part of the country. No matter at what point the work has been started, we have had force enough to carry it on. I believe that it would have been utterly impossible to have carried on this work without the help of the Bible Institute. It may be that God raised it up for such a time, even as Esther was raised up for the time of her country's peril and need."

THE NEED OF THE INSTITUTION

The need of an institution of this kind became evident to Mr. Moody as he went about, holding evangelistic services in various places. There was constant difficulty in getting persons who were able to deal directly with inquirers or who were trained sufficiently in the knowledge of the Word of God to point the soul to Christ. In every meeting there would be great numbers of the poor and of the outcast whose hearts would be reached by the message, and when there was any great number of such inquirers it was quite impossible for him to deal personally with them all. On one occasion, Mr. Moody said, "One of the great purposes we have in view in the Bible Institute is to raise up men and women who will put their lives alongside the life of the poor and the laboring classes, and bring the influence of the Gospel to bear upon them." Out of a little Mission Sunday School, which had been organized by Mr. Moody, grew the Chicago Avenue Church, and it was in this church that the first steps were taken toward the founding of such an institute as Mr. Moody had in mind. In the spring of 1889, the Chicago Evangelization Society came into existence, and Mr. Moody was its president. From the experiment made at the church it was clearly demonstrated that it would be possible to have a Bible Institute conducted on practical lines in the City of Chicago. Ground and buildings near the church were purchased, and the organization was effected in October, 1889, when the Institute opened for regular work.

The Beginning

At the beginning something like eighty students were enrolled, fifty of them being men and thirty women. Three houses had been already purchased by the Institution, and another brick structure was at once begun, which was finished the following year. The attendance during this year was three times as great as the first year. The students came from all parts of the world. They held religious opinions of every type, and they came to the Institute with different objects. Some of them intended to continue their studies after leaving the Institute; others expected to enter immediately upon active work when they left. Indeed, there were many pastors of churches, who came there in order that they might increase their knowledge of practical ways of working in their own churches.

MR. MOODY DRIVING WITH HIS GRANDDAUGHTER EMMA FITT, ON HIS KNEE.

Perhaps in no institution of the country would there be manifest a more intense zeal for work than would be found there. The main object of the institution was both practical and simple; it was to give all the students a thorough working knowledge of the Scriptures, in order that they might be equipped for personal Christian work, and at the same time have their own spiritual lives stimulated.

There are, in all, accommodations for about three hundred students. The two departments are kept separate except at the time of lectures, when all come together in the lecture hall of the main building.

The Object in View

One is not a guest at the Institute for any great length of time without discovering the object which the Institute has in view. He will see here 200 or 300 bright and earnest Christian young men and women from all parts of the world. As a rule, they come from that class of people which the Institute is training them to help.

They have no fortune back of them, few of them have had the advantages of an education beyond that afforded by the common schools. They come there with strong convictions that God has called them to some special service which needs special training such as the Institute can give them. One feels the influence of the spiritual atmosphere which pervades the Institute as soon as the door is opened to receive him, and, if he were spending some little time among these young people so consecrated to their work, he could not come away without having received great personal blessing.

The Ordinary Routine

The ordinary routine of the Institute is systematic and orderly to a high degree. The hour for breakfast is seven o'clock. All take part in asking God's blessing upon the food, for grace is "sung" and not "said". When the breakfast is finished the chairs are pushed back from the tables and a short exposition is made of the Scripture chosen for the morning devotions. As a rule this Scripture is read by Mr. John H. Hunter, who has a general oversight of the men's department; if not by him, then by some one of the visiting lecturers who is living temporarily at the Institute. At eight o'clock they assemble for prayer, and at nine o'clock the young men and young women assemble together for the first lecture of the day. From ten to eleven o'clock the time is given to thorough instruction, under competent teachers, in vocal and instrumental music. The second lecture hour is at eleven o'clock, and dinner at 12.30. At four o'clock in the afternoon comes the fourth lecture, and the evenings are invariably taken up by the students who are assigned to various places for practical work. It would seem to be one object of these students to bring theory and practice close together, for as in the morning they are shown where to find the Scriptures which would point the way to Christ, they are in the evening sent out with those same Scriptures to make a practical application of them upon the unsaved.

THE PRACTICAL NATURE OF THE WORK

The practical part of the education which is given to those who study here is of the most important character. Every student is required to do a certain proportion of practical work each week that he is in the Institute. Sometimes he will be obliged to visit the homes in some section of the city designated to him. At other times he will be obliged to organize and carry on cottage prayer meetings. Then, nearly all the missions of Chicago are supplied more or less by students from the Institute. Children's meetings are held, industrial schools are also carried on, and in almost every case where students are sent to conduct meetings they are obliged also to hold inquiry meetings, so that they get hold not only of theories, but also are shown how to put these theories into operation.

The course of study is most varied, though the main object constantly adhered to is that all the students may get a thorough knowledge of the Word of God and be taught how they may skillfully apply it. The doctrines of the Scriptures are studied in a thorough and careful manner. Several books are taken up and an analytic study made of these. Each year some of the best known Bible students of the country are brought in to reinforce the regular staff, and these give daily lectures on some biblical theme. As I have before stated, one of the most impressive features of the Institute life is the spiritual atmosphere which pervades it.

Touching Requests for Prayer

After the supper hour, and just before the students scatter in all directions to visit the homes and missions and other places of assignment, they meet together for prayer, and those who have some special burden upon their hearts send up a written request to the leader. It is most touching sometimes to hear the words of these requests for prayer. Sometimes they are like this, "Please pray for that unsaved man with whom I am to speak to-night;" or "Pray for me that I may conduct the services in my mission to-night in all the power of the Holy Spirit;" or "Pray for me that I may be led to do the right thing in striving to arrange for that series of cottage meetings." One by one these requests are read by the leader, and then the most fervent prayers are offered up that these desires may be heard and granted. The students insist upon it, that they have the most remarkable answers to prayer, and no one could be present at one of these meetings and notice the nature of the requests, and the fervent spirit in which they are presented to God, without believing that these prayers would be answered.

The teacher from the outside has, as a rule, rare opportunities to get into close and intimate relationship with the young men of the Institute. If he can succeed in interesting these men with his Bible theme, he will be sure to be visited by large numbers, sometimes as many as twenty, who come to him for some further light upon questions which are troubling them. The students are frank and open-hearted, and are earnestly seeking whatever light God will give them. They seem to have a burning desire to be fitted properly for any work to which God may call them.

The Rev. R. A. Torrey, who is the superintendent of the Institute, is without question the most capable man that Mr. Moody could have found for this very important position. He has preeminent endowments which qualify him in a very special manner to conduct this work which has been in his charge from its inception. He is a man of most delightful spirit, and has a profound knowledge of the Word of God, which he has wrought up in a most thorough form, and which is with intense earnestness taught the students, who are subjected to a very thorough examination at the end of their course.

Mr. Torrey's Influence Upon the Institute

Mr. Torrey is not only the superintendent of the Institute, but also the pastor of the Chicago Avenue Church. He is loved by all the students, who accept as absolute his word, from which it is dangerous for any strange teacher to digress.

He has had from the beginning a most profound influence upon the character of the Institute, as well as of the students who have gone from it. These students are trained for special spheres of work, spheres which would never be filled, if it were necessary to depend upon the ordinary theological seminaries. The theological student prepares himself for the ordinary ministry; those who come to the Moody Institute are seeking to become pastors' assistants, mission workers in the slums, secretaries to Young Peoples' Societies or Young Men's Christian Associations, Sunday school workers, and evangelists. That there is need of such workers is clearly evident from the large number of requests which are constantly coming in to the superintendent for men to supply vacancies. It has been impossible hitherto to meet the demand, but nevertheless, year after year, there has been put into the world by this Institute a large number of consecrated Christian workers for fields which are considered by no means easy.

A Steady Increase

The Institute is accomplishing the very object which Mr. Moody had in mind at the time of its organization, This object has been held to unswervingly from the beginning, and in the ten years' history of the Institute it would be impossible to overestimate the value of the work which has been accomplished by it. Steadily from the beginning, the number of students in attendance has increased, and this increase is noticeable not only in the men's department, but also in the women's department.

During these first ten years of its organization nearly three thousand students have studied at the Institute, and at least a third of these are now engaged in active Christian work throughout the country. The Institute has not only provided home workers, but is represented also by a large number in the field of foreign missions, and some of those who have come from foreign lands to be educated here have returned to their own homes and are loyally serving Christ there.

Since the organization three other buildings have been purchased for the work of the Institute, and in connection with the Institute a Colportage Association has been established, which has published millions of books, and distributed them widely in all parts of the world. The purpose of this Association is to send out sound Christian literature at low prices. The work has no denominational connection, and all Christians are expected to give their sympathy and co-operation to the work in order that the vast influence of vicious literature, which is now so widely circulated, may be counteracted. Thousands of these books are distributed free, and it has been the special desire of Mr. Moody to put these books within the reach of the prisoners in the penal institutions of the country.

Let us Multiply Such Institutes

So long as the Institute endures, it cannot be said of Chicago, at least, that there is not a large number of intelligent, consecrated, Christians who are both willing and eager to go down in the slums and dark places and put their lives alongside the lives of the outcast and fallen. So deeply impressed was Mr. Moody with the importance of this work that he thought it desirable that such institutes should be started in other sections of the country, and I believe that he cherished the hope that, at no distant day, there might be institutes of this character in all of our great centres of population. It is the unique and splendid work which is being accomplished by the Institute that kept it close to Mr. Moody's heart, and just so far as our sympathies go out toward the poor and the unsaved masses, we will seek by all the influence we possess to perpetuate this, and to multiply in our land institutes of a similar character.

It is most interesting to notice the peculiar and deep influence which Mr. Moody had, not only upon the students in the Institute, but also upon those who gathered together at Northfield and Mt.

Hermon. Not always at once were students drawn to him, but it would not be long before his tremendous magnetism would be felt in their lives. He held a unique position in all the schools that were under his direction; both at Northfield and Chicago he came to be regarded as a father, and no one would be able to estimate the influence exerted upon the character of the students by Mr. Moody's broad sympathy.

The Institution Was Born of Necessity.

While the Northfield schools were ever near to his heart, there was a special sense in which the work that was being carried on at the Institute appealed to him. Possibly too, his heart was drawn out more toward the Chicago work, because this more than the other depended upon the personal interest of Mr. Moody for its maintenance. It is in no sense a theological seminary; it was never designed to be; it was not even designed to supplement the education that might be obtained at a theological seminary. The institution was born of the necessity of bringing into the field workers who would be skilled to meet the needs and difficulties of those who never would come within the reach of the graduate of the theological school.

If, however, the Institute does not cover the ground of theoretical study, which is ordinarily taken up by the technical school, it is nevertheless in its own way giving a thorough training for those who are to do a special work in the world. The Bible itself is the book upon which the attention of the student is constantly centred. The book is approached from various standpoints. All the great doctrines are most carefully and systematically taught the students. It would be a strange thing for any young man or woman to pass through the course of studies without having at the end a very clear conception of the great truth of salvation; and also a clear idea as to how salvation might be presented to other men. Whoever has had the privilege of working in the Institute of Chicago, or in any other place where graduates of this institution have assisted in the work, would see as no other how much real value lies in an institution of this kind. It would not be too much to say that the effectiveness of any evangelistic campaign would be quadrupled if there could be distributed through the audience a number of trained workers such as are to be found in the Chicago Bible Institute.

The Women's Department

The splendid services of Mrs. S. B. Capron, for so long the superintendent of the womens' department, ought not to be passed by without notice. Coming as she did, enriched in experience, she brought a peculiar ability and a devotion of spirit to the work of the Institute. The same delightful spiritual atmosphere which pervades the men's department, is noticeable in the buildings of the women's department. These consecrated young women are, by no means, behind the young men in their zeal for the work which is laid out for them. They, too, are sent out upon the streets to work. They go to the police stations; they are to be found in the halls and tents; they go from house to house in visitation of the poor and the sick, and are especially equipped with the right answer for those who may be inquiring the way of salvation.

As a rule the students are assigned to their different sections in pairs. They hold a mothers' meeting on Wednesday at the Institute and, in their house to house visitation, invite the mothers to this meeting, telling them to bring their children too, and these little ones are entertained and taught by kindergarten methods, while the poor mothers have their bodies refreshed and their souls brought into contact with a higher spiritual plane. Then they are invited also to the great Sunday afternoon Bible class, to which they come, and again the children are taken care of

REV. R. A. TORREY, Superintendent of the Moody Bible Institute.

in the primary departments. Often they can be induced also to attend the evening service, and all these tremendous results are being achieved, home and character being transformed by this noble band of young women who have given up their whole lives to consecrated service of this kind.

Development of the Student's Character

The object of the Institute is not altogether defined by, or limited to, the study of the Bible or practical Christian work. There is another design, namely, that the character of the students themselves may be developed on spiritual and symmetrical lines. Many a one has come to the Institute with little conception of the possibilities lying within himself, or of the possibilites of service lying without him, who here, under the spiritual influence of the home, has had these things dawn upon him and has gone forth with some wide and noble plan of action.

No wonder that this Institution, with its noble aim and its already accomplished good, was the joy and delight of Mr. Moody's heart. It means the perpetuation of that work to which he had consecrated his own life; it means that after him will be raised up generations of men and women who will, so far as God will give them strength, do what he has done, by putting their lives alongside the lives of the poor and wretched and miserable and outcast. No man in all the world has so closely touched the lowly classes as did Mr. Moody. It might almost be said of him as it was said of his Master, "The common people heard him gladly," and his great design in the establishing of the Bible Institute was that it might ever be in the interests of the common people. In the interests of the common people it has been and doubtless will continue to be, for whatever of training may be gained by the students is immediately utilized, not in the behalf of the rich, but in behalf of those whom sin has marred, and who are in special need of personal sympathy such as they can give. Nowhere in all the world will there stand a whiter monument to the memory of Mr. Moody than this great training school of Christian workers. This is no finished work, but one that will live on, and one which, by reason of its peculiar need, will have a peculiar claim upon the sympathy and prayer of those who are interested in it.

It was one of the cherished desires of Mr. Moody's heart that this Institution might be put upon a basis that would make it possible for the work to continue without a constant appeal to its devoted friends for an annual deficit. No more fitting tribute can be paid to the founder of the Institution than to fulfill this desire of his heart, and raise a sufficient endowment to perpetuate this, one of his greatest works.

At Mr. Moody's special request, I, a few years ago, became Vice-President of the Bible Institute. He was desirous at that time that I should give much of my life to it, and I was very strongly tempted to do so. But the call of duty was clearer in another direction, and so I was obliged to turn aside, although nothing would have given me greater pleasure than to have been associated with him in this great work. I desire to commend it to my readers everywhere, and I believe the blessing of God will be especially upon them, if they should help, not only with their prayers, but by the contribution of their money, to the firmer establishment of this important work. Young men and women who could not possibly secure training for Christian work elsewhere, have been given opportunities for study here, and to my personal knowledge hundreds of them have been helped by Mr. Moody when there was no one else to help. I pray God, that in Chicago the Bible Institute may ever stand as a memorial of the work of this consecrated man of God.

CHAPTER XVII.

The World's Fair Campaign.

WHEN the World's Columbian Exposition became an assured fact, and Chicago was finally selected as the place of the celebration, Mr. Moody was quick to notice the possibility which would arise to carry the Gospel to the multitudes likely to be attracted there. Other men might have been blind to this, but not this mighty man of God. When he came to Chicago his mind was clear as to the necessity of a wide opportunity for evangelistic movement, and he was in a position to command the services of those men upon whom God had set the special seal of His approval. His heart had for some time been fixed upon this work, as is evident from the address he made after his memorable experience on the steamship *Spree*, in which he says:

A Vow to God

"As I was preparing to leave London after my last visit there, I called upon a famous physician. He told me that my heart was weakening and that I would have to ease up on my work, that I would have to be more careful of myself; and I was going home with an idea that I would ease up a little. During the voyage, the announcement came that our vessel, the *Spree*, was sinking, and we rolled there for two days helplessly. No one on earth knows what I passed through at the thought that probably my work was finished, and that I would never again have the privilege of preaching the Gospel of Jesus Christ; and on that first dark night after the accident, I made a vow that if God would let me live and bring me back to America, I would go back to Chicago, and at this World's Fair, preach the Gospel with all the power He would give me. And God has made it possible for me to keep that vow during the past five months. It seems as if I went to the very gates of Heaven during that two days on the sinking ship, and God permitted me to come back and preach His Son a little longer." After landing on these shores he went to his Northfield home, and having brought the students of Mt. Hermon and Northfield together at six o'clock in the morning, he said to them, "If you have any regard for me, if you love me, pray for me that God may anoint me for the work in Chicago; I want to be filled with the Spirit that I may preach the Gospel as I never preached it before; we want to see the salvation of God as we have never seen it before."

Not only to the students of Northfield and Mt. Hermon did he emphasize the importance and value of prayer, but he insisted upon it in other directions so that in all regions there was rising continuous prayer that the blessing of God might be poured out upon the unsaved masses which would throng the streets of Chicago.

The First Meeting of the Campaign.

It was a most fitting thing that the first meeting of this campaign should be held in the Chicago Avenue Church, known as Moody's church. On the first Sunday of May, which was bright and beautiful, a great congregation came together in the church and waited patiently for the appearance of the evangelist. He came in, followed by Mr. Sankey and other distinguished leaders. When the time arrived for Mr. Moody to speak, he took for his theme the elder brother in the story of the prodigal son. If, in his description, he pictured the elder brother as the meanest man on earth, and unworthy of a father's love, on the other hand he showed how graciously God received those who, through repenting of their sins, turned back to Him. The yearning of his own heart that the lost sinner might be found, was a key note, and gave the characteristics of all the sermons that were subsequently preached by Mr. Moody and his co-workers in this campaign. All were animated with the one spirit, that Christ might be presented lovingly, earnestly, and persistently as the friend of sinners. The vast number of those who accepted the invitation invariably offered, shows how God set His seal to simple testimony of this character.

A Marked Characteristic of His Faith.

Afternoon services were held in this same church, and again there was another crowd to hear Mr. Moody, who spoke on the subject of Praise. He had such a full assurance that God would send a wave of blessing over the city that his heart was filled with praise in anticipation of it. The invariable desire on the part of Mr. Moody to praise God with his whole heart for anticipated blessings was one of the marked characteristics of his faith. This is as rare as it is beautiful, and it was the theme of that afternoon meeting. At night the church was thronged again, while services were also held in other places. Special meetings in different parts of the city were also conducted by the students of the Institute. So passed the first day of the great campaign in Chicago. The sins and sorrows of the city lay like a heavy burden on Mr. Moody's heart, and it became evident, as his plans matured, that his design was not merely to reach the multitude of strangers who were pouring into the city, but that he might also influence the citizens themselves. The moral condition of the city was beyond description. Sunday was the great holiday of the week; all the places of amusement were open; the worst features of a Sunday on the Continent were observed, and nothing but the outpouring of the Holy Spirit could check the tide.

It is no easy matter to plan and carry into execution the details of a great campaign like this, but Mr. Moody was in perfect command of the situation. He spent hour after hour waiting upon God, and God in response opened door after door of opportunity. Difficulties vanished as they were approached, and what had seemed to be utterly impossible was accomplished. As the days went by the magnitude of the work was very much increased. The great buildings were secured in different sections of the city, theatres, halls, churches and missions were opened. The large circus tent of Forepaugh was also secured. Five other great tent tabernacles were moved from section to section, and sometimes great crowds assembled in the open air. Speakers were assigned to these places, and day after day for months there went out a testimony for God such as perhaps no other city of the world has had.

Song, a Feature of the Meetings

Mr. Moody had surrounded himself with a company of men with whom it was one of the greatest privileges to be associated. The men most used of God in evangelistic work went there, as well as a large number of others who had been gifted with the power of Gospel singing. The singing was one of the strong features in all the meetings, and contributed largely to their success. Mr. Moody always made the most careful arrangements for the song services in connection with the meetings. Indeed the singing was a feature of no small importance in all these meetings. Where it was possible, great choirs were organized under skilfull directors, and these, together with great congregations who were once wrought up into the spirit of praise, would fill the buildings with such music as is rarely heard. Wherever Mr. Moody conducted evangelistic services he paid the same careful thought to the services of praise, and the meetings in the Chicago campaign will by many be remembered best for the magnificent singing.

As a rule when the services of the day were over, Mr. Moody would meet with his co-workers at the Bible Institute. Each speaker, as he came in from some different section of the city, would be greeted with a cordial word from Mr. Moody and an inquiry as to the nature of the services. Almost without exception, the reports were of the most encouraging character. Not only were the audiences large, but often the aisles were filled with chairs, great crowds as well being turned from the doors, unable to get in. Often the report was that large numbers had definitely accepted Christ.

The Reports of Co-Workers

At all such reports Mr. Moody's face would be lighted up with a look of intense pleasure. From the beginning, the only reason that he had for holding these services was in order that sinners might be saved. While he was always glad if Christians were reached and lifted up into a higher level of experience, still the deeper joy came to his heart when some lost man or woman might be through his, or his colleagues', preaching led to accept Christ. Rarely an evening passed that such news was not brought in to the great joy of Mr. Moody. God had so singularly owned the work from the beginning that scarcely a meeting passed without some being led by the Spirit of God to a definite surrender of themselves to His service. It was a privilege to look upon Mr. Moody's face when these reports were brought in by different speakers. When the last one had reported, the meetings would close with praise and prayer. No one who was privileged to attend these after-services in the Institute will ever forget the delightful fellowship of these godly men. They had come from all parts of the world. They had been most largely used of God, and were men of wide and varied experiences. The evening would be spent, not merely in the giving of reports of the special services from which they had come, but other things drawn out of past experience would be brought in, so that one would feel that he was in some special way connected with the carrying out of God's purpose, as he might listen or contribute something to these meetings.

By reason of the work connected with the meetings themselves, the men might come in very much exhausted, yet, after such a meeting as has been spoken of, there would come a sense of a new baptism of the Spirit, and in their waiting upon God there would be a renewal of strength for whatever service might lie before them.

The Monday Conferences

In accordance with the custom of the Institute, Mondays were set aside as days of conference and rest. Mr. Moody would meet the workers from all parts of the city and put to them questions as to the results of the week's work. These meetings, by reason of the suggestions and comments that were offered, were not only deeply interesting, but also exceedingly profitable. Mr. Moody himself would put questions to those who had been conducting the meetings. He would inquire about the progress of the work, ask the number of people that had been present, and how many of them had made up their minds to serve the Lord Jesus Christ. He would also want to know the different nationalities that might be represented, as to the proportion of the working men and of the poor, desiring to learn, if possible, how many of those attending were representatives of visitors to the World's Fair. Then these workers would be asked to give their opinion as to the value of the meetings compared with others which had been held by these same workers at other places. Questions of this kind,

AN AUTHENTIC PORTRAIT OF D. L. MOODY, from a photograph taken in Paris, and loaned to one of our authors, Dr. H. M. Wharton, by Mrs. Moody.

and answers given by trained and skillful workmen, would bring out the most useful suggestions. It was also discovered that at the tents, congregations were a thousand or more at the evening services, and perhaps half as large in the day services. These audiences were made up not only of Protestants but also of Roman Catholics. In some sections, the neighborhood being almost altogether Roman Catholic, perhaps more than three-fourths of the great audiences would belong to that faith. In some of the tents were large numbers of workingmen who would sit with intense interest expressed in their faces, and when the invitation was given, individuals among these would make decision for Christ.

As a rule, all the churches in the immediate vicinity of the tent meetings were in perfect sympathy with the work, the ministers attending the meetings and sitting on the platform, and the largest number of workers were secured from these churches.

Meetings For Children

Some of the most interesting reports were made concerning the children's meetings. Oftentimes Sunday school teachers would be drawn to these meetings where they would find their classes assembled, and in many instances, if the members of the class were not reached, Sunday school teachers would be, and those who had not hitherto made a profession of faith would come out definitely for Christ in these meetings.

In all the sections where these meetings were held, the spiritual power of the neighboring churches was intensely magnified. The prayer meetings of the local churches grew in attendance, and the Sunday services were far better attended than ever before.

It was most interesting also to hear the reports of the men who had charge of the great meetings in the theatres. Sometimes, as for example at the Empire Theatre, nearly the whole congregation would consist of men only, and a very large proportion of these men would be not only out of work, but drinking men. For these, temperance meetings were held, and hundreds of pledges were signed by these men, while hundreds of others yielded themselves altogether to Christ.

Great Throngs at the Meetings

While there were large audiences at nearly all the services, some of them reached enormous proportions. Dr. J. Munro Gibson, of London, who was associated with Mr. Moody in his campaign, said on returning to London, "While the Fair grounds were quite deserted on Sundays the churches were full. There was little use trying to get into the churches where Mr. Moody or Mr. McNeill preached unless you went an hour or two before the time, but even with only a preacher of ordinary abilities the church would be filled, not only in the morning but also at the evening service, and it is not an easy thing to secure a good attendance for evening services in Chicago." It was not only on Sunday nights, but on week nights as well. Many of the great buildings were thronged long before the hour of opening. At the Haymarket Theatre, in West Madison Street, where Mr. Moody was to preach, a great throng would stand in the streets long before the doors were opened, and when they were opened every available inch of space would be filled in an almost incredibly short time, and those who failed to gain entrance would be directed to some place for an overflow meeting, to which, however, they could by no possibility be induced to go until assured that Mr. Moody would speak there.

Perhaps the most extraordinary meetings in point of number, were those held in Forepaugh's circus tent, and those in Tattersall's Hall. When Mr. Moody was arranging to secure the use of the mammoth tent, he had difficulties in making an agreement with the manager, who expected Sunday to be his great day in Chicago, but he was finally prevailed upon to allow him the use of it for Sunday morning, reserving Sunday afternoon and evening for his show. When these arrangements were being made, one of the circus men contemptuously asked him if he supposed it would be possible to get an audience of 3,000. What must have been his surprise when, arriving on the scene Sunday morning, he found assembled a vast congregation of 18,000 people, whereas the attendance at the circus in the afternoon and evening was so poor that the performances had to be given up altogether on Sundays. This was perhaps the greatest throng that attended any one service. After an hour of singing by the great choir and congregation, Mr. Moody spoke from the text, "The Son of Man is come to seek and to save that which was lost." His whole being seemed to be under the control of the power and Spirit of God, and never perhaps did he speak with so much earnestness as to this vast multitude.

Encouraging Features of the Work

It was at this service that the pathetic incident happened where a little child was lost, and Mr. Moody taking the little one in his arms made an effort to discover the parents. As the anxious father made his way toward the platform, Mr. Moody, still holding the child, said, with tears streaming down his cheeks, "this is what Jesus Christ came to do, he came to seek and save sinners, and to restore them to their heavenly Father's embrace." It was a most solemn service and will never be forgotten by any one who had the privilege of attending.

Toward the close of the meetings Mr. Moody said, "We have to-day everything to encourage us, and nothing to discourage us. This has been by far the best week we have had. The Gospel has through this agency been brought to 150,000 people during the week. I have never seen greater eagerness to hear the word of God. The largest halls are too small for the crowds that come to many of the services. One night, for instance, on my way to the Fair Grounds, I beheld one of the most beautiful sights I have ever seen on earth. It was a wonderful display of fireworks and illuminations, tens of thousands of people gazing on the scene. It seemed useless to expect any one to come away from that scene and sit down in a tabernacle to hear the Gospel; but the house was filled, and we had a blessed meeting. The following nights though cold and rainy, with a damp, uncomfortable room, the people crowded in until every inch of space was occupied. I thank God that I am living in Chicago to-day; these have been the happiest moments of my life; what a work He has given us to-day; what encouragements He has given us; how He has blessed us. Perhaps never in your life will some of you have an opportunity to do as much for Christ as now.

Though it required a vast sum of money, Mr. Moody was equal to the occasion, and raised every dollar. Northfield was deeply interested in the work, and contributed largely. The work being presented by Dr. Gordon, of Boston, a contribution of about $10,000 was sent to Mr. Moody from Northfield after Dr. Gordon's appeal. Mr. Moody himself had great skill in getting good collections. When he had to leave the Haymarket Theatre, he said to the audience, "How many people believe we ought to go on? Just lift your hands." And when they had their hands up, he said, "Now put them down deep into your pockets, and help us to carry it on."

No work of this kind can be measured in terms of money. I am sure that in the days to come there will still be great harvests gathered from this sowing, and this World's Fair campaign will doubtless be numbered among the greatest ever conducted by Mr. Moody.

CHAPTER XVIII.

The Last Campaign.

THE last public appearance of Mr. Moody was in Kansas City, Missouri. He began a series of meetings there November 12, 1899. Earlier in the autumn a meeting of the ministers of the evangelical churches had sent an invitation to the great evangelist to captain a religious campaign in the young and vigorous western city. The preliminary discussions of the proposed meetings afforded proof of the confidence reposed in Mr. Moody by many men of many minds. About him the religious forces of the city crystallized with enthusiasm. His name was a power, making for Christian unity. The executive committee of ministers represented the Presbyterian, Methodist, Episcopal, Congregational, Christian, Methodist Episcopal, South and Baptist denominations.

How the Expenses Were Defrayed.

When the laymen were informed of the proposed meetings they sent word to the ministers that they would raise the funds necessary to defray all expenses—a pledge that was abundantly fulfilled. Several of the large business establishments announced that they would pay for one day each the rental of the hall where the meetings were held. The general gratification over the coming of Mr. Moody was a splendid testimonial to his recognized leadership in soul-winning.

Mr. Moody arrived in the city on Saturday morning, in readiness to inaugurate the campaign on the day following. Immediately after breakfast he went with members of the local committee, to have a look at Convention Hall, the mammoth building where the meetings were to be held. He stood upon the stage and tried his voice. He was more than satisfied with the result, declaring that he had come 1,500 miles from New York to find the best hall he had spoken in in this country. The hall had been dedicated only in February of that year. It has a seating capacity of between 15,000 and 20,000. In the interior there are four floors commanding the stage, and here the famous evangelist in his last meetings preached the Gospel to some of the largest audiences ever reached at one time by his voice.

Mr. Moody's Large Human Interest.

One secret of Mr. Moody's hold upon the public was illustrated by a characteristic conversation on the occasion of his first visit to Convention Hall. He had a large human interest, even in secular movements and institutions. One of the reporters of the party said to him: "Do you know, Mr. Moody, how this building was put up? Do you know what it means to this city?" "No," said Mr. Moody, "I supposed some wealthy man owned it." "Kansas City owns it," was the answer. "Nearly every man and woman, and hundreds of children contributed to its building, and own stock in it. It was built by the gifts of the poor, as well as of the rich. It was built voluntarily by the people, and not by taxes. And it stands to-day as it stood the day it was finished, without a dollar of debt."

At once Mr. Moody was intensely interested and demanded the story of the building. It was given him. "That is the sort of thing that annihilates anarchy," said Mr. Moody, in a burst of enthusiasm. "When I laid eyes on the hall, I said that there was no other such hall in this country. But now that I know the sentiment and feeling that have been put into the hall, I know there is no other such building in the world. Do you know that when men are induced to unite as this city has united, where all classes of people behave as if they had common interests, a great lesson has been taught. The value of your hall, it strikes me, is not in dollars and cents, but in its moral significance. I did not believe that such a thing could be done in this generation. It has never been done before." It was this cordial sympathy and hearty appreciation of everything that influenced or manifested the life of a community that made the people feel that Mr. Moody was one with them, and upon this common ground of vantage he gained the public ear for his message.

The First Service at Kansas City.

The first meeting of the memorable series was held on Sunday afternoon. The singing was led by a great chorus of more than 500 voices, organized for the occasion. This was in charge of Prof. C. C. Case, who accompanied Mr. Moody. In his characteristic way Mr. Moody said, "There's good material in that choir. They sing famously well. At first, I am told, there was some difference between the Methodists and Presbyterians in the manner of their singing. The Methodists sang fast, and the Presbyterians sang slow. The result was peculiar. But we have taught them to pull together pretty well now." Another feature of the singing that pleased Mr. Moody was an Old Men's Quartette, which sang several times.

The happy faculty possessed by the evangelist of securing desired action on the part of a vast audience, was shown in this first meeting in connection with the singing. The hymns to be used were printed in sheet form, and were in the hands of the audience. The noise made in handling them threatened to drown the speaker's voice. Just before he began his sermon Mr. Moody said: "All who have sheet hymns please hold them up high." At once 5,000 hands were uplifted, holding the rustling sheets of paper. The effect was that of a Chautauqua salute. "Now shake them," he said. They all did, and the result was an indescribably noisy confusion. "Now sit on them," he said, with a laugh. "I only wanted you to see what a noise they would make, if you kept handling them." The result of this felicitous admonition was a reign of silence.

The service was to begin at three o'clock, but before that time the great auditorium was filled, and it was necessary to close and lock the doors. Several thousand people were turned away. At night an overflow meeting crowded the Second Presbyterian Church near by, and great crowds of people went home, unable to get into either meeting. There had been notable gatherings in the great Convention Hall on former occasions, but even the dedication services, with the attraction of Sousa's Band and the appeal to civic pride, failed to bring together such a throng as that assembled to hear the man of God preach his plain, direct Gospel. It was the greatest meeting in point of attendance in the history of the Mississippi Valley. It was evidence of the fact that, as some one has said, "man is incurably religious," and of the further fact, that there is attractiveness in the message of a recognized ambassador for Christ.

Deep Effect of the Opening Sermons.

The subject of the opening sermons, afternoon and evening, was the same, "Sowing and Reaping." Mr. Moody looked down into the thousands of upturned faces, and amidst intense silence, began the delivery of his last series of sermons by saying: "In after years, as you go by this building, I want you to remember this text that I am going to read to you. I pray that God will

RECENT PICTURE OF MR. MOODY IN HIS ROAD WAGON. It was with this wagon that the noted preacher went to market, and sometimes met the students at the depot and hauled them up to their boarding-houses.

AUDITORIUM HALL. Main building of the Northfield Schools

write it on every heart. It appeals to men and women of every sort and condition; to the priests and the ministers and the reporters: 'Be not deceived; God is not mocked: for whatsoever a man soweth, that shall he also reap. For he that soweth to his flesh shall of the flesh reap corruption; but he that soweth to the Spirit shall of the Spirit reap life everlasting.'" Then followed such a sermon as has won thousands for Christ. Terse, direct sentences, freighted with convicting truth, were dropped deliberately from his lips. He was the master of the assemblies. The people sat in rapt attention, and upon their faces could be traced the effects of varying phases of thought. Toward the close the preacher made an appeal, tender as a young mother's love, and unnoticed tears fell from thousands of eyes. In solemn silence, at the last, the benediction dismissed audiences whose souls had been stirred to deepest depths.

Appeals to the Unconverted

The meetings on Monday fulfilled the expectations aroused by Sunday's services. Following the evening sermon an after-meeting was held in the Second Presbyterian Church, just across the street from Convention Hall. The church was crowded, many standing. As Mr. Moody took his place, the old hymn, "Just as I am," was sung, and then, with no preamble, he began one of his face to face dealings with inquirers. In a simple, conversational way, he presented the truth, just as though he were sitting by the side of each one before him. He closed with an effective incident from his army experience, illustrating his appeal. Then the evangelist paused a moment. The church was still. The ticking of the clock could be distinctly heard. Then he spoke:

"Will any one say he will trust Christ? If so, say 'I will'." He paused, but no reply came, and then again he put the question quietly, "Who will say he will trust Christ?" A moment of silence again, and far back in the church there came a low, but firm, response, "I will." At the sound Mr. Moody advanced quickly to the edge of the platform, and with his eyes questioned those before him. The responses came fast and faster, and in a few minutes fully fifty had said "I will." The after-meeting on Tuesday evening was a repetition of the one the night before. It was marked by the conversion of one of the most prominent business men of the city. His action, which was without reserve of any sort, made the timid confident, and the result was decision on the part of many.

The Beginning of the End

On Wednesday came the first indications of a break-down. The great strain of speaking twice a day in so large a building as Convention Hall began to tell on Mr. Moody. After the night meeting he told the ministers that he was almost exhausted; that he must have some rest, and that it would be impossible for him to lead the inquirers' meeting in the church. He went at once to his room at the Coate's House, that he might rest and be ready for the great meetings of the next day. On Thursday afternoon he gave signs of exhaustion, though anything like a total physical collapse was not apprehended. To a sympathetic inquiry on the part of one of the city ministers, who asked him how he felt, the answer was, "Not big." At night his appearance had changed. His face was flushed, and he perspired profusely. He appeared at times hardly able to support himself, and it seemed sometimes as though he would fall from weakness. The pauses after making his telling points were lengthened, but otherwise his presentation of the truth was as usual. "Then cometh the end." The benediction was pronounced. The public personal work of Dwight L. Moody was finished.

For tens of thousands of people whose lives were touched by the evangel of this soul-winner every incident of that last day will possess a deep interest. There was one circumstance of the afternoon that, in the light of what followed, seemed prophetic in its significance. When Mr. Moody sat in his chair, so tired, during the song service, before beginning his sermon, he asked Mr. Case to sing "Saved by Grace," Fanny J. Crosby's beautiful hymn. In it is the stanza:

> "Some day the silver cord will break,
> And I, no more, as now, shall sing;
> But O, the joy when I shall wake
> Within the palace of the King.
> Then I shall see Him, face to face,
> And tell the story, Saved by Grace."

But if Mr. Moody had any premonition of the approaching end, it passed away as he became possessed of his subject, "The Grace of God." He warned the older Christians to avoid living in the past. He denounced the pessimistic tendencies of those who were sure the former days were better than these. "I have no sympathy," he said, "with the idea that our best days are behind us. In a hopeful, cheery mood he spoke of the shock he had experienced some time before, when he picked up a paper and saw himself alluded to as "old Moody." "Why," he said, "I'm not old. I'm only a baby when considered in comparison with the great eternity which is to come."

The last sermon on Thursday night was on the parable of "The Great Supper." In it he dealt especially with the excuses men made for staying out of the Kingdom of God. Mr. Moody closed his sermon in a peculiarly effective way. He said that, if an excuse were written out by one of the reporters, asking God, "I pray Thee have me excused from the marriage feast," that no one in the house would sign it. If the note were written to go direct to

God, "I will be there," all would want to sign it. "Now," said the preacher, "how many will accept this invitation? How many will say, 'I will?'" Then, as a number responded, the request was repeated. Still he lingered, his energies exhausted, and made one more appeal. "I'll wait a few minutes longer to see if anyone else, any man, woman or child, will say the word. I could stand here all night and listen to these 'I wills.'" So he went away to his long rest with the sound of "I will" spoken by those who were moved by his words still in his ears.

Utterances During the Last Sermon

Some of the utterances of that last day are peculiarly worthy of preservation. Among them were such statements as these: "I've worn God's yoke for over forty years, and I've always found it easy." "There's nothing sweeter than to obey God's will. He is not a severe task-master." "You may trust God. I can believe in God rather than in D. L. Moody. My heart has deceived me a thousand times, but God has never deceived me once." "If you have a good impulse act on it. Don't be afraid. I say that most of the good done in the world is done by men who act on impulses. I am sixty-two, and I have acted on impulses all my life. I never made a mistake by acting on an impulse I felt to be good." "The natural growth of the Christian is toward more kindness and a more beautiful nature. Have you ever noticed how many old people seem cross and crabbed these days? That is because they have not been good Christians." "I am not old. I'm only an infant compared with the ages that will roll over me when I am gone." "Those who live in Christ will live forever. The glory is not past, but to come."

Friday morning, toward noon, Mr. Moody went out driving. He came back thoroughly exhausted. Not until then did he relinquish the hope of preaching that day. He sent for one of the ministers of the committee, Rev. Dr. Matt. S. Hughes, of the Independence Avenue Methodist Episcopal Church, to preach that afternoon, saying, as he made his request, with a flash of his old spirit, "You Methodists are always prepared to preach." Mr. Moody told those who were near him that he had never felt so feeble before. For the first time in forty years he was obliged to abandon his services. He had not been able to lie in bed for three nights, but had taken all his rest in his chair, sleeping only a few minutes at a time. It was decided, upon consultation with his physician, Dr. Schauffler, that he should go home at once.

Mr. Moody was sitting in his armchair. He was breathing heavily, and his face seemed puffy and bloated. He said his limbs were swelling, and he had a feeling of oppression about his heart. "I'm afraid I shall have to give up the meetings," he said. "It's too bad." He was silent. "It's the first time in forty years of preaching that I have had to give up my meetings." He did not say anything for a while. Then he spoke in a low voice. "It is more painful to me to give up those audiences than it is to suffer from my ailments." How regretfully he relinquished his labors! But he could at least lay down his life with the knowledge that his steps had never lagged.

BACK TO NORTHFIELD

An effort was made to get a special car, but none being available at once, the Gospel car, "The Messenger of Peace," belonging to the American Baptist Publication Society, and in charge of Rev. S. G. Neil, the railroad evangelist, was offered for the trip to Northfield. At nine o'clock on Thursday evening, accompanied by a physician and friends, the homeward journey was begun. The next day a cheery telegram came from Mr. Moody, saying that he had had the best night for a week, and thanking "the good people of Kansas City for all their kindnesses".

Charles M. Vining tells an interesting story of the trip home with Mr. Moody. When the train pulled into Detroit it was over an hour late, and unless at least half of this time could be made up, the eastern connection for the through Boston train could not be made. As the train was standing in the station at Detroit, the engineer came back along the train until he reached the Gospel car. "Whose car is this?" he asked one of the party who was standing outside. "It's a special taking Mr. Moody, the evangelist, to his home," was the reply. "Where has he been?" came the question. "He was holding meetings in Kansas City, where he was taken ill, and now we are taking him home. We are about an hour late, and if we don't make up the time, we won't make the proper connections for Boston." "Look here," said the engineer, "fifteen years ago I was converted by Moody, and I have lived a better and happier life ever since. I didn't know Moody's car was on to-night, but if you want me to make up the time for you I'll do it. Just tell Mr. Moody that one of his friends is on the engine, and then hold your breath." As soon as the train got clear of the city the engineer pulled the throttle open, and it is said that he made the fastest time ever made over this division. Connections were made, and when the party awakened the next morning they were on the Boston train. When Mr. Vining left East Northfield for Kansas City, Mr. Moody said: "Tell them they have caged the old lion at last."

While the influences of his work were still active in the churches of the city, came the tidings that he had entered into rest, and Kansas City, the recipient of his latest toil, bowed its head in sorrow over the common bereavement that had come to the Christian world.

CHAPTER XIX.

Mr. Moody as an Evangelist.

IN the ancient Church there were men whose special call and labors were to save her decaying life from extinction, and reinforce it with fresh spiritual power. If time permitted, the names of patriarchs and prophets in the Old Testament might be mentioned, and the names of New Testament apostles might be spoken, for all of these were evangelists in the truest sense of the word. The word "evangelist" means "the bringer of good tidings." This being true, D. L. Moody was an evangelist in the truest sense of the word. The office, being of divine appointment is distinct from that of the pastor, the teacher, and the prophet, and as a rule in all the history of the Church has been given to those who have no stated pastoral charge, but have traveled from place to place as they had opportunity to work.

He Led Them to Christ

Among all the men whom the world has ever known as evangelists D. L. Moody takes no secondary place. One has but to study the history of the Church to learn the value of regligious awakenings in general, and he who states that their effect upon the Church is not helpful makes a statement which cannot be supported by the facts. I once heard Mr. Moody say that when some one in the City of Boston had criticised the meetings he had held, he determined that he would go back to the city and call for all those who had been converted in his meetings to be present at a service which he would announce. The great building was filled to overflowing and at least ten years after his services had closed he had the joy of hearing literally thousands give testimony to the fact that he had led them to Christ.

A little before the middle of the eighteenth century began what may be called the First Era of Revivals in this country, part of a religious movement that affected and moulded in a most remarkable manner the entire English-speaking world for three-quarters of a century.

The leaders of this movement in England were Whitefield and the Wesleys. The leader in America was Jonathan Edwards.

Remarkable Revivals in America

*"The second Era of Revivals in this country dates from about 1797. Among the honored leaders in the earlier phase of the movement were Dr. Edward Dorr Griffin and President Dwight, associated with such men as the elder Mills. In its later phase, in what may be called the supplement to the Revival of 1797, the revivalists Nettleton and Finney were prominent."

It is an interesting fact in revivals that they frequently succeed some great calamity. It was so with the wonderful work of grace known as The Revival of 1859. The churches, to an alarming extent, were characterized by indifference and conformity to the world. Speculation was running rife, and men were entering recklessly in the race for riches. As a natural result, frauds and failures were very common, and in a day the most fanciful dreams would perish and millionaires would become paupers.

But God was working in it all, and as a direct result there was a call sent forth to the Christians of the Nation for united prayer, and the result was the mighty awakening.

---

* "The Church in America and its baptisms of fire," by D. S. Gregory.

(Copyright.)
D. L. MOODY SPEAKING IN COOPER UNION HALL, NEW YORK, IN 1896.
"I want you to pray earnestly for the text I tried to bring out yesterday. It has gone into all the morning papers. Just the text; no matter about the sermon.—'Whatsoever a man soweth that also shall he reap.' There will be millions of people see that text to-day."

Its history can never be known perfectly. It is written in Heaven, and when we stand there we shall know the full story.

But no history of revivals in this generation would be complete without due consideration being given to the man whose name is a household word, and who has been a blessing to Christians throughout the world, Mr. Dwight L. Moody,

Mr. Moody may be regarded as being, in his career and work, the representative of lay activity in the work of evangelization—especially of the Young Men's Christian Association as embodying and organizing this activity. That association had largely to do with opening the way for him into the various churches and communities in the early stages of his work, and with awakening and sustaining enthusiasm in his various evangelistic enterprises

Representative Evangelists

It would be difficult to imagine men more unlike than these representative evangelists. Jonathan Edwards was a mighty logician, and his great theme was *The sovereignty of God's Grace in the Salvation of Sinners.*

His sermons stirred the souls of men to their very depths, and sometimes resulted in remarkable outward manifestations of feeling, as when, during the preaching at Enfield, of the sermon entitled 'Sinners in the Hands of an Angry God,' the audience rose up in agony to cry out for mercy.

George Whitefield was an orator of great power. Indeed, many of those who heard Whitefield regarded him as the most eloquent of men, and the traditions of the remarkable effects produced, not only by his sermons but by the very tones of his voice, are still handed down.

Dr. Asahel Nettleton was very different from either of the two just mentioned. The following general estimate of his life has been given by some one:

Dr. Nettleton's life was marvelously useful and helpful. I never heard the opinion expressed that he was either a great or a very learned man; but I never heard those who knew him intimately question his goodness. He was a most godly man, serious, circumspect, discreet, and gifted with rare discrimination, enabling him to know and read men, and greatly aiding him to adapt himself and his instructions to men in their various moods, with their different peculiarities, prejudices, conditions, and prepossessions. He had power to prevail with God and man. His rare success is not to be attributed to his greatness, nor to his native sagacity, nor to the happy combination of gifts constitutional or natural, nor to everything combined in him, so much as to his holiness. He walked with God, knew and trusted God. He had a mighty faith. He found out how much God loved men, and he was brought into sympathy with God for the salvation of men. His perception of the guilt and doom of sinners was intense and absorbed him. He was a man whose religious development would lead him to cry out while prostrated on the cold ground at the midnight hour, "Give me souls or I die!"

Charles G. Finney

Charles G. Finney was still another type of man, but few men have been more mightily used of God than he. Sometimes he could proceed no farther in the service than the reading of his text when the power of God would fall upon his audience and scores of people would profess conversion.

But with all their greatness none of them outshine Dwight L. Moody, who stands out among all men as God's chosen instrument to show what one consecrated layman may accomplish when filled with the Holy Ghost.

He was mightily moved when Henry Varley, the English evangelist, said to him as they were "visiting at a friend's house together in England some years ago: "It remains for the world to see what the Lord can do with a man wholly consecrated to Christ.' Mr. Moody soon returned to America, but those words clung to him with such power that he was induced to return to England and commence that wonderful series of labors in Scotland and England. Mr. Moody said to Henry Varley on returning to England, 'Those were the words of the Lord through your lips to my soul."

Strangers sometimes thought him difficult to approach, and he was, if you were trying to seek him out to say flattering words to him; but no man in all the world was more approachable than he when he knew that you had an unselfish desire with him to extend the bounds of the Kingdom of God.

Especially Adapted to His Work

Mr. Moody was especially adapted to his work, first, because he was pre-eminently practical in this practical age. He was most direct in his speech; every one knew exactly what he meant; there was no mistake in his utterance. His energy was literally boundless; day and night and night and day he toiled, never seeming to be weary. His earnestness and enthusiasm were contagious and wherever he found an audience dull and lifeless he had only to speak to them a few minutes until they were ready to do anything that he might command. He preached to larger crowds than any man in his generation, and yet it was ever his object and aim to reach the individual rather than the people in a mass. He was a born organizer, and in this century which has been specially distinguished for its progress in organization he took high rank. He was the world's greatest evangelist because with all these qualities he knew men through and through, and he was able to move them at his own will,

A distinguished southern Presbyterian minister writes me the following, which illustrates my thought.

"I first knew Mr. Moody in Louisville, Kentucky during a great campaign that he was conducting there. I first had some conversation with him in regard to some work which we were setting on foot at the time. I found him a most sympathetic listener, and wonderfully helpful, but the moment any allusion was made to his own work, and what great things it was doing for Louisville he instantly shifted the conversation.

An Embarrassing Incident

"After the work had been in progress for some days, and the great Tabernacle on Broadway had been crowded from day to day, and at every meeting, an incident occurred which troubled me greatly, and which I did not fully understand until many months later. The after-meeting was held one morning in the Warren Memorial Church. At the conclusion of the service a great many workers in the meeting tarried for a moment of conference. A gentleman approached Mr. Moody, 'See this group of ladies on the right of the platform, they are among our prominent women of the City, and supports of our movement, both with their means and their personal work. They have not yet had the pleasure of shaking hands with you, and they have tarried for this purpose.' 'Where are they?' asked Mr. Moody. The gentleman pointed them out, saying, 'I will tell them you will see them in a few moments.' And in a little while I saw Mr. Moody reach under the pulpit stand for his little felt hat, go out a back door, and taking a cab, drive to his hotel.

"The ladies waited for some time, and finally left with the greatest feeling of indignation, and many, of them, declaring that they would not again be seen in the meetings, and work with a man who could be so rude. I confessed I was puzzled myself, and did not know what explanation could possibly be offered for the strange action.

"Some year or so after this I was in Chicago with him on the platform. Again a woman came to the foot of the stair, and said she wished to see Mr. Moody. 'He was used of God for the salvation of my husband, I want to shake hands with him, and tell him how grateful I feel toward him.' I said, 'Why certainly, wait and I will see that you have the privilege of seeing him,' when finally I called his attention to her, and when she had given him her reason for wishing to shake hands with him, without one word he turned and left her. Again, I thought, here is a type of the same thing we saw in Louisville. I comforted the poor woman as best I could.

Guard Against Flattery

"A few days later in his conference with young men, he spoke of how we should guard against flattery, and how many strange things we had to do, to prevent the devil's getting a hold upon us. After this conversation I told him of the injustice I had done him in my mind, in the incidents above alluded to. His explanation was very brief, but equally satisfactory and to the point. 'If I had shaken hands with those women, I wouldn't have been half through before the devil would have made me believe that I was some great man, and from that time I would have to do as he bid.

"I was present with him in a meeting for a month after this time, and studied him in the light of this explanation, and no one thing has ever helped me more to explain his closeness to God, and his humility of Spirit than the facts alluded to."

His messages had no uncertain sound, concerning the Gospel.

He believed that men were lost without Christ. He told the story of the mother who came into the Eye Infirmary in Chicago and said: "Doctor, there is something wrong with my baby's eyes." He described how the doctor took the child in his arms and carried it to the window, looked at the eyes only a moment, then, shaking his head, gave the child back again to its mother. "Well, Doctor, what is it?" she said. "Poor woman" he replied, "your baby is going blind; in three months' time he will be stone blind, and no power on earth can ever make him see." Mr. Moody told how the mother held the baby close against her heart and then fell on the floor with a shriek, crying out, "My God! My baby blind! My baby blind!"

On Sudden Conversion

I can see his face now as he said, the tears rolling down his cheeks: "Would to God, we might all be as much moved as that when we know that our friends are spiritually blind as well as lost!" Because he believed this, he preached as he did, and it was this spirit that literally drove him to Kansas City to preach his last sermon, and then turn his face home to die. He believed in instantaneous conversion; he had no patience at all with the man who thought he must grow better to be saved. He once said:

"When Mr. Sankey and myself were in one place in Europe, a man preached a sermon against the pernicious doctrines that we were going to preach, one of which was sudden conversion. He said conversion was a matter of time and growth. Do you know what I do when any man preaches against the doctrines I preach? I go to the Bible and find out what it says, and if I am right I give them more of the same kind. I preached more on sudden conversion in that town than in any town I was in, in my life. I would like to know how long it took the Lord to convert Zaccheus? How long did it take the Lord to convert that woman whom He met at the well of Sychar? How long to convert that adulterous woman in the temple, who was caught in the very act of adultery?

How long to convert that woman who anointed His feet and wiped them with the hairs of her head? Didn't she go with the Word of God ringing in her ears, 'Go in peace?'"

He was a master in the conduct of evangelistic meetings. I well remember, during the recent Armenian massacres, some one interrupted him in one of his services, saying, "Mr. Moody, I want to ask permission to present a petition, and to ask the people to sign it. This petition is to be sent to the President of the United States, asking him to take some action which may help to stop this dreadful slaughter of innocent people."

The man who made the request, was of considerable prominence, and many a leader would have yielded to his entreaty.

A Better Plan

But Mr. Moody was always true to his convictions, and said, "My friend, I have a better plan than yours. I always believe in approaching any difficulty by the way of the throne of God. Will some one lead us in prayer?" It is sufficient to say that there was no petition presented, and everybody was satisfied, that his was the better way.

He was at his best in the Inquiry Meeting. He knew just what Scripture to use, and it was a rare privilege to be anywhere near him when he talked with one who wanted to be a Christian.

He was never easily discouraged; circumstances that would greatly hinder others, had no effect upon him, except to lead him closer to Christ. Mr. William Phillips Hall, the Business Men's Evangelist, relates the following:

In Mr. Moody's early evangelistic career, he began a series of meetings in a church across the sea. There was nothing remarkable about the first service except that it was formal and cold. In the evening the attendance had increased, and when the invitation was given to those to stand, who desired to express an interest in their souls' salvation, so many stood that the evangelist feared they had not understood his invitation, so he gave it again more plainly, only to have a larger number stand. And when the after-meeting was called, there was a most remarkable manifestation of the power of God, and it was the beginning of a great and memorable work of grace.

An Incident From His Early Career

One of the members of that church went home to tell an invalid member of the family, that two Americans, by the names of Moody and Sankey, had conducted services in the church that day. The invalid burst into tears, and reaching for her purse took out a piece of an English newspaper, which contained the large announcement that Dwight L. Moody and Ira D. Sankey were being greatly used of God in Chicago. So she had read it and had cut it out of the paper, and from that moment began to pray that God would send those two men to her church.

I have heard Mr. Moody relate the incident myself and then say:

"I believe when the rewards are given out in Heaven, that that invalid woman will share with us in the glory and honor of that grand campaign."

No one this side of Heaven can ever estimate the number of people he won to Christ in his evangelistic services. It has been estimated that he preached to millions. It is safe to say that he must, under the power of God, have led hundreds of thousands to a decision.

Margin annotations (top): Ps 91 ("My lodging") The shadow of His wings ("My habitation") The most High ("My Covering") His wings ("My Shield") His truth ("My Keepers) His angels

Margin (left side): Blessings God will give to those that do these 3 things

Margin (bottom left): Some think it was written by Moses of the fairy Respents

---

Security of believers. **PSALMS, XCI.—XCIV.** Folly of atheists and oppressors.

PSALM XCI.

1 HE that dwelleth in the secret place of the Most High, shall abide under the shadow of the Almighty.
2 I will say of the LORD, *He is* my refuge, and my fortress: my God; in him will I trust.
3 Surely he shall deliver thee from the snare of the fowler, *and* from the noisome pestilence.
4 He shall cover thee with his feathers, and under his wings shalt thou trust: his truth *shall be thy* shield and buckler.
5 Thou shalt not be afraid for the terror by night, *nor* for the arrow that flieth by day;
6 *Nor* for the pestilence *that* walketh in darkness, *nor* for the destruction *that* wasteth at noonday.
7 A thousand shall fall at thy side, and ten thousand at thy right hand; *but* it shall not come nigh thee.
8 Only with thine eyes shalt thou behold, and see the reward of the wicked.
9 Because thou hast made the LORD, *which is* my refuge, *even* the Most High, thy habitation,
10 There shall no evil befall thee, neither shall any plague come nigh thy dwelling.
11 For he shall give his angels charge over thee, to keep thee in all thy ways.
12 They shall bear thee up in *their* hands, lest thou dash thy foot against a stone.
13 Thou shalt tread upon the lion and adder: the young lion and the dragon shalt thou trample under feet.
14 Because he hath set his love upon me, therefore will I deliver him: I will set him on high, because he hath known my name.
15 He shall call upon me, and I will answer him: I will be with him in trouble; I will deliver him, and honour him.
16 With a long life will I satisfy him, and shew him my salvation.

PSALM XCII.
A Psalm or Song for the Sabbath day.

1 IT is a good thing to give thanks unto the LORD, and to sing praises unto thy name, O Most High:
2 To shew forth thy lovingkindness in the morning, and thy faithfulness every night,
3 Upon an instrument of ten strings, and upon the psaltery; upon the harp with a solemn sound.
4 For thou, LORD, hast made me glad through thy work; I will triumph in the works of thy hands.
5 O LORD, how great are thy works! *and* thy thoughts are very deep.
6 A brutish man knoweth not; neither doth a fool understand this.
7 When the wicked spring as the grass, and when all the workers of iniquity do flourish, *it is* that they shall be destroyed for ever:
8 But thou, LORD, *art most* high for evermore.
9 For, lo, thine enemies, O LORD, for, lo, thine enemies shall perish; all the workers of iniquity shall be scattered;
10 But my horn shalt thou exalt like the horn of an unicorn: I shall be anointed with fresh oil.
11 Mine eye also shall see *my desire* on mine enemies; *and* mine ears shall hear *my desire* of the wicked that rise up against me.

12 The righteous shall flourish like the palm tree: he shall grow like a cedar in Lebanon.
13 Those that be planted in the house of the LORD shall flourish in the courts of our God.
14 They shall still bring forth fruit in old age; they shall be fat and flourishing;
15 To shew that the LORD is upright: *he is* my rock, and *there is* no unrighteousness in him.

PSALM XCIII.

1 THE LORD reigneth; he is clothed with majesty; the LORD is clothed with strength, *wherewith* he hath girded himself: the world also is stablished, that it cannot be moved.
2 Thy throne *is* established of old: thou *art* from everlasting.
3 The floods have lifted up, O LORD, the floods have lifted up their voice; the floods lift up their waves.
4 The LORD on high *is* mightier than the noise of many waters, *yea, than* the mighty waves of the sea.
5 Thy testimonies are very sure: holiness becometh thine house, O LORD, for ever.

PSALM XCIV.

1 O LORD God, to whom vengeance belongeth; O God, to whom vengeance belongeth, shew thyself.
2 Lift up thyself, thou judge of the earth: render a reward to the proud.
3 LORD, how long shall the wicked, how long shall the wicked triumph?
4 *How long* shall they utter *and* speak hard things? *and* all the workers of iniquity boast themselves?
5 They break in pieces thy people, O LORD, and afflict thine heritage.
6 They slay the widow and the stranger, and murder the fatherless.
7 Yet they say, The LORD shall not see, neither shall the God of Jacob regard *it*.
8 Understand, ye brutish among the people; and, *ye* fools, when will ye be wise?
9 He that planted the ear, shall he not hear? he that formed the eye, shall he not see?
10 He that chastiseth the heathen, shall not he correct? he that teacheth man knowledge, *shall* not he know?
11 The LORD knoweth the thoughts of man, that they *are* vanity.
12 Blessed *is* the man whom thou chastenest, O LORD, and teachest him out of thy law;
13 That thou mayest give him rest from the days of adversity, until the pit be digged for the wicked.
14 For the LORD will not cast off his people, neither will he forsake his inheritance.
15 But judgment shall return unto righteousness: and all the upright in heart shall follow it.
16 Who will rise up for me against the evildoers? *or* who will stand up for me against the workers of iniquity?
17 Unless the LORD *had been* my help, my soul had almost dwelt in silence.
18 When I said, My foot slippeth; thy mercy, O LORD, held me up.
19 In the multitude of my thoughts within me thy comforts delight my soul.
20 Shall the throne of iniquity have fellowship with thee, which frameth mischief by a law?

COPYRIGHTED 1895
BY JOHN F. WINSTON

A PAGE FROM MR. MOODY'S BIBLE, containing the 91st Psalm with his original annotations. It was from this page that Mr. Moody preached his famous "Life and Death" sermon, and it is also from this that he spoke to the passengers on board the steamship *Spree* in November, 1892, while crossing the Atlantic from London to New York, when it was thought that the steamship was about to founder. Photograph was taken by permission of Mrs. Fitt day before the funeral.

CHAPTER XX

His Bible.

MR. MOODY loved his Bible. He knew it so well that his eyes and fingers could find any passage that he wanted from Genesis to Revelation, and it mattered not how hurriedly he was speaking, it was as easy for him to find the text he wished as for the master musician to find the notes on the keyboard of a piano, and yet, he tells us himself that, when he first entered the Sunday-school class in Boston, he did not know the difference between the Old Testament and the New.

More Than Precious to Him

The Bible as a book was more than precious to him. His own Bible was a storehouse of richest treasure. He was never heard even by his closest friends to make a play on Bible words and phrases, and he was always quick to rebuke those who did. He really had no patience at all with the so-called higher criticism of God's word. He was one day approached by a newspaper reporter who asked for some word from him regarding the higher criticism. "I'm not up to that sort of thing," he said, with a twinkle in his eye. "You see, I never studied theology, and I'm precious glad I didn't. There are so many things in the Bible that everybody can understand that I'm going to preach about them until they are exhausted, and then, if I have any time left, I'll take up the texts I don't understand." "Aren't you ever asked to discuss difficult passages of Scripture?" was the inquiry. "Mercy, yes," answered Mr. Moody, "almost every day, but I always answer people just as I have answered you, and tell them that there is satisfaction and consolation enough in the promises of the Saviour, all that anybody can want. The single verse, 'Come unto Me, all ye that labor and are heavy laden and I will give you rest,' contains all the theology and religion that I need, or any other man or woman."

The page taken from the Bible he studied, and giving us a picture of his notes made on the ninety-first Psalm, is but an illustration of the entire book. Almost every page contained an illustration or reference to an incident which shed light upon the truth of God.

A Valuable Advice

Years ago Harry Moorehouse, the English Bible reader, said to him while visiting his church in Chicago, "If you will stop preaching your own words and preach God's Word, you will make yourself a great power for good." This prophecy made a deep impression on Mr. Moody's mind, and from that day he devoted himself to the study of the Bible as he had never done before. He had been accustomed to draw his sermons from the experiences of Christians and the life of the streets, now he began to follow the counsel of his friend, and preach the *Word*.

His first series of sermons on characters of the Bible was preached during the summer before the Chicago fire, and at once attracted great attention. He also began to compare Scripture with Scripture. "If I don't understand a text," said his friend Moorehouse, "I ask another text to explain it, and then, if it is too hard for me, I take it to the Lord and ask Him to explain it for me." This method Mr. Moody adopted, and this was one of the secrets of his power. He was mighty in the Scriptures, and spoke as with authority from God.

He had a large library at his house at Northfield, much of which had been presented to him by admiring friends; but it is safe to say that there are not half a dozen books in the world, besides the books of the Old and New Testaments, of which he could give the names and a general outline of their contents; hence there was room in his head for God's Word, and with it he kept himself continually full and running over. His method of Bible study was like the method of a humming bird studying a clover blossom. From the cells of sweetness down into which he thrust his questions and his prayers, he brought up the honey which God has stored away; he reveled in the profusion and preciousness of the promises, like a robin in a tree full of ripe cherries. It was enjoyable just to see how heartily he enjoyed the Word of God, and almost convincing to see with what absolute faith he clung to it for his own salvation, and with what absolute assurance he urged others to do the same. To Mr. Moody the Word of God was food, drink, lodging, and clothes; he climbed by it toward Heaven, as a sailor climbs the rigging; it was an anchor to hold him; a gale to drive him; it was health, hope, happiness, eternal life.

Comments on Hope and Faith

It was by his loving, prayerful, trustful study of the Scriptures that he had acquired his skill as a practical commentator. Take, as a specimen of his off-hand comments, this from one of the Bible readings on Hope: "Hope is the anchor of the soul. Now none of you ever saw an anchor but was used to hold something *down*. It goes down to the bottom of the sea, and takes hold of the ground, and holds the ship to it. But this anchor, this hope, is to hold us *up:* it enters within the veil; it takes hold of the throne of God."

On the text, "Faith cometh by hearing, and hearing by the Word of God," he said: "A great many people are mourning their want of faith; but there is no wonder that they haven't any faith; they don't study the Word of God How do you suppose you are to have faith in God when you don't know anything about Him? It is those who haven't any acquaintance with God that stumble and fall; but those who know Him can trust Him and lean heavy on His arm. If a man would rather read the Sunday newspapers than read God's Word, I don't see how Christ is going to save him. There is no room in him for the Gospel when he has filled himself with the newspapers. For years I have not touched a Sunday newspaper, or a weekly religious paper either, on Sunday. Some people lay aside those religious papers for Sunday reading, but that is not a good way. Let us lay aside all other reading for one day in the week, and devote ourselves to the study of God's Word. But you say, 'O, we must study science and literature, and such things, in order to understand the Bible.' What can a botanist tell you about the 'Rose of Sharon' and the 'Lily of the Valley'? What can the geologist tell you about the 'Rock of Ages'? What can the astronomer tell you about the 'Bright and Morning Star'?

Get Rid of Doubts

"A good many people are asking, 'Will this work hold out?' Now I am not a prophet, nor the son of a prophet, but there is one thing I can predict, and that is, that every one of these young converts who studies his Bible till he learns to love it better than anything else, will be sure to hold out; the world will have no charms for him. What all these young converts want is to be in love with the Word of God; to feed upon it till it comes to be sweeter than honey and the honeycomb.

"One day when my old employer, C. N. Henderson, was sending me out to make some collections, he gave me some notes on which he had made some private marks. Some were marked 'B'.

bad, and I was to get anything I could for them. Others were marked 'D', doubtful; I was to get all the security I could. And others were marked 'G', good, and these I was to treat accordingly. Now people take God's notes or promises, and some of them they mark 'B', because they don't believe in them; others they mark 'D', because they don't feel sure of them; but if there happens to be one which has been fulfilled to themselves, that one they mark 'G'.

"Now that isn't the way to treat God's promises. You ought to mark every one of them G–O–O–D, good. Heaven and earth shall pass away before any one of them shall fail. If we could only get these Christians out of Doubting Castle, how rich they would be, and what a work of grace there might be. O, these Devils, Ifs! When shall we ever get rid of them?"

Mr. Moody's Bible was a real storehouse of treasure. Every page of it was marked—almost every verse had some special illustration connected with it, so that he had only to open the book to have a perfect flood of light upon its pages. It was for this reason that he was always helpful and always interesting.

The following is one of his most characteristic statements, and really was the beginning of my marking my own Bible. He always practiced what he preached, and he advised other people to mark their Bibles because it had been such a blessing to him:

"When the preacher gives out a text, mark it; as he goes on preaching, put a few words in the margin, key-words that shall bring back the whole sermon again. By that plan of making a few marginal notes, I can remember sermons I heard years and years ago. Every man ought to take down some of the preacher's words and ideas, and go into some lane or byway, and preach them again to others. We ought to have four ears—two for ourselves and two for other people. Then, if you are in a new town, and have nothing else to say, jump up and say: 'I heard some one say so and so;' and men will always be glad to hear you if you give them heavenly food. The world is perishing for lack of it."

He had many references to the twenty-third Psalm; this is one of the best. "I suppose I have heard as many good sermons on the twenty-third Psalm as on any other six verses in the Bible. I wish I had begun to take notes upon them years ago when I heard the first one. Things slip away from you when you get to be fifty years of age.

"With me, the Lord.

"Beneath me, green pastures.

"Beside me, still waters.

"Before me, a table.

"Around me, mine enemies.

"After me, goodness and mercy.

"Ahead of me, the house of the Lord.

"'Blessed is the day,' says an old divine, 'when Psalm twenty-three was born!' It has been more used than almost any other passage in the Bible.'"

Mr. Moody was never more interesting, than when giving his Bible readings. He could hold his great audiences spellbound with his plain, practical, and yet powerful interpretations of the Scripture. He had no use at all for the so-called *higher criticism*. At one of the last conferences held in New York, he said to a company of ministers:

"I don't see why you men are talking about 'two Isaiah's; half the people in the country do not know that there is one Isaiah yet; let's make them know about one, before we begin to tell them about two."

The last conversation of any length, that I had with him, he must have talked for half an hour, concerning his absolute confidence in the Bible and his growing love for it.

CHAPTER XXI.

His Co-Workers.

MR, MOODY was a great general not only in faculties of organization, but also in his shrewd choice of the right men for the right work. Thus, from the beginning of his labors, he associated with himself the most competent assistants, and it is by no means depreciatory of his own efforts to say that his success was in no small measure dependent upon those who helped him. It is not depreciatory, I say; for one of the greatest gifts is this ability to choose worthy helpers. Napoleon could not conduct in person all his campaigns, but he surrounded himself with a staff of generals so brilliant in their abilities that they were able to help him maintain his prestige for fifteen years.

IRA DAVID SANKEY.

In speaking of Mr. Moody's co-workers, I realize that space is obliging me to leave out the names of many who are worthy of mention, so I have endeavored to confine my choice to those whose names are most prominently associated with his work in the ears of the public. One name is indissolubly connected with Mr. Moody's, and of its bearer I would speak first.

Ira David Sankey was born August 28, 1840, in the village of Edinburgh, in western Pennsylvania. His parents were Methodists. His father was well-off in worldly circumstances, and in such good repute among his neighbors that they repeatedly elected him member of the State Legislature; he was, moreover, a licensed exhorter in his own church.

From childhood Ira was known for a joyous spirit and trustful disposition. The gift of singing developed in him at a very early age. Reared in a genial, religious atmosphere, liked and respected by all who knew him, he lived on, till past his fifteenth year, before he was converted. His conviction occurred during a series of special services, and after a week's hard struggle he found peace in accepting Jesus as his Saviour. Soon afterward he joined the church, and, about the same time, his father having removed to Newcastle, he entered the Academy at that place. The young man had developed from his gift of song a rich talent of expression, through his wonderful voice, of the hymns of the church. After his conversion it became his delight to devote this precious gift to the service of the Lord, and it was his continual prayer that the Holy Spirit would make use of the words sung to the conversion of those who flocked to the services. Before he attained his majority, he was appointed superintendent of the Sunday school, which contained more than 300 pupils. His singing of Gospel invitations in solos dates from this time. The faith of the singer was rewarded with repeated blessings. A class of seventy Christians was committed to his charge, a responsibility which made him a more earnest student of the Bible The choir of the congregation also came under his leadership.

Elsewhere in this book is described the meeting between Mr. Moody and Mr. Sankey and their subsequent labors together. It is sufficient to add concerning Mr. Sankey that his gift is still used in the service of his Master.

Paul P. Bliss

There are many who still remember the shock to Christian workers throughout the country when on the night of December 29, 1876, Mr. Paul P. Bliss and his wife perished in the terrible railroad accident at Ashtabula, Ohio. They had been spending

DISTINGUISHED BIBLE TEACHERS, Rev. A. C. Dixon, Rev. G. Campbell Morgan, Rev. G. H. C. Macgregor, with their wives and friends at Northfield.

the Christmas holidays in Pennsylvania, and, leaving their little ones at the house of a relative in Avon, N. Y., set out for Chicago to help Major Whittle in the revival work which was following the great meetings of Mr. Moody in that city. After they started on their journey, Mr. Bliss telegraphed to Major Whittle, "We are going home to-morrow." They did go home—to their home above.

P. P. Bliss, like his associate in Gospel songs, Mr. Sankey, was a native of Pennsylvania. In early life he had few opportunities for culture, but, through a noble nature, God helped him to a place of great usefulness. He was married young, and through the influence of his wife, who was possessed of deep religious principles, was converted and led to consecrate his gifts to the service of his Master. Moving to Chicago, he united with the First Congregational Church, where, form any years, he was leader of the choir and superintendent of the Sunday school, also becoming widely known by his work in musical conventions. His voice was a rich baritone. As a composer he will long be remembered; he was the author of many of the best known Gospel songs, such as, "Hold the Fort," "What Shall the Harvest Be," "More to Follow," "Only an Armor Bearer," "Let the Lower Lights be Burning," "Pull for the Shore," etc.

Major D. W. Whittle

When Major Whittle entered upon revival work Mr. Bliss decided to give up business and accompany him. During the years 1874-6, they traveled together through the West and South. Mr. Bliss devoted his share of the royalty from the Gospel Songs, a sum amounting to more than $60,000, to charity; this in spite of the fact that he had no private fortune. During the last three months of his life, in connection with Major Whittle, he held revival services at Kalamazoo, Mich., and afterward at Peoria, Ill.

The voice of this sweet singer still lives in his songs, for those who heard him will never forget the pleading, tender, sympathetic quality of his voice. No singer in the history of evangelistic work has made a deeper impression on the Christian world.

Major D. W. Whittle was for many years a well-known business man of Chicago. His prospects were large, and he had won a wide reputation for integrity and ability, when he gave up everything that might be counted of worldly advantage to enter upon evangelistic work. He was known, in earlier years, in his connection with Mr. Bliss. His career during the past few years is well known to the public; for a long time he has been one of Mr. Moody's valued helpers, and the tie between the two men was cemented the more closely by the marriage of Major Whittle's daughter, Mary, to Mr. Moody's son, Mr. Will R. Moody.

Major Whittle is especially at home in the inquiry room. The exercise of marvelous tact, and the use of excellent judgment, make his personal instruction clear as well as convincing, and his sympathy and love for those whom he tries to serve are unmistakable. Of special value were his services during the recent war with Spain. He toiled when he was too weary to preach, but always with that zeal which has so commended him to churches everywhere. I do not think I have ever known a more godly man. I never think of him without blessing.

Henry Varley.

Mr. Varley was born in Lincolnshire, England, in 1835. In boyhood his health was poor, and he came especially under the influence of his mother, who, although she died when he was only ten, gave him from her own strong nature and training the foundations of good character.

It was not long after that he began to live in London, barren of worldly possessions and condemned to very many trying experiences. At fifteen he was converted, and scarcely a year later made his own first public address in the large Sunday school of the John Street Church, with which he had united. From this time various services yielded occasion for the development the gifts which the Lord had placed with His young servant.

He was only nineteen when he secured a business partnership, but in 1854 he went to Australia to the gold fields. There he would preach on Sundays, and about the glowing fires in the evenings would lead his rough comrades to approach their Father's throne in prayer. He did not succeed as a miner, and soon returned to Melbourne. In spite of flattering business offers he went back to London, where, in 1857, he married a daughter of his friend and former employer. Mr. Varley then purchased a large business at the West End of London, where for many years he resided. His position as preacher to a regular congregation began in 1859, and the spirit of revival soon appeared in his meetings.

The Free Tabernacle Opened

In 1862 was opened the Free Tabernacle, Notting Hill, to the erection of which Mr. Varley had consecrated the first £1,000 he ever made in business. In a short time 600 or 700 believers were gathered into the fellowship of this church. For twenty years Mr. Varley was the pastor of this people. The building was enlarged later to make room for hundreds who had been clamoring unsuccessfully for admission. It is now known as the West London Tabernacle. In 1868 Mr. Varley disposed of his large business and gave himself up entirely to religious work. From that time his revival efforts throughout the world are common knowledge. His work in Melbourne, Australia, in 1877, will never be forgotten, and his services in New York filled the great Hippodrome in Madison Square. In 1883 he resigned his pastorate in order to devote his whole strength to evangelistic work.

It was Mr. Varley, who suggested to Mr. Moody, that God was waiting to find a man through whom He might speak to the world. On the day when Mr. Moody receives his reward, Henry Varley will have no small share in it.

John McNeill

Visitors to the great World's Fair at Chicago will never forget the great midday meetings conducted in Central Music Hall by the Rev. John McNeill. He is a Scotchman of the true type, as one writer says, with a converted soul, a granite mind, and a great big loving heart. Essentially, he is a man of the people and has no use for ecclesiastical formalism. In his introduction to one of the volumes of Mr. McNeill's sermons, the Rev. Dr. A. T. Pierson says; "Some men, like their Master, cannot be tied; John McNeill is one of them. He needs no introduction. On both sides of the sea he has won men as any man will win them who thinks and speaks in dead earnest. There is a great difference between having to say something and having something to say. He has shown that he has much that is worth saying, and therefore much that is worth hearing. Those who read his sermons will not need to be told that the man who followed Dr. Dikes at Regent Square, is a free, fresh, truthful, helpful preacher."

It was found in Chicago that some people were forgetting the World's Fair in their great desire to hear John McNeill speak at Central Music Hall. He is considered by many to be the greatest preacher that has ever come to our shores from abroad. He is a delightful man socially, and wins all to him, as they hear him talk in his own inimitable way.

Daniel B. Towner was born in Rome, Bradford County, Pennsylvania, March 5, 1850. As a boy he began the study of music with his father, who was a teacher of music, and at nineteen he began to teach singing classes. From 1873 to 1875 most of his time was devoted to conducting musical conventions and institutes. In this work he was eminently succesful. In Cincinnati, in 1885, Mr. Moody held a series of meetings. Mr. Towner was assisting in the music, and the evangelist saw in him a man whose services would be invaluable. From that time Mr. Towner was associated with the work of Mr. Moody. He has a baritone voice of wonderful power and compass, and his heart is in the work. As a composer of Gospel music he ranks among the best. Mr. Towner is a most accomplished musician, and his voice has a sweetness about it that is never lost, even under the stress of continuous and exacting service.

George C. Stebbins

Another singer who is known wherever the Gospel message is carried by song is Mr. George C. Stebbins. He is a native of New York State, and was born February 26, 1846, of Christian parents, the hallowed influence of whose lives is in his work to-day. At twenty he took charge of a choir, and also taught singing school for several years. At twenty-three he was converted. In 1869 he moved to Chicago and was soon employed by the First Baptist Church to lead the choir. During this time he met Mr. Moody, and often sang with Mr. Sankey and Mr. Bliss, who were his personal friends. Going to Boston for the further culture of his voice, he was employed in Dr. Gordon's Church, the Clarendon Street Chapel, where he remained one year, when he went to Tremont Temple as director of music. Becoming more deeply interested in the evangelistic work, he joined the rank of singing evangelists, and on the death of Mr. Bliss was called upon to aid Major Whittle in Chicago. For a long time he was associated with Dr. George F. Pentecost. He accompanied Mr. Moody to California, and was with him in 1892 in closing his work in Great Britain. Mr. Stebbins wrote many of the best known songs in the Gospel Hymns, among others, "Saviour, Breathe an Evening Blessing," "Must I Go and Empty Handed," "The Home-land," etc. But I doubt not he will be longest known as the author of "Saved by Grace." Mr. and Mrs. Stebbins sing together beautifully, and of all my own assistants none have been more helpful than these sweet singers.

Ferdinand Schiverea.

As a younger man Ferdinand Schiverea was an actor, but he was led providentially to attend a meeting which Mr. Moody was conducting in Brooklyn. There the Spirit of God took hold of him mightily. For days he had no rest, but finally the light came. He went at once to his mother with the news and she said, "I have asked God for this, dear child; I have given you to God, and He has just done what He said He would, if I only would believe." The first effort of Mr. Schiverea was to lead his brothers to Christ. He then reached out for the neighbors, and every night for months held services of prayer in a small rear room in his poor home. During all this time, and for four years, he worked in a large furniture house, packing goods for shipment. The first work that God especially blessed him in was in Brooklyn, where for twelve months he held meetings nearly every night. He has labored in the principal cities and towns of the United States, as well as in most of the important cities and towns in Canada. In Toronto alone he held twenty different series of meetings. Mr. Schiverea is particularly strong in his ability to reach the masses; he is now in the very midst of his useful life, and his "love abides in strength." There is a future of increasing usefulness before him.

He was a particular favorite with Mr. Moody, who never lost an opportunity to say a kind word about his work.

H. M. WHARTON.

Of the men who stood very close to Mr. Moody, none was more highly esteemed by him, than the subject of this sketch. They came together first in a southern city where good words concerning Dr. Wharton had been spoken to Mr. Moody by the people of the city, and he did with him what he frequently did with many others—called him out of the audience and insisted that he should preach, and then announced that he would conduct subsequent services. I first saw these two men of God together in the days of the World's Fair, when Dr. Wharton always sat on Mr. Moody's right. He is an inimitable story-teller, and Mr. Moody's sides would shake and the tears run down his face as Dr. Wharton would tell some of his southern experiences, or recall some of the events of his boyhood days. As, for example, when he told one morning, which happened to be his birthday, of his great delight in the workmen that were digging some ditches near his boyhood's home. A large number of Irishmen were in the company, and young Wharton had been punished for staying too long in their presence. He had been designed by his family to preach, and after the punishment he declared that he would not be a minister, but surely intended to be an Irishman. I can see Mr. Moody laugh now, as the story was told. Dr. Wharton is a magnificent preacher, and one of the best evangelists in the country. He has made himself poor in taking care of orphan children both at Luray and in other places, and the blessing of God will surely ever abide upon him. Mr. Moody considered him one of the most skilful workers in the after-meetings he had ever come in contact with, and to his ability in this direction I bear hearty testimony.

R. A. TORREY

Mr. Torrey was born January 28, 1856, in Hoboken, N. J. At fifteen he entered Yale College, and four years later the Yale Theological Seminary, whence he was graduated in 1878. During his last year in the Seminary he worked for six weeks in the inquiry room in Mr. Moody's meetings in New Haven. In 1882 he resigned his charge and went to Germany for a year of study. Returning in 1883, he accepted a pastorate in Minneapolis, becoming later the superintendent of the City Missionary Society in that city, and after a time founded an independent people's church. Several years later he accepted the invitation to become superintendent of Mr. Moody's Bible Institute, entering on the charge in 1889. Most of the phenomenal success of the Institute is due to his wise administration. He was very close to Mr. Moody during the later years. No man, really, had Mr. Moody's confidence more completely, and justly so, for no man could ever be more loyal to another than R. A. Torrey to D. L. Moody.

A. C. DIXON.

Dr. Dixon is a typical southerner, fiery, intense, dramatic, eloquent. His father was a frontier preacher, and the son was converted and joined his father's church when eleven years old. At fifteen he entered Wake Forest College, and after graduation decided to study law, but the need of some country churches in his neighborhood persuaded him to accept the ministry of different congregations. During nine months he baptized 100 converts. After an incumbency of three years in a small church he entered upon a new charge in Asheville, N. C., where, within three months of his aggressive ministry, 250 persons were converted. Three-and-

REV. F. B. MEYER, OF LONDON, AT NORTHFIELD.

a-half years later he was elected president of the Wake Forest College, but he declined the election, accepting instead the pastorate of a large Baptist church in Baltimore. His church began to expand, and soon a large tabernacle had to be erected to accommodate the crowds who pressed forward to enjoy his ministry. Later he was called to Brooklyn, where he has already won a high position as preacher and pastor of his church. Dr. Dixon is a man of deep convictions. The Bible is to him the book of life. He is a man of prayer, a believer in the Holy Spirit, tender and gentle in dealing with inquirers, ever beseeching sinners to become reconciled to God. Mr. Moody was devoted to him, and had the greatest confidence in his ability.

HENRY DRUMMOND.

The death of Henry Drummond a few years ago took from the world a gentle, ministering spirit whose influences had been turned to Christian work by the help of Mr. Moody's meetings in Glasgow, twenty-six years ago. What this one man, who was led to the Master by Mr. Moody, accomplished in his too brief period of service, it is impossible to estimate, but his forceful words, and the example of his shining life have been an inspiration to thousands. He was born in 1851, in Sterling, Scotland. He was well educated, and prepared himself for the ministry. His culture was wide Science unlocked her doors to him; advanced thought had no terrors for him,—nor did these work any insidious undermining of his faith. When Mr. Moody and Mr. Sankey were conducting their great mission in Scotland, Henry Drummond felt the burden of their message and became an earnest assistant at the meetings. He was one of the band of helpers who followed in Mr. Moody's wake, and aided in continuing the work which the evangelists had begun. In later years he traveled widely, visiting the United States, and spending some time in East Central Africa. In 1877 he became lecturer on Natural Science in the Second Free Church College in Glasgow. He was the author of a number of important books, most of which tended to disabuse the public mind of any supposed conflict between science and religion. Acquaintance with him was a great stimulous to his friends. Several times he worked with Mr. Moody, and his opinion of the great evangelist was apparent in the words he uttered a few weeks before his death in 1897. He said, "Moody was the biggest human I ever met." And D. L. Moody was heard to say again and again that he loved Henry Drummond.

G. CAMPBELL MORGAN.

Mr. Morgan was born December 9, 1863, at Tetbury, Gloucestershire, England. He was of nonconformist ancestry, his father being a Baptist minister. The young man was educated at Cheltingham, and at twenty was appointed to a mastership in the Jewish Collegiate School in Birmingham. Three years later he abandoned his profession of teaching to become an evangelist. He went to Hull to hold services for two weeks, but they proved so successful that they ran for many months, and he finally left, in 1887, on account of ill health. He continued his evangelistic work, however, and at last became pastor of the Congregational Church in Stone, in 1889, and in 1891 pastor of the Rugeley Congregational Church. In 1893 he went to Westminster Road Church at Birchfield, a suburb of Birmingham. It was in 1896, while pastor of this church, that he first went to the United States, and visited Northfield. In 1897 he became pastor of the Newcourt Congregational Church, Tollington Park, London. He visited Northfield in 1897, 1898 and 1899. Mr. Moody had the greatest delight in Mr. Morgan's ability. He had him travel through many of our cities in September and October of 1899.

The last time I ever saw Mr. Moody was when he was sitting on the platform with Mr. Morgan.

George H. Macgregor.

Mr. Macgregor was born in Scotland thirty-six years ago. His father was a minister. The boy attended the University of Edinburgh and New College of Divinity in the same city, and even before he completed his theological studies he was called to a church in Aberdeen, in 1888, gaining experience which proved invaluable. In 1889 he visited Keswick, and under the influences of the dwellers on that consecrated ground came into a closer walk with God. In 1891 he was invited to the Keswick platform. Mr. Macgregor bears in his style all the evidences of his fine culture, a culture which, like that of Henry Drummond, is consecrated to the Work of God. His zeal is inspiring. As a winner of souls he is not excelled. I do not think any one has ever visited Northfield who was really more helpful to the people than Mr. Macgregor. He is a most charming man, and as thoroughly consecrated as any one I have ever met.

F. B. Meyer.

Mr. Meyer began his ministry twenty-seven years ago, in Richmond, Surrey, England, even before he had completed his studies, which he was then carrying on at Regent Park College; but after his graduation he went as assistant to the Rev. C. M. Birrell, of Pembroke Chapel, Liverpool, and later transferred his interests to York, where, during the meetings of Mr. Moody and Mr. Sankey, in 1873, the young minister was profoundly stirred by the message of the American Evangelists. Mr. Meyer is best known, aside from his spiritual literature, as pastor of Christ Church, West London. This great institutional house of God was completed twenty-two years ago to perpetuate the Surrey Chapel work of Rowland Hill. Mr. Meyer followed Dr. Newman Hall in this pastorate. Dr. Hall was the successor of James Sherman, who, in his turn, succeeded Mr. Hill. It is doubtful if any other church in the world employs so wide a range of activities as Christ Church, London.

Mr. Meyer's name is known wherever the English language is spoken, and Bible students everywhere are devoted to him, for his own as well as his work's sake.

CHAPTER XXII.

Three Characteristic Sermons

IF one has known Mr. Moody for any great length of time, there are three sermons which doubtless would come before his mind as being more intimately associated with the great evangelist than any other sermons he has preached.

The first has to do with the love of God.

The second, with the excuses of men.

The third, with his special appeal made to men in every part of the English speaking world on "Sowing and Reaping."

CHARACTERISTICS OF THE THREE SERMONS

The first sermon is remarkable because for a long time Mr. Moody felt called to preach the law, and was constantly crying out, after the manner of an Old Testament prophet, against sin, but under the influence of Harry Moorehouse, as suggested in another part of this volume, he seemed to come out from under the power of law into the power of grace, and his preaching was altogether different.

His sermon on the excuses is very characteristic of him, and one has but to shut his eyes as he reads, to see the greatest evangelist of the generation pleading with men, as he alone could do,—now moving his audience to tears, and then almost instantly having them convulsed with laughter, but as a result of it all, leading multitudes to Christ.

The third sermon is one which a host of men throughout the world will ever remember. It was the first sermon I ever heard him preach. Under the power of it, I saw my own heart as never before, and under the power of the Holy Ghost, as manifested in the preacher's sermon, I began to feel the power of Christ to make me clean.

The sermons follow in the order mentioned:

GOD'S LOVE

I have often thought I would like to have but one text; and if I thought I could only make the world believe that God is love, I would only take that text and go up and down the earth trying to counteract what Satan has been telling them—that God is not love. He has made the world believe it effectually. It would not take twenty-four hours to make the world come to God, if you can only make them believe God is love. If you can really make a man believe you love him, you have won him; and if I could only make people really believe that God loves them, what a rush we would see for the Kingdom of God! Oh, how they would rush in! But man has got a false idea about God, and he will not believe that He is a God of love. It is because he don't know Him.

Now, in Paul's farewell letter to the Corinthians, in the 13th chapter, 2d Corinthians, he says: "Finally, brethren, farewell. Be perfect. Be of good comfort. Be of one mind. Live in peace, and the God of love"—he calls Him the God of love—"and peace shall be with you." Then John, who was better acquainted with Christ, telling us about the love God has for this perishing world, writes in this epistle, in the evening of his life, these words: "Beloved, let us love one another, for love is of God, and every one that loveth is born of God and knoweth God, and he that loveth not knoweth no God, for God is love." We built a Church in Chicago a number of years ago, and we were so anxious to make people believe that God is love, that we thought if we could not preach it into their hearts, we would burn it in, and so right over the pulpit we had the words put in gas jets, "God is love," and every night we had it there. A man going along there one night glanced in through the door and saw the text. He was a poor prodigal, and he passed on, and as he walked away, he said to himself, "God is love? No. God is not love. God does not love me. He does not love me, for I am a poor, miserable sinner. If God was love, He would love me. God is not love." Yet there the text was, burning down into his soul. And he went on a little further, and turned around and came back and went into the meeting. He didn't hear what the sermon was, but the text got into his heart, and that is what we want. It is of very little account what men say, if God's word only gets into the heart. And he stayed after meeting was over, and I found him there weeping like a child; but as I unfolded the Scripture, and told him how God had loved him from his earliest childhood all along, the light of the Gospel broke into his mind, and he went away rejoicing. This would be the best meeting to-day we have had yet, if we could only make this audience believe that God is love.

Now turn a moment to the 13th chapter of John's Gospel, first verse: "Now, before the feast of the Passover, when Jesus knew that His hour was come that He should depart out of this world unto the Father, having loved His own which were in the world He loved them unto the end." His love is unchangeable. That night He knew very well what was going to happen. Judas had gone out to betray Him. He knew it. He had already left that little band to go out and sell Christ. Do you tell me Christ did not love Judas? That very night He said to him, "Judas, what thou doest, do quickly;" and when Judas, meeting Him in the garden, kissed Him, and He said, " Betrayest thou thy Master with a kiss?" was it not the voice of love and compassion that ought to have broken Judas' heart? He loved him in the very hour that he betrayed Him; and that is what is going to make hell so terrible, that you go there with the love of God beneath your feet. It is not that He don't love you, but you despise His love. It is a terrible thing to despise love. He loved them unto the end. He knew very well that Peter was going to deny Him that night and curse and swear because he was mistaken for Jesus' companion. He knew all His disciples would forsake Him, and leave Him to suffer alone, and yet He says He loved them unto the end. And the sweetest words that fell from the lips of the Son of God were that night when they were going to leave Him. Those words that fell from his lips that night will live forever. How they will live in the hearts of God's people! We could not get on very well without the 14th of John and the 15th and 16th. It was on that memorable night that He uttered those blessed words, and on that very night that He told them how much God loved them. It seems as if that particular night, when He was about to be deserted by all, His heart was bursting with love for His flock.

Just let us look at the 16th chapter and the 27th verse and see what He says: "For the Father Himself loveth you because ye have loved me and have believed that I came from God." I don't know but what Christ felt that there might be some of His disciples that would not love the Father as they loved Him. I remember for the first few years after I was converted I had a good deal more love for Christ than for God the Father, whom I looked upon as the stern Judge, while I regarded Christ as the Mediator who had come between me and that stern Judge, and had appeased His wrath, but when I got a little better acquainted with my Bible those views all fled. After I became a father, and woke up to the realization of what it cost God to have His Son die,

MR. MOODY'S STUDY. At this desk the evangelist says the best inspirations of his life came to him. The portrait hanging on the wall is that of his mother.

I began to see that God was to be loved just as much as His Son was. Why, it took more love for God to give His Son to die than it would to die Himself. You would a thousand times sooner die yourself in your son's place than have him taken away. If the executioner was about to take your son to the gallows, you would say, "Let me die in his stead, let my son be spared." Oh, think of the love God must have had for this world that He gave His only begotten Son to die for it, and that is what I want you to understand. "The Father Himself loveth you because you have loved Me." If a man has loved Christ, God will set His love upon him. Then in the 17th chapter, 23d verse, in that wonderful prayer He made that night, "I in them, and Thou in Me, that they may be made perfect in one, and that the world may know Thou hast sent Me and hast loved them as Thou hast loved Me." God could look down from Heaven and see His Son fulfilling His will, and He said, "This is my beloved Son, in whom I am well pleased." But when it is said, "God loved us as He loved His own Son," it used to seem to me to be downright blasphemy, until I found it was in the Word of God. That was the wonderful prayer He made on the night of His betrayal. Is there any love in the world like that? Is there anything to be compared to the love of God? Well may Paul say, "It passeth knowledge."

And then, I can imagine some of you saying, "Well, He loved his disciples and He loves those who serve Him faithfully, but then I have been untrue." I may be speaking now to some backsliders, but if I am, I want to say to everyone here: "The Lord loves you." Now, it says in John, first chapter: "He loved them unto the end." That is, His love was unchangeable and you may have forgotten Him and betrayed Him and denied Him, but nevertheless He loves you, He loves the backslider. There is not a man here that has wandered from God and betrayed Him but what the Lord Jesus loves him and wants him to come back. Now in this 14th chapter of Hosea He says, "I will heal every backslider. I will love them freely." So the Lord tells the backsliders, "If you will only come back to Me I will forgive you." It was thus with Peter who denied his Lord; the Saviour forgave him, and sent him to preach His glorious Gospel on the day of Pentecost, when three thousand were won to Christ under one sermon of a backslider.

Just turn to the 31st chapter of Jeremiah and the 3d verse. "He hath loved us," he says, "with an everlasting love."

Now there is a difference between human and divine love. The one is fleeting, the other is everlasting. There is no end of God's love. I can imagine some of you saying: "If God has loved us with an everlasting love, why does it say that God is angry with the sinner every day?" Why, dear friends, that very word "anger" in the Scriptures is one of the very strongest evidences and expressions of God's love. Suppose I have got two boys, and one of them goes out and lies and swears and steals and gets drunk; if I have no love for him I don't care what he does; but just because I do love him it makes me angry to see him take that course, and it is because God loves the sinner that he gets angry with him. That very passage shows how strong God's love is. Let me tell you, dear friends, God loves you in all your backslidings and wanderings. You may despise His love and trample it under your feet and go down to ruin, but it wont be because God don't love you. I once heard of a father, who had a prodigal boy, and the boy had sent his mother down to the grave with a broken heart, and one evening the boy started out as usual to spend the night in drinking and gambling, and his old father as he was leaving said, "My son, I want to ask a favor of you to-night. You have not spent an evening with me since your mother died, and now I want you to spend this night at home. I have been very lonely since your mother died. Now, wont you gratify your old father by staying at home with him?" "No," said the young man, "it is lonely here, and there is nothing to interest me, and I am going out." And the old man prayed and wept, and at last he said, "My boy, you are just killing me, as you have killed your mother. These hairs are growing whiter, and you are sending me, too, to the grave." Still the boy would not stay, and the old man said, "If your are determined to go to ruin, you must go over this old body to-night. I cannot resist you. You are stronger than I, but if you go out you must go over this body." And he laid himself down before the door, and that son walked over the form of his father, trampled the love of his father under foot and went out.

And that is the way with sinners. You have got to trample the blood of God's Son under your feet if you go down to death, to make light of the blood of the innocent, to make light of the wonderful love of God, to despise it. But whether you do or not, He loves you still. I can imagine some of you saying, "Why does He not show His love to us?" Why, how can it be any further shown than it is? You say so because you won't read His Word and find out how much He loves you. If any man will take a concordance and run through the Scriptures with the one word "love," you will find out how much He loves you; you will find out that it is all one great assurance of His love. He is continually trying to teach you this one lesson, and to win you to Himself by a cross of love. All the burdens He has placed upon the sons of men have been out of pure love, to bring you to Himself. Those who do not believe that God is love are under the power of the Evil One. He has blinded you, and you have been deceived with his lies. God's dealing has been all love, love, love, from the fall of Adam to the present hour. Adam's calamity brought down

God's love. No sooner did the news reach Heaven than God came down after Adam with His love. That voice that rang through Eden was the voice of love, hunting after the fallen one—"Adam, where art thou?" For all these thousand years that voice of love has been sounding down the ages. Out of His love He made a way of escape for Adam. God saved him out of His pity and love.

In the 63d chapter of Isaiah, and the 9th verse, we read: "In all their affliction, He was afflicted, and the angel of His presence saved them. In His love and in His pity He redeemed them; and He bare them, and carried them all the days of old." In all their afflictions He was afflicted You cannot afflict one of God's creatures without afflicting Him. He takes the place of a living father. There a man has a sick child burning with fever. How gladly the father or the mother would take that fever and put it into their own bosoms. The mother would take from a child its loathsome disease right out of its body, and put it into her own—such is a mother's love. How she pities the child, and how gladly she would suffer in the place of the child! That illustration has been often used here—"As a mother pitieth her children." You cannot afflict any of God's creatures, but God feels it. The Son of His bosom came to redeem us from the cares of the world. I do not see how any man with an open Bible before him can get up and say to me that he does not see how God is love. "Greater love hath no man than this, that a man will lay down his life for his friend." Christ laid down His life on the cross, and cried in His agony, "Father, forgive them, they know not what they do." That was wonderful love. You and I would have called fire down from Heaven to consume them. We would have sent them all down into the hot pavement of hell. But the Son of God lifted up His cry, "Father, forgive them, they know not what they do."

I hear some one say, "I do not see, I do not understand how it is that He loves us." What more proof do you want that God loves you? You say, "I am not worthy to be loved." That is true. I will admit that. And He does not love you because you deserve it. It will help us to get at the Divine love to look a little into our own families, and at our human love. Take a mother with nine children, and they are all good children save one. One is a prodigal, and he has wandered off, and he is everything that is bad. That mother will probably love that prodigal boy as much or more than all the rest put together. It will be with a love mingled with pity. A friend of mine was visiting at a house some time ago, where quite a company were assembled and were talking pleasantly together. He noticed that the mother seemed agitated, and was all the while going out and coming in. He went to her aside and asked her what troubled her, and she took him out into another room and introduced him to her boy. There he was, a poor wretched boy, all mangled and bruised with the fall of sin. She said, "I have much more trouble with him than with all the rest. He has wandered far, but he is my boy yet." She loved him still. So God loves you still.

That love, it ought to break your hearts to hear of, and it ought to bring you right to Him. You may say you do not deserve it, and that is true; but because you do not deserve it, God offers it to you. You may say, "If I could get rid of my sins, God would love me," In Revelation, 1st chapter, 5th verse, it says: "Unto Him that loved us and washed us from our sins in His own blood." It does not say He washed us from our sins and then loved us. He loved us first, and then washed us clean. Some people say, you must turn away from sin, and then Christ will love you. But how can you get rid of it until you come to Him? He takes us into His own bosom, and then He cleanses us from sin.

He has shed His blood for you; He wants you and He will redeem you to-day if you will.

An Englishman told me a story once that may serve to illustrate this truth, that God loves men in their sin. He does not love sin, but He loves men even in their sin. He seeks to save them from sin. There was a boy a great many years ago, stolen in London the same as Charley Ross was stolen here. Long months and years passed away, and the mother had prayed and prayed, as that mother of Charley Ross has prayed, I suppose, and all her efforts had failed, and they had given up all hope; but the mother did not quite give up her hope. One day a little boy was sent up into the neighboring house to sweep the chimney, and by some mistake he got down again through the wrong chimney. When he came down, he came in by the sitting room chimney. His memory began at once to travel back through the years that had passed. He thought that things looked strange and familiar. The scenes of the early days of youth were dawning upon him; and as he stood there surveying the place, his mother came into the room. He stood there covered with rags and soot. Did she wait until she had sent him to be washed before she took him into her arms? No, indeed; it was her own boy. She took him to her arms, all black and smoke, and hugged him to her bosom, and shed tears of joy upon his head. You have wandered very far from Him; there may not be a sound spot upon you, but if you will just come to God, He will forgive and receive you.

There is a verse in Isaiah xxxviii,—the 17th verse,—that I think a good deal of. It reads: "Thou has in love to my soul delivered it from the pit of corruption, for Thou hast cast all my sins behind Thy back." Mark you, the love comes first. He did not say that He had taken away sins and cast them behind Him. He loved us first, and then He took our sins away. I like that little word m-y "my" there. The reason we do not get any benefit from Scripture is because we are always talking about generalizations. We say: "God loves nations, God loves churches, and loves certain classes of people. But here it reads: "Out of love to my soul He has taken all my sins and cast them behind His back." If they are behind His back they are gone from me forever. If they are cast behind His back, how can Satan ever get at them again? I will defy any fiend from hell to find them. Satan can torment me with them no more.

There are four expressions wherein God put our sins away. The first is, He has blotted out our sins like a thick cloud. You remember, don't you, how in the morning we wake and sometimes find the sky covered with clouds, and by the afternoon there is not a cloud to be seen. Can any one tell where the clouds go to? They vanish and we see them no more, and no one can tell what has become of them. God has blotted out our sins like these clouds. Another verse is: "I will remove them as far as she east is from the west," Another is: "I will roll them into the depths of the sea." And there is this one which reads: "Who will take them out of love to my soul and cast them behind his back." They are gone through time and eternity. Bear in mind, it is out of love He does it, not out of justice. It is not justice we want, but mercy. God feels wonderful love, which it ought to break every heart here to contemplate, and the love of God ought to sweep over this audience, and bow every head here to-night, and fill our hearts full of gratitude and praise that God so loved us, and gave himself for us. It says in Galatians, 2d chapter, 20th verse, "Who loved me and gave Himself for me." Take that verse in Isaiah, "Who loved my soul" and put it with this verse, "Who loved me and gave Himself for me," and you have it all. Christ shed every drop of his precious blood for sinners. Some people say "only one single drop of

Christ's blood is enough to cleanse you from sin." It is not true. If one drop would have done it, He would have shed but one drop; but it took every drop of blood that His life had, and He gave it all up to save us. Paul says, "He loved me and gave Himself for me," and so Paul loved Him in return. If you could but get that thought in your mind that Christ has loved you so much as to give Himself for you, you cannot help loving Him in return.

EXCUSES OF MEN

"And they all with one consent began to make excuse."—St. Luke, xiv., part of 18th verse.

We read in the 14th chapter of Luke that Christ is invited by one of the chief Pharisees to take supper with him on the Sabbath. I think by reading it carefully you will find it was a snare that the Pharisees were setting for Christ, that they were trying to get Him into some trouble, in order to get some reason that they might put Him out of the way. The law was that a man should not work on the Sabbath day, and the Pharisees were all the time bringing charges against Christ, because He was, as they said, working on the Sabbath! And so this Pharisee invited Him to his house, and there was a great company there. They had a certain man there who had the dropsy. Undoubtedly they had sent a servant out to get the man in so as to have him ready for the occasion. They had him sitting right opposite to Christ. Christ said to the Pharisees and the others sitting by, "Is it lawful to heal on the Sabbath day?" And there wouldn't one of them answer Him a word.

One after another, I can imagine, looked down, and it was as if they had said, "Keep still now," and they held their peace. Christ said to the man who had the dropsy, "You may be healed," and the man got up and walked home a perfectly sound man. Christ said to the Pharisees, "If any of you have an ass or an ox fallen into

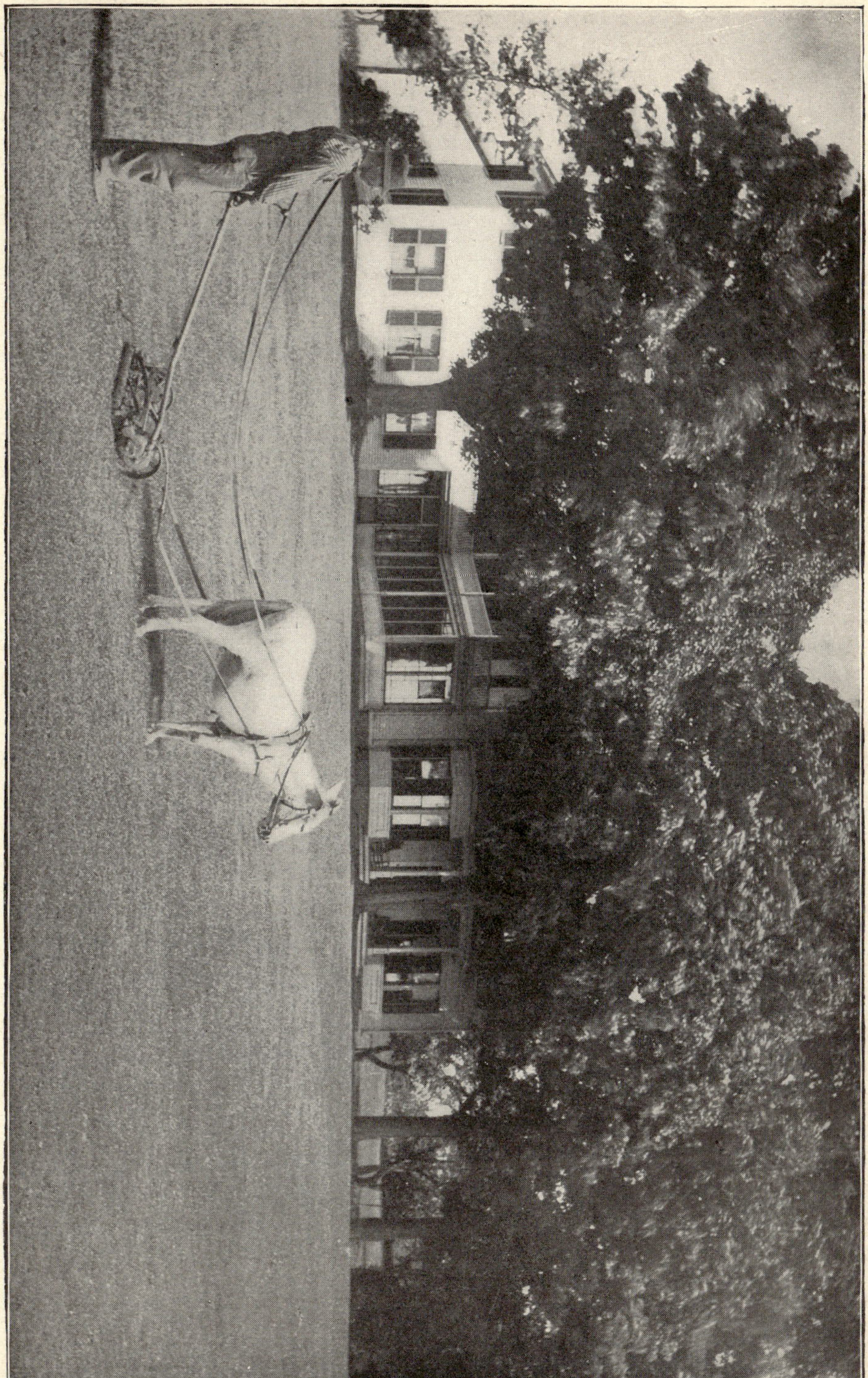

the pit, will you not straightway pull him out on the Sabbath day?" And they said not a word. They knew very well that if any of them had an ox or an ass fallen into the pit they would save him if it was on the Sabbath day. But they said nothing. They were all the time putting questions to Him; but see how Christ answered all these questions. It would be well for you to take your Bible and go through the Scriptures and see with what wisdom and tact those questions were answered that were put to Christ.

He said to the Pharisees gathered there—for he noticed that there was a great rush to see who was going to get the best seats. There they were pushing and elbowing each other back in order to get the best seats. Christ said, "Let me give you counsel. When you are invited to a feast take the lowest place. Do not be so ambitious to get the best place, to get to the head of the table; because if you get there, and a more honorable person comes, the head of the feast will make you sit further down, and you will be mortified and ashamed." Then He turned to the chief of the Pharisees who invited Him and said: "When you get up a feast, do not go and invite the rich, or you will be looking for them to invite you again." Isn't it the same thing to-day in the world? When people get up a feast, they invite the rich and influential, so by that means they will get into society, and their invitations will be returned. But, He said, go to the lame, the halt, the dumb, the blind, and ask them, and you will be well rewarded for what you do by our Father in Heaven. A man sitting at the table burst out and said, "Blessed is the man that shall eat bread in the Kingdom of God." Then Christ said, "A certain man made a great supper and bade many;" here He described the great spiritual feast—"and sent his servant at supper time to say to them that were bidden, 'Come, for all things are now ready.' And they began to make excuses." They made excuse. They did not have any to offer without making them. "And they all with one consent began to make excuses." A man gets up a feast, and his friends make no excuses; but God gets up a feast, and not only prepares a table, but He goes forth and invites them all to come. They cannot go; they would like to go, they say, but cannot possibly, they have so much to do. Let me show you what these excuses are, and you will see on the face of them that they are downright lies. The Scripture says, "One after one they began to make excuses." If those men had been invited to go out and walk, if they had been invited to go to a hospital to witness some terrible operation, or if they had been invited to an execution, they would have had some reason for giving excuses; but these men were invited to a royal feast. It is not often that common people like us get an invitation to a royal feast. If Queen Victoria were to invite us to a feast at Windsor Castle, do you suppose we would not regard it as a great honor? Do you suppose you would make excuses? O, my friends, I have an invitation to-day that is a thousand times beyond that. It is from the very King of Kings and Lord of Lords. It is the Marriage Supper of God's own Son. Blessed is he that shall be at the Marriage Supper of the Lamb. He wants to see you all there. The invitation is to every one here. All are invited—the lowest, the highest, the richest, the poorest, all can come if they will.

Do you ever think what would take place in a city like New York if God should take men at their word when they make excuses, and should say to-night, "Well, I will excuse you," and so, with one stroke of Providence should sweep them all away, and cease to care for those who refused Him? Why, the grass would right away begin to grow in your streets. There would be very few stores open to-morrow. Most of the merchants would want to be excused; their stores would be closed up, every solitary one of them. The rumsellers would all want to be excused. You cannot find a rumseller in all New York but wants to be excused. Every man that is carrying on a dishonest business would want to be excused. I do not think there would be any crowd here to-morrow, if that should take place in the next twenty-four hours. What desolation would reign in the streets of New York, and how many of all classes would make excuses! If I should step down from this place, and go right down the aisle among the audience, beginning with that little boy, and asking every one down the line, if you had not an excuse, how many of you would not have them? You would begin to find one before I got to you, and if you could not find one, you would make up one, and if you could not easily think of one, Satan would help you to get up one.

Let us take up the excuses of those three men mentioned here. The first man had bought some ground, and he must needs go and see it. Why didn't he see the ground before he bought it? If he had been a good business man, he would have seen it first. If he had been, he would have been looking at the title. That would have been the better way. But he said he must go and see his ground. He had an invitation to the supper, and said, "I would like to go, but I cannot." And he said to the servant, "Tell the Lord I would be delighted to be there. I do not know anything that would please me more than to go, but business is so pressing it will be utterly impossible for me to go." If the devil can only get us off into some cradle of excuses and rock us off to sleep, that is all he wants. If would have been better if this man had been honest and said to the servant, "Tell the Lord I don't want to go to the feast." It is better to be honest than to seek a refuge of lies and false excuses.

And the other man could not accept the invitation either. I suppose he thought to himself, "How shall I get out of it?" So he said, "I have just bought five yoke of oxen. I will give them as my excuse." I suppose, perhaps he asked his wife, "What shall I tell him?" Perhaps his wife told him, "Say you have just bought five yoke of oxen, and that you have to go and prove them." Now, why didn't he prove them before he bought them? And besides, did he not have plenty of time to prove them? It was not necessary for him to go just at the hour of the feast to prove his oxen. He manufactured the excuse. The third man's excuse is more absurd, if possible, than the others. He said, "I have just married a wife." What difference did that make about his going? Why didn't he take his wife along? You can see that that excuse was a downright lie. So these three men made excuses, and when the messenger came back and gave them to the Lord, he said, "Not one of those that were bidden and have refused shall taste of my supper. Go and get the beggars from the highways and hedges, and the tramps and the poor, the lame, the maimed, the dumb, the blind, and if these men won't accept the invitation, let those who will, come." Let those that will accept of the invitation and press into the Kingdom. Thank God that His Gospel is for the poor as well as for the rich. If the rich won't have it, thank God that the poor are pressing into the Kingdom.

I want to call your attention to the fact, that since these 1900 years have worn away, men are becoming very wise, or think they are, and they say, "We have now outgrown this old Bible, and are now living in a more intellectual age. Men are wiser than they used to be. They have got a great deal more culture; they have a great deal more refinement." But, my friends, with all your culture and all your refinement, can you find one man who has any better excuse than these three men had? I have met hundreds here in New York, in the inquiry room and outside of it, during the past few weeks, and I have yet to find the first man who has a better excuse. My friend, what is your excuse? Have you got a better one? Why do you not accept the invitation? God invites you.

I have often heard people say "I would like to be a Christian very much, but O, it is so hard to serve God." Is that true? Is God a hard master? Is the devil an easy one? Is it true that those who have served both masters have found that God is such a hard master? Is He austere? Does He require us to perform more tan we can? Does He reap where He has not sown? O, ye saints of the living God, is that your testimony? There never was a greater lie forged in hell and told on earth, than that. "The way of the transgressor is hard." Ask the men in prison, ask the drunkard, if the way of the transgressor is one of ease.

Go down to the Tombs. I am told that that little bridge over the prison yard over which the prisoners are led has written on one side the words, "The way of the trangressor is hard." If that is not true, how do they dare put it on there? They ought to take it off. There is not a man in all New York but knows as he goes down deep in his heart that the way of the transgressor is hard. On the other side of that bridge it is written, "The Bridge of Sighs;" and over that the young men pass every day, and every one of them will testify that that portion of the Bible is true where it says the way of the transgressor is hard. So don't give that as an excuse.

There is another class that say, "I believe that. I believe the most delightful service in the world is serving Christ. That is not my excuse, but my excuse is this: There are so many things in that Bible that are dark and mysterious. I don't understand the Bible from Genesis to Revelation. If I could understand the Bible on reading it through once, I could accept the invitation; but there are so many dark and mysterious things that I cannot accept the invitation," and so we find a good many giving the Bible

18

as an excuse. I contend there is no book under the sun that has been so misjudged as the Bible. Of all the skeptics and infidels I have ever met, I have yet to meet the first one that has read the Bible through from beginning to end. Now, if a book comes out and you have not read all of it, and you are asked your opinion of it, you say, "I have not read it through yet, and don't like to express my opinion until I have more carefully read it." But people are not afraid of expressing their opinion of God's book after having read a few chapters, and because they don't understand what they have read, they condemn the whole.

I have a boy about say four or five years, and I send him to school to-morrow, and he comes home, and I ask him, "Willie, can you read and write and spell? Do you understand all about geometry? Have you finished your algebra?" "Why, papa," he says, "why do you talk that way? I have been all the time trying to learn what A, B and C are." "What!" I say, "have you not finished your education? I will take you right away from that school if you have not." Now there is just as much reason in my doing that as there is in a man's taking up the Bible and condemning it before he has studied it, and that excuse that these men are giving that they cannot accept the invitation because they don't understand the Bible, will not sland before Christ's tribunal.

When they go up and stand before the Lord they will say, "I was very anxious to accept the invitation to be at the marriage service of your Son, but there were many things in the Bible that were dark and mysterious, and so I could not accept the invitation." That excuse sounds very well here, but up there you can't tell that. You will be speechless when you stand before God's bar.

"Well," says another, "my trouble is not with the Bible, which I believe in from end to end, nor do I have any trouble about that other excuse about serving Christ; but the trouble I have is in seeing so many hypocrites, and I am not going to join the Church, there are so many hypocrites. I know a person who cheated me out of $5. and that same person pretends to be a Christian, and so you must not ask me to associate with hypocrites." Well, I say, if you don't want to associate with hypocrites, you had better get out of the world as soon as you can. You will find one hundred hypocrites outside of the Church where you will find one in it. If you don't want to associate with hypocrites, you had better accept this invitation at once. If I ever find a man who is a hypocrite, and betrays the cause of Christ, it only makes me want the love of Christ all the more, and I want to serve Him all the better. Because this or that man is untrue, is it any reason that I should like less the cause they betray? That is no excuse either, then. It is a personal, an individual matter with you. Suppose almost all men on the face of the earth are hypocrites, it is no sign that I or you should be so. Is that any reason why you should not become Christ's follower?

There is a young man over there who says, "Mr. Moody has not touched my case at all. My trouble is different. I would like to become a Christian, but if I become one, I am afraid I won't hold out." That is a very common excuse. We have it in the inquiry room every night. "There is no one in New York that feels more anxious to become a Christian than I do," said a young man the other night, "but I am afraid that I will not hold out." Now, is it our work to keep ourselves, or is it the work of the shepherd to keep the sheep? The keeper of Israel never slumbers and sleeps, and is not the God of Israel able to keep us? The work of the shepherd is to take care of the sheep, and not the sheep to take care of the shepherd.

Now the question comes, will you trust Him to-day? You will be able to stand if God stands with you. When I was talking with that young man, it reminded me of a boy whom I knew some years ago, whose father was a miserable drunken wretch and infidel, and he would not allow a praying man under his roof, for he said a man that prayed was nothing but a blackhearted hypocrite. Somebody got hold of his little boy, and got him into the Sabbath school, and he was converted. One day afterward, the old man caught him praying, and he caught him by the collar and jerked him to his feet, commanding him with oaths never to be caught doing that again, or he would have to leave home forever. Twice after that he caught him in the act of praying, and the last time told him to leave his house forever. The little fellow packed up his things in a handkerchief, went down into the kitchen where his mother was, and bade her good-bye, then went and bade his little brother and sisters good-bye, and as he passed his father on his way to the door, he reached up his arms to put them around his father's neck, and said, "Good-bye, father. As long as I live, I will pray for you," and he went down the street, but he had not gone a great while, before his father came after him, and said, "If that is Christianity, I want it." And the boy went back and prayed with his father, and led him to Christ. So you see you cannot give any excuse for not coming to Jesus, so accept His invitation this hour and be saved.

But there is another excuse, and a good many of the young people give it. I have no doubt many of these little boys and girls here say, "I don't want to be a Christian, for if I do, I shall have to be gloomy." I know that was one of my excuses before I was converted. I thought if I became a Christian, I had got to put on a long face, and walk on through the world, looking neither to the right nor to the left, and have no more joy until I got into the other world. In other words, that Christianity was to make me sad and gloomy and despondent. But no; that is not religion, for religion should make you happy and joyful. See this man on the

REV. F. B. MEYER, OF ENGLAND, PREACHING AT THE CAMP GROUND, NORTHFIELD.

way to execution. A pardon from the Governor is put into his hands, and the poor man goes home to his family. Do you think that is going to make him gloomy? That is what the Gospel is. A pardon comes from the throne of Heaven, and that is not going to make us gloomy, is it? If a man dying for bread is given bread, is that going to make him gloomy? That is what the Gospel is— bread to the soul. If you give water to a man dying of thirst, a clear draught from the spring, isn't that going to make him happy? Christ is the water of life. My friends, it does not make people gloomy. It makes people gloomy to want Christ. There are many who profess Christianity that don't have a living Christ in them, and those are the people who are gloomy. But when Christ is with us a living well of water gushing up, it is a living well of gladness. And so, little boy, little girl, young man, young maiden, don't give that for an excuse. Don't say, "I will not accept of this invitation because it will make me gloomy and sad." That is not the experience of the true Christian. If you want to see a person truly happy, with a joy that the world does not know anything about, you must go to those that have been Christ's, and have caught the spirit, for He brings us joy and true peace and happiness.

Then another thing. There are a great many men that want to come, and they say, "Wait until I am a better man, and then I will come." I never knew a man to be saved that came to Christ in that way. You cannot make yourselves any better. You cannot cleanse yourselves. Every day and hour that you are staying from Christ you are getting worse instead of better. The very act of your staying away is a sin, and so instead of trying to get better, and get ready to come, just come as you are and be clothed with the garments of salvation. He will clothe you with His own righteousness. I noticed when our war was going on, men used to come to enlist, and the man who came with a fine suit of clothes on, and the hod-carrier in his dirty garments, would both have to take off their clothes and put on the uniform of the Government. And so, when men go into the Kingdom of God, they have to put on the livery of Heaven. You need not dress up for Christ, because He will strip you when you come and put on you the robes of His righteousness. My friends, you cannot stand before God in your own righteousness. Come to God as a poor beggar, and He will have mercy upon you.

I heard some years ago of an artist who wanted a model for the Prodigal. He went to many institutions and prisons, but could not get a man who suited his ideas of the Prodigal. One day, however, while walking down the street, he met a poor miserable tramp, and he suited the artist's eye, so he asked him if he would be willing to sit for his portrait. The tramp said he would, if the artist would pay him for it. The artist promised and set a day and hour for him to come. At the appointed time, when the artist was sitting in his studio, the man came in, but he was so well dressed, the artist didn't know him, and told him he had no appointment with him. When the beggar told him the circumstances, the artist said, "What have you been doing?" "Why,' said the man, " I thought if I was going to sit for my portrait, I would get a new suit of clothes." " Ah," said the artist, " you wont do; I wanted you just as you were." So, when you go to Christ, go just as you are, with all your rags, your filth, and your sin, and He will receive you. I don't care how bad you are. He came for that purpose, and there is not a man or woman in this hall to-night that is so bad that Christ would not have you if you will only come. You may be a thief, a drunkard, a libertine, polluted witn sin, and corrupt as the devil would have you, and yet the Lord Jesus Christ will receive you if you will just come, and come without delay, just as you are.

But I need not go on enumerating excuses; if you drive a man from behind one excuse, he takes immediate refuge behind another. If you drive him from that, he gets behind another like a flash. You cannot exhaust excuses. They are more numerous than the hairs upon your head. I will tell you what you can do with them. You can take them up and bind them in one bundle, and mark it, "Lies, lies, lies," in great big letters. God will sweep away those refuges of lies. It is only a question of time. By and by you will be left without an excuse. He that believeth not, will be without God, without hope, without excuse. Do not think of giving excuses here. If you have any excuse that you call good, if you have any excuse that you think will stand the light of eternity and of the judgment day, if you think you have any excuse that God will accept, do not give it up for anything I have said. Take it into the grave with you. Let it be buried with you, and when you come before Him, tell it out. If not, then give your excuses to us here to-day. It is easy to excuse yourself into hell, but you cannot excuse yourself out of it. It is easy to take a seat here, and to make light of everything you hear, and go away laughing and scoffing at the whole thing; but ah, it will be terrible to stand before God without an excuse.

One of the most solemn things in Scripture is that not one of these men that were bidden to the feast of the Lamb and refused should taste of the supper. That is to say, that God would excuse them, taking them at their word. It will be a terrible thing to be excused from that feast. Do you really want to be excused? Is there a man or woman here that will say honestly that he or she would willingly be excused? Why not accept of the invitation now? Let the plough stand in the furrow, let the oxen stand in the stall until you accept the invitation. Let your business go until this question of eternity is settled with you. It is better for you to press into the Kingdom than it is for you to attend to any other duty. That is the first thing. A man must first attend to the soul's salvation. If your wife won't go, leave her at home. If you cannot get your family to join you, go alone. Make up your mind that to-day you will be up and pursuing that one object. If your companions make light of it, let them do it. It is Christ that invites you. Did you ever stop to think who will be there? Not one who has washed in the blood of the Lamb will be missing on that occasion. I would rather have my heart torn out of my body here on this platform, and go from here right straight to Heaven and be with Him at last, than live a hundred years and lose that opportunity. I want to be at the Marriage Supper of the Lamb. I want to sit with Abraham and Isaac and Jacob. I want to be in the presence of the King of Kings. Do not make light of it.

I can imagine some of you saying, "I never yet got so low that I have been willing to make light of religion and serious things." Let me ask you: Suppose a man invites me to his house. Suppose he sends me a note and invites me to dinner with him, and I read it and simply tear it up or throw it aside and pay no more attention to it. Is not that making light of it? How many will thus walk out of this hall, and make light of everything they have heard? Suppose here we just write out a refusal of the invitation. "To the King of Heaven: While sitting in the church on a beautiful day, January, 1899, I received a pressing invitation from one of Your servants to be present at the marriage supper of Your only begotten Son. I pray Thee accept my excuses." Now, who would come forward and take a pen, and dip it in the ink and put his name to that? I can imagine you saying,

"Let this right hand forget its cunning and this tongue cleave to the roof of my mouth, before I would be guilty of such a thing; ten thousand times, No!" But I will tell you what you will do. You will get up and go out and make light of the whole thing. Let us write out an acceptance: "To the King of Heaven: January, 1899. While sitting in the meeting, I received a very pressing invitation from one of Your messengers to be present at the marriage supper of Your only begotten Son. I hasten to reply. By the grace of God I will be present." Who will sign that? Will you say from the depth of your heart, "I will do that?" Some one up there says, "Yes, I will." Thank God for that! Why should not the one person speak for the whole audience?

REAPING WHATSOEVER WE SOW

"Be not deceived: God is not mocked: for whatsoever a man soweth, that shall he also reap. For he that soweth to his flesh shall of the flesh reap corruption; but he that soweth to the Spirit shall of the Spirit reap life everlasting."—Galatians, 6th Chapter, 7th and 8th verses.

It is very easy for us to deceive ourselves and one another, and there is a good deal of deception in the world. But you cannot deceive God.

When we try to deceive Him, we are thinking all the time that He is like us. We are told in Jeremiah that "the heart is deceitful above all things, and desperately wicked." Any man who leans on his own understanding will be deceived. How many times have we deceived others, and because we succeeded in doing so, thought we could deceive God; but we cannot do it. You may mock us, but whatever you do in that way, don't mock God. I was reading some time ago of a young man who had just come out of a saloon. He had mounted his horse. As a certain deacon passed on his way to church he followed the deacon and said,

"Deacon, can you tell me how far it is to hell?" The deacon's heart was pained to think that a young man like that should talk so lightly; he passed on and said nothing. When he came round the corner to the church he found that the horse had thrown that young man, and he was dead. So you may be nearer the judgment than you think. Now, in the first place, a man expects to reap. That is true in the natural world. Men are sowing and planting, and what for? Why, to reap. And so it holds true, you will find, in the spiritual world. Not only that, when he sows he expects to reap more than he sows, and the same that he sows. If he sows wheat, he doesn't expect to get potatoes; if he wants wheat, he sows wheat. If a man learns the trade of a carpenter, he doesn't expect to be a blacksmith. It says in the 5th chapter of Matthew: "Blessed are they that mourn, for they shall be comforted. Blessed are the merciful, for they shall obtain mercy." See how God has dealt with the nations. See if they have not reaped what they sowed. What has become of the monarchs and empires of the world? What brought ruin to Babylon? Why, her king and people would not obey God, and ruin came upon them. What has become of Greece and all its power? It once ruled the world. What has become of Rome and all its greatness? When their cup of iniquity was full, it was dashed to the ground. What has become of the Jews? They rejected salvation, persecuted God's messengers, and crucified their Redeemer, and we find eleven hundred thousand of them perished at one time. O, my friends, it is only a question of time!

Look at the history of this country. With an open Bible our forefathers planted slavery; but judgment came at last. There is not a family North or South that has not to mourn over some one taken from them. Instead of that war humbling us, how defiant we became. Look and see how crime has increased during the past few years.

Ah, this fair republic will go to pieces, if there is not more righteousness; it will perish like the other nations, if we don't repent in time. I happened to be in France in 1867, and I confess I could not tell the difference between Sunday and any other day; and did not God punish France for her sins? She went down from her high station very quickly. But a few years ago she stood shoulder to shoulder with the leading nations of the earth.

Why have those nations fallen? Just because God made them reap what they sowed. Now if a man sows for this life, why, he will reap in this life; and if he sows for eternity, he will reap in eternity. If he sows to the Spirit, he will have his harvest up yonder. If he sows to the flesh he will reap disappointment and despair; he will reap gloom, and death and hell; but if he sows to the Spirit, he will reap joy and peace and long-suffering and gladness, for these are the fruits of the Spirit; and not only that, but he has everlasting life. Now just ask yourself to-night what are you sowing? Are you sowing for time, or are you sowing for eternity? Are you sowing good seed, or are you sowing bad seed?

You must remember the judgment sometimes comes down very suddenly, and sometimes it is deferred; but all through Scripture we find that God deals in grace before He deals in judgment. I have showed you that God dealt in judgment with Lot, and what a bitter end his was. Just take up your Bible, and, all through it, you will see that God deals in grace and government. Take that priest of His, Eli; he had two sons who didn't care for God. He failed to bring them up right. They sold what was offered to God, and became very wealthy; but they were slain in battle against the Philistines, and Eli himself, when he heard the news, fell back and broke his neck. God sent a message twenty years before that sentence was carried out, that judgment would come. Look at the sons of Jacob. They sold Joseph and deceived their father.

Twenty long years rolled away, and away down in Egypt their sin followed them; for they said: "We are guilty of the blood of our brother." The reaping time had come at last for those ten boys that sold their brother. If God will punish His own priest, Eli, one of His own children, won't He punish those who have not accepted the offer of salvation?

Mr. Moody proceeded at length to show that Jacob and David, though children of God, were severely judged in this life for their sins, and so continued. So keep this in mind that God has got a government. He may forgive us, He may give us eternal life, but it is the law of high Heaven that a man must reap what he sows.

Now bear in mind that these three men were men of grace. We will see them in Heaven, there is no doubt about that. Now some of you will say, "If God is going to forgive me my sins, how does he make me reap what I have sown?" Well, I will illustrate it. Suppose I send out a man to sow wheat; he neglects to do his duty and sows tares. When the wheat grows up I find it out, and call him to account. "Well, to be honest with you," he says, "I got mad and sowed a lot of tares, but I am very sorry for it." I forgive him for sowing the tares, but when the reaping time comes, I make him reap them. Why, one of those men who spoke here to-day was a drunkard for thirty years. I have no doubt his sins are forgiven, but O, how he is reaping what he has sown! His wife and his children are away from him; he has not seen his little boy for fifteen years! I see a man in this audience to-night, and O, how he is reaping, how I pity him. I few months ago he was in a happy home in England. He gambled his employer's money all away, and now he is an exile, a stranger in a strange land. God may forgive him, but he must reap what he has sown. Some men think that is hard, but it cannot be otherwise.

THE COUNCIL MEET, showing stone pulpit from which Mr. Moody spoke to the students in camp.

HOTEL NORTHFIELD. Used as home of the Northfield Training School in winter.

I tried to help a poor man in Philadelphia. He had been in prison, and I could not help but try to lift him up. He betrayed my confidence, so we don't know whom to help. Now suppose here is a father; he has got a boy who has gone out and stolen some money. His conscience is thoroughly roused, and he goes and confesses it. "Yes, my boy," the father says, "I will forgive you, but you must go and confess it." He don't want to do that, but he must do it; he has got to reap what he has sown. Do you think God would punish Jacob and his own children and let unbelieving sinners go unpunished? Do you think the ten thousand rumsellers of New York are not going to be punished? I would not take the place of one of them, if you gave me all the world. Look at that little, weak, pale, thin girl, only six or seven years old; she went into a saloon and went to the bar and said to the saloonkeeper: "O, sir, don't sell papa any more liquor, for we are starving." The rumseller ordered her out. You think there was no God to witness that? O, there is a just God yonder, and men are going to be gathered there to give an account of their stewardship by and by. Do you think that libertine who has gone and lied to that lady, and then ruined her and fled—do you think he is going unpunished? He may escape the law on earth, but he will be tried at God's bar, bound hand and foot, and cast into hell. There is a day of grace now. He will forgive you the sin, though He will make you reap what you sow. He will give you your eternal life, if you will only come to Him and confess your sin, and is it not the very best thing you can do to come to God to-night?

While preaching this sermon in a western city, and saying over and over the text, "Whatsoever a man sow, that shall he also reap," one man in the audience was deeply impressed. He sought Mr. Moody at the close of the sermon, and when he could speak to him, he said, "I am a defaulter. I have taken a great amount of money from my old place of employment in the State of Missouri. I have a wife and three children, and under your sermon to-night I have been convicted. Now what must I do? The penitentiary faces me if I return to Missouri." Mr. Moody said to me, when the man came to me I was on the eve of telling him instantly to go back and confess his sin and pay the penalty, but when I thought of my own wife and three children, I said, let me think about it until to-morrow, and then see me at my hotel. I met him next day at the hotel, and as soon as he entered my room, he said, "The question is settled. I have decided to go back." Sometime afterward when he had been sentenced to the penetentiary, he wrote me a letter in which he said that he had gone back to his old home; had stolen into the city in the night-time and after the children were asleep, had gotten into his house. He desired to spend a few days in fellowship with his wife, and he knew, if the children were aware of his presence, that the law would come down upon him, and so he remained hidden in his own home. Each night, when his wife would put the children to bed, he would stand near the door of an adjoining room and listen to their prayers and innocent talk. Finally he said, "Mr. Moody, I heard my little boy say, 'Papa does not love us any more; he has gone away, and he never writes us. I am sure he doesn't love us,' and Mr. Moody," said he, "I thought my heart would break, but it is true, as you have said, I am reaping what I have sown." He confessed his sin; was sentenced to the penitentiary and was pardoned out, after some little time of penal servitude.

Mr. Moody was one day giving this illustration in the State of Missouri, and he said, "Some people have been disposed to question the truth of this." When he made that statement, a gentleman arose in the audience and said, "I am a former Governor of the State of Missouri." It was Governor Francis, who was speaking. "I can vouch for the truth of all Mr. Moody says, for I pardoned the man out myself." "But, in the sad story of the broken-hearted man," said the great evangelist, "we have a perfect illustration of the text, 'whatsoever a man soweth, that shall he also reap.'"

CHAPTER XXIII.

His Best Illustrations

MR. MOODY was a master in the use of illustrations. He saw in everything on which his eye rested something, that would make the Word of God more easily understood. What other men would pass by, he seized upon, and, under his skillful touch, told in his inimitable way, it became powerful in illustrating the statements of the Bible. His illustrations always moved him, and for that reason they took firm hold upon his hearers. I have, again and again, seen the tears roll down his face as he would tell some touching story of a father's love for his child, or give some wonderful picture of the passing of a saint into the presence of God. There are those who criticise the use of illustrations in sermons, but Jesus used them, and was ever and again saying, "Whereunto shall I liken it," and would then tell the story of a prodigal son, or a broken-hearted mother, or a demoniac boy —"and the common people heard him gladly"

The Fervor of His Eloquence

The Honorable James A. Mount, Governor of Indiana, thus writes of him:

"I unhesitatingly pronounce Dwight L. Moody the greatest preacher of the century. Classical scholars and literary critics may not agree with this estimate. Mr. Moody did not preach to please the ear, but to save the soul, yet he moved thousands to repentance by the fervor of his eloquence and the earnestness of his appeal.

"He had a message from the Holy Spirit to dying men, and with love to God and love to men he delivered that message. More enduring than if perpetuated by marble shaft will be the name of Moody, for it is embalmed in the memory of loving hearts whom he led out of darkness into light, and from the power of sin to salvation through faith in Christ. 'He being dead yet speaketh'."

And whatever may be given by men as the secret of his power as a preacher, all will agree in this, that his superb power in the use of illustration, contributed, in no small degree, to his ability to hold and to sway the millions of people to whom he preached.

The following illustration I have often heard him use:

It is said that Whitfield once preached a sermon, in the midst of which a sudden thunder storm of terrific force burst upon them, and, taking advantage of the storm to illustrate the Judgment, the effect of his preaching was profound. A request was sent to him to print the sermon for distribution; he agreed to do so on condition that the thunder storm be printed with it.

To appreciate D. L. Moody's illustrations you should have seen his audience moved by them, and you should have looked up into his face, all aglow with the power of his message, as I have done in the use of my story here given. The following are only a few of the hundreds he used when I have heard him preach:

Infidel Books

People read infidel books and wonder why they are unbelievers. I ask, why do they read such books? They think they must read both sides. I ask, if that book is a lie, how can it be one side? It is not one side.

Suppose a man tells lies about my family, and I read them so as to hear both sides; it would not be long before some suspicion would creep into my mind.

I said to a man once, "Have you got a wife?"

"Yes, and a good one."

I asked: "Now what if I should come to you and cast out insinuations against her?"

And he said, "Well your life would not be safe long if you did."

I told him just to treat the devil as he would treat a man who went around with such stories.

Doubts

I remember laboring with a man in Chicago. It was past midnight before he got down on his knees, but down he went, and was converted. I said: "Now, don't think you are going to get out of the devil's territory without trouble. The devil will come to you to-morrow morning and say it was all feeling; that you only imagined you were accepted by God. When he does, don't fight him with your own opinions, but fight him with John vi. 37 : "Him that cometh to me I will in no wise cast out.' Let that be the "sword of the Spirit."

"The struggle came sooner than I thought. When he was on his way home the devil assailed him. He used this text, but the devil put this thought into his mind: 'How do you know Christ ever said that after all? Perhaps the translators made a mistake.' Into darkness he went again. He was in trouble till about two in the morning. At last he came to this conclusion. Said he: 'I will believe it anyway; and when I get to Heaven, if it isn't true, I will just tell the Lord *I* didn't make the mistake—the translators made it.'

Let the Lower Lights be Burning

A few years ago, at the mouth of Cleveland harbor, there were two lights, one at each side of the bay, called the upper and lower lights; and to enter the harbor safely by night, vessels must sight both of the lights.

These western lakes are sometimes more dangerous than the great ocean. One wild, stormy night, a steamer was trying to make her way into the harbor. The captain and pilot were anxiously watching for the lights. By and by the pilot was heard to say, "Do you see the lower light?"

"No," was the reply: "I fear we have passed them."

"Ah, there are the lights," said the pilot; "and they must be, from the bluff on which they stand, the upper lights. We have passed the lower lights, and have lost our chance of getting into the harbor."

What was to be done? They looked back, and saw the dim outline of the lower lighthouse against the sky. The lights had gone out.

"Can't you turn your head around?"

"No; the night is too wild for that. She wont answer to her helm."

The storm was so fearful that they could do nothing. They tried again to make for the harbor, but they went crash against the rocks, and sank to the bottom. Very few escaped; the great majority found a watery grave. Why? Simply because the lower lights had gone out.

Now with us the upper light is all right. Christ himself is the upper light, and we are the lower lights, and the cry to us is, *Keep the lower lights burning;* that is what we have to do.

They are Old Enough.

I have no sympathy with the idea that our children have to grow up before they are converted. Once I saw a lady with three daughters at her side, and I stepped up to her and asked her if she was a Christian.

"Yes, sir."

Then I asked the oldest daughter if she was a Christian. The chin began to quiver, and the tears came into her eyes, and she said: "I wish I was."

The mother looked very angrily at me and said, "I don't want you to speak to my children on that subject. They don't understand." And in great rage she took them away from me. One daughter was fourteen years old, one twelve, and the other ten, but they were not old enough to be talked to about religion! Let them drift into the world and plunge into worldly amusements, and then see how hard it is to reach them. Many a mother is mourning to-day because her boy has gone beyond her reach, and will not allow her to pray with him. She may pray for him, but he will not let her pray or talk with him. In those early days when his mind was tender and young, she might have led him to Christ. Bring them in. "Suffer the little children to come unto Me."

Is there a prayerless father reading this? May God let the arrow go down into your soul! Make up your mind that, God helping you you, will get the children converted. God's order is to the father first, but if he isn't true to his duty, then the mother should be true, and save the children from the wreck. Now is the time to do it while you have them under your roof. Exert your parental influence over them.

"For Charlie's Sake."

Some years ago at a convention, an old judge was telling about the mighty power Christians summon to their aid in this petition "for Christ's sake;" "in Jesus' name;" and he told a story that made a great impression on me. When the war came on, he said, his only son left for the army, and he became suddenly interested in soldiers. Every soldier that passed by brought his son to remembrance; he could see his son in him. He went to work for

MR. MOODY CHRISTENING THE TWINS OF THE PRINCIPAL OF MT. HERMON SCHOOL. Mr. Morgan of England stands by the chair at the left of the picture.

soldiers. When a sick soldier came there to Columbus one day, so weak he couldn't walk, the judge took him in a carriage, and got him into the Soldiers' Home. Soon he became president of the Soldiers' Home in Columbus, and used to go down every day and spend hours in looking after those soldiers, and seeing that they had every comfort. He spent on them a great deal of time and a great deal of money.

One day he said to his wife; "I'm giving too much time to these soldiers. I've got to stop it. There's an important case coming on in court, and I've got to attend to my own business."

He said he went down to the office that morning resolved in future to let the soldiers alone. He went to his desk, and then to writing. Pretty soon the door opened, and he saw a soldier hobble slowly in. He started at sight of him. The man was fumbling at something in his breast, and pretty soon he got out an old soiled paper. The father saw it was his own son's wirting.

"Dear Father:—

"This young man belongs to my company. He has lost his leg and his health in defense of his country, and he is going home to his mother to die. If he calls on you, treat him kindly,

"For Charlie's Sake."

"For Charlie's Sake." The moment he saw that, a pang went to his heart. He sent for a carriage, lifted the maimed soldier in, drove home, put him into Charlie's room, sent for the family physician, kept him in the family and treated him for his own son. When the young soldier got well enough to go to the train to go home to his mother, he took him to the railway station, put him in the nicest, most comfortable place in the carriage, and sent him on his way.

"I did it," said the old judge, "for Charlie's sake."

Now whatsoever you do, my friend, do it for the Lord Jesus' sake. Do and ask everything in the name of Him "who loved us and gave Himself for us."

A Beautiful Legend.

There is a beautiful tradition connected with the site on which the temple of Solomon was erected. It is said to have been occupied in common by two brothers, one of whom had a family, the other had none. On this spot was sown a field of wheat. On the evening succeeding the harvest—the wheat having been gathered in separate shocks—the elder brother said to his wife:

"My younger brother is unable to bear the burden and heat of the day; I will arise, take of my shocks and place with his without his knowledge."

The younger brother being actuated by the same benevolent motives, said within himself;

"My elder brother has a family; and I have none. I will arise, take of my shocks and place with his."

Judge of their mutual astonishment, when, on the following day, they found their respective shocks undiminished. This transpired for several nights, when each resolved in his own mind to stand guard and solve the mystery. They did so; and on the following night they met each other half-way between their respective shocks with their arms full. Upon ground hallowed by such associations as this was the temple of Solomon erected—of the world! Alas! in these days, how many would sooner steal their brother's whole shock than add to it a single sheaf!

"Dinna Ye Hear Them?"

During the Indian mutiny, the English were besieged in the city of Lucknow, and were in momentary expectation of perishing at the hands of the fiends that surrounded them. A little Scotch lassie was in this fort, and, while lying on the ground, she suddenly shouted, her face aglow with joy:

"Dinna ye hear them comin'? dinna ye hear them comin'?"

"Hear what?" they asked.

"Dinna ye hear them comin?"

She sprang to her feet. It was the bagpipes of her native Scotland she heard. It was a native air she heard that was being played by a regiment of her countrymen marching to the relief of those captives, and these deliverers made them free.

Oh, friend, don't you hear the voice of Jesus Christ calling to you now?

"Throw the Reins to Christ"

An interesting story is told of Professor Drummond. He was staying with a lady whose coachman had signed the pledge, but afterward gave way to drink. This lady said to the professor, "Now this man will drive you to the station; say a word to him if you can. He is a good man and really wants to reform; but he is weak."

While they were driving to the station, the professor tried to think how he could introduce the subject. Suddenly the horses were frightened and tried to run away. The driver held on to the reins and managed them well. The carriage swayed about, and the professor expected every moment to be upset, but after a little the man got the better of the team, and as he drew them up at the station, streaming with perspiration, he exclaimed: "That was a close shave. sir! Our trap might have been smashed into matchwood, and you wouldn't have given any more addresses."

"Well," said Professor Drummond, "how was it that it did not happen?"

"Why," was the reply, "because I knew how to manage the horses."

"Now," said the professor, "look here, my friend, I will give you a bit of advice. Here's my train coming. I hear you have been signing the pledge and breaking out again. Now I want to give you a bit of advice. Throw the reins of your life to Jesus Christ." And he jumped down, and got into the train.

The driver saw in a flash where he had made the mistake, and from that day ceased to try to live in his own strength.

A Remarkable Picture

Some years ago a remarkable picture was exhibited in London. As you looked at it from a distance, you seemed to see a monk engaged in prayer, his hands clasped, his head bowed. As you came nearer, however, and examined the painting more closely, you saw that in reality he was squeezing a lemon into a punch bowl.

What a picture that is of the human heart! Superficially examined, it is thought to be the seat of all that is good and noble and pleasing in a man; whereas in reality, until regenerated by the Holy Ghost, it is the seat of all corruption. "This is the condemnation, that light is come into the world, and men loved darkness rather than light."

"He Is My Brother"

A fearful storm was raging, when the cry was heard, "Man overboard!"

A human form was seen manfully breasting the furious elements in the direction of the shore; but the raging waves bore the struggler rapidly outward, and ere the boats could be lowered, a fearful space separated the victim from help. Above the shriek of the storm and the roar of the waters rose his rending cry. It was an agonizing moment. With bated breath and blanched cheek, every eye was strained to the struggling man. Manfully did the brave rowers strain every nerve in this race of mercy; but all their efforts were in vain. One wild shriek of despair, and the victim went down. A piercing cry, "Save him, save him!" rang through the hushed crowd; and into their midst darted an agitated man; throwing his arms wildly in the air, shouting, "A thousand pounds for the man who saves his life!" but his staring eyes rested only on the spot where the waves rolled remorselessly over the perished. He whose strong cry broke the stillness of the crowd was captain of the ship from whence the drowned man fell, and was his brother.

This is the feeling we should have in the various ranks of those bearing commission under the great Captain of our salvation, "Save him! he is my brother."

The fact is, men do not believe in Christianity because they think we are not in earnest about it. When the people see that we are in earnest in all that we undertake for God, they will begin to tremble; men and women will be inquiring the way to Zion.

A Fragrant Act

There is a preacher in Edinburgh, but I never think of him as a preacher, although he is one of the finest preachers in Scotland. There is just one act associated with that man that I will carry in remembrance to the grave.

There is a hospital for little children in Edinburgh, and that great minister, with a large parish and a large congregation, goes one afternoon every week and sits down and talks with those little children—a good many of them there for life; they are incurable. One day he found a little boy, only six years old, who had been brought over from Fife. The little fellow was in great distress because the doctors were coming to take off his leg. Think how you would feel, if you had a little brother six years old and he was taken off to the hospital, and the doctor said that he was coming forty-eight hours afterward to take off his leg!

Well, that minister tried to comfort the boy, and said: "Your father will come to be with you."

"No," he said, "my father is dead; he cannot be here."

"Well, your mother will come."

"My mother is over in Fife. She is sick and cannot come."

The minister himself could not come, so he said, "Well, you know the matron here is a mother; she has got a great big heart."

The little chin began to quiver as the little boy said: "Perhaps Jesus will be with me."

Do you have any doubt of it? Next Friday the man of God went to the hospital; but he found the cot was empty. The poor boy was gone: the Saviour had come and taken him to His bosom.

One little act of kindness will often live a good deal longer than a most magnificent sermon.

Calling on God

Some old divine has pictured Peter preaching on the day of Pentecost. A man pushed his way through the crowd, and said, "Peter, do you think there is hope for me? I am the man who made that crown of thorns and placed them upon Christ's brow; do you think He will save me?"

"Yes," said Peter, "'Whosoever shall call upon the name of the Lord shall be saved.' You are a 'whosoever;' if you call He will hear your cry. He will answer your prayer and save you." The man might have cried then and there, and the Lord saved him.

Another man pushed his way up and said to Peter, "I am the man who took that reed out of His hand, and drove it down upon that cruel crown of thorns, sending it into His brow; do you think He will save me?"

"Yes," said Peter, "He told us to go into the world and preach the Gospel to every creature, and He did not mean any to be left out; salvation is for you. He did not come to condemn men; He came to get His arm under the vilest sinner and lift him up toward Heaven."

Another man, elbowing his way through the crowd, pushed up to Peter, and said, "I am the Roman soldier who took the spear and drove it to His heart, when there came out blood and water; do you think there is hope for me?"

"Yes," said Peter, "there's a nearer way of reaching His heart than that; 'whosoever shall call upon the name of the Lord shall be saved.'" And the Roman soldier might have cried then and there, and might have obtained forgiveness and salvation.

If the Lord heard the cry of those Jerusalem sinners whose hands were dripping with the blood of the Son of God—if He heard their cry and saved them, do you not think he will hear your cry and save you?

A Penalty Necessary

A person once said to me: "I hate your God; your God demands blood. I don't believe in such a God. My God is merciful to all. I do not know your God."

If you turn to Lev. xvii. 11, you will find why God demands blood: "For the life of the flesh is in the blood; and I have given it to you upon the altar to make an atonement for your souls; for it is the blood that maketh an atonement for the souls."

Suppose there was a law that man should not steal, but no penalty was attached to stealing; some man would have my pocket-book before dinner. If I threatened to have him arrested, he would snap his fingers in my face. He would not fear the law, if there was no penalty. It is not the law that people are afraid of; it is the penalty attached.

Do you suppose God has made a law without a penalty. What an absurd thing it would be. Now the penalty for sin is death; "The soul that sinneth it shall die." I must die, or get somebody to die for me. If the Bible doesn't teach that, it doesn't teach anything. And that is where the atonement of Jesus Christ comes in.

Grip of Promise

Mr. Moody once told me that he was conducting meetings in Scotland, passing through an inquiry meeting he saw two little girls crying as if their hearts would break. He stopped long enough to ask them their difficulty, and one of them replied that she wanted to be a Christian. The great evangelist took his Bible and, opening it at the fifth chapter of John, the 24th verse, he asked her if she could receive that, and, with her face brightening, she said she thought she could and would. The next night, passing through the same room, he saw the same two girls upon their knees, and one of them crying bitterly. He was greatly perplexed, and, coming near enough to hear their conversation, he heard the child of the night before saying to her companion, "I say, lassie, you do just as I did, grip a promise and hold on to it, and he will save you, for he saved me." And this is true not only for the Scotch girl, but for every one who will simply take God's Word and trust Him fully.

One Year's Record

The following illustration of Dr. Gordon was much loved by Mr. Moody.

Very tiny and pale the little girl looked as she stood before those three grave and dignified gentlemen. She had been ushered into the Rev. Dr. Gordon's study, where he was holding counsel with two of his deacons, and now, upon inquiry into the nature of her errand, a little shyly preferred the request to be allowed to become a member of his church.

"You are quite too young to join the church," said one of the deacons, "you had better run home, and let us talk to your mother."

She showed no sign of running, however, as her wistful blue eyes traveled from one face to another of the three gentlemen sitting in their comfortable chairs; she only drew a little step nearer to Dr. Gordon. He arose, and with the gentle courtesy that ever marked him, placed her in a small chair close beside himself.

"Now, my child, tell me your name, and where you live?"

"Annie Graham, sir, and I live on K——— Street. I go to your Sunday-school."

"You do; and who is your teacher?"

"Miss B———. She is very good to me."

"And you want to join my church?"

The child's face glowed as she leaned eagerly towards him, clasping her hands, but all she said was, "Yes, sir."

"She cannot be more than six years old," said one of the deacons, disapprovingly.

Dr. Gordon said nothing, but quietly regarded the small, earnest face, now becoming a little downcast.

"I am ten years old; older than I look," she said.

"It is not usual for us to admit anyone so young to membership," he said, thoughtfully. "We never have done so; still———"

"It may make an undesirable precedent," remarked the other deacon.

The Doctor did not seem to hear, as he asked, "You know what joining the church is, Annie?"

"Yes, sir;" and she answered a few questions that proved she comprehended the meaning of the step she wished to take. She had slipped off her chair, and now stood close to Dr. Gordon's knee.

"You said, last Sabbath, sir, that the lambs should be in the fold——."

"I did," he answered. "It is surely not for us to keep them out. Go home now, my child. I will see your friends and arrange to take you into membership very soon."

The cloud lifted from the child's face, and her expression, as she passed through the door he opened for her, was one of entire peace.

Inquiries made of Annie's Sabbath school teacher proving satisfactory, she was baptized the following week, and, except for occasional information from Miss B., that she was doing well, Dr. Gordon heard no more of her for about a year.

Then he was summoned to her funeral.

It was one of June's hottest days, and as the doctor made his way along the narrow street on which Annie had lived, he wished, for a moment, that he had asked his assistant to come instead of himself, but as he neared the house, the crowd filled him with wonder; progress was hindered, and as perforce he paused for a moment, his eye fell on a crippled lad crying bitterly as he sat on a low doorstep.

"Do you know Annie Graham, my lad?" he asked.

"Know her, is it, sir? Niver a week passed but what she came twice or thrice with a picture or book, mayhap an apple for me, an' its owin' to her an' no clargy at all that I'll ever follow her blessed footsteps to Heaven. She'd read me from her own Bible whiniver she came, an' now she's gone there'll be none at all to help me, for mother's dead an' dad's drunk, an' the sunshine's gone from Mike's sky with Annie, sir."

A burst of sobs choked the boy. Dr. Gordon passed on, after promising him a visit soon, making his way through the crowd of tear-stained, sorrowful faces. The doctor came to a stop again in the narrow passageway of the little house. A woman stood beside him drying her fast-falling tears, while a wee child hid his face in her skirts and wept.

"Was Annie a relative of yours?" the doctor asked.

"No, sir; but the blessed child was at our house constantly, and when Bob here was sick she nursed and tended him, and her hymns quieted him when nothing else seemed to do it. It was just the same with all the neighbors. What she's been to us no one but the Lord will ever know, and now she lies there."

Recognized at last, Dr. Gordon was led to the room where the child lay at rest, looking almost younger than when he had seen her in his study a year ago. An old bent woman was crying aloud by the coffin.

"I never thought she'd go afore I did. She used to run in regular to read an' sing to me every evening, an' it was her talk an' prayers that made a Christian of me. You could a'most go to Heaven on one of her prayers."

"Mother, mother, come home," said a young man, putting his arm around her to lead her away. "You'll see her again."

"I know, I know; she said she'd wait for me at the gate," she sobbed, as she followed him; "but I miss her sore now."

A silence fell on those assembled, and, marvelling at such testimony, Dr. Gordon proceeded with the service, feeling as if there was little more he could say of one whose deeds thus spoke for her. Loving hands had laid flowers all around the child who had lead them. One young girl had placed a dandelion in the small waxen fingers and now stood, abandoned to grief, beside the still form that bore the impress of absolute purity. The service over, again and again was the coffin lid waved back by some one longing for one more look, and they seemed as if they could not let her go.

The next day a good-looking man came to Dr. Gordon's house and was admitted into his study.

"I am Annie's uncle, sir," he said simply. "She never rested till she made me promise to join the church, and I've come."

Dr. Gordon sat in the twilight, resting, after his visitor had left. The summer breeze blew in through the windows, and his thoughts turned backward and dwelt on what his little parishioner had done.

"Truly a marvelous record for one year. It is well said, Their angels do ever behold His face."

CHAPTER XXIV.

Revival Conventions.

IN the early days of Mr. Moody's evangelistic experience, frequent revival conventions were held, when questions were asked by the people and answered by the great leader, as a result of which hundreds of Christian workers were instructed in the special conduct of evangelistic services, and many ministers went out to do the work which they felt themselves before unable to perform. No wiser counsel was ever given. I remember in one of these conventions, Mr. Moody spoke as follows:

WHAT IS EVANGELISTIC SERVICE?

"Some one said to me, 'What do you mean by evangelistic services? Is not all service evangelistic? And what do you mean by preaching the Gospel? Are not all services in the churches and all meetings preaching the Gospel?' "By no means. There is the greatest difference. There are really three services in every church; at least there ought to be; there is worshipping God; this is not preaching the Gospel at all. We come to the house of God to worship at times when we meet around the Lord's table. Then there is teaching, that is building up the church, but it is not preaching the Gospel. Then there is the proclaiming the good news to the world, that is, to the unsaved; that is really Gospel preaching. Now the question we have before us is how can these services be conducted to make them profitable? Well, I should say first of all, you must make them interesting. If people go to sleep in church, they certainly need to be roused up, and if one method fails, try another, but I think we ought to use our common sense in all this work. We talk a great deal about this, but I think it is about the least sense we have, especially in the Lord's work. This preaching to empty seats don't pay. If people do not come to hear us, let us go where they are, and I have come to this conclusion, that if we are going to have successful Gospel meetings, we have got to have a little more life in them. Life is found in singing new hymns. For instance, I know some churches that have been singing about a dozen hymns for the last twenty years, such hymns as "Rock of Ages," "Jesus, Lover of my Soul." These hymns are always good, but we want a variety. We want new hymns as well as old ones.

We Want New Hymns

I find it wakes up a congregation tremendously to bring in now and then a new hymn, and if we cannot wake them up by preaching, let us sing the Gospel into them. I believe the secret of John Wesley's success was that he sent every man to work as soon as he was converted, and if people cannot speak, let us make them sing.

Then, again, the question is asked as to whether we ought, in holding revival services, to change the minister every evening? I frequently receive letters telling me about special meetings, how the people turned out well, but there were no results, and I found out that they had a Methodist minister one night, a Baptist minister another, an Episcopal minister another, a Congregational minister another, in order to keep all denominations in, and the result was, they preached everybody out of doors. One man gets the people all interested, and just at the point where he needs to continue his own ministrations, another steps in, he goes out, and the people frequently go out with him. Then these meetings ought to be made short. I find a great many are killed because they are too long. The minister speaks five minutes, and a minister's five minutes is generally ten, and his ten minutes quite often twenty, and the result is often long sermons drive people out of the spirit before the meeting is over. When the people leave they are glad to go home, and ought to go home. Now, you send the people away hungry and they will want to come back. There was a man in London who preached in the open air until everybody left him, and somebody said, "Why did you preach so long?" and he said, "I thought it would be a pity to stop while anybody was listening." It is a great deal better to cut right off. Then the people will want to come back.

The Most Apt Replies to Questions

At this point, Mr. Moody paused for questions, and he was always at his best when answering these questions in such services. He had the keenest mind and the most apt replies possible.

Q:—Would you start a meeting where there is no special interest in the church?

Mr. Moody:—Certainly I would. So many people are saying to-day that they are waiting for God to favor Zion, and the fact is God has been waiting to favor Zion ever since Pentecost. They have no calendar in Heaven. God can work one month as well as another, and he is always ready when we are ready.

Q:—Suppose a minister is interested, and there is no special feeling among the people. Would you call in outside help?

Mr. Moody:—That is a very important question. If I were a minister in a community or a church, and could not get more than one or two to sympathize with me, I would just get them around to my study, and we would pray and go forth in the name of the

Lord, and say, "We are going to have a meeting." Three men filled with the Spirit of God can move any town in this country.

Q:—Suppose the congregation is alive and the minister is dead?

Mr. Moody:—Then let the congregation go on without the minister.

Q:—Suppose the minister wont permit them?

Mr. Moody:—He cannot prevent it. A man that wants to work for God can do so; nobody can stop him.

Q:—Suppose there is a difficulty in the church which cannot be removed?

Mr. Moody:—I do not know of anything that is too difficult for God. The trouble is we are trying to remove these difficulties ourselves instead of going to God in prayer.

Q:—Why was it the Lord Jesus could not do anything at Nazareth?

Mr. Moody:—On account of their unbelief, but that was the world, not the Church.

Q:—Is it best to put the test question in a church, asking those who are anxious to arise, or rather to go to another room?

Mr. Moody:—I think so. If any man is going to be saved, he is going to take up his cross, and if it is a cross, I would like to ask him to do it. What you want is to get them to do something they dont want to do, and it is a great cross generally for people to rise for prayer, but in the very act of doing it, they are very often blessed. I do not think I should attempt to have meetings without the inquiry-room. People are impressed under the sermon, but what you want is to deal with them personally. Here and there one is converted under the sermon, but for every one converted under the sermon, hundreds are converted in the inquiry-room.

MR. MOODY AT GLASGOW, preaching to fully 40,000 people who could not enter the Great Crystal Palace, already filled for his farewell meeting.

Q:—Do you advocate "anxious seats?"

Mr. Moody:—I would rather call it seats of decision; but in union meetings you know we have to lay aside a good many of the different denominational peculiarities. The "anxious seat" is known to the Methodists, but if we should call it that, the Presbyterians would be afraid, and the Episcopalians would be so shocked that they would leave, and I find in the union meetings, it is best to ask them to go right into the other room, and talk to them there.

Q:—What would you say to a person who replies, "I can be a Christian without rising for prayer"?

Mr. Moody:—I should say, most certainly he could, but as a general thing, he won't.

Q:—What method would you recommend to get people on their feet to testify for Christ?

Mr. Moody:—In the first place, I would bury all stiffness. If a meeting has a formal manner, it throws a stiffness over it, so that it would take almost an earthquake to get a man up, but if it is free and social, just as you would go into a man's house and talk with him, you will find people will appreciate it and get up.

Q:—If the world has got in and is stronger than the church, what then?

Mr. Moody:—Then I would organize another church. The mistake in all this is in taking unconverted people into the church. We really must be more careful.

Q:—How far is it wise to encourage young converts to labor with inquirers in the inquiry-room?

Mr. Moody:—I always encourage them. I believe a man who has been a great drunkard, for instance, and been reclaimed, is just the man to go to work among his class.

Q:—When a man feels he must preach the Gospel, and the church doesn't want to hear it, must he go out?

Mr. Moody:—A great many have got the idea that they can preach the Gospel, when they cannot, and some have got the idea that they cannot preach the Gospel, and they can to a certain class, and then they are just the ones to speak in that church. Now, I have tried that. When I was first converted, I thought I must talk to them about Christ, but I saw they did not like it, and finally they came and told me, I could serve the Lord better by keeping still. Then I went out into the street, and God blessed me, and I got to preaching before I knew it. If the people don't want you, don't force yourself upon them. Go out and preach to the ragged and the destitute.

Then some question was asked about the inquiry-meeting, in the conduct of which Dwight L. Moody was a master. To this inquiry Mr. Moody made answer: "If the ministers would encourage their members to be scattered among the audience, to never mind their pew, but sit back by the door if need be, or in the gallery, where they can watch the faces of the audience, it would be a good thing. In Scotland I met a man who, with his wife, would go and sit among the people, as they said, to watch for souls. When they saw anyone who seemed impressed, they would go to him after the meeting and talk with him. Nearly all the conversions in that church during the last fifteen months had been made through that influence. Now, if we could only have from thirty to fifty members of the church, whose business it is just to watch for those who are impressed, and lead them into an inquiry meeting when the pastor announces it, the results would be magnificent. The best way in our regular churches is to let the workers all help pull the net in. When the people have come into the after-service, let some one who knows his Bible sit down beside them and give them God's Word. I have very little confidence in the man who simply states his own experience, for, as a rule, that experience might discourage the one to whom he speaks, but if he points out God's Word, the Spirit is pledged to apply that word to the seeking soul, and the result is salvation.

It is an awful thing for a man to preach a sermon on coming to Jesus and then dismiss his audience without giving them a chance to come. Instruct your people in the knowledge of God's Word, and teach them how to explain that word to the man who is saying, "What must I do to be saved?"

CHAPTER XXV.

How to Study the Bible.

NO more interesting services were ever conducted by Mr. Moody than his Bible Readings.

I remember riding on the train with him at one time, and as we came into New York City, where he was to conduct a service, I said to him, "let me see your Bible," he had it in his hands, turning over the leaves, he laughingly replied, "Oh, no, if I should give you this, you would have my sermon for to-night, and then you might preach it before I could." And yet no one was more willing to give help to others than Mr. Moody. He was always receiving from his friends, but he was ever giving to them in return; and as for myself, it has been difficult for me to preach without saying, "Mr. Moody said this," or "I once heard Mr. Moody say," and I have ever found that illustrations on which he had set his seal of approval, were received by all classes of people as authentic.

Mr. Moody was peculiar in this, that however many times you might hear him say anything it never lost its freshness, and somehow you felt that you were hearing it for the first time.

The following is a characteristic Bible reading—the theme being one, in which he was always at his best:

A Characteristic Bible Reading

In Ephesians, 5th chapter and 18th verse, we are commanded to be filled with the Holy Ghost. A person who is full of the Holy Spirit deals much with the Scriptures. One of the things we lack in the present day is more Bible study. I think this nation is just waking up to the fact that we have had a famine. It is not the man now that makes a fine oration in the pulpit so much as it is a man that expounds the Word of God that we need. A boy once asked another boy how it was that he caught all the pigeons that were in the neighborhood. He said: 'Well, I tell you, it is because I feed them well.' If you feed the people well they will come; and people have got tired hearing a little more or less eloquence. The preachers have hitherto used the Bible merely as a text-book. They have taken their texts out of the Bible, and they have gone all over Christendom for their sermons. The result is that our churches are weak in spiritual power. But it is beginning to improve already. The churches are not now hunting after a man that will make a grand oration, so much as they are for a man that will unfold to them the Word of God. That is what the people want. If they can only get back to the Word of God, then we will have not just here and there a revival, but we will be in a revival all the time. The church will be constantly in a revived state. It is those Christians that are feeding on the Word of God that are revived all the while. There is something fresh about them, and people are glad to hear them talk.

"That Book Made me a Good Man"

As we come to study this Word of God, we want to keep in mind that it is the Word of God, not the Word of man; and that as the Word of God, it is true. I think the colored man was about as near the truth as one need be, when some infidel came to him and told him the Bible was not true. 'That Book not true? Massa, I was once a murderer, and a thief, and a blasphemer, and that Book made me a good man. That book must be true! If it is a bad book, it could not make such a bad man good.' That is argument enough; we do not need any more. Look around us;

if a man becomes a profligate, he begins to talk against the Bible; if he is upright he takes it as a lamp to his feet. We are never afraid of a man that tries to live according to the teachings of this book. This book is God's Word, and it will stand. Over the new Bible House recently built in London, England, are written these words, 'The Word of the Lord endureth forever.' That building will pass away, that city may pass away, like Babylon and Nineveh, and other cities that once flourished, but the Word of God shall endure forever. Not one word that God has spoken shall fall to the ground. We want also to bear in mind that the Bible is not a dry, uninteresting book, as a great many skeptics try to make out. They say, 'We want something new; we have outgrown that.' Why, the Word of God is the only new book in the world. All that the newspapers can do is to tell of things as they have taken place, but the Bible will tell of things that will take place. We do not consider the Bible enough as a whole. We just take up a word here and a word there, and a verse here and there, and a chapter here and there, and never take it up in any systematic way. We, therefore know very little about the Bible. I will guarantee that the bulk of Christians in America only read the Bible at family worship; and you will notice, too, that they have to put in a book-mark to tell where they left off the day before. You ask them an hour after what they have read, and they have forgotten all about it. Of course we cannot get much knowledge of the Bible in that way. When I was a boy I worked on a farm, and I hoed corn so poorly that when I left off I had to take a stick and mark the place, so I could tell next morning where I had stopped the night before. If I didn't, I would likely as not hoe the same row over again.

In order to understand the Bible we will have to study it carefully. I was told in California that the purest and best gold that they get they have to dig the deepest for; and so, in studying the Bible, we must dig deep. And there are a great many Christians walking on crutches in their Bible studying. They do not dare to examine for themselves. They go wondering what others say, what Edwards says, what the commentators say. Suppose you look and see for yourselves. God has given you your own mind to use. If we will go to the Word of God, and be willing to be taught by the Holy Ghost, God will teach us, and will unfold His blessed truth to us.

There are three books that every Christian ought to have, if he cannot have but three. The first is a Bible—one with good plain print that you can easily read. I am sick of these little fine types. It is a good thing to get a good-sized Bible, because you will grow old by and by, and your sight may grow poor and you won't want to give up the one you have been used to reading in after it has come to seem like a sort of a life-long companion. The next book to get is Cruden's Concordance. You cannot get on very well in Bible study without that. There is another book printed in this country by the Tract Society called the Scriptural Text Book. It was brought out first in London. These three books will be a wonderful help to you in studying the Word of God.

Do Not Read the Bible to Ease Your Conscience

Another thing: do not read the Word of God as I used to, just to ease your conscience. I had a rule to read two or three chapters every day. If I had not done it through the day, I would read them just before I went to bed to ease my conscience. I did not remember it perhaps an hour, but I kept the rule. You will never get much out of it in that way. It is a good way to hunt for something when you read it. Two words will give you the key to the whole Bible—Christ and Jesus. The Christ of the Old

Testament the Jesus of the New, and the two books explain each other. You may search for these words in your study.

Some time ago I went through the building where Prang's chromos are produced in Boston. They were bringing out a chromo of a prominent public man, and he showed me this picture in its different stages of progress. In the first stone there was no trace of a man's face; only a little tinge of color that did not suggest any shape. I saw the next stone, and still no face, and the third, and so on, and not until the fourth or fifth stone was there any likeness of a face at all. After a little it began to show, and yet not until I came to the fourteenth or fifteenth stone did it look at all like the man himself, and not until the twenty-sixth stone did it look as natural as life. That is the way it is when we read the Scripture. We take it up and do not see anything in it; we read it again, but see nothing. Again and again, and after you have read it twenty-five times, you will see the man Christ Jesus stamped on every page.

Study One Book at a Time

The Old Testament was written only to teach us who Christ was. Moses, the law, the prophets, they all testify to Christ. You take Christ out of the Old Testament and it is a sealed book to you. It has been a great help to me in studying the Bible to study one book at a time. Suppose you spend six months reading Genesis. Getting the key of that, you get the key to the whole Bible. Death, resurrection, and the whole story are told in Genesis. All in types, to be sure, and shadows that are brought out further on. There are eight great beginnings in Genesis—the beginning of creation, the beginning of marriage, the beginning of sin and death, of sacrifices, of the convenant, of the nation, and human race and Hebrew race. Take up these

CAMBERWELL HALL, LONDON, WHICH WAS BUILT EXPRESSLY FOR MR. MOODY'S MEETINGS.

eight beginnings, and see what they teach, and this key will unlock to you the rest of the Bible.

If you just take the Bible itself alone, without any other book to help you to interpret it, one passage will explain another. Instead of running after the interpretations of different men, let God interpret it to your soul. As Stephens said, Do not study it in the blue light of Presbyterianism, or the red light of Methodism, or the violet light of Episcopalianism, but study it in the light of Calvary. One man says, "I am a Romanist, and it has got to teach what Romanism teaches;" another says, "I am a Protestant, and it has got to teach me what Protestantism teaches." Take it up independent of these, and after you have dug its meaning out for yourself it will be so much sweeter to you.

Take The Bible Topically

Another way is to take it up topically. Suppose you spend three or four months reading all you can find about love; after that you will be full of love. Then take the word grace, and run through the Bible, reading all there is about grace. After I had been studying grace for two or three weeks, I got so full that one day I could not stay in my study any longer, and went out on the street and asked the first man I saw, if he knew anything about the grace of God. I suppose he thought I was crazy, but I was so full I had to talk to somebody. Then take up the subject of the blood, then the subject of Heaven. Some are troubled about assurance, and do not know whether they may have assurance of being saved or not; but take up the Bible, and let God speak to you about it. If you go into court, you will find that the lawyer just gets all the testimony he can on one point and he heaps it before the jury. If you want to convince men of any grand truth, just stick to that one point. Take up the Word, and get all the testimony you can. Bring in Moses and David and Joshua, and every apostle you can, and make them testify. If you read all the Bible says of forgiveness, before you have studied it a week, you will want to forgive every one.

Not Enough Bibles

People do not have enough Bibles. Once in my own Sunday school I asked all the children who had on borrowed boots to rise; no one rose. Then I asked all those who had on borrowed coats to rise; no one rose. Then I asked all those who had borrowed Testaments in their hands to rise, and they all went up; and I said I want you all to bring your Bibles with you, and about two months after that it would have done your soul good to see every child come with a Bible. A great many people carry their hymn-books, but it is better to carry your Bible. When I was in Scotland I had to keep my eyes open, and preach exactly according to the Word, or some old Scotchman would rise and draw his Bible on me, and I would know it pretty quick. A man got up in Parliament a few years ago and made a grand speech full of eloquence, that took over four hours. He carried all the people with him in one voice. When he got through a man got up and read two or three lines of the law of England, and bursted the whole speech in a minute.

Some men are very eloquent when there is not one word of truth in what they say, but you cannot know it, because you have not the Bible knowledge. There are a good many people who wonder that they do not have joy in their religion. The reason is that they do not feed upon the Word; that is where they get the joy. If we neglect the manna that God has given us for our soul's nourishment, of course we won't have joy; but people whine and say it is a great mystery to them that they do not have joy as others do. See how happy some are! Why? They feed upon the Word of God. That is why. They are not living upon the old stale matter of the conversion that they had long ago. It makes me sick to hear men tell how happy they were long ago when they were first converted. The idea that they should not be happier since then! We ought to grow in grace and be advancing. Suppose I should keep telling my wife, "I loved you very much when I married you!" That is the way many treat the Lord, telling Him how much they loved Him once.

Have a Bible You Can Mark

About bringing your Bibles with you—just have a Bible you can mark. If I should go and hear one of my friends preach, and he unfolded some grand and glorious truth, I would put a few words down upon the margin of the Bible that would just give me the key to the whole, and I would not forget it. By doing this, when you heard a good sermon you could go and preach it to other people. I hope the day will come when if a man hears a good sermon in the morning, he will be so full of it he will have to go and preach it over again in some locality where they have not heard it. If the lawyers and merchants would only do that they would make better missionaries than the hired ones. I think more of this Bible in my hand than of all the other Bibles in New York. If I had come without this Bible I would have been lonesome. I have carried it so long I have got used to it. Buy a good Bible, one that won't wear out, with a good flexible cover that will fold around you. Button up your coat over it and keep it close to your heart. You can mark your texts in it and know where to look for them at any time, and they will all be glad to see you in any prayer-meeting. There will be something fresh about you that will make you always welcome.

An Englishman said to me, "Did you ever study the book of Job?" "No," I said, "not particularly." "You ought to," said he; "it is a wonderful book; if you get the key to that, you get the key to the whole Bible." "That is singular," said I. "I thought Job was more of a poetical book; how do you make it out?" He said the first division represents Adam in Eden, a perfect man untried; the second head represents his fall; the third says "The wisdom of the world came to restore Job." You cannot," he said, "find any wisdom in all the books equal to the wisdom of those three men, but they could not help poor Job out of his difficulty."

Just so is the world trying to put Adam back again; they try to amend him but they cannot do it. Your philosophers cannot restore Adam to his original perfection. What can the geologist tell you about the Rock of Ages? What can the astronomer tell you of the Bright and Morning Star? The fact is Job could not stand their treatment. He could stand his boils and his scolding wife, but he could not stand the way the wise men treated him. The fourth head is about Elihu; he came and brought grace and that is what Job wanted. He did not want law; Job was a righteous man in his own conceit up to this time. He said, I have fed the hungry, I have clothed the naked, I did this and that—I! I! I!—that was Job's cry then. He was a great man; if we had him now we would make him a leader in some Presbyterian Church and be glad to get him.

God Speaks

Under the fifth head God speaks. He says, "Gird up your loins like a man, I will put a few questions to you." The moment Job got a glimpse of God he was a different man; his self-righteousness was gone. When I go into the inquiry-rooms some days some have their heads down on their hands, and I cannot get a word out of them. I say to myself, such persons are near to God. But some are flippant and glib, and say, Why does God do this and why does God do that? God alone restores Adam to his lost state, and in his restoration he is better than he was at the beginning, because his last state is eternal. When he is restored to Heaven there is no more banishment.

Jesus the Key to the New Testament

Up to this point I have tried to show you that Christ was the key to the Old Testament, now I will show that Jesus is the key to the New. Christ was tempted as we are, but He had not the same enemy to overcome. He that knew no sin took upon Him ours. One of the saddest mistakes that young converts make, is that of merely feeding upon sermons instead of the Word of God. You know it is quite an event in the family when the child gets so it can feed itself. We want to learn as quick as possible to feed ourselves. If we will only take our Bible and make up our minds that we will depend upon our own study of the Bible, He will help us understand it. If we try to study it in one way, and we find we do not like it, let us take up another, and if that fails, try another. Some time ago my wife was very anxious that I should learn to like tomatoes. She liked them and she wanted me to like them. So she got me to try them, first raw, with vinegar, and sugar and pepper, but I could not bear them; then she fixed them another way, but still I could not eat them. One day I came home, and she said, "I have cooked the tomatoes a new way." Well, I tried them again once more, and I thought they were the best things I ever tasted. So, if you take up the Bible one way and don't like it, take it up another way, and keep trying until you find a way in which it will unfold itself to you. You won't find people that are in love with the study of this Word carrying a dime novel through the street. They won't walk up Fifth Avenue with a trashy book in their hands. They will be reading books that will help them understand the Bible. You will be so anxious to get off alone and have a feast upon it, that you will have to reprove yourself for not going out and working more.

There is Danger on That Head

There are a great many who are all the time feeding upon the Word—not in this country, I am sorry to say. I would rather be as they are elsewhere than as they are in this country, where they neither feed on the Word, nor study either. But some people are always taking in, taking in, and not as if they intended to give it out. Some one said we ought to fill our minds like they fill a vessel in the Mississippi river. A vessel goes up the Mississippi river, and takes in its cargo on the way, always with a view to taking it out. They put the freight that is coming out first on top. So let us store away our knowledge with a view of getting it out again, and not just to lumber up our heads with a lot of stuff that we never intend to use. Let us try to put these truths where we can get them out and give them to some one else. Now, I see some people who are here every night. They get the best seats every solitary night, and for the last six weeks they have been here every night, regularly. And when they go into the inquiry-room, you cannot get a word out of them; they won't as much as lift a little finger; their arms are folded. They are always standing round the building an hour before the doors are open. Here they are every night, always taking in and never giving anything out. But if we get a good thing let us go and give it to some one else.

Some one said he always studied the Bible with three R's in his mind—Ruin, Redemption, and Regeneration. When I open the Word of God I keep that idea in view. There are three corner-stones that a man must know—first, that he is ruined, or he does not want a redeemer; second, there is redemption through the blood; and third, regeneration by the Holy Ghost, born of the Spirit.

The Four Gospels

I have in my Bible here the keynotes to the four books of the New Testament. I will give you my idea of a few of them. Matthew, when he wrote about Christ, writes of Him as the Son of David. He writes from the standpoint of a man that had belonged to the government. If you want to find out about Christ as the Son of David, you will have to turn to Matthew. These four men, Matthew, Mark, Luke and John, wrote from different standpoints. Matthew brings out Christ as the Royal Son of David, as the Heir, as Abraham's successor, or from the line of Abraham to take the throne of David. Mark takes Him as a servant. You will find Him going here and there as a servant doing His master's will. Luke brings Him out as the Son of Man, as coming in contact with man; and then we find in the Gospel of John he brings Him out as the Son of God. Luke and Matthew and Mark do not go and trace Him back as John does. John goes past Adam and Abraham and Zachariah and Malachi—sweeps past them all, and brings Him out of the bosom of the Father; and he has with one stroke of the pen settled the question of the divinity of Jesus Christ. No one can read the Gospel of John and believe it, and still doubt the divinity of Jesus Christ, and believe Him to have been a mere man. He spoke of Him as the Son of God, a stranger starting out in the world alone. All through John, He was meeting sinners alone. He met Nicodemus alone, and the woman at the well. I have been interested, some time ago, in taking up for study the characters that had personal interviews with the Son of God. There were nineteen. Peter had two such interviews. No one knows what they said. Take up the history of these nineteen persons and see how they were blessed, unless, indeed, they rejected Him, as Pilate did?

One Word at a Time

Take one word at a time, and run through the Bible and read all you can find on that point. Take words "I Am." When the Lord sent Moses to Egypt, Moses was reluctant to go, and he said as a last excuse, "If I tell them that I have been sent, whom shall I tell them has sent me?" And the Lord said, "Tell them I Am." Some one said that was the same as a blank check given to Moses; and that when he got down in Egypt and they wanted water, he just filled in the check with water, and they got it. Take the word "verily" of St. John. Whenever you see that word, you may feel sure there is some great truth coming after it. Some time ago I was blessed in taking up the seven blessings of Revelation for study. Some people say you cannot understand Revelation. They say the deep theologians can understand it, but common people cannot. Why, it is the one book that tells of the downfall of the devil, and the devil does not want us to find that out, so he says to us, "You cannot understand Revelation." It is the one book in the Bible that opens with a benediction. It tells us of the marriage supper of the Lamb. We get a great deal in Revelation that is not found in any other part of the Bible. All Scripture is given by inspiration, and all is profitable for reproof and correction, that a man of God may be thoroughly furnished. We want to take the Bible from Genesis to Revelation. Do not let us join the unbelieving, scoffing world that says we cannot understand Revelation. "Blessed are those that watch. Blessed are those that keep from the world. Blessed are the dead that die in the Lord, for they shall rest from their labors. Blessed are they that have part in the first resurrection." Let us have a part in the first resurrection

And the last is, "Blessed are they that shall be at the marriage supper of the Lamb." Take these seven blessings and put them together and study them.

Six Things Worth Knowing

I take up one chapter in the Epistle of John with the word "know." There are six things worth knowing. The first verse and third chapter says, "We know He is manifested to take away sin." That is what Jesus came for. We know it because God said it. Some people say it makes no difference what a man believes if he is sincere in his belief. Why it makes all the difference in the world. What we believe we know to be true. We are not deluded and deceived into believing it. The Spirit of God has borne witness to its truth.

Take the third thing worth knowing, in the 14th verse. "We know that we have passed from death unto life." How many in this audience to-night know that. Suppose I should ask this audience, how many could say they knew it? Some people think it is not the privilege of any one to know that. But this is a great mistake. If I did not know it now I would not go to my dinner this day or to my bed this night until I did know it. It is worth knowing. Christ came to call us from death to life. Do you think we have to go on in this terrible uncertainty not knowing whether we are saved or not. God does not leave us with that uncertainty. But if you have malice and hatred against some one, that is a sure sign that you have not got the spirit of Christ. You may know you have not been born of God, for God is love.

The fifth thing worth knowing is in the 24th verse, "We know that He abideth with us, by the Spirit which He hath given us." If we are out backbiting our neighbors, and living like the world, it is good evidence that we have not been born of God.

The sixth thing worth knowing is the best of all. It is in the 2d verse: "Beloved, now are we the sons of God." John wanted to disabuse them of the idea that they were not sons of Heaven. I heard a man pray in a prayer-meeting: "When we come to die may we be the sons of God." But "now are we the sons of God," it says. "It does not yet appear what we shall be," The world does not yet know the difference, but it will be revealed by-and-by. There was a little boy in Boston who was probably the richest person in all Boston. The little child did not know that he was heir to a great estate. So, Christians, many of them, don't know that they are heirs to all things. We will come into possession of our inheritance by-and-by. What God wants is to have us live for that inheritance. He has had it in store for us where He dwells. Satan cannot get there to get it out, though he would like to if he could. It is kept for us, and He keeps us for it. The day I first got hold of those truths I could not hold my peace. When people came in I said to them, "I have got some honey out of the rock," and I gave it to my friends. So we can help one another in our wilderness journey.

Whom is it Written to?

The power of the Holy One is unlimited. If you have relatives who have no faith, and they are running down these meetings, do not get discouraged. The Lord God is able to save them. In the first twelve chapters of John, you will find Christ dealing with sinners altogether. In the 8th chapter of John, they are going to tell Him that they doubt His word. In the 10th chapter, He is going to have His sheep in spite of those unbelieving Jews. In the 11th chapter, the Jews are going to put Lazarus out of the way, because on account of Lazarus's testimony all men were believing. From the 13th to the 17th chapters, you will find Christ dealing with His Church. When you take a chapter like that, you should consider whom the chapter is addressed to. We would not have any trouble about the doctrine of election if we considered that it was addressed to the Church, to believers. Suppose I should find a dispatch on the floor, saying, "Your wife is dead," I would say, "My wife dead! How can that be, and I not know of it?" But suppose I should find on the back of the envelope that it was addressed to some one else, and not to me, the case would be different. We must understand whom it is written to. The whole Bible is **not** directed to sinners. A good deal of it is addressed to certain classes and individuals, and a great deal is addressed to the whole world. In the 13th of John, he has Christ dealing with the disciples.

How Christ Dealt With Sinners

There are certain passages addressed to the wicked, and certain passages to God's people. Very often a sinner will get hold of some comforting word addressed to a Christian, and he will go and take comfort in it when he has no right to, any more than I would have a right to read some one's letters. In the 17th chapter of John, Christ is with the Father. In the 18th chapter of John, Christ is in the hands of His enemies. And so you just take any one book and divide it up like that. Take the subject of the gifts of Christ and, with the word gifts, learn all that is written of the gifts of Christ and the gifts of Satan. For Christ's gifts there are the bread of Life and the Holy Spirit and peace, and joy, and love, and mercy, and the morning star, and mansions. Take these gifts and put them down, and then put down beside them the gifts of Satan for serving him, and compare them. See if you will turn your back upon all these blessed gifts of God for the sake of the few fleeting moments of time here, and the baubles which, when you have got them, do not satisfy you.

I want to speak of the seven different characters in John, and how Christ dealt with them.

Suppose we could divide up these sinners here under these seven heads. Turn to the 7th chapter of John, and see how Christ dealt with that respectable sinner, Nicodemus. He set him aside entirely. He did not put a new piece into the old garment; the Lord does not patch a man's coat. He gives him a new coat throughout. He told Nicodemus he must be born again. In the 4th chapter, see how Christ deals with one who has fallen. She is not very respectable, but He gives her the water of life. We cannot find any class of people in New York that has not its representative in the Bible, and Christ's dealings with them. A nobleman came to Him, whose child was ill. He told him to go home, his child would live; He did not give the nobleman any medicine for his child, but the man took His word, and when he got home he found the child was nearly well, and that it was better from the seventh hour, when he had spoken to Christ.

"Take up Thy Bed And Walk"

If some poor tramp should read these words who has not got any friends, or anywhere to lay his head, a poor miserable sinner, if he will turn to the 5th chapter of John, he will know how Christ will deal with him. There was just such a poor beggar at the pool. Christ asked him if he would like to touch the waters; he said, "I would like to be put in, but I haven't any one to help me; I am lame;" and the Lord said, "Take up thy bed and walk." He cured him by a word.

I can imagine in the gallery there is a man who says: "I wish there was some class in the Bible that represented me. I have broken the law. If the law should get hold of me I would have to go to prison for twenty years; the police do not know; I have covered up my sin. I wish there was something in the Bible for me." Well, there is; there is. Turn to the 8th chapter of John. You will see how Christ dealt with a woman whom the law would have stoned to death. They dragged her into the presence of Christ, saying, "The law of Moses says, 'stone her to death;' what sayest thou?" He stooped and wrote on the ground as if He paid no attention; then He raised up and said, "He that is without sin among you, let him cast the first stone," and He went on writing on the ground. When He looked up again the crowd had disappeared. He said, "Where are thy accusers? Go thou and sin no more." If you want to know how Christ dealt with sinners, go to the Bible. There is no sinner here who has not his representative in the Bible.

CHAPTER XXVI.

His Creed—Three Cardinal Truths

MR. MOODY was the most faithful advocate of every truth presented in the Word of God. He seemed to have the most wonderful conception of all the great principles underlying the plan of salvation. His belief in the atonement was never to be shaken, and his uncompromising position as touching the inspiration of the Scriptures was always commented upon by those who heard him preach for any length of time, but there are three special truths with which his ministry was particularly identified in the judgment of many of his friends.

His View Concerning The Word of God.

The first was his view concerning the Word of God in itself. The last time I heard him speak in Philadelphia he said: " It is always the greatest pleasure to me to speak on the subject of the Bible. I think I would rather preach about the Word of God than anything else, because I think it is the best thing in the world, and we cannot possibly overestimate the value of Bible study. One must keep constantly drinking at this fountain if he is to be used of God. A man stood up in one of our meetings and said he hoped for enough out of the series of meetings to last him all his life. I told him, that was perfect nonsense; he might as well try to eat enough breakfast at one time to last him his lifetime. These meetings are a failure, if they do not bring you in touch with God's Word, and enable you to drink deeply there." When I was with him in Pittsburg, I took the following notes from his morning address.

"We do not ask men and women to believe in the Bible without inquiry. It is not natural to man to accept the things of God without question, and, if you are to be ready to give an answer or a reason for your faith to every one that asks you, you must first of all be a diligent student of the Word of God yourself. Do not be a doubter because you think it is intellectual. 'Give us your covictions,' said a German writer; 'we have enough doubts of our own,' and if you are filled with the Word of God there will not be any doubts. But some one will say, 'I wish you would prove to me that the Bible is true.' My answer is, the Book will prove itself if you will let it. There is real power in it. 'For this cause also we thank God without ceasing, because when ye received the Word of God which ye heard of us, ye received it not as the word of men, but as it is, in truth, the Word of God, which continually worketh also in you that believe.'

"It is not the work of men to make other men believe; but it is the work of the Holy Ghost. It is an awful responsibility to have a Bible and to neglect its teachings. What if God should withdraw it and say, I will not trouble you with it longer?

What To Do With Difficult Passages

"But some one else asks, 'what am I going to do when I come to a thing that I cannot understand?' I answer, 'I thank God that there are heights in it that I have never scaled, and depths in it that I have never sounded, because if I could understand it all, I would know that a man not greater than myself had written it. When it is beyond me in places, I know that God must have written it. 'It is one of the strongest proofs that the Bible must have come from God, that the wise men in all the ages have been digging down into it, and never yet have sounded its depths.'

"A man came to me with a difficult passage some time ago and said, 'Moody, what would you do with that?' I answered, 'I don't do anything with it.' 'How do you understand it?' I don't understand it.' 'How do you explain it?' 'I don't explain it.' 'Well, then, what do yon do with it?' 'I don't do anything with it.' 'But you believe it, don't you?' 'O, yes, I believe it, but there are lots of things that I believe that I cannot understand and that I cannot make plain. **I do** not know anything about higher mathematics but I believe in them, with all my heart. I do not understand astronomy, but I certainly believe in astronomy.'

He was always most intense when he said, "But somebody will say, 'You surely do not believe in the story of Jonah and the whale. That's entirely out of date.' I want to say most emphatically that I do not believe it, and when men turn away from this story, I think it is the master stroke of Satan to try to make us doubt the resurrection, for Jesus used it as an illustration of this doctrine. The book of Jonah says, 'God prepared a great fish to swallow Jonah.' Couldn't God make a fish large enough to swallow him? If God can create a world out of nothing, I think he can create a fish large enough to swallow a million men. Don't you?

Don't Cut Anything Out of the Bible

"Then there are other people who say, 'I believe in the Bible, but not in the supernatural side of it.' They go on reading the Bible with a pen-knife, cutting out this and that and the other thing. Now, if I have a right to cut out a certain portion of the Bible, I think my friend has the same right, and you would have a queer book, if everybody cut out what he wanted to. Every liar would cut out everything about lying. Every drunkard would cut out what he did not like. It is a most absurd statement for a man to say he will have nothing to do with the supernatural. If you are going to throw off the supernatural, you might as well burn your Bibles at once. For if you take the supernatural out of the book, you take Jesus Christ out of it.

"Then, I want to say, also, that it is absurd for any one to say that he believes in the New Testament and not in the Old. Do you not know that of the thirty-nine books of the Old Testament, it is recorded that our Lord made quotations from over twenty? Over 800 passages in the Old Testament are quoted or mentioned in the New. In Matthew there are about 100 quotations from twenty books in the Old Testament. In Luke, thirty-four quotations from thirteen books, and in John eleven quotations from six books. In the four Gospels there are more than 160 quotations from the Old Testament.

Christ Referred to the Old Testament

"If the Old Testament Scriptures are not true, do you think Christ would have so often referred to them, and said, 'The Scriptures must be fulfilled,' and, if He could use the Old Testament, let us use it. May God deliver us from the one-sided Christian who reads only the New Testament and talks against the Old.

"It is a great thing to study the Bible. I once heard Dr. Pierson say there are four things necessary in studying the Bible: Admit, submit, commit and transmit.

"First: Admit its truth.

"Second: Submit to its teachings.

"Third: Commit it to memory, and

"Fourth: Transmit to someone else.

"And, if we are to study the Bible, there are three books which I think every Christian ought to have. First is a Bible with large print; the second, a Cruden's Concordance; the third, a topical text book; and if we have these three books, anyone of us might become successful students of this old book.

"Dr. Pierson also says, whenever we read any portion of the Bible we ought to remember the five P's:

"Place where written.

"Person by whom written.

"People to whom written.

"Purpose for which written.

"Period at which written.

"Let me indicate some suggestions:

1st. Always carry a Bible with you.
2nd. Mark it.
3rd. Set apart a portion of each day to study it.
4th. Ask God to open your eyes to its truth.
5th. Believe that God wrote this word to you, and act accordingly.
6th. Commit some portion of the Bible to memory each day.
7th. Do not be satisfied with simply reading a chapter daily; study the meaning of at least one verse in it.

"But remember this, that the Bible is every whit inspired. God has said it, and God always speaks the truth. 'Heaven and earth shall pass away, but My Word shall not pass away.'"

The Second Coming of Christ

The second great cardinal truth with which Mr. Moody was so closely identified in his world-wide ministry was the second coming of Christ. He firmly believed that Christ was coming before the Millennium, and not after it. He was never more eloquent than when he was speaking of prophecy and its fulfillment. "Some people tell us," he said, "that it is useless to try to understand prophecy. 'The Church is not agreed about it; better let it alone, and deal only with those things that have been fulfilled.' Paul did not say that. He said, 'All Scripture is profitable.' If these people are right, he ought to have said, 'Some Scripture is profitable, but you cannot understand the prophecies, so better let them alone.' 'And you can't understand about this second coming,' what nonsense this is! If God did not mean to have us study the prophecies, He would not have put them in the Bible. Some of them have been fulfilled. Some are being fulfilled, and all shall be. The three great comings are foretold in the Word of God. First, that Christ should come; that has been fulfilled. Second, that the Holy Ghost should come, and that has been fulfilled. Third, that our Lord should return from Heaven, and for this we are told to watch and wait.

" Whoever neglects this truth has only a mutilated Gospel, for the Bible deals not only with the death and sufferings of Christ, but also of his return to reign in honor and glory. His second coming is mentioned and referred to over three hundred times, and yet I was in the Church fifteen or sixteen years before I ever heard a sermon on it. Every church makes much of baptism, but in all of Paul's epistles baptism is spoken of only thirteen times; the return of the Lord fifty times.

"We are also told in the Scriptures just how He is to come. The angel said, in like manner as you have seen him go. We know that He went up with His flesh and bones, and we certainly know that when He comes back again, He shall come just as He went away from His disciples; but it is also true that of that day and hour no man knoweth, but it is well for us that we do not know. If Christ had said, 'I will not come back for eighteen hundred years,' none of His disciples would have begun to watch for Him until the time was near. The last chapter of John gives us a text which seems to settle the whole matter. Peter asks the question about John : 'Lord, what shall this man do?' Jesus said unto him, 'If I will that he tarry till I come, what is that to thee? Follow thou me.' Then this saying went abroad among the brethren that that disciple should not die. They certainly did not think that the coming of the Lord meant death. There was a great difference between these two things in their minds, and when any one says that the coming of Christ means the death of the Christian, he has only to put this thought into the Bible as he reads, to see how ridiculous it is. Look at that account of the last hour of Christ with His disciples. What does He say to them? 'If I go away I will send death for you to bring you to me, or that I will send an angel after you?' Not at all. He says, '*I* will come again and receive you unto myself.'

Will the World Grow Better or Worse?

"Some people shake their heads and say that this thought is too deep for the most of us; such things ought not to be told to young converts. Paul wrote these things to young converts among the Thessalonians, and I believe there is no Christian to-day, whether he be young or old, but what he can get a great inspiration out of this truth. At one time I thought the world would grow better and better until Christ could stay away no longer, but in studying the Bible, I do not find any place where God says so. I find that the world is to grow worse and worse, then, after a while, Christ is to come in power and glory. Some people think this is a new and strange doctrine, but I say that it is not. Many of the most spiritual men in the world are firm in this faith. Spurgeon preached it, and I know of no reason why Christ might not come before I finish this sermon.

"There is another thought I want to bring to your attention, and that is, that Christ will bring our friends with Him when He comes; all who have died in the Lord are to be with Him when He descends from His Father's throne into the air. 'Behold, I come quickly,' said Christ to John. Three times it is repeated in the last chapter of the Bible, and almost the closing words of the Bible are the prayer, 'Even so, come, Lord Jesus.'

"The world waited for the first coming four thousand years, and then He came. He was here only thirty-three years and went away, when He left us a promise that He would come again, and, as the world watched for His first coming, so we wait for His appearing the second time unto salvation. But you also read, 'for in such an hour as we think not, the Son of Man cometh.'"

The Work of the Holy Ghost.

The third great truth for which Mr. Moody stood, and of which his own great life was a powerful illustration was the truth touching the work of the Holy Ghost.

"When I was first converted, I spoke in a Sabbath school, and there seemed to be a great deal of interest, and quite a number rose for prayer, and I remember I went out quite rejoiced; but an old man followed me out—I have never seen him since. I never had seen him before, and don't even know his name—but he caught hold of my hand and gave me a little bit of advice. I didn't know what he meant at the time, but he said, 'Young man, when you speak again, honor the Holy Ghost.' I was hastening off to another church to speak, and all the way over, it kept ringing in my ears, 'Honor the Holy Ghost,' and I said to myself, 'I wonder what the old man means.' I have found out since what he meant, and I think that all that have been to work in the vineyard of the Lord have learned that lesson, that if we honor Him in our efforts to do good, He will honor us and work through us; but if we don't honor Him, we will surely break down.

"The only work that is going to stand to eternity is the work done by the Holy Ghost, and not by any one of us. We may be used as His instruments, but the work that will stand to eternity is that done by the Holy Ghost; and every conversion in these meetings, that is not by the power of the Holy Ghost, will not stand. They may be impressions that will last for a few weeks or months, but then they will pass away like the morning cloud; and I firmly believe that if a man or woman be not converted by the Holy Ghost, we will not see them in Heaven.

The Holy Ghost a Person

"I really believe I was a Christian ten years before I believed it. I went into a church once and heard an old minister say that the Holy Ghost was a person. I thought the old man was wrong, and could not believe that the Holy Ghost was a person. I did not know my Bible then as well as I do now, but I went home and got my Bible, and went to work to study it out; and I have been thoroughly convinced ever since that the Holy Ghost is a person as much as God the Father is, and as much as Jesus Christ the Son is. Some may say that it is a mystery, and there are a good many things that are mysterious on their face. Now turn to the 14th chapter of John, 16th and 17th verses: 'And I will pray the Father, and He shall give you another Comforter, that He may abide with you forever. Even the Spirit of Truth, whom the world cannot receive because it seeth Him not, neither knoweth Him; but ye know Him, for He dwelleth with you, and shall be in you.'

Now, if the Holy Ghost were not a person, Christ would not have said 'Who.' To be sure He is a spirit, but at the same time He is a person, the same as God the Father is. God is a spirit, and yet He is a person. Three times in this last verse it says 'Him' and once 'Who.' Then in the 26th verse of the same chapter: 'But the Comforter, which is the Holy Ghost, whom the Father will send in my name, He shall teach you all things, and bring all things to your remembrance whatsoever I have said unto you.' Then there are a good many other verses, and I want to call your attention to one or two more, just to show this fact, that He is a person. Whenever Christ spoke of the Holy Ghost, He always spoke of Him as 'He' or 'Him,' and we won't honor the Holy Ghost unless we make Him a person, and one of the persons of the Trinity—the Father, Son and Holy Ghost.

The Real Fruit is Love.

"It is the work of the Holy Ghost to impart love. Just turn to Romans v. 5: 'And hope maketh not ashamed; because the love of God is shed abroad in our hearts by the Holy Ghost, which is given unto us.' The real fruit that we look for in a young convert is love, and I think it is one of the strongest proofs that this religion of Jesus Christ is divine, that it is the same all the world over. Even in the heart of China you will find, if a man is converted, he will love his enemies. The love of God is in that man's heart. What do we as Christians feel and want to-day? What is the great lack of the Church? Why are so many complaining about the coldness of the Church? It is because we have not got this love. If the Holy Ghost is a power in the Church, shedding abroad love in our hearts, there won't be any complaint.

"A great many Christians are like Lazarus when he came forth—he was bound hand and foot; but Christ said, 'Loose him and let him go.' And so Christians want to feel that liberty they should feel when Christ calls them to be His disciples. Where the Spirit of the Lord is, there is liberty. Many think to themselves before they get up to speak: 'Now, what will Mrs. B. say when I get up, if I don't talk as well as the minister?' and 'Oh, if I could talk as well as Brother A., wouldn't I give my testimony quickly! But I haven't any eloquence, and cannot speak like an orator.'

"Don't you know, my friend, it is not the most fluent man that has the greatest effect with a jury? It is the man who tells the truth. And in speaking of your experience, God will help you if you trust in Him, and you will find after a simple trial that you have perfect liberty. The trouble is we have a great many Christians who have only got as far as the 3d chapter of John, and so far as liberty to come out and speak up for God is concerned, they don't know anything about it. We want this spirit of liberty so as to be qualified for God's work. A friend of mine told me once that when he went to a boarding-house he could always tell who the boarders were, for they never alluded to family matters, but sat down to the table and talked of outside matters; but when the son came in, he would go into the sitting-room to see if there were any letters, and inquire after the family, and show in many ways his interest in the household. It doesn't take five minutes to tell that he is not a boarder, and that the others are. And so it is with the Church of God. You see these boarders in church every Sunday morning, but they don't take any interest. They come to criticise, and that is about all that constitutes a Christian nowadays. They are boarders in the House of God, and we have got too many boarders. What we want is liberty.

How the Judge Became a Working Christian.

"A friend of mine asked a judge in his church to go out to a schoolhouse in the country with him one day, where he was going to preach. He said to the judge that he would like to have him go, and the judge said he would like to go along. He told the judge he would like to have him speak to the people. The judge said, 'Oh, I could not do that.' 'Why can't you? You can

CONGREGATIONAL CHURCH, EAST NORTHFIELD, which Mr. Moody attended and where the funeral services were held.

speak in your court well enough without any trouble. Why cannot you speak here? Suppose you just try it?' When they got out there, the judge refused to do so, but the minister said, 'I want to put the judge into the witness box and question him.' And the judge got his lips open at last, and told how he was converted, and how the Spirit of God came down upon him. And there was a mighty power in what he said, and the result was that many were converted, and the judge has been a working Christian ever since. I think there are hundreds bound, as he was, by station.

"A man who had been a professing Christian for three years I met at a meeting, and I knew he had been a professing Christian, and I supposed, of course, he had prayed in public. I noticed that he hesitated when I asked him, but he rose, and as soon as he opened his lips, the words came easily. I heard him tell a friend afterward that that night he felt as if he had been converted a second time.

The Holy Ghost Testifies of Christ.

"I believe the world would have forgotten Christ's death as soon as they forgot His birth, if it had not been for the Holy Ghost. It had only been thirty years since His birth, and all those wonderful scenes had happened in Bethlehem and it was well known in Jerusalem; yet, it seems to have been forgotten until Christ came. And they would have forgotten His death if it had not been for the Holy Ghost. He came to testify for Jesus Christ that He had risen. He saw Him in Heaven, and He came to tell us that He was there at the right hand of God. He convinced men on the day of Pentecost, three thousand of them. He does not talk of Himself, but of Christ. In the 15th chapter of John, the 26th verse, it says, 'But when the Comforter is come, whom I will send unto you from the Father, even the Spirit of Truth, which proceedeth from the Father, He shall testify of me.'

"A man came to me the other day and said he was going where my wife and family are, and wanted to know if I had any message to send. Well, I sent them a message; but suppose when that man went down there, that he should go and see my wife and should begin to talk about himself, and not say a word about me. That would not cheer their hearts; they would want to hear about me. That would make their hearts warm. The Holy Ghost teaches us this lesson of self-forgetfulness. Every one of us Christians wants more of the Holy Ghost. Let us all give ourselves up to the influence of His Spirit, who will lead us on to liberty and life and peace and joy.

Three Classes of Christians.

"It seems to me that we have got about three classes of Christians. The first class in the 3d chapter of John, were those who had got to Calvary and there got life. They believed on the Son and were saved, and there they rested satisfied. They did not seek anything higher. Then, in the 4th chapter of John, we come to a better class of Christians. There it was a well of living water bubbling up. There are a few of these, but they are not a hundredth part of the first class. But the best class is in the 7th chapter of John, 'Out of his belly shall flow rivers of living water.' That is the kind of Christian we ought to be.

"When I was a boy, I used to have to pump water for the cattle. Ah, how many times I have pumped with that old right hand until it ached! and how many times I used to pump when I could not get any water, and I was taught that when the pump was dry I must pour a pail of water down the pump, and then I could get the water up. And that is what Christians want—a well of living water. We will have plenty of grace to spare; all we need ourselves and plenty for others. We have got into the way now of digging artesian wells better. They don't pump now to get the water, but when they dig the well they cut down through the gravel and through the clay, perhaps one thousand or two thousand feet, not stopping when they can pump the water up, but they cut to a lower stratum, and the water flows up abundantly of itself. And so we ought, every one of us to be like artesian wells. God has got grace enough for every one of us, and if we were only full of the Holy Ghost what power we would have! The influence of these meetings would be felt through the whole country. A learned doctor said once, speaking of Christ's holiness, 'You fill a tumbler of water to the brim and then just touch it, and the water flows out; and so Christ was so full of truth that when the woman touched Him, virtue flowed out and healed her.' Every one of us should be as full of the Holy Ghost as this, and then men will see that we have an unseen power. We must not be satisfied with just having life, but we want this power. How many times we have preached and taught, and it has been like the wind! And why? Because our hearts were not full, and we did not have that anointing.

We Have to be Very Humble.

"Some one asked a minister, if he had ever received a second blessing since he was converted. 'What do you mean?' was his reply, 'I have received ten thousand since the first.' A great many think because they have been filled once, they are going to be full for all time after; but O, my friends, we are leaky vessels, and have to be kept right under the fountain all the time in order to keep full. If we are going to be used by God we have to be very humble. A man that lives close to God will be the humblest of men. I heard a man say that God always chooses the vessel that is close at hand. Let us keep near Him. But we will have to keep down in the dust; God won't choose a man that is conceited.

The moment we lift up our head and think we are something and somebody, He lays us aside. If we want this power, we have to give God all the glory. I believe the reason we do not get this power more than we do, is because we do not know how to use it. We would be taking all the credit to ourselves and saying, 'Don't I do a great work?' and begin and boast about it. There are hundreds and thousands I believe that God would take up and use and give us a great baptism if we would only give Him the glory. We have not learned the lesson of humility yet, that we are nothing and God is everything."

A Blessed Experience.

In the city of Glasgow, some years ago, Mr. Moody related an incident which is given here in his own words, from which we get a glimpse of his superior life, and from which we are led to believe that in this, as in everything else, he was a great illustration of the truths he taught to others:

"I can myself go back almost twelve years and remember two holy women who used to come to my meetings. It was delightful to see them there, for when I began to preach, I could tell by the expression of their faces they were praying for me. At the close of the Sabbath evening services they would say to me, 'We have been praying for you.' I said, 'Why don't you pray for the people?' They answered, 'You need power,' 'I need power,' I said to myself; 'why, I thought I had power.' I had a large Sabbath school and the largest congregation in Chicago. There were some conversions at the time, and I was in a sense satisfied. But right along these two godly women kept praying for me, and their earnest talk about 'the anointing for special service' set me thinking. I asked them to come and talk with me, and we got down on our knees. They poured out their hearts, that I might receive the anointing of the Holy Ghost. And there came a great hunger into my soul. I knew not what it was. I began to cry as I never did before. The hunger increased. I really felt that I did not want to live any longer if I could not have this power for service. I kept on crying all the time that God would fill me with His Spirit. Well, one day, in the city of New York—O, what a day! I cannot describe it; I seldom refer to it; it is almost too sacred an experience to me. Paul had an experience of which he never spoke for fourteen years. I can only say, God revealed himself to me, and I had such an experience of His love that I had to ask Him to stay His hand.

"I went to preaching again. The sermons were not different; I did not present any new truths, and yet hundreds were converted. I would not be placed back where I was before that blessed experience if you would give me all Glasgow. It is a sad day when the convert goes into the church, and that is the last you hear of him. If, however, you want this power for some selfish end, as for example, to gratify your ambition, you will not get it. 'No flesh,' says God, 'shall glory in my presence.' May he empty us of self and fill us with His presence."

CHAPTER XXVII.

The Funeral

IT would be difficult to imagine a more representative company of Christian workers than that which assembled about the casket holding all that was mortal of him who was said by many to have been the most remarkable man of this generation. The friends had been gathering for two days. The Holiday joys in their own homes and the natural desire that every man has to be with his own family at such a season of the year could not keep them from paying this last tribute to the man who had been a friend, indeed more than a friend to every one of them; for, if ever any one came to know D. L. Moody well, he loved him. Paul once wrote in his Epistle to the Philippians, "I thank my God for every remembrance of you," and all who came close to this man of God could write the same concerning him.

So Like Mr. Moody Himself

The Hotel Northfield had been opened by the family of Mr. Moody for the accommodation of those who would come to the services, and Mr. Ambert G. Moody, his nephew, who has been so closely associated with Mr. Moody's Northfield work, was there to receive the coming friends and bid them welcome, just as his distinguished uncle would have had it done. It was so like Mr. Moody himself to care for the comfort of these sad-hearted pilgrims. I found myself, as I was planning for the journey and had received notification that the Northfield was opened for us, saying,

"Well, that is like him in all his careful thought for others. I suppose that he has ordered that the house be thrown open, and that it be made comfortable for all who would accept the invitation to come," and then it came to me like a shock that *D. L. Moody was dead*, and could care for us no more except as the influence of his sainted memory would guide and control for many a long day. Many of his co-laborers were in Northfield the evening of Christmas Day, and the life of this dear friend was talked over; always with love, and frequently with tears blinding the eyes of those who would attempt to speak. Those who were qualified to testify told of his last days and the closing hours of his life. One said, "It was just such an experience as we would have supposed he might have. It was glorious."

His Last Moments and His Will

Another told how just before the last he said, "Can't a man die sitting up as well as lying down," and when the doctor said yes, they took him up and let him rest for a moment or two in his chair, but it was only for a little while, and then they put him back again in his bed. It was the last time he was to rise, and he who told it said with a sob, "I cannot bring myself to realize that he has gone from us." Another told how, when he was aroused from his stupor and saw all his loved ones about him, he said in his old way, so characteristic of himself, "What's going on here," and when they told him that he had been worse for a little time, and that they had come to be with him, he closed his eyes and seemed to fall asleep again.

Still another told of the will he made, unlike any other will that any man had ever made; when he gave the care of Mt. Hermon to his son, William R. Moody; the Northfield Young Ladies' School to the care of Paul, his son, a junior in Yale; the special oversight of the Bible Institute to Mrs. Fitt and her husband, Mr. A. P. Fitt, the latter having for years been Mr. Moody's closest and most confidential helper, particularly in the Bible Institute in Chicago and the Colportage Library work. The Northfield Training School was to be the care of Mr. Ambert G. Moody, his nephew. And when something was said about Mrs. Moody, he had said she was the mother of them all, and they must all care for her. An old friend gave the account of his words to his boys when he said, "I have always been an ambitious man, not ambitious to lay up money, but ambitious to leave you all work to be done, which is the greatest heritage one can leave to his children."

A Triumphant Passing Away

Still another gave the picture of his last hours. No more memorable sentences on one's deathbed have ever been spoken. It was just such a triumphant passing away as his dear friends would have wished. Where have you ever read better sayings than these:

"Is this dying? Why this is bliss.

"There is no valley.

"I have been within the gates.

"Earth is receding; Heaven is opening; God is calling; I must go."

And when he went away from them for a little time and came back, he said that he had seen his loved ones in Heaven, giving their names, and when it was suggested that he had been dreaming, he assured them it was not so, but that he had actually been within the gates of Heaven. Thus his noble life went out, but he being dead yet speaketh, and is continuing to speak, and tens of thousands rise up to call him blessed. Such intimate associates as Mr. Ira D. Sankey, Mr. George C. Stebbins, Rev. George

MOUNT HERMON STUDENTS WAITING FOR THE CASKET AT MR. MOODY'S HOME.

C. Needham, Prof, W. W. White, Mr. William Phillips Hall, Mr. John R. Mott, Mr. Richard C. Morse, Rev. George A. Hall, and many others talked until the evening was gone, and then retired each to feel that his was a personal bereavement, because D. L. Moody was dead.

Wanted to see His Face Once More

Special trains were run from the surrounding New England towns, and they were filled with people who wanted to see his face once more. Farmers drove from distances of twenty miles away that they might pay respect to the memory of him in whom they all believed. The students were many of them away for their Christmas vacations, but there was a sufficient number present to bear his body from the house, which had become so much a part of himself, to the church in which he was so deeply interested.

At last the day of the funeral came. It was a sad company of friends that met in the Grand Central Station in New York City the morning of the funeral. There was the Hon. John Wanamaker, who had been in close fellowship with him for years; the Rev. A. C. Dixon, D.D., who had been as near to him in Christian work as any man in the country, who showed by every expression of his face that he was in sorrow, yet "not as others who have no hope;" Mr. and Mrs. Janeway, of New Brunswick, New Jersey, devoted friends of the great Evangelist for years, and intimately and officially connected with the Northfield work. There were very many others, but notably, there was the veteran evangelist, the Rev. Dr. E. P. Hammond, who had known Mr. Moody as long as any one in the company. It was a sad group of people that journeyed toward the little town where the devoted friend was lying dead. Many of them had not seen Northfield in winter. They had visited it when the trees were in full foliage, when the grass was green on the hillsides, and when the birds sang their joyous welcome, but at this visit all nature seemed in sympathy with the many who sorrowed because their friend was not, but rejoiced as well because God had taken him, and because of the abundant entrance given him into His presence.

At last the church was reached. Special seats were reserved for the late coming friends, and the most memorable funeral service in all the experience of the most of those who knew him began.

During the morning Mr. Moody's family had been with the body, which had been lying in the death-chamber since the time of death. But soon after ten o'clock the body was laid in the heavy broadcloth casket and removed to the parlor of the home, where a simple service of prayer was conducted by Mr. Moody's pastor, the Rev. C. I. Scofield, assisted by the Rev. R. A. Torrey, of Chicago.

Funeral Services at The Church

At the close of this service the casket was placed on a massive bier, and thirty-two Mt. Hermon students bore it to the Congregational Church, where it was to lie in state. During the next three hours fully three thousand persons looked for the last time at the face of the great, good man. The casket was placed directly in front of the altar, and around it were banked many floral tributes.

The gathering at the church for the funeral service at 2:30 was notable. Men from all walks of life—clergymen, business men, tillers of the soil—came side by side to pay a last tribute. The services were as simple and as impressive as if he himself had planned them. The voice of the loved one was still, but his presence was felt.

The hymn, "A Little While and He Shall Come," was followed by the Rev. C. I. Scofield's prayer. The Rev. A. T. Pierson read the Scripture lesson from II Corinthians, iv. ii. This was followed by a prayer by Rev. George C. Needham, after which the congregation sang "Emmanuel's Land," the music being directed by Mr. A. B. Phillips, Professor of Music in the Northfield Institute.

The Rev. Dr. Scofield then pronounced the eulogy, saying:

"'We know,' 'We are always confident,' That is the Christian attitude toward the mystery of death. 'We know,' so far as the present body is concerned, that it is a tent in which we dwell. It is a convenience for this present life. Death threatens it, so far as we can see, with utter destruction. Soul and spirit instinctively cling to this present body. At that point revelation steps in with one of the great foundational certainties and teaches us to say· 'We know that if our earthly house of this tabernacle were dissolved, we have a building of God, a house not made with hands, eternal in the heavens.'

"There is a natural body, and there is a spiritual body. But that is not all. Whither after all shall we go when this earthly tent dwelling is gone? To what scenes does death introduce us? What, in a word, lies for the Christian just across that little trench which we call a grave? Here is a new and most serious cause of solicitude. And here again revelation brings to faith the needed word: 'We are confident, I say, and willing rather to be absent from the body and to be at home with the Lord.'

"Note, now, how that assurance gives confidence. First, in that the transition is instantaneous. To be absent from the body is to be at home with the Lord. And secondly, every question of the soul which might bring back an answer of fear is satisfied with that one little word 'home.'

"And this is the Christian doctrine of death. 'We know.' 'We are always confident.' In this triumphant assurance Dwight L. Moody lived, and at high noon last Friday he died. We are not met, dear friends, to mourn a defeat, but to celebrate a triumph.

He 'walked with God and he was not, for God took him.' There in the West, in the presence of great audiences of 12,000 of his fellow-men, God spoke to him to lay it all down and come home. He would have planned it so.

"This is not the place, nor am I the man to present a study of the life and character of Dwight L. Moody. No one will ever question that we are laying to-day in the kindly bosom of earth the mortal body of a great man. Whether we measure greatness by quality of character or by qualities of intellect, Dwight L. Moody must be accounted great.

"The basis of Mr. Moody's character was sincerity, genuineness. He had an inveterate aversion to all forms of sham, unreality and pretence. Most of all did he detest religious pretence or cant. Along with this fundamental quality, Mr. Moody cherished a great love of righteousness. His first question concerning any proposed action was: 'Is it right?' But these two qualities, necessarily at the bottom of all noble characters, were in him suffused and transfigured by divine grace, Besides all this, Mr. Moody was in a wonderful degree brave, magnanimous and unselfish.

"Doubtless this unlettered New England country boy became what he was by the grace of God. The secrets of Dwight L. Moody's power were: First, in a definite experience of Christ's saving grace. He had passed out of death into life, and he knew it. Secondly, Mr. Moody believed in the divine authority of the Scriptures. The Bible was, to him, the voice of God, and he made it resound as such in the consciences of men. Thirdly, he was baptized with the Holy Spirit, and he knew it. It was to him as definite an experience as his conversion. Fourthly, he was a man of prayer; he believed in a divine and unfettered God. Fifthly, Mr. Moody believed in work, in ceaseless effort, in wise provision, in the power of organization, of publicity.

"I like to think of D. L. Moody in Heaven. I like to think of him with his Lord and with Elijah, Daniel, Paul, Augustine, Luther, Wesley and Finney.

"Farewell for a little time, great heart, may a double portion of the spirit be vouchsafed to us who remain."

The next address was by the Rev. H. B. Weston, of Crozier Theological Seminary, Chester, Pa., who said:

Rev. H. B. Weston's Address

"I counted it among one of the greatest pleasures of my life that I had the acquaintance of Mr. Moody; that I was placed under his influence, and that I was permitted to study God's words and work through him.

"He was the greatest religious character of this century. When we see men who are eminent among their fellows, we always attribute it to some special natural gift with which they are endowed, some special education they have received, or some magnetic personality with which they are blessed. Mr. Moody had none of these, and yet, no man had such power of drawing the multitude. No man could surpass him in teaching and influencing individuals —individuals of brain, of executive power. I am speaking to some of such this afternoon. Mr. Moody had the power of grouping them to himself with hooks of steel, and many of them were good workers with him many years; and they will carry on his work now that he has passed away.

"Mr. Moody had none of the gifts and qualifications that I have mentioned: no promise, and apparently no possibiltity, in his early life; no early promise, if he had any promise, of the life he had to lead. What had he? There was nothing else as interesting in Northfield as Mr. Moody to me. I listened to him with profound and great interest and profit, as the one who could draw the multitude as no one else in the world. He entered fully into the words, ' Man shall not live by bread alone, but by every word that proceedeth out of the mouth of God.' So he fed upon that word; his life was instantly a growth, because he fed on the Word of God, so that he might have it ready for every emergency.

"All this was not for himself, but for others. He did not study the Bible for himself alone, but that he might add to his stock of knowledge. He did not study his Bible in order to criticise, but to make men partakers of that light which had enlarged his own soul, and that, I appeal to you, was the first desire of his heart, that other men might live.

"With this one conception in his heart he dots his plain all over with buildings which will stand until the millennium. His soul was full of joy, and that definite joy finds its expression like the Hebrew prophet. I don't think he himself sang, but he wanted the Gospel sung, and I used to listen to song after song and remember all the time this was simply the expression of that joy that welled up in his heart, the joy of the Lord Jesus Christ.

"You remember last summer how hopeful he was, constantly, as he compared himself to 'that old man of eighty years, and I am only sixty-two, and I have so much before me to live for.' Because D. L. Moody had mastered, or the power of Christ had so mastered, every fibre of his being; because of that completeness of consecration—I hardly dare say it—were Jesus Christ given the same body, the same mental caliber and surroundings, He would fill up his life much as Moody did, and that is the reason to-day that I would rather be Dwight L. Moody in his coffin than any living man on earth."

The next speaker was the Rev. R. A. Torrey, who said:

"It is often the first duty of a pastor to speak words of comfort to those whose hearts are aching with sorrow and breaking underneath the burden of death, but this is utterly unnecessary to-day. The God of all comfort has already abundantly comforted them, and they will be able to comfort others. I have spent hours in the past few days with those who were nearest to our departed friend, and the words I have heard from them have been words of 'Rest in God and triumph.'

Rev. R. A. Torrey's Estimate of Mr. Moody

"As one of them has said: 'God must be answering the prayers that are going up for us all over the world. We are being so wonderfully sustained.' Another has said: 'His last four glorious hours of life have taken all the sting out of death,' and still another, 'Be sure that every word to-day is a word of triumph.'

"Two thoughts has God laid upon my heart this hour. The first is that wonderful letter of Paul in I Corinthians, xv. 10: 'By the grace of God I am what I am.' God wonderfully magnified His grace in the life of D. L. Moody. God was magnified in his birth. The babe that was born sixty-two years ago—the wonderful soul was God's gift to the world. How much that meant to the world; how much the world has been blessed and benefited by it we shall never know this side the coming of Christ. God's grace was magnified in his conversion. He was born in sin, as we are, but God, by tbe power of His word, the regenerating power of His Holy Spirit, made him a mighty man of God. How much the conversion of that boy in Boston forty-three years ago meant to the world no man can tell, but it was God's grace that did it.

"God's grace and love were magnified again in the development of that character. He had the strength of body that was possessed by few sons of men.

"It was all from God. To God alone was it due that he differed from other men. That character was God's gift to a world that sorely needed men like him. God's grace and love were magnified again in his service. The great secret of his success was supernatural power, given in answer to prayer.

"Time and again has the question been asked, What was the secret of his wonderful power? The question is easily answered. There were doubtless secondary things that contributed to it, but the great central secret of his power was the anointing of the Holy Ghost. It was simply another fulfilment by God of the promise that has been realized throughout the centuries of the Church's history: 'Ye shall receive power, after that the Holy Ghost shall come upon you.'

"God was magnified again in his marvelous triumph over death, but what we call death had absolutely no terrors for him. He calmly looked death in the face and said, 'Earth is receding. Heaven is opening. God is calling me. Is this death? It isn't bad at all. It is sweet. No pain. No valley. I have been within the gates! It is beautiful. It is glorious. Do not call me back. God is calling me.'

"This was God's grace in Christ that was thus magnified in our brother's triumph over that last enemy, Death. From beginning to end, from the hour of his birth until he is laid at rest on yonder hilltop, Mr. Moody's life has been a promulgation of God's everlasting grace and love.

"The other thought, that God has laid upon my heart in these last few hours are those words of Joshua i. 2: 'Moses my servant is dead. Now, therefore, arise, go over this Jordan, thou, and all this people, unto the land which I do give to them.'

"The death of Mr. Moody is a call to his children, his associates, ministers of the Word everywhere, and to the whole Church: 'Go forward. Our leader has fallen.' 'Let us give up the work,' some would say. Not for a moment. Listen to what God

FUNERAL OF DWIGHT L. MOODY. Head of the procession leaving the house. Thirty-two Mt. Hermon students carrying the bier on which rests the casket.

Copyright

says: 'Our leader has fallen. Move forward. Moses my servant is dead, therefore arise, go in and possess the land. As I was with D. L. Moody, so I will be with you. I will not fail thee nor forsake thee.'

"It is remarkable how unanimous all those who have been associated with Mr. Moody are upon this point. The great institutions that he has established at Northfield, Mt. Hermon, and Chicago, and the work they represent, must be pushed to the front as never before. Many men are looking for a great revival.

"Mr. Moody himself said when he felt the call of death at Kansas City: 'I know how much better it would be for me to go, but we are on the verge of a great revival, like that of 1857, and I want to have a hand in it.' He will have a mighty hand in it. His death, with the triumphal scenes that surround it, are part of God's way of answering the prayers that have been going on for so long in our land for a revival.

"From this bier there goes up to-day a call to the ministry, to the Church: 'Forward!' Seek, claim, receive the anointing of the Holy Ghost, and then go forthwith, to every corner, preach in public and in private to every man, woman, and child the infallible Word of God."

The Words of Bishop Mallalieu.

The Rev. W. F. Mallalieu, bishop of the Methodist church, said:

"'Servant of God, well done,
Thy glorious warfare's past,
The battle's fought, the race is won,
And thou art crowned at last.'

"I first met and became acquainted with him, whose death we mourn, in London in the summer of 1875. From that day, when he moved the masses of the world's metropolis, to the hour when he answered the call of God to come up higher, I have known him, esteemed him and loved him. Surely we may say, and the world will endorse the affirmation, that in his death one of the truest, bravest, purest and most influential men of this wonderful 19th century has passed to his rest and his reward. With feelings of unspeakable loss and desolation we gather about the casket that contains all that was mortal of Dwight L. Moody. And yet a mighty uplift and inspiration must come to each one of us as we think of his character and his achievements, for he was:

> 'One, who never turned his back but marched breast forward,
> Never doubted clouds would break,
> Never dreamed, though right were worsted, wrong would triumph.'

"In bone and brawn and brain he was a typical New Englander; he was descended from the choicest New England stock; he was born of a New England mother, and from his earliest life he breathed the free air of his native hills and was carefully nurtured in the knowledge of God and the holy traditions and histories of the glorious past. It was to be expected of him that he would become a Christian of pronounced characteristics, for he consecrated himself thoroughly and completely and irrevocably to the service of God and humanity. The heart of no disciple of the Master ever beat with more genuine, sympathetic and utterly unselfish loyalty than did the great, generous, loving heart of our translated friend. Because he held fast to the absolute truth of the Bible, and unequivocally and intensely believed it to be the unerrant Word of God; because he preached the Gospel rather than talked about the Gospel; because he used his mother tongue, the terse, clear, ringing, straightforward Saxon; because he had the profoundest sense of brotherhood with all poor, unfortunate and even outcast people; because he was unaffectedly tender and patient with the weak and sinful; because he hated evil as thoroughly as he loved goodness; because he knew right how to lead penitent souls to the Saviour; because he had the happy art of arousing Christian people to a vivid sense of their obligations and inciting them to the performance of their duties; because he had in his own soul a conscious, joyous experience of personal salvation—the people flocked to his services, they heard him gladly, they were led to Christ, and he came to be prized and honored by all denominations, so that to-day all Protestantism recognizes the fact that he was God's servant, an embassador of Christ, and indeed a chosen vessel to bear the name of Jesus to the nations.

"We shall not again behold his manly form animated with life, hear his thrilling voice or be moved by his consecrated personality but if we are true and faithful to our Lord, we shall see him in glory, for already he walks the streets of the heavenly city, he mingles in the song of the innumerable company of white-robed saints, sees the King in his beauty, and waits our coming. May God grant that in due time we may meet him over yonder."

Dr. Chapman's Address.

The Rev. J. Wilbur Chapman of New York, the next speaker, said:

"I cannot bring myself to feel this afternoon that this service is a reality. It seems to me that we must awake from some dream and see again the face of this dear man of God, which we have so many times seen. It is a new picture to me this afternoon. I never before saw Mr. Moody with his eyes closed. They were always open, and it seemed to me open not only to see where he could help others, but where he could help me. His hands were always outstretched to help others. I never came near him without his helping me."

At this point the sun came through a crack in a blind, and the rays fell directly on Mr. Moody's face, and nowhere else in the darkened church did a single beam of sunshine fall.

"The only thing that seems natural is the sunlight now on his face. There was always a halo around him. I can only give a slight tribute of the help he has done me, I can only especially dedicate myself to God, that I, with others, may preach the Gospel he taught.

"When I was a student, Mr. Moody found me. I had no object in Christ. He pointed me to the hope in God; he saw my heart, and I saw his Saviour. I have had a definite life since then. When perplexities have arisen, from those lips came the words, 'Who are you doubting? If you believe in God's Word, who are you doubting?' I was a pastor, a preacher, without much result. One day Mr. Moody came to me, and, with one hand on my shoulder and the other on the open Word of God, he said: 'Young man, you had better get more of this into your life,' and when I became an evangelist myself, in perplexity I would still sit at his feet, and every perplexity would vanish just as mist before the rising sun. And, indeed, I never came without the desire to be a better man, and be more like him, as he was like Jesus Christ. If my own father were lying in the coffin I could not feel more the sense of loss."

Rev. A. T. Pierson's Address.

The Rev. A. T. Pierson spoke next, saying:

"When a great tree falls, you know, not only by its branches, but by its roots, how much soil it drew up as it fell. I know of no other man who has fallen in this country having as wide a tract of uprooting as this man who has just left us.

"I have been thinking of the four departures during the last quarter of a century, of Charles Spurgeon of London, A. J. Gordon of Boston, Catherine Booth, mother of the Salvation Army, and

George Müller of Bristol, England, and not one made the world-wide commotion in their departures that Dwight L. Moody has caused.

"Now, I think we ought to be very careful of what is said. There is a temptation to say more than ought to be said, and we should be careful to speak as in the presence of God. This is a time to glorify God.

"Dwight L. Moody was a great man. That man when he entered the church in 1856 in Boston, after ten months of probation, was told by his pastor that he was not a sound believer. That pastor, taking him aside, told him he had better keep still in prayer meeting. The man the church held out at arm's length has become the preacher of preachers, the teacher of teachers, the evangelist of evangelists. It is a most humiliating lesson for the Church of God.

"When, in 1858, he decided to give all his time, he gave the key to his future. I say everything D. L. Moody has touched has been a success. Do you know that with careful reckoning he has reached 100,000,000 of people since he first became a Christian? You may take all the years of public services in this land and Great Britain, take into consideration all the addresses he delivered, and the audiences of his churches, and it will reach 100,000,000. Take into consideration all the people his books have reached and the languages into which they have been translated; look beyond his evangelistic work to the work of education, the schools, the Chicago Bible Institute, and the Bible Institute here. Thousands of people in the world owe their hope to Dwight L. Moody who was the means of their consecration.

"I want to say a word of Mr. Moody's entrance into Heaven. When he entered into Heaven there must have been an unusual commotion. I want to ask you to-day whether you can think of any other man of the last half-century whose coming so many souls would have welcomed at the gates of Heaven. It was a triumphal entrance into glory.

"No man who has been associated with him in Christian work has not seen that there is but one way to live, and that way to live wholly for God. The thing that D. L. Moody stood and will stand for centuries to come was his living only for God. He made mistakes, no doubt, and if any of us is without sin in this respect, we might cast a stone at him, but I am satisfied that the mistakes of D. L. Moody were the mistakes of a stream that overflowed its banks. It is a great deal better to be full and overflowing than to be empty and have nothing to overflow.

"I feel myself called to-day by the presence of God to give eye that what is left shall be consecrated more wholly to him. Mr. Moody, John Wanamaker, James Spurgeon (brother of Charles), and myself were born in the same year. Only two of us are still alive. John Wanamaker, let us still live wholly for God."

Rev. H. M. Wharton's Words

The Rev. H. M. Wharton, of Philadelphia, spoke in behalf of the southern States. He said:

"I am sure, dear friends, that if the people of the South could express their feeling to-day, they would ask me to say we all loved Mr. Moody; we did love him with all our hearts. It seems to me that when he went inside the gates of Heaven he left the gates open a little, and a little of the light fell upon us all.

"As I go from this place to-day, I am more convinced that I desire to live and be a more faithful minister and more earnest Christian, and more consecrated in my life. We will not say 'Good night, dear Mr. Moody,' for in the morning we will meet again."

As Mr. Wharton ceased, Mr. William Moody rose in the pew, and said he would like to speak of his father as a parent. He said:

Mr. W. R. Moody's Tribute to His Father

"As a son, I want to say a few words of him as a father. We have heard from his pastor, his associates and friends, and he was just as true a father. I don't think he showed up in any way better than when, on one or two occasions, in dealing with us as children, with his impulsive nature, he spoke rather sharply. We have known him to come to us and say: 'My children, my son, my daughter, I spoke quickly; I did wrong; I want you to forgive me.' That was D. L. Moody as a father.

"He was not yearning to go; he loved his work. Life was very attractive; it seems as though on that early morning as he had one foot upon the threshold it was given him for our sake to give us a word of comfort. He said: 'This is bliss; it is like a trance. If this is death it is beautiful.' And his face lighted up as he mentioned those whom he saw.

"We could not call him back; we tried to, for a moment, but we could not. We thank God for his home life, for his true life, and we thank God that he was our father, and that he led each one of his children to know Jesus Christ."

Mr. John Wanamaker's Remarks

Dr. Scofield then called upon the Hon. John Wanamaker, of Philadelphia, who said:

"If I had any words to say, it would be that the best commentary on the Scriptures, the best pictures of the Lord Jesus Christ, were in our knowledge of the beautiful man who is sleeping in our presence to-day. For the first time I can understand well the kind of a man Paul was, and Nehemiah, and Oliver Cromwell. I think of Mr. Moody as a Stonewall Jackson of the Church of God of this century. But, the sweetest of all thoughts of him are his prayers and his kindnesses. It was as if we were all taken into his family and he had a familiarity with every one and we were his closest friends.

"There is not any place in this country where you can go without seeing the work of this man of God. It seems to make every man seem small, because he lived so far above us, as we crept close to his feet. It is true of every one who sought to be like him.

"I can run back into the beginning of his manhood, and there have the privilege of being close to him. I can call up personal friends that were at the head of railroads, that were distinguished in finance and business, and I declare to you, great as their successes were, I don't believe that there is one of them who would not gladly have changed place with D. L. Moody.

"The Christian laborer, I believe, to-day looms up more luminous than any man who lived in the century. It seems as if it were a vision when the one who has passed away stood in Philadelphia last month, when, on his way to Kansas City, and, with tears in his eyes, he said to me with a sigh : 'If I could only hold one great city in the East before I die, I think it might help other cities to do the same.' Still trusting God, he turned his back on his home and family, and went 1,000 miles carrying that burden, and it was too much for him. A great many of the people of the sixties are quitting work, and if anything is to be done for God, it is time we consecrate ourselves to Him."

SENIOR GLEN, EAST NORTHFIELD, where Mr. Moody met the students of the Senior Class at 6 A.M., daily during the sessions of the school.

ROUND TOP. The Hill where Mr. Moody frequently held Meetings, and where he now lies burried.

CHAPTER XXVIII.

Roundtop, where Mr. Moody Loved to Speak and where he was Buried.

THE funeral services in the church were over. In every way it was the most remarkable gathering that could possibly be imagined on any such occasion, and one friend was heard to say to another as we passed out of the Congregational Church, "I would not have missed this privilege for any consideration. My faith in God and in His promises is stronger to-day than ever; my fear of death is all taken away. Did you ever in all your experience attend a service in which the power of God was more mightily manifest?" One distinguished man said to a brother minister as they walked in solemn procession toward the grave, "If it had been possible to repeat that service with all its attending circumstances and surroundings in all the cities of the land, D. L. Moody would have been greater in his death than in his life, and thousands and tens of thousands would have been brought to Christ."

A Most Notable Service

It was a notable service because there was a spirit of victory in it all. From where we sat on the platform we could look down into the faces of those who had been bereaved, and while there were marks of tears upon their faces, yet there was such evident joy in the thought that they had had him so long, and that he had brought so much of blessing into the lives of countless numbers of people, that one really forgot that he was attending a funeral and thanked God that he was sitting together with dear friends in heavenly places in Christ Jesus.

It was notable also, because not very often on funeral occasions do the bereaved ones join in the singing of the hymns, and yet at this funeral very frequently you could see that the lips of the members of the family were moving, and you knew they were singing the songs that Mr. Moody loved, and singing them just in the way that would have been pleasing to him.

A Ray of Sunlight

It was notable also, because of the fact that just in the midst of the services one single ray of sunlight from the setting sun came through the window, but the only face in all the building that was touched with the glory of that streak of light was the face of the man of God lying in his coffin. It was just what all could have wished for him, for to those who knew him and loved him, there was always a kind of a halo of glory about him, and this touch of sunlight was just a hint to us as to how his face would appear when in the better country we should see him once again with the redemption body transfigured into the likeness of Christ. I seriously question if any man in the present generation ever walked closer with God than did Mr. Moody. He was my ideal in this respect as in many others. His was a story like that of Enoch of old, and when he died we could understand it all, he simply was not, for God took him.

All the funerals associated with Mr. Moody's family have ever been most touching. When his mother was carried to the tomb, she was not taken away until her son had said what only a devoted and godly son could say concerning the life of a consistent Christian mother, and of her it was true as the wise man said, "Her children rise up and call her blessed."

When the children of his eldest son, Mr. W. R. Moody, were buried, once again did he speak such words as he only was able to speak. Quite recently, at the funeral of Irene Moody, he said the most touching words concerning his love for his grandchild, told how she had always greeted him with a smile, and then told how she had influenced his life as very few people had—no one could have said these words with such tenderness and sweetness as Mr. Moody, but it was just like him to say them for the grief of his son was as if it had been his own.

While holding services in my Church, Rev. B. Fay Mills spoke concerning the funeral of the brother of Mr. Moody, as contrasted with the funeral of Mr. Robert Ingersoll's brother, and the picture is most striking in its contrasts:

A Most Striking Picture

"It was in June, 1879. This brother had died in Washington, and Colonel Ingersoll stood by the coffin and tried to read his address, which he had carefully prepared. His voice became agitated, his form trembled, and his emotion overcame him. Finally he put down the paper, and, bowing himself upon the coffin, as if he would throw his arms about it, he gave vent to uncontrollable grief. When at last he was able to proceed he raised himself up, and among other words he said these: 'Whether in mid-ocean or 'mid the breakers of the farther shore, a wreck must mark at last the end of each and all; and every life, no matter if its every hour be filled with love and every moment jeweled with a joy, will at the last become a tragedy as sad and dark and deep as can be woven of the warp and woof of mystery and death. * * * Life is a dark and barren vale between the cold and ice-clad peaks of two eternities. We strive in vain to look beyond the heights. We lift our wailing voice in the silence of the night, and hear no answer but the bitter echo of our cry.'

"Could ever words more sadly hopeless have been uttered at a time like that? And then he added what to me were the most pathetic words of all—something about 'hope trying to see a star, and listening for the rustle of an angel's wings.'

"Mrs. Browning most truly writes:

> "'There is no God,' the foolish saith,
> But none, 'There is no sorrow.'
> And nature oft in bitter need
> The cry of faith will borrow.
> Eyes which the preacher could not school,
> By wayside graves are raised;
> And lips cry, 'God be pitiful!'
> Which ne'er said, 'God be praised!'

"I think I should like a greater comfort and a better hope than that.

His Brother's Funeral

"Dwight Moody had a brother, and after his own conversion he earnestly pleaded with him, until the brother also yielded himself to Christ, and became such an earnest worker that he was the means of leading a number of his friends at his home into the kingdom. And then this brother died and was buried. A few years ago", Mr. Mills said, "as I spent a day in Northfield, and was driven through its beautiful streets by one of the old residents, I said, 'I wish you would tell me something about Mr. Moody that may not be generally known.' And as we passed the old white Church he said, 'I remember his brother's funeral.' He said that there were a number of ministers in the pulpit, and that after they had finished the usual services and the coffin-lid was about to be put in its place, Mr. Moody arose, and stepping forward from the seat where he had been sitting, with a shining face, he laid one hand upon the coffin, and then, lifting the other, he poured out such a stream of thanksgiving unto God for the life that was gone and for the wonderful comfort and joy and hope that came to him in Jesus Christ, that it was said by this onlooker that it almost seemed as if the heavens were opened and they could see the angels of God ascending and descending upon the Son of man. At last he ceased, the coffin-lid was placed in its position, and the body was carried out and laid in the grave. On one side of the sepulcher stood a large number of young men, many of them led to Christ through the influence of this one who was gone, and they held in their hands beautiful white flowers, which they cast down upon the coffin in token of the glorious resurrection. And on the other side of the grave stood Mr. Moody; and he said that as he stood there and thought of how his brother, being dead, was yet speaking, he felt that if he were silent the very stones would cry out, and he cried with a loud voice, 'Glory to God! Glory be to God! O death where is thy sting? O grave, where is thy victory?'"

On the Procession to Roundtop

When the last hymn had been sung on this day of the funeral of D. L. Moody, the audience was requested to remain seated until the family had passed out and also until the pallbearers had taken from the Church the precious remains of this servant of God. As we passed along in solemn procession towards Roundtop, it was my privilege to hear something of the conversation of those who followed the students who had been given the privilege of bearing him to his tomb. One gentleman said to his friend, "When Mr. Moody's little grandchild was buried only a short time ago, the students carried her from the house to her grave, and Mr. Moody said to his son, 'I think I should like to be carried like that myself,'" and so the students bore him carefully to the place where he is to rest until the Lord himself shall descend from Heaven with a shout, with the voice of the archangel and the trump of God, and he shall rise.

Roundtop was reached in the dusk of that winter day. The grave was lined with evergreen, and the resting place made as comfortable as possible. After a moment's gazing at the grave, all but the immediate family and the specially invited guests were requested to withdraw, but before they went away some one started the following old hymn which Mr. Moody ever loved to have sung in his meetings. One voice was added to another until at last a great volume of song rose towards God:

>Jesus, Lover of my soul,
>   Let me to Thy bosom fly,
>While the nearer waters roll,
>   While the tempest still is high;
>Hide me, O my Saviour, hide,
>   Till the storm of life is past;
>Safe into the haven guide,
>   Oh, receive my soul at last.
>
>Other refuge have I none,
>   Hangs my helpless soul on Thee:
>Leave, oh, leave me not alone,
>   Still support and comfort me.
>All my trust on Thee is stayed,
>   All my help from Thee I bring;
>Cover my defenceless head
>   With the shadow of Thy wing.
>
>Thou, O Christ, art all I want;
>   More than all in Thee I find;
>Raise the fallen, cheer the faint,
>   Heal the sick, and lead the blind.
>Just and holy is Thy Name,
>   I am all unrighteousness:
>Vile, and full of sin I am,
>   Thou art full of truth and grace.

> Plenteous grace with Thee is found—
> Grace to cover all my sin:
> Let the healing streams abound;
> Make me, keep me pure, within.
> Thou of life the Fountain art,
> Freely let me take of Thee;
> Spring Thou up within my heart,
> Rise to all eternity.

With heads solemnly bowed for a moment, the benediction was pronounced, and all that was mortal of D. L. Moody, the greatest evangelist of modern times, and one of the best men that ever lived was lying in the grave.

A Place of Blessing

Roundtop has ever been a place of blessing to the Northfield visitors. There each evening, when the conferences are in session, as the day is dying out of the sky, Bible students gather to talk of the things concerning the Kingdom. At this point many of the young men and women of the various students' gatherings, which have been so intimately associated with Northfield, have decided their life work, and forth from this point they have gone to the ends of the earth to preach the Gospel. The old haystack at Williamstown figures no more conspicuously in the history of missions than Roundtop figures in the lives of a countless number of Christians throughout the whole world.

A. J. Gordon, of sainted memory, delivered some of his most telling addresses from this point. I recall one evening when he spoke of the Lord's return, and just as he finished he stood for a moment with his kindly face, all aglow with the power of his theme, and said, "I wish He might come now," and as we looked towards the west and saw the sunset glow upon everything it came to us as a regret that the Lord did not come at that instant, and that we must go down from this mount of privilege to work and to wait, possibly through weary years until He should appear.

From this point Mr. S. H. Hadley, Jerry Macauley's successor in the old Water Street Mission has told the story of his remarkable conversion, until people first sobbed in sympathy for him because of all that he had suffered through strong drink, and then praised God that He had raised him up such a miracle of grace and such a monument to His keeping power.

Here Mr. John Willis Baer has met the young people who were seeking to know what they must do to be used of God, and under the influence of the Spirit of God has pointed many a young man and young woman to the Spirit of God who could fill their lives and make them useful in every way.

Indeed, every visitor to Northfield journeys to Roundtop, and every speaker at Northfield counted himself fortunate if he were permitted to gather the people about him and speak as once the Master did when He went up into a mountain.

Roundtop Particularly Identified With Mr. Moody

But Roundtop is particularly identified with Mr. Moody himself. It is situated just back of his home. It was the place where often he used to go for meditation and prayer, and whatever it has been to friends of Northfield in the past, it shall be more sacred to them in the future, because it is the last resting place of the man whom they devotedly loved.

I recall one picture which can never be effaced from my memory. It was just at the close of one of the first days of the Northfield conference proper when it was announced that Mr. Moody would lead the Roundtop services, and as we were all gathered together singing, he came up. I can see him as plainly as I see my friend of to-day. He was carrying a chair in

DWIGHT L. MOODY LYING IN STATE at the Second Congregational Church, East Northfield. Taken one hour before the service by permission of the pastor.

his hand upon which he was to sit in the midst of his people. He had his old, worn Bible in the one hand, and with his face beaming with delight because so many people were there at the beginning of the conference, he said, "I will ask Mr. Jacobs to sing," and the great strong voice of the singer sounded out from that hilltop and came back to us like an echo from the hills, until some of us wondered whether we were in the body or not. "Now, some one lead us in prayer," said the leader. "Now, let us sing," and there altogether we sang, he keeping time with his hymn-book. The hymn was "Christ Returneth":

> It may be at morn, when the day is awaking,
> When sunlight through darkness and shadow is breaking,
> That Jesus will come in the fulness of glory,
> To receive from the world "His own".
>
> *Chorus—*
> O Lord Jesus, how long, how long
> Ere we shout the glad song,
> Christ returneth; Hallelujah, Hallelujah, Amen.
> Hallelujah, Amen.

As the blessed words rolled out from the lips of those assembled there on that sacred hill, I remember how transported we all were with the bliss of that great truth, "Christ returneth!" The faces of those about me shone with joy, and there before us sat our beloved leader, the great factor of modern evangelism. He always seemed ready for Christ's coming, and I doubt if his joyful demeanor would have altered in the least, if at that moment the Heavens had opened. He was always ready because his consecration of himself to God was renewed with every breath, and attested by each succeeding act in his life.

When the singing was at an end, Mr. Moody opened his Bible, and said: "I have come up to-night, dear friends, in a spirit of praise and thankfulness, to give you just a few nuggets from the margin of my Bible; you can take them down if you like, and if I go too fast for you just stop me." I stood just behind his chair, and beginning at Genesis he turned over the pages of his Bible, and quickly I wrote down what he had to say. The following is almost an exact report of that Roundtop meeting, and everything recorded here I have, at one time or another, heard him say:

"Turn to Genesis and put this down," he said.

Genesis.

Adam	illustrates	Human nature.
Cain	"	The carnal mind.
Abel	"	The spiritual mind.
Enoch	"	Communion.
Noah	"	Regeneration.
Abraham	"	Faith.
Isaac	"	Sonship.
Jacob.	'	Service.
Joseph	'	Suffering and glory.

"Now, let us go on to Exodus the third chapter, maybe you would like this.

Objections raised by Moses for declining and avoiding God's call:—

Lack of fitness. V. 11.
" " words. V. 13.
" " authority. Chap. 4 : 1.
" " powers of speech. 4 : 10.
" " special adaptation. 4 : 13.
" " success at first attempt. 5 : 23.
" " acceptance by Israelites. 6 : 12.

"Have you ever noticed the seven feasts in Leviticus, twenty-third chapter? I have long had it in my Bible.

"Seven feasts:—
1. Sabbath—Rest.
2. Passover—Death of Christ.
3. First-fruits—Resurrection.
4. Pentecost—Descent of the Holy Spirit.
5. Trumpets—Ingathering of Israel.
6. Atonement—Mourning for sin.
7. Tabernacles—Christ's indwelling in the Christian.

"Sin is an awful thing, let every man make a note of this. Joshua 7 : 21.

"Steps in Achan's sin :—
1. 'I saw.'
2. 'I coveted.'
3. 'I took.'
4. 'I hid.'

Compare Eve, Gen. 3 : 6; Ananias, Acts 5 : 1–10.

"How mean was the sin of Achan! He saw the Babylonish garment, and all the soldier in him withered up and he became a sneaking thief.

"Here is a good thing on forgiven sin. Psalm 32.

"Seven steps to blessedness of forgiven sin :—
Conviction. Vs. 3, 4.
Confession. V. 5.
Forgiveness. V. 5.
Prayer. V. 6.
Protection. V. 7.
Guidance. Vs. 8, 9.
Joy. Vs. 10, 11.

"Here are seven things God will do for the believer. I find them in the 91st Psalm.

'I will deliver him.' Vs. 14, 15.

'I will set him on high.' V. 14.
'I will answer his call.' V. 15.
'I will be with him in trouble.' V. 15.
'I will honor him.' V. 15.
'I will satisfy him.' V. 16.
'I will show him my salvation.' V. 16.

"Now let us find something in the New Testament. Look at Matt. 7.

"In this chapter we have :—

Two gates—strait, and wide ;
Two ways—broad, and narrow ;
Two classes—many, and few ;
Two destinations—life, and destruction ;
Two trees—good, and corrupt ;
Two fruits—good, and evil ;
Two things done to trees—hewn down, and cast out ;
Two houses ;
Two foundations—rock, and sand ;
Two builders—wise, and foolish ;
Two storms ;
Two results—the one house stood, the other fell.

"I found this somewhere ; does anyone want it ?

"Christ was foretold to :—

Adam—as a man. Gen: 3 : 15.
Abraham—as to His nation. Gen. 22 : 18.
Jacob—as to His tribe. Gen. 49 : 10.
Isaiah—as to His family. Isa. 11 : 1–5.
Micah—as to His town. Micah 5 : 2.
Daniel—as to His time. Dan. 9 : 25.
Mary—as to His person. Luke 1 : 30.

By angels—as to His date. Luke 2 : 11.

By a star—as to His birthplace. Matt. 2 : 9.

"Here is an outline for a sermon. Let the ministers put it down. Luke 10 : 42.

'One thing is needful'—the Gospel.

'One thing I know.' John 9 : 25.

'One thing have I desired.' Ps. 27 : 4.

'One thing I do.' Phil. 3 : 13, 14.

'Not one thing hath failed.' Josh. 23 : 14.

'Be not ignorant of this one thing.' 2 Peter 3 : 8

'One thing thou lackest.' Mark 10 : 21.

"Here is something about the Prodigal Son." Luke 15.

His condition—'in want.' V. 14.

His conviction—'came to himself.' V. 17

His confidence—'I will arise.' V. 18.

His confession—'I have sinned.' V. 18.

His contrition—'no more worthy.' V. 19.

His conversion—'He arose and came.' V. 20.

"Turning-points in his life :—

Sick of home. Vs. 12, 13.

Homesick. Vs. 17–19.

Home. Vs. 20–24.

Sequel. Vs. 25–32.

"Six cases of men 'afar off' from God :—

The prodigal. Chap. 15 : 13.

The rich man. Chap. 16 : 23.

The ten lepers. Chap. 17 : 12.

The publican. Chap. 18 : 13.

The beggar. Chap. 18 : 40.

Peter. Chap. 22 : 54.

"God's Word gives us a picture such as we find in no other place, turn to John, sixth chapter.

"Seven classes of people :
1. Curious. V. 2.
2. Admiring. V. 14.
3. Greedy. V. 26.
4. Skeptical. V. 36.
5. Murmurers. V. 41.
6. Scoffers. V. 52,
7. Backsliders. V. 66..

"I have found much help in Hebrews. Note this :—
Sin is met by Atonement. Chap. 1 : 3.
Guilt is met by justification. 2 : 9.
Defilement is met by sanctification. 2 : 11.
Alienation is met by reconciliation. 2 : 17.
Temptation is met by succor. 2 : 18.

"Christ communicates eternity of existence to everything he touches : —
His throne is for ever and ever. Heb. 1 : 8.
His salvation is eternal. 5 : 9.
His priesthood is unchangeable. 7 : 24.
His redemption is eternal. 9 : 12.
His inheritance is eternal. 9 : 15.
His kingdom cannot be moved. 12 : 28.
His covenant is everlasting. 13 : 20.

"The key word of Hebrews is 'better;' see how many times it occurs.
Better hope. Chap. 7 : 19.
Better Testament. 7 : 22.
Better covenant. 8 : 6.
Better promises. 8 : 6.

Better sacrifices.   9 : 23.
Better substance.   10 : 34.
Better resurrection.   11 : 35.
Better country.   11 : 16.
Better things.   12 : 24."

When it was too dark for him to see, the well-marked Bible was closed, and he offered such a prayer as I have rarely heard, thanking God that He had permitted us to come to Northfield, and asking Him that He might make it more of a blessing than ever before in all its history.   This is but a specimen service of Roundtop, and if the trees which stand there could speak, they would tell as thrilling a story of scenes witnessed there as has ever been pressed into human language, and now from this time on, pilgrims will journey to Northfield and to this the new heart of the old town, because in this grave lies the body of a man who yielded himself absolutely to God, who had only one supreme desire, and that was that he might glorify Him.   The words of the poet certainly describe him in his life :

> "The strong man's strength to toil for Christ,
> The fervent preacher's skill,
> I sometimes wish but better far
> To be just what God will.
> No service in itself is small,
> None great, though earth it fill,
> But that is small which seeks its own,
> That great which seeks God's will."

D. L. Moody was a mighty man, because, he sought, as nearly as any man I have ever seen, to do the will of God.

CHAPTER XXIX.

Memorial Services.

THE announcement of the death of Mr. Moody was a shock to many thousands. Numerous telegrams of condolence which were sent to the bereaved family from all the quarters of the world expressed but faintly the sense of loss which affected not only those who had known him personally, but also a great following of those who had known him only through his work. Hundreds of memorial services were held. The great meeting in New York, on Monday afternoon, January 8, 1900, brought out so much of interest in regard to Mr. Moody and in regard to the sentiment entertained toward him on all sides that I believe an account of the services worthy of permanent record in this place.

The Great Meeting in New York

At the hour appointed for the opening of the services, Mr. Wm. E. Dodge, the presiding officer, announced a favorite hymn of Mr. Moody's, "In the Cross of Christ I Glory." After the singing, the Rev. Dr. A. T. Pierson read a number of selections from the Bible, being those verses of which Mr. Moody was especially fond. The Rev. John Balcolm Shaw then led in prayer.

Dr. David H. Greer then spoke. He said:

"In the history of the Church of Christ very few have touched so many hearts and influenced so many lives as the dear friend we come to remember and to thank God for to-day.

"I am sure it is no exaggeration to say that if all those whom

FUNERAL OF DWIGHT L. MOODY at the Second Congregational Church, East Northfield. Rev. Dr. Needham offering prayer. Photograph taken by our special photographer by permission of the pastor Rev. Dr. Schofield. Dr. Chapman will be noticed about the centre of the front row.

he has led to a better life were to be gathered together, a half-dozen halls of this size would not hold them. In the tender services held at Northfield last week, Mr. Moody's pastor said, that they were not gathered to mourn a defeat but to rejoice in a victory. So to-day there is not the note of sadness in our gathering nor a funeral gloom. We are gathered together this afternoon only to thank God with all our hearts for so fruitful and successful a life, and to pray that that influence which he exercised while here among us, shall continue. He is not dead, he has gone to the better life above, and he lives with us to-day and will live on, by his example and by the inspiration that came from his words and his life.

His Conversion Like That of St. Paul

"When Mr. Moody became a Christian man it was like the conversion of St. Paul,—clear, decisive, and full. When the blessed message came to him, that God had offered pardon and peace and life here and eternal, he accepted it in all its fullness, and he wondered with great astonishment that anyone could turn away from such a message and such an offer, and he longed to bring men to accept it and believe in it. From the very beginning his theology was very simple. His creed was: 'God so loved the world that He sent His only begotten Son, that whosoever believeth in Him shall have eternal life.' And this message he repeated with all his courage and manliness and strength through all his life, and so earnestly that it told wherever he carried it.

"Mr. Moody's early work was a very simple one. He had very few opportunities of education. At that time he had no gift of utterance, but he found fellowship and help in the Young Men's Christian Association, and he commenced his work among a few poor children in Chicago when he was a mere clerk there. I remember nearly forty years ago going with him one Sunday morning to that poor little school across the river, and I caught sight then of the peculiar character of the man, his directness, manliness, and hence his great influence upon those children and upon their parents.

"There were two early influences that directed his life more than any others. One was the companionship and help that came to him from the brotherhood of the Young Men's Christian Association. All his life he acknowledged that as having formed part of his character, and all his life he was a warm friend of the Associations and aided them in every way. But the stronger and greater influence was his beginning to study the English Bible. He had the idea that a great many other good men have that, if God wanted him to do work and speak for Him, God would put words in his mouth. In his earliest efforts his talks were repetitions of each other, and without much effect. A kind, earnest Christian man who influenced him very much talked with him and urged him that, if he wanted to do God's work, he must fit himself in the best way for such service and prepare himself to do his Master's work. He urged him, therefore, as the best means for so fitting himself, to study the Bible. Mr. Moody paid heed to the advice; he shut himself up for a long time and devoted himself to a thorough and intense study of the Bible. From this study he acquired two qualities, which in later years added much to his power: first that clear-cut, plain, simple, Anglo-Saxon of the King James version, which gave him such immense power over people everywhere; second, he acquired from his study of the Bible an arsenal of promise and warning, which he used through all his life with magnificent power and effect. There was something wonderful about his simple directness. To you, my friends, who are here this afternoon, I could give you, by the hour, instances of the keen way he went to a point. I remember when I first met him in

Chicago he went to call on one occasion on a leading merchant and most influential man in that city, and when he went out he turned to him and said: 'If you were only a Christian man, what a grand influence you would have in this great city!' That man has been a communicant of the Church for years, and he was Moody's best friend for many years afterward. There was a manliness about Moody, a hatred of cant and mere religious form. He had the most intense and superb enthusiasm of any man I ever knew, tempered by strong human common sense. He had a wonderful intuitive knowledge of men.

"We all know very much of his wonderful successes as a preacher, but those who knew him best and were closest to him know that the great power of his life was in personal conversation with men. The greatest sermon I ever heard from Mr. Moody was one night when we were coming along Madison Avenue at half-past twelve o'clock, going home from one of those great meetings in Madison Square. We had been kept there by those who insisted upon getting advice from Mr. Moody, and, as we were moving along, a gentleman came up from behind and said, 'Mr. Moody, how shall I accept Christ and change my life?' He turned in the moonlight, and standing there on the corner he said a few sharply-cut, kindly words, and he put the truth so earnestly to that man that there was no getting away from it, and the man's heart was changed from that day.

"I was privileged to be with him at those great meetings at the Haymarket, London, and what struck me and surprised me most was the number of educated and cultivated people who came there—the large number of literary people who came there to hear Mr. Moody. The great majority of them did not believe in religion, and they came to hear and enjoy his clean-cut English phraseology. His work at Cambridge and Oxford and in the universities was simply wonderful. When he went to Oxford and Cambridge they determined to run him out of the town; they did not want that kind of a man there, and before they knew him and had heard him they were utterly opposed to his methods. But his courage and his straightforwardness conquered them, and the number of young men, not only in those universities but over all the world, whose lives have been influenced for the better by Mr. Moody's work we will never know until we get into another and better world. His schools at Northfield are models of organization and thoughtfulness. I trust that they will be carried on as a memorial to him.

"What touched me more than anything else in Mr. Moody's character was his extreme modesty about himself. He was the most masterful man I ever knew; when it came to the guidance and instruction of others, he was like a general, managing his army; but when it came to himself he was a most modest man. I was privileged to be in the house with him during all the time of those great meetings at Madison Square. I never heard him appreciate himself once; you would never have known he had anything to do with those meetings; time after time he said to his friends: 'My only wonder is that God can use so feeble an instrument as I, to do his work.' His views became broader as he grew older, and his prejudices, of which he had many in his early life, were thrown off. I have heard him say, 'I am ashamed of myself; you know I have always talked about the extravagance and worldliness of the women in New York; it has been the theme of many of my talks in many places, but I have been here now several days; I have been on the East Side and on the West Side; I have been where the schools are which these women are conducting, and I want to say that I have never known so much self-sacrifice and devotion as is shown by these women, and I am ashamed of what I have said.' I have heard him say, 'You know that I have had great prejudice against the Roman Catholic Church, but I am ashamed of it; I have had some opportunity of noting lately that among the churches where Christ is preached there is none where He is preached so simply and where His cross is held up as it is in the Catholic churches.' I mention these incidents simply to show how he had thrown off his earlier prejudices."

The next speaker was to have been the Hon. John Wanamaker, but illness prevented his attendance, and at his request Mr. Sankey was asked to take his place. After leading the hymn, "Saved by Grace," Mr. Sankey gave the audience an account of the funeral services at Northfield and the incidents attending that ceremony.

Mr. John R. Mott's Address

Mr. John R. Mott, the next speaker, one of the leading Christian Association workers in the world said:

"Among some people the impression exists that Mr. Moody did not exert a great and marked influence upon thinking young men and women. This is a great mistake; there is no class over which Mr. Moody exerted a greater and more helpful or more continuous influence than over the students of this and other countries. He was one of the main factors of that great spiritual awakening at Princeton in 1876 and 1877, resulting in the conversion of 100 young men, and marked the impulse of the movement that led to the Christian Association among the colleges of this country and Canada. When the suggestion was made that an actual conference of college men should be held, it was the influence, co-operation, and leadership of Mr. Moody that made it a fact, and the gathering at Mount Hermon in 1886, which has since convened from year to year, has extended from Northfield to other parts of the country; until now we have some 1,200 young men from the universities and colleges meeting together every year in the United States and Canada, and nearly 1,000 college women, while the movement has spread from this country into Great Britain, Switzerland, France, Germany, Australasia, even into China and Japan, and year by year the inter-collegiate gatherings are held for the training of young men and young women for leadership in the work of Christ.

"Possibly no greater influence has gone out from Mr. Moody's life than that of these conferences. Be it understood that these are conferences, not of the rank and file of the students, but of the young men and women selected by the other students to become leaders in the organized work of Christ in the colleges and universities. Yale will send this year fifty, or one hundred, young men to be leaders in the committees and Christian societies; Harvard will send a large delegation, and Princeton will send hardly less than forty. Bryn Mawr and other young women's schools will send their full delegations to take their part as leaders in the work of Christ. The Student's Volunteer Mission movement had its origin in these meetings, and under the leadership of Mr. Moody. God used Mr. Moody for the purpose, and he seemed to generate the atmosphere which created this Divine movement as projected into foreign fields. The great increase in our Bible classes from 2,000 to 12,000 within a comparatively short time is traceable directly to these annual conferences under Mr. Moody's leadership. There is no sign which is attended with greater promise to the Church of God than this one.

"By his services to students, has the work of evangelism been most advanced. The greatest revivals ever known at Oxford and Cambridge were led by Moody. The most notable awakening at the University of Virginia was during the work of Mr. Moody. The last work among students which he performed, the last work of this description, was at the Yale revival, where twenty or thirty young men acknowledged their faith in Jesus Christ as Lord. Who can measure what he accomplished! Henry Drummond worked among students, and we might add twenty other names; and many of these men to-day are having access to lives and hearts of college men in this and other countries for the reason of Mr. Moody's lasting influence upon them.

"You ask me what is the secret of this influence of his among thinking young men and young women. I find it more especially in his matchless knowledge of the human heart. After that it seems to me that his most marked influence was in his wonderful honesty. If he didn't know a thing he said, 'I don't know.' That gave him the intelligent confidence of the students. Then again his freedom from cant or professionalism gave them additional confidence in him. I have known students to go to his meetings in a critical frame of mind with the purpose of analyzing his methods; I have seen them subdued, almost without exception, by his matchless sympathy and heart power. He appealed to the heroic and self-sacrificing in young men, and then there was over all this and through it all that without which his results and work would be unexplainable, the fact of his abounding fidelity and spiritual life, due to the fact that he was a God-possessed man. I find in these the secret of his great success.

"It was most proper and fitting that his body should be placed at rest on Roundtop; that one spot in all the wide world most gloriously and sacredly associated with his teachings and the influences of his life-work.

"His going from us leaves a great gap; but I am reminded of the words of Henry Drummond on the death of a friend, when he wrote to a classmate: 'We must close up the ranks and work hard.'"

The Chairman introduced the Rev. Dr. Theodore Cuyler as one of Mr. Moody's earliest friends and co-laborers. Dr. Cuyler said:

"The most unique and extraordinary Gospel preacher that America has produced in this century has gone up to his resplendent crown. It was accorded to our Moody to meet and influence more men and women than any other man in modern times. Spurgeon, in his fearless way, spoke once a week, but Moody spoke seven times a week—to 40,000 or 50,000 souls in a week. Our dear brother was more endeared to us because he was such a thorough typical American. He had tasted of the soil, and smelt of the New England fields.

Dr. Cuyler Compares Moody and Lincoln

"If I were called on to name the two most typical Americans of the century-men who have risen from obscurity to worldwide renown—the one a brilliant statesman and the other a model preacher—I should not hesitate to name Abraham Lincoln and Dwight L. Moody. When a nation's life is to be preserved and its liberties maintained, Almighty God calls a poor boy from the log cabin in Kentucky; cradles him in the school of hardship and gives him the Great West for his only university, and then annoints him to lead us through a sea of blood to the Canaan of freedom. In like manner God called the humble farmer boy from the banks of the Connecticut, gave him as his education only one book—the book which schooled him with the spirit of Jesus Christ—and then sent him out as a herald of salvation. Lincoln and Moody were alike in the gift of a remarkable common sense. Neither one of them ever committed a serious mistake. They were alike in being masters of simple, strong, Anglo-Saxon speech, the language of the Bible and of Bunyan, the language of the plain people. Lincoln's heart gushed out in sympathy to all sorts and conditions of men and made him the best loved man in American history. Moody's big loving heart,

PREPARING MR. MOODY'S GRAVE on Round Top. It was from here that Mr. Moody best loved to speak; two of these men were converted under Mr. Moody's

fired with a love of Jesus Christ, made him a master of human emotions, touching the fount of tears in thousands of hearts, and often bringing weeping multitudes before his pulpit. Finally, Lincoln, the liberator, went up to his martyred crown, holding the shattered manacles in his hand. Moody, the liberator, the liberator of immortal souls, fell the other day as a martyr from overwhelming work—went to be greeted at the gates of glory by the thousands he had led from the cross to the crown.

"Ere I take my seat, let me say what may not be known to all of you. On the Sabbath before our brother started for Kansas City he delivered his last sermon in New York in yonder Fifth Avenue Presbyterian Church. In that discourse, as if already the preliminary shadow was falling, he uttered this wonderful sentence: 'You may read in the papers that Moody is dead! It will not be so! God has given me the gift of life everlasting.'

"Thank God, Moody is alive! Moody lives! His spirit is to-day in this hall where he lifted up Jesus. I hear that trumpet voice calling on the pastors and churches of New York to seek the seat of prayer, the baptism of fire, that shall kindle this city and set, perhaps, the nation aflame.

"One other message and I am done. Our beloved brother who has just left us said: 'Five and twenty years ago, in my native village of Northfield, I planted two Christian schools for the training of boys and maidens in Christian living and consecration as teachers and missionaries of Jesus Christ. I bequeath as my legacy those training schools for Jesus to the churches of America, and I only ask, I only ask that visitors to the beautiful native village where I shall slumber on consecrated ground, when they go there shall not be pained by the melancholy sight of the ruins of these schools, but rather that they shall be rejoiced by seeing them as two glorious lighthouses of the Lord beaming out truth and kindness over the world.' My beloved brother, the answer of the Churches of God in America will be: 'We will! We will! We will perpetuate those training schools of Jesus as a splendid, magnificent, fervent memorial of our beloved Dwight Lyman Moody.'"

Mr. R. F. Cutting's Remarks

The next speaker was Mr. Robert Fulton Cutting. He said: "It is a good many years since I last saw Mr. Moody, in his own home, surrounded by his family, and I have been a great deal richer man since I had that experience. I do not know any man who touched me more than he did. He lacked many of those elements of eloquence which go to make up a great public speaker. He did not have much of poetic fire, glowing rhetoric, or elocutionary cadence, but his manner was so direct, so straightforward, so honest, that he seemed to speak to everything human in his audience—everything that was righteous. He seemed to know mankind as very few people do. And he came to this knowledge not by exhaustive analysis, not by psychological formulæ, but he seemed to be able to see into a man's heart because of the transparency of his own nature; because he was so unconsciously honest, so perfectly frank, so courteous, that men and women showed to him what they would not show to others, because they could not hide it from him. He knew mankind, he knew what human life was, and the brilliancy of his own work shone through and through them.

"I was especially impressed at the Northfield conference by one incident. Mr. Moody had been speaking at one of the meetings, and had gone to one of the rooms. Mr. Sankey, who will probably remember the incident, gave out as one of the hymns—one, I think, that belongs to the old Gospel Hymn Book No. 2,—'I feel like singing all the time.' 'I only give that hymn out because

Mr. Moody has left the room', he said. 'He won't let me sing that hymn; he does not believe in singing all the time.' So it was that Mr. Moody knew perfectly well that the men or women whose lives were made up of uninterrupted singing knew very little of the gravity of human life, and was waiting for experiences which would temporarily chill them. He gained access to the hearts of men and women because he dealt with them in a common-sense way. That is the way he completely disarmed all criticism. No man who has played so large a part on the stage of our religious history was so far above criticism as was Mr. Moody. He knew only one doctrine—that 'God so loved the world that He gave his only begotten Son that whosoever believeth in Him should not perish but have eternal life.' He knew only one heretic in the world, and that was the unconverted man or woman. Every man with the love of God in his heart was at home with him. In the midst of all his successes, what a wonderful testimony it was to that man's greatness that he never seemed to have any perception of himself. Like the great master, Michael Angelo, he always so arranged the lights in his life that his own shadow should not fall upon his work. He did not know himself. He knew his field; he knew his God; but he did not know himself,—because he forgot himself when he first made up his mind what his life work was to be. That was the source of his power.

"We are going now to lay our little tributes upon his tomb. If he is gone out of our natural life, he has not gone out of our eternal memories. What he has done for us in making us richer, we will endeavor, in our way, to do for others also."

The Rev. Dr. David J. Burrell, of the Marble Collegiate Church, was the next speaker. His words were:

"A good man has gone and we cannot be sorry. We cannot repeat the liturgy of death, 'Man that is born of woman is of few days and full of trouble; he cometh up as a flower and is cut down.' We are saying, 'Bless the Lord, O my Soul, and all that is within me bless His Holy Name. Bless the Lord, O my Soul, and forget not all His benefits.' It was a wonderful death, was it not? 'Earth is receding; Heaven is opening; God is calling.' Was he thinking of the poet's words:

> " 'The world recedes; it disappears;
> Heaven opens on mine eyes; mine ears
> With sounds seraphic ring?
> Lend, lend your wings! I mount! I fly!
> O grave where is thy victory,
> O death, where is thy sting?'

"It should have been a wonderful death, for it was a wonderful life that went before it. As I have been sitting here, the words that Dr. Pierson read out of Moody's book have been hammering at my heart, 'One thing I do; one thing I do.' This was the dominating power in Mr. Moody's life, an absolute singleness of purpose. He looked into the face of Jesus Christ, who came into the world to do one thing; and, following the Master's text, he said, 'This one thing I also do.'

"I met Mr. Moody when I was a Theological student, thirty-one years ago, in Chicago. I roomed in Farwell Hall, in which Mr. Moody preached, and his apartments were on the floor below me. The Hall took fire one morning, and burned slowly but surely through the forenoon. I busied myself in removing personal effects and otherwise, until at last, driven out, I found myself coatless and hatless in the street. A cordon had formed around in front, but there stood Mr. Moody with a bundle of handbills under his arms; he called me, saying, 'Take these and distribute them.' I looked at the bill. It read, 'Our Beautiful House is Burned; The Noon-day Meeting will be held at the Clark Street

Methodist Church.' I asked, 'Where are your wife and children?' He replied, 'I saw them safe.' 'And your personal effects?' 'O, never mind them,' he said, 'Our meeting must go on.' This was the spirit of the man, 'One thing I do.'

"We cannot better perpetuate his memory than by copying his enthusiasm. I mean to build him a monument, please God, in my ministerial life, by devoting myself most earnestly to the Master's work. I believe I shall love the Bible better, because he loved it so; I believe I shall honor the Holy Ghost more, because he honored Him so; I believe I shall look more affectionately upon the Face so marred, yet so divinely beautiful, because he loved it so. My brethren in the service of Christ, if we revere the memory of this man, let us do the one great thing with more earnestness than ever.

"'Time worketh; Let me work too!
Time undoeth; Let me do!
Busy as time my work I'll ply
Till I rest in the rest of Eternity.

Sin worketh; Let me work too!
Sin undoeth; Let me do!
Busy as sin my work I'll ply
Till I rest in the rest of Eternity!

Death worketh; Let me work too!
Death undoeth; Let me do!
Busy as death my work I'll ply
Till I rest in the rest of Eternity.'"

Dr. Dixon's Eloquent Tribute

The Rev. A. C. Dixon, who for years had been close to Mr. Moody, was the next speaker. He said:

"There was no need that D. L. Moody should ever perform a miracle. He was a miracle. Miracle is God at work; and God

Almighty worked through Dwight L. Moody, who showed to the world, as it seems to me no other man has shown in this generation, the difference between influence and power. He began without influence; he became influential through power. He did not magnify the influences of power and of money and of organization, education and position; but his trust was in God, and the power of Moody's life was God Himself at work. Jesus was not a man of influence; He made Himself of no reputation but of power. Paul and Silas did not have enough influence to keep out of jail, but they had power enough after they were in jail to shake the doors open and walk out; and Moody was gifted with the power that could shake the doors open. I always felt when I left Moody, not like praising Moody, but like praising God. It seemed to me that I could feel and see the throbbing of God, of God's love, God's sympathy, God's great-heartedness, as I came in contact with this wonderful man. He incarnated those words: 'God is able; God is powerful, all powerful.' And God did mighty works through Moody because of his belief. He enabled God—I speak it reverently. Omnipotence stood helpless because of unbelief; but God worked through Moody because he believed. I saw some time ago a great steam-engine, throbbing with power, but it could do nothing because a bolt was broken and the power was cut off. Moody furnished the bolt; he linked himself with Almighty God, and God worked through him because he trusted in His word and in His Spirit and in His Son.

"The life work of our friend was so simple. He had a heart that took him into the great assemblies, into the great cities, the great countries and the great world, making not only a sphere but an atmosphere for Jesus. We speak of the modesty and humility of Moody; and the philosophy of his humility, I am impressed, was this: He always stood in the presence of some great undertaking, some wonderful unfinished work of God, and the work before him was so big that he could hardly see Moody; he could simply see the work to be done and the God that could do it, and he felt honored in being the instrument of God in its execution. Brethren, he always considered himself as the mere instrument of God, and he never thought to take any of the glory of his work to himself. I am afraid that many of us are too well satisfied; we get puffed up with vanity and pride, with the little bit that we have done; we have not undertaken enough for God. Moody fought for evangelization of the cities and of the world, and if God will lift us unto his feet and just let us see Him as Moody saw Him, we shall be humiliated, expecting a blessing from Him.

"I believe in the educational work established by Mr. Moody. God prosper the schools! May God lead some of the millionaires to lay millions upon that altar, and do it quickly, the more quickly the better for the glory of God. But education with Mr. Moody was the result of evangelism, and not evangelism the result of education. Education was an incident of his life, and education was established through his evangelism; and my prayer is that Moody may be projected into the future, and that those schools may be supported by evangelism. Not only by wealthy men giving their millions, but by pastors praying for them, do I hope that this two-fold work of Moody's will be continued until we shall meet him in glory.

"'Within the next twelve months,' if Moody were standing on this platform, I believe he would say, 'Within the next twelve months we shall preach the Gospel to every creature in Greater New York.' Let that be the watch-word for 1900! The politicians can reach all the voters in three months, and I believe that Christian people can reach every sinner in Greater New York within the next twelve months. We can bring the Gospel to the people in the home and on the street—the Word of God Himself—and the work of the Church will make God wake them up. Let us bring the Gospel to the people everywhere—in the homes, in the churches, in the theatres, on the streets. If we are to perpetuate Moody's work, it will be by taking Christ into the homes and the hearts of the people.

"Remember the Word of God to Joshua, the man who was to meet danger: 'Be strong and of good courage;' and it needs courage to meet swords and bullets. Remember God's words to Solomon, the man who was to meet difficulties in building the temple: 'Be strong and of good courage;' and it takes a finer fibre of courage to meet obstacles than to meet bullets, it takes more real bravery to overcome the obstacles that beset the Christian's path than to climb San Juan Hill or storm Manila or Santiago; it takes more than courage to meet the obstacles and labor of carrying the Gospel to the millions. Moody never faltered under difficulty, because he believed his God was equal to any emergency. Listen to these words of God, 'Moses, my servant, is dead; arise therefore and pass over Jordan.'

"God help us to carry on the work that he laid down and do it in the strength of his Almighty God!"

The Characterization by Dr. Buckley

The Rev. Dr. J. M. Buckley then spoke as follows:

"We go to the Bible for sublime passages, and those who understand the great book go to it for strange passages. The strangest memorial note in all literature is to be found in the Bible concerning a certain king who reigned in Israel eight years, and the epitaph proposed for him is this, 'and he departed without being desired.'

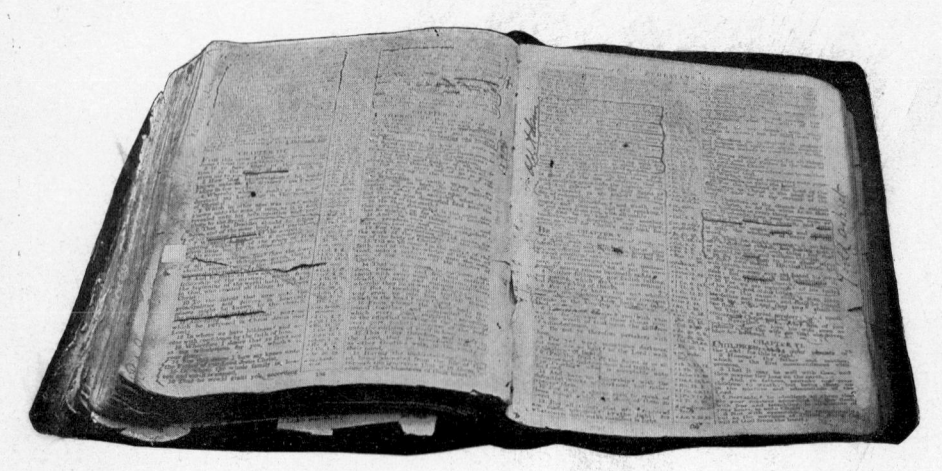

MR. MOODY'S BIBLE showing marks and annotations by the evangelist.

MR. MOODY'S DOG. Everyone who saw the evangelist on the streets of Northfield during recent years will remember this faithful dog, always at his heels.

"What a contrast between such a career and that which has called us here! Our friend died when he was most desired; desired to maintain those wondrous Bible Conferences; desired as a nucleus of undenominational activity; desired to sustain those educational institutions which he had founded; desired to raise up more workers imbued with his spirit; desired to dart to and fro through the country to awaken communities, to snap the chains of conventionalism, to elicit and evoke the tremendous latent forces of the Church, and to unite Christians in the only way in which they can ever be united;—by a firm and unswerving belief in the fundamental principles of the Gospel he developed, and in active, soul-saving, consecrated labor. At this hour D. L. Moody was called away.

"To attend a meeting of this sort sometimes produces singular effects. Persons are heated by the Scriptures, and by their own rhetoric, until at last one would think it a jubilation, and from a great memorial meeting in this city a gentleman retired saying, 'I was sad when I went there, but I don't know now that it makes any great difference.' According to these speeches, God is going to take care of His own work. The fact is the New Testament never teaches that we should not be sad. On the contrary, when Epaphroditus was sick, St. Paul wrote to the Philippians and told them that Epaphroditus longed after them because they had heard that he had been sick. And the Apostle said, 'indeed he was sick, nigh unto death; but God had mercy on him, and not on him only, but on me also, lest I should have sorrow upon sorrow.' The real feeling is midway between jubilation and the sorrow of the world that worketh death. It is a great loss; to human eyes it is a dreadful and in a certain aspect of the case an irreparable loss.

"How are we going to prove that any preacher has the Spirit of God? Will oratorical preaching, will pathetic preaching, will persuasive preaching demonstrate that he has the Spirit? Is the power of discerning spirits left in the Church? Did not some of the most famous evangelists the world ever saw fall into the very depths of iniquity and sin? Did not the author of that wondrous hymn, 'Come, ye sinners, poor and needy', spend twelve years in the most dreadful depth of depravity, and go mourning all his days after he emerged from it? Have we not in our day known men absolutely to renounce the doctrines they held when they were most prosperous as evangelists, and confess with brazen face that in the very midst of their greatest efforts and success they did not believe what they were supposed to believe? How then shall a man prove that he has the Spirit of God? He must prove it by a long career, by a spotless reputation, by meeting men face to face as well as upon the rostrum, and by the men who have slept with him, and traveled with him, and prayed with him, and suffered in evil report as well as in good report. These men must stand up, and be able to declare in the face of God, and in the presence of men, that this man all through this period lived as he professed, prayed as he professed, preached as he professed, denied himself as he professed. And then, if God gives such a wondrous death to that man as this, we have evidence probable and conclusive that he was a man of God.

"But, my brethren, you cannot undertake to show that D. L. Moody did just what any other man could do, if he only had enough of the Spirit. Could God do as much by Peter in the same way that He could with Paul? What kind of a speech would Peter have made at Mars Hill to the Epicureans and the Stoics? He would, perhaps unconsciously, unless a special miracle had been wrought, have gotten himself into very great difficulty. He did it on several occasions, and had not learned better until the threshold of the crucifixion, when he smote off an ear in the excess of ill-regulated zeal. The fact in the case is that God by nature endowed Mr. Moody in an astonishing manner with regard to his mere body. There was a man in Connecticut who loved and adored Mr. Moody, and he invariably amused himself in this way, sitting in the cars. When Mr. Moody came in he would say, 'Do you know him? That is Huntington, the greatest railroad man in this country.' Never did he hear one word of question from the men who had never seen Huntington. At other times he would suggest he was a Western Judge. In every case every man seemed to think it exactly right. They saw that tremendous head, monster chest, prompt, intense, direct action, a man obviously born to command. This same man invariably told people afterward before they left him, for he was a Christian, 'No, that is not Mr. Huntington; it is Mr. Moody;' and their curiosity was greatly excited. But D. L. Moody never reminded any other man of another man, in the ordinary sense of the term. All the humility of Mr. Moody was before God. He never was humble in his dealings with Mr. Sankey. He never was humble in his dealings with any man that he undertook to deal with. If ever there was a man self-confident under God, D. L. Moody was the man.

"Physically many men reminded other men of Mr. Moody. That undefinable personality that will not show in a photograph, and cannot be painted in oil, was in Mr. Moody, and it went out of his eyes, and out of his head. He came up to me one day in a parlor car, and struck me on the shoulder and said, 'You look about the same as you did when,'—and he mentioned a long period of time that need not be repeated here. A man came up and said, 'Who was that?' Said I, 'That is D. L. Moody.' 'I thought,' said the stranger, 'it was Henry Wilson,' and there was a very great physical resemblance between the Vice-President and Mr. Moody.

"Then this man had what is seldom found in men inclined to corpulence,—immense activity. He was more active than the average man of medium size.

"He could improve, and that was one of his glories. Two hundred years from now the extreme higher critics will be trying to prove that there were two Moodys, and they will do it by getting up the language word by word, and sentence by sentence, that Mr. Moody used when he began in Chicago. They will make a parallel of that with the highly improved style of his later years. Some persons say Mr. Moody was not a cultivated orator. Note that passage quoted by Drummond, observe that when in London he described the ascension of Elijah several parliamentary orators arose to their feet and looked in the air after the ascending prophet. Take his sublime eulogy of Joseph of Arimathea, delivered in this house less than a year ago. Not far from yonder box sat a bishop noted for sound judgment, and he said, 'That is a piece of work any man might be proud of.'

"Nearly twenty-five years ago the gentleman who presides to-day sat on the platform in the Hippodrome. A very strange scene took place in the City of New York. We have read the Arabian Nights' entertainment, we remember that a certain Caliph used to go about in disguise, and marvelous are the extraordinary tales told of him. But at that time New York beheld an emperor, an emperor of a great territory, which is to be in the future one of the greatest empires of the world, unless it remains permanently republican. I refer to Dom Pedro, the Emperor of Brazil. He went on the platform and took the seat vacated by Mr. Dodge and sat there. Two-thirds of the audience knew who he was, but the man of the occasion was Mr. Moody, and he was preaching then and there. What did he do? Did he exhibit that fawning and obsequious bow that many persons do when the President appears, or even a Secretary of State? Mr. Moody never referred to Dom Pedro, but he introduced into the midst of his discourse these words: 'What will you do with Jesus? What will you do with Jesus? An emperor cannot buy Heaven, but he can have it as a free gift,' and after he said that he paused, and Dom Pedro bowed his assent, and afterwards remarked to the gentleman who wrote the account, 'That is a man to be heard and to be believed.'

"Mr. Moody was a personality. That personality is now invisible. It will disappear. You and I will remember him, and those who have seen him will remember him, but we belong to a vanishing generation. Who can go through Westminster Abbey without a guide-book, and know much about a great many that are there? Very few. The personality of Mr. Moody will be totally forgotten, as has been the personality to a large extent of Jacob Knapp, and of Charles G. Finney, and a great many others; to the present generation they are but names. There is but one way to prevent the personality of Moody from entirely disappearing. It is by the perpetuation of those schools, and the maintenance of their spirit. God forbid that those schools should ever follow in the wake of Harvard Divinity School and of some others! Mr. Moody had his prejudices, but I heard him declare that he would fellowship with everybody who believed himself a sinner and trusted in Christ. 'But,' said he, 'God being my helper, I never will fellowship a man who denies the Deity of my God and Saviour, Jesus Christ, or sneers at His atonement.'

"There was a man who spent his life in traducing the Bible, in caricaturing the ministry, in making audiences as large as this, laugh at our holy faith. That man boasted that he would have his stenographer with him when he died, that none could misrepresent his last words. He had a painless death. He never had to meet the king of terrors. No man whispered in his ear, 'You are about to die. Does your faith sustain you?' He died and left the most deplorable scene of unconsolable grief that the world ever saw. Our Moody was told that he must die. What then? O, the blessing of the manner of his death to the Church! God showed, I believe, in a peculiar way for the Church and for him that 'Precious in the sight of the Lord is the death of his saints.' There is something worse in this world than agnosticism, something worse than blank infidelity. It is the practical effects of a belief that we cannot be sure of the future. There are some hopeless words from 'In a Persian Garden', that I heard sung with sweeter voices than are often heard in the sanctuary, at a private entertainment, and at the close a young lady was heard to say, 'Well, perhaps that is all there is to it.'

" There were those in the time of Paul who said, ' Let us eat, drink, and be merry, for to-morrow we die.' Ah, if there were no life afterward I too would drink anything that would make me oblivious of my doom! But listen! listen! listen! 'I heard a voice from Heaven saying to me, Write: Blessed are the dead which die in the Lord from henceforth. Yea, saith the Spirit, that they may rest from their labors and their works do follow them.'

" Farewell, beloved brother! Farewell, stalwart friend! Farewell, all men's friend! We shall see thee at last, but not in the flesh; for didst thou not thyself say, ' My body to the dust, my soul to the God who gave it.' "

At the conclusion of Dr. Buckley's remarks, Mr. Sankey sang a memorial hymn, written by him for the occasion, the whole assemblage joining in the chorus. The ceremonies were then closed with the benediction by the Rev. J. Balcolm Shaw.

CHAPTER XXX.

Appreciations by Eminent Friends

THE estimation in which Mr. Moody was held by his co-workers, and others who knew him, will testify perhaps most fittingly to his wonderful personality. Many of the following tributes were written in response to inquiries made by *The Christian Endeavor World.*

"He was a convincing example of the priesthood of the people, and led out the laity into fields of unsuspected Christian usefulness. Edwards, Payson, Caughey, Inskip, Moody: the greatest of these was Moody."—*Rev. D. H. Moore, D. D., Cincinnati, Ohio.*

"Mr. Moody was a man of the utmost sincerity, clear faith and strong constitution. He knew men, and was a man of common sense. He was a preacher, simple, direct and interesting. I believe that he gave a strong uplift to the religious life of America and Great Britain."—*William Lawrence, Protestant Episcopal Bishop of Massachusetts.*

"In the most entire and utmost way, Mr. Moody exhibited and lived for and preached Jesus Christ at once God and Brother. His success in that preaching is only an illustration of the fact that such Gospel appeals to and meets as nothing else can, the needs of the human heart. His last words were: 'The earth recedes, Heaven opens.' Those may be our last words also if, as he did, we trust and serve his Lord, who is at once Lord and Brother."—*Rev. Wayland Hoyt, D. D., Philadelphia, Pa.*

"In Christ
His life was a good fight of faith.
His work was a long labor of love.
His death was a full triumph of hope.
His memory is a strong inspiration to service.
His reward is an inheritance of glory
With Christ."
—*Rev. Henry Van Dyke, D. D.* *New York, N. Y.*

"He is, in my opinion, the greatest evangelist since Whitefield, and since the Apostle Paul there has been no man who has preached to so great a multitude and led so many to Christ. To the end of time Mr. Moody's teachings will last. The simplicity of his words went direct to the heart of common men. His conscientiousness, his enthusiasm, his inspired common sense, his kindness—all made him especially fitted for his work."—*Rev. Newell Dwight Hillis, D. D., Brooklyn, N. Y.*

"He was, under God, the prime inspirer and director of the evangelistic trend, which has marked the last third of the nineteenth century. He has done more than any clergyman or layman of his generation in changing the style and method of the pulpit and in making it, as it ought to be, more direct, practical and sympathetic. To say that Mr. Moody was an uneducated man is wide of the mark. He was well educated, although self-educated, through the constant use of all the varied resources, which lay around him, for thorough and continuous preparation for his divinely designated mission."—*Rev. Robert Hunter, D.D., Philadelphia, Pa.*

"I have known Mr. Moody for twenty-five years, and have met him on many occasions. He was one of the purest and truest men I ever knew. He was a most thoughtful and careful student

REV. F. B. MEYER, OF LONDON.

of the Bible. He was a great friend of young men, and his influence over them was remarkable. He was a devoted and laborious worker, and, so far as I know, the money he received nearly all went to aid poor young men or struggling colleges or churches. Mr. Moody was a remarkable reader of human nature and seemed intuitively to understand how to apply the truth to men in keeping with their disposition and nature. The Church of Jesus Christ has lost one of the most effective workers it ever had in the death of Mr. Moody."—*Rev. I. W. Joyce, D.D., LLD., Bishop of the M. E. Church.*

"Mr. Moody was a man of tender compassion and unbounded sympathy, of deep humility and abounding charity, of tireless energy and unflagging hope. Faith in a God who answers prayer and who can save the most hopeless, faith in the Bible as the Word of God from the beginning to the end, faith in the present power of the Holy Spirit, was the secret of his strong, beautiful and wondrous service."—*Rev. R. A. Torrey, Chicago, Ill.*

"Mr. Moody has taken his place among the immortals. In his own sphere his work was owned by God as truly as was that of Mr. Spurgeon in his sphere. Mr. Moody gave great prominence and power to the work of the laity. He emphasized the gentler rather than the sterner elements of the Gospel. His ministry was one of declaration rather than one of argumentation. His educational work is the most enduring feature of his unique service and his consecrated life."—*Rev. R. S. MacArthur, D.D., New York, N. Y.*

"In the death of Mr. Moody, the world suffers a loss which no other man's services, however invaluable, can neutralize. His speculations concerning things beyond this earth were not peculiarly his and were not the measure of his great worth. His value was his amazing gift for identifying the whole human side of his religion with the whole human side of his life, and for kindling other souls from the fires of his mighty devotion. May these things live after him forever."—*George W. Cable, Northampton, Mass.*

"My heart aches over the loss that comes to us in the death of Mr. Moody. He has always been an inspiration to me in preparing hymns for gospel work; not that he was a musician or claimed to be, but I early learned to prize his judgment as to the value and usefulness of a hymn for the work. What moved him was sure to move others, and what failed to do so could be safely omitted. I have esteemed it one of my highest privileges to share in preparing songs for his work, and, now that he has gone, how lonely it seems!"—*James McGranahan, Kinsman, O.*

"D. L. Moody believed the Bible to be the Word of God, and preached its truths with the authority of a messenger intrusted with a revelation. He believed in the Holy Spirit, and depended upon Him for power. His love for Jesus was a passion; and he loved people, good and bad, because Jesus loved them.

"In the inner circle of his family and intimate friends he was as tender as a child, or gentle as a woman, at times as frolicsome as a boy, and as cheerful as morning sunshine. There was in him a rare union of spiritual fervor and common sense. His enthusiasm never ran away with his judgment. He was truly great in the Christlike sense of ministry to others."—*Rev. A. C. Dixon, D.D., Brooklyn, N. Y.*

"The rounded fulness of Dwight L. Moody's life is answer to the oft-repeated question, Is life worth living? It is not worth living if lived for self; it is if lived for others. And, when I think of the countless many who have been lifted to higher things by his earnest words and self-denying life, I am sure that his life was worth living. Only the recording angel can tell the number of those who, when the news of his death was telegraphed, responded with the expression, unrecorded on earth, 'Thank God for Dwight L. Moody's life!'

"His end was peace. His message to all is service. 'Whosoever will be chief among you let him be your servant.' The world needs a successor. Who will he be?"—*David J. Brewer, Associate Justice of the Supreme Court of the United States, Washington, D. C.*

"He preached a positive Gospel to an age of doubt, and moved the popular heart and life as no other man of the age has done, unless it be Charles H. Spurgeon. The great preacher was ever true to the Bible doctrines concerning God, sin, punishment, repentance, Heaven and hell He stood firmly for the divinity of Christ and the inspiration of the Scriptures and the authority of the Book of books. He was a large-hearted, sympathetic, noble, manly man. His Gospel was full of sunshine and joy. 'God is love' was the magnet which he used to draw men to Christ and a new life. His power was due to his positive faith, his life in close touch with the spirit of God, his rare good sense, his sympathy and love for all classes, his insight into human nature and his ability to manage men. He has shown what one can be and do who is wholly devoted to God and his work."—*Rev. P. H. Swift, D.D., Chicago, Ill.*

"Very few men have been so close to the strength and weaknesses of humanity. He saw and dealt with all classes—the high and the low, the rich and the poor—and as he came close to them they also were drawn close to him. This was because all believed in his love and truth, in his sincerity and absolute unselfishness. This was never shown perhaps to a greater degree than in the early life of this association, when full of faith, hope and perseverance he gave to this organization that spiritualizing force which is to-day the great source of strength and vitality.

"Two of my childish recollections of Sunday are of sitting in one of the pews of the old 'spotted church,' as it was called, and going with my father to the mission Sunday school in North Market Hall, where Mr. Moody was the chief spirit. I remember how he inspired me with confidence as a child, and how my love and respect grew with the passing years."—*J. V. Farwell, Jr., Chicago. Ill.*

"Any tribute I might give to the memory of Mr. Moody would be largely influenced by personal affection as well as admiration, for during the well-nigh quarter of a century I have been associated with him and his work, both my love and my admiration for him have grown with the passing years, and his taking away therefore comes as a personal grief.

"He combined in a most extraordinary degree great strength and force of character with great sympathy and tenderness of heart, and with these a most generous nature, always considering the welfare of others rather than his own comfort and happiness.

"It may be truly said of him that 'a prince in Israel has fallen.' and those who know him best and are best able to estimate his services to his generation will say, what they believe time will reveal to all, Dwight L. Moody was one of the greatest men of the century now closing."—*George C. Stebbins, Brooklyn, N. Y,*

"The lines along which he won success are worthy of very careful attention. First, his life was a constructive force. He was in the world to build up, construct, to save. He could say, with Christ: 'I am come not to destroy men's lives, but to save them.' He dealt with the positive, the known and settled in religion.

"Second, he was thoroughly sincere. He believed his messsage to be absolutely true. There was no doubt in his heart, consequently none found expression on his lips. He was evidently so honest, so true, outspoken and frank that all men were convinced that he believed through and through every word he preached, and that he loved his fellow-men and desired their salvation above everything else; and that he was in the work, not to satisfy a selfish ambition, or for ease or fame, but because from conviction he had to be there.

"The next element of power in Moody was a childlike simplicity that was marvellous. He was a man of remarkable wisdom, but there was no cunning in him. He was as absolutely free from duplicity as a man can be."—*Rev. Charles C. Earle, Boston, Mass.*

"His life was spent for Jesus Christ, his Master. Self was kept back, while Christian power within was his guide.

"God chose Moody, I have no doubt, because there was in his nature all the fire and enthusiam that would break out and electrify mankind. He was anxious for the souls of men. Moody was a layman, but his ministry has been as successful as any man in orders. Others have saved their hundreds, he his thousands. Moody was a born leader and was one of the greatest generals we have ever had. If he had been a soldier he would have stood side by side with Grant or Wellington.

"Moody unified humanity. He wanted all denominations to get together. He knew that the way to have a union was not by creeds but by work. Let us take Moody's idea of work as a unifying force."—*Rev. George C. Lorimer, D.D., Boston, Mass.*

"Dwight L. Moody was as undeniably the most extraordinary Gospel preacher that America has produced in this century as Spurgeon was the most extraordinary that Britain has produced. Both had all Christendom for their congregations. I am glad that, like Abraham Lincoln, he never went to any college; both formed their own racy Saxon styles for themselves.

"With my beloved Brother Moody I had much personal intimacy for twenty-eight years. He delivered his first Bible readings in our little mission chapel in the winter of 1872. A few months later, when I was in London, he came into my room one day and said, 'They want me to stay and preach here; what shall I do?' My quick answer was, '*Come.*' He went with Mr. Sankey, and thus began his world-wide career in Britain.

"One of his last sermons was delivered from my old pulpit here a few weeks ago. I said to him, 'Last night you were *at your best*; you were not talking to Christians, but calling the unconverted to Jesus; *stick to that* as long as you live.' Who will be the Elisha to follow our translated Elijah?"—*Rev. Theodore L. Cuyler, D.D., Brooklyn, N. Y.*

Dwight L. Moody, the most divinely ordained Christian evangelist of the nineteenth century, sleeps well. He was girt with greatness all around. A great intellect was his. For, although unlearned in the classics and sciences, he was deeply schooled in the science of God and of His Son Jesus Christ, whom to know aright is life eternal. Other knowledges than this pass away, and are liable to puff up while they last.

"Mr. Moody's greatness of intellect was evidenced by the fact that his sermons repeated a thousand and more times were always as fresh and fascinating as they were at first. Only extraordinary minds can speak often on the same theme without becoming stale. He had also a great heart. He loved everything that was good. I do not believe he ever felt hateful toward any man. Supremely he loved Jesus Christ as we read of Him in the Word. Mr. Moody was as certain that the Holy Scriptures, as we have them, were fully inspired by the Holy Spirit, as he was that his pulse-beat came from his heart's throb. I recall no other one in my day whose departure and 'abundant entrance' above have brought Heaven so sensibly near. He was the friend of the whole world, and all lands will lament the loss of his measureless influence for human welfare."—*Rev. John Lindsay Withrow, D. D., Boston, Mass.*

"Moody and I met for the first time in Cleveland, East Tennessee. It was about the middle of April, 1864. I was bringing together my Fourth Army Corps. Two divisions had already arrived, and were encamped in and near the village. Moody was then fresh and hearty, full of enthusiasm for the Master's work. Our soldiers were just about to set out on what we all felt promised a hard and bloody campaign, and I think were especially desirous of strong preaching. Crowds turned out to hear the glad tidings from Moody's lips. He showed them how a soldier would give his heart to God. His preaching was direct and effective, and multitudes responded with a confession and promise to follow Christ.

"From that time on throughout his useful career I have had association with him. On the steamer Spree, during our remarkable wreck and rescue, I was with him. Who could have held up Christ with more fearlessness and fidelity than he did then to over seven hundred passengers?

"In Chicago he acted as a general, and I became his subordinate during the World's Fair. Thousands upon thousands crowded the theatres, tents, halls, churches, and other public buildings, by his provisions, to hear the simple Gospel.

"His work, again, in our war with Spain, by sending evangelical speakers to the front, whom he knew the soldiers would heed and hear, will never be measured by us who were mere helpers. He planned, selected his messengers, and sent them, and raised funds to give to our soldiers the bread of life.

"With tears we read his last words: 'Heaven opens. Earth recedes. God is calling me.' But O the triumph, Stephen-like, of such a departure."—*General O. O. Howard., Burlington, Vt.*

"I first knew Mr. Moody in 1857. It was at a Sunday school convention at a Clark Street mission in Chicago that I met him. He was then twenty-one years old, and was just entering the career in which he has done so much of good. He was a stout, robust, ardent young fellow, shaking hands with everybody and smiling on them in his cheerful way, and the smile was not put on either—it was genuine.

"I crossed the continent with him in 1871 to attend the California Sunday school Convention, and again in 1872 I crossed the Atlantic in his company when he first went to London to hold evangelistic services. At the invitation of Mr. Buley, the originator of the Dublin tax system, and a philanthropic gentleman of large means, I spent several days at Mr. Buley's home, near Dublin, in company with Mr. Moody, and there I became better acquainted with the man himself. Since then I have met him many times.

"Mr. Moody was bold, courageous in his advocacy of the things which he believed. He did not know what self-consciousness was. He was never embarrassed—at least he never showed it. He had unlimited faith in the divine power to carry him through difficulties. To be sure he sometimes failed in his plans—things did not go just as he wanted them to, but he never worried over such things. Once in Ireland I made fun of some of his old stories. I said, 'See here, Moody, I have heard you tell these same stories over and over again, and now I'd like to hear some new ones.' He looked at me in a hurt sort of way and with tears in his eyes he said, 'Don't say that. I have to use them.' I made up my mind then that if any man could use an old sword as effectively as D. L. Moody did, I would never criticise him for it.

"While fixed in his own faith, he was liberal towards people of diverse faiths. Once in Chicago he went to call on a Roman Catholic bishop. 'I have talked religion with almost everybody,' said

G. CAMPBELL MORGAN AND G. H. C. MAC GREGOR, pastors of Congregational and Presbyterian Churches in London,

REV. DR. SCOFIELD, pastor of the Second Congregational Church at East Northfield, who conducted the funeral services. On

Moody, 'and I thought I would come and talk to you. Besides, some of your boys throw stones at a mission over on the north side.' 'That's very wrong in them,' said the bishop, 'and I will tell them they must not do so.' So they talked about religion for a while, and Moody said, 'You pray, bishop?' 'Yes, said the bishop.' 'Let's pray now,' said Moody, and they did, and they parted fast friends. Moody had largeness of soul while he had positiveness of faith. It would be good if we had more like him.

"No man has died in this country in years for whom there has been a wider, greater, intenser affection than there was for Dwight L. Moody."—*Rev. John H. Vincent, D.D., L.L. D., Bishop of the M. E. Church.*

"1. A man of prayer—the chief secret of his wisdom, usefulness and success.

"2. A man of the Book—unwearied in Biblical study, he wore out several Bibles; absorbed the very atmosphere as well as the spiritual texts of Scripture.

"3. A man of soundest evangelical faith, with a mighty grasp of essentials in the answer to the question, 'What must I do to be saved?'

"4. A man of extraordinary practical sagacity, organizing power, and aptness for leadership. He used to say that it was better to set ten men at work than to do yourself the work of ten men. But he was accustomed to do both.

"5. A man of combined courage and tenderness—bold as any lion, tender as any drop of dew.

"6. A man endowed by his unusually powerful but balanced emotions with greatness of character, and by his caution and trenchant common sense with strategic strength of character.

"7. A man of commanding spiritual manliness, everywhere inspiring confidence.

"8. A man of remarkable business and executive talent, he was trusted by men of affairs.

"9. A man working easily with associates whose endowments filled out his own, like Professor Drummond and Mr. Sankey, the three together making a globe of capacities and aptitudes for the work they undertook.

"10. A man whose career has been a spiritual link between England and America and all English-speaking lands. Mr. Moody has had no equal as an evangelist since President Finney was laid in his grave; and, as he had no real predecessor like himself, so he is not likely to have a successor. The Chicago and the Northfield schools ought to continue through his sons his unmatched work. 'I wonder,' said a young minister to Professor Park, 'that Providence can accomplish so much through a man of only moderate endowments.' 'I wish to speak respectfully of Providence,' said Professor Park, in reply, 'but I call Mr. Moody a great man.' 'I wish I had your shoulders,' said Mr. Gladstone. 'I wish I had your head,' said Mr. Moody, in answer."—*Joseph Cook, L.L. D., Boston, Mass.*

"My acquaintance with Mr. Moody runs back forty years or more, when he was just emerging from business and attracting attention in Chicago by his resolute and resistless efforts in religious work. We came together often. My house was his home, especially after the Chicago fire, when he walked out from his flame-lit house with his little family, saving nothing but his personal Bible. We were together several months at the time, and gathered the money mainly in New England for the rebuilding of the Illinois Street Mission. Soon after the fire he made the acquaintance of Mr. Sankey and founded the connection with which work in England began at York.

"Stretching over the years that intervened, up to Monday night, November 13th of this year, I have enjoyed the inspiration of his life. The freshest memory I have of him is the night above referred to, when he got off the Pennsylvania Railroad train to keep an appointment he had made with me by telegraph, to spend a short time between trains on his way to Kansas City for his last meetings. I remarked that same night, after he had left me, how heavy a burden seemed to rest upon his heart as he said again and again: 'I wish that I might be moved of God to move one large Eastern city. For I think if one Eastern city could be thoroughly revived, the others would feel the influence and be stirred likewise.' As I looked into the face of the man, whose eyes and voice were full of tears, it seemed as if a prophet like unto Elijah had come back again. He left behind him that night his comfortable home at Northfield and the hospitality which so many friends would have been glad to give him; laid himself down in a sleeping-berth of a Pullman car, rattling over a thousand miles to Kansas City; and rose with a heavy load of concern for the kingdom of his Master, and under the weight of it he staggered into his grave.

"In summing up the distinctly great things of this great century no man stands out more prominently who has spent so many continuous years in superhuman labor for the public good as Dwight L. Moody, the Christian American layman. Uncrowned, without title of any kind, he wears the first honors among the men who loved their fellow men."—*The Honorable John Wanamaker.*

"In D. L. Moody's death the world has lost one of the most remarkable men of the century. He was especially distinguished for his great devotion to the cause of Christianity and of preaching the gospel to the world. To me one of his most distinguishing characteristics was his consecrated common sense; this, together with a burning zeal for winning men to the service of Christ, and his ability to do the work of ten or a dozen ordinary men, made him the most successful and powerful evangelist of his day. He was as tender as a woman, and yet as strong and brave as a lion. It was my happy lot to have been with him for over twenty-eight years, in our own country and in lands beyond the sea; and my love and admiration for him increased as the years passed by.

"The news of his death came as a great shock, as we had been led to believe that he was slowly gaining ground and likely to recover. A week before he passed away, I went to Northfield to see him, and, if possible, to cheer him up, but found him so weak and nervous that I decided not to risk an interview, lest harm might come to him; and thus I failed to bid him good-by. The last time I saw and talked with Mr. Moody was on the occasion of his last visit to Dr. John Hall's church in New York City. We spent most of that Sabbath day together talking over the work in this country, and also the old days of our labors together across the sea. He seemed quite happy as we spoke of many kind friends with whom we had worked in Great Britain; but, when I suggested to him that we might go once more to that country and hold a few farewell meetings, even for a month or two, an expression of sadness came into his face such as I had seldom seen before, as he said, 'I should like to go, but I have a feeling that I shall not live to cross the sea again.' This was the first intimation I had ever received that he had any thought that he might not be with us long. Little did I dream that I was having my last talk with my beloved friend.

"It is a pleasant thought that Mr. Moody's body has been laid to rest on beautiful 'Round Top,' where he has spent so many of the happiest hours of his life with those who had gathered there to hear his words of wisdom and grace. This spot might very appropriately be called Missionary Hill, for it is believed that from it more young men and women have decided to go to foreign lands as missionaries than from any other single spot in the world."—*Ira D. Sankey., Brooklyn, N. Y.*

CHAPTER XXXI

Editorial Estimates of His Character.

FEW men who have labored in the field of evangelism have won their deserved recognition so completely as Mr. Moody. Association with Mr. Moody very quickly convinced one that he stood pre-eminent among millions for his earnestness, his singleness of purpose, his unaffected piety,—for all that combination of principles and faculties which went to make up his marvelous personality. But it was not necessary to be associated with him to understand in some measure his greatness. His work stands as a monument to abilities which were far above the ordinary. Tens of thousands of men cry out, "He helped me!" Great buildings in various parts of the country attest his foresight in educational matters, and the practical bent of his mind.

His Greatness Recognized Everywhere

These visible signs, this great mass of cumulative evidence of his greatness it is impossible to ignore. Even persons who were so unfortunate as not to come into sympathy with his efforts cannot refuse to recognize that he accomplished, with God's help, great things for the betterment of mankind.

Here, then, I quote a few extracts from editorials in various journals, published immediately after Mr. Moody's death. The unanimity of opinion is remarkable. I doubt very much if any other great man who has died within the past few years has received after his death such a shower of glad tributes. Those who have followed Mr. Moody's career know how well deserved the tributes are, and yet, how much they fall short of recognizing the full measure of his greatness.

"Mr. Moody undoubtedly exerted a powerful and stimulating influence, not only on the masses but on many of those who were his superiors in birth, breeding or intellect."—The London *Spectator*.

"Wherever Moody spoke, whether in his own country or in other English-speaking lands, he invariably commanded attention and aroused interest. He retained to the very last of his public career the qualities which marked him from the outset as a potent preacher."—The Boston *Globe*.

"Mr. Moody's claim to greatness did not rest on his intellectual strength, but on his goodness. The standard of his character was his unqualified and immovable faith in God and in the Bible. With this faith he combined simplicity, honesty, sincerity, humility, zeal, an abhorrence of egotism, and a broad charity."—The Chicago *Inter-Ocean*.

"His going leaves a great void behind, and the world will seem lonely without him to many in every land. His death will send a wave of sincere sorrow over millions of humanity without distinction of race, creed or church. Here was a man whose soul was pure goodness, who was ruled by loftier motives than commonly govern men, whose crown was Christlike character, and men, even irreligious men, instinctively yield his memory the homage of their respect and reverence."—*The Presbyterian Banner*.

"Mr. Moody's life teaches us that, while the Church needs scholars, what she needs most of all is the impulse of Christian devotion, that force which compelled St. Paul, and has compelled a thousand others in all branches of the Church on whom was laid the burden of a lost world, and who have said, 'Woe is me if I preach not the Gospel.' Mr. Moody's life was well filled out with work nobly accomplished, and his death was the fit end of a life of faith and service. His memory is one of the treasures of the Christian Church."—*The Independent.*

"He combined, as only his countrymen can, a remarkably keen business intelligence with unflagging enthusiasm. To the last he was very much what he had been at first; he attempted to be no more or better; he had no precise "views" or "opinions" about abtruse matters; and probably he did not himself know very well whether he was a Calvinist or not, or what were his exact theological bearings. But some gift within him, some influence which he gave out, had more efficacy with certain minds in certain moods than learning or eloquence or wit or pathos. The note of sincerity, the unflinchingly literal way in which he took things which others understood symbolically or spiritually, had a prodigious effect on people who wanted to see and hear and touch with their hands; people by no means necessarily unintelligent."—*The London Times.*

"According to common agreement, Mr. Moody was not a great preacher, so far as greatness depends upon and is manifested in extensive learning or lofty flights of eloquence. There was in his appeals to sinners that mysterious something which is expressed neither in fine phrases nor in deep philosophic reflections. His magnetism and convincing force seem to have lain in an earnestness which left no doubt, and which affected the emotions like a whirlwind. By his death the evangelization movement has sustained a tremendous, perhaps irreparable, loss."—*The Baltimore Herald.*

"Chicago at one time claimed this mighty preacher. But when he died the whole world claimed him, so wide was the range of his evangelizing activities. He stirred the hearts of the two great English-speaking nations with his militant enthusiasm. He was the field marshal of the hosts that cling to the belief that the Gospel itself suffices for all the spiritual needs of humanity. The moral effect of his life-work upon humanity was greater than that of any other man of the nineteenth century."—*The Chicago Times-Herald*.

"Mr. Moody's strength lay in his simplicity and his earnestness. He has been described as magnetic, but simple earnestness always is magnetic. He had the faculty of impressing his hearers with his absolute and undeviating belief in the truth of all he said. He went straight to the point. There was no concession to oratorical effect or to literary polish. He said nothing simply because it sounded well, confining himself to straightforward, fearless statements of what he believed and what he wanted others to believe, and such apparent absolute faith necessarily carried conviction with it."—*The Chicago Evening Post*.

"He preached the Bible only and he lived in accordance with his preaching. For dogma, he cared little and in theology he was a tyro. He never preached over the heads of his audience. The wayfarer, though a fool, could not fail to understand him, and his earnestness was so great and his personal appeal so forcible that every one felt Moody was talking to him alone. Such honesty, sincerity and strength of purpose could not but have their reward, and few expounders of divine truth have looked upon a harvest so rich in sheaves as his."—*The Chicago Tribune*.

"He seemed to care little for any business but his Master's. It was this unflagging energy, this faith in his vocation, that brought him the confidence of men to whom like energy and faith had brought like success in the pursuit of wealth. He combined strangely the old and the new. He was perhaps the last great revivalist on the old theological lines, and he was the first to use wholly modern methods of publicity and appeal. In his earnestness, his unselfishness and his sanctified common sense he was one of the most remarkable men of our generation, for whose life the world has been better."—*The Churchman*.

"What was the secret of his power? First and foremost, it was his intense religious earnestness. He knew God. The vision of the Eternal had risen in his soul. This deep and definite experience was an offset to his lack of literary culture. It made him profoundly anxious to do something for the souls of his fellow-men. Nature had endowed him also with a sturdy and sober commonsense. He cut no fantastic tricks, adopted no sensational methods, avoided even the appearance of smartness, and relied solely on the truth of God as spoken in plain and simple words and as vivified by the Holy Spirit."—*The Nashville Christian Advocate.*

"The story of the outward life of such a man as Mr. Moody can be condensed after a fashion into a paragraph, and this has frequently been done; but the ramifications of its influence no pen can describe, no imagination can conceive. Its effect upon theology have been its least effects; but they have been incalculable. For though Mr. Moody has done little directly to change the theological thought of his time, he has done a great deal to inspire its religious life: and those who believe that theology must always be the outgrowth of religion will believe that his theological influence is far greater and far more wholesome, because more vital, than either he or his contemporaries have imagined."—*The Outlook.*

"In nearly all the great cities of this country and in many of the towns of Great Britain, the footsteps of Dwight L. Moody have been marked by the upspringing of schools, of helpful agencies, of aids to raise the fallen, to lighten the dark places, to help human beings in all that makes for righteousness. Although a lay evangelist, he was a great preacher, eloquent, soul-stirring, convincing and ministering to others the faith that made him whole, but great as he was as a preacher, he was greater as a worker, and his works live after him, vitalized and given enduring substance by the spirit which created them."—*The Philadelphia Telegraph.*

"Farewell, Brother Moody! Thousands upon thousands will mourn thy departure; thousands upon thousands will look back to the time when they were first warned to return to the fold by the words of entreaty, while future generations will be blest by the influence of thy searching teaching of the truth as it is in Jesus. The Church will learn all too soon of the greatness of the prophet who has left them. But all work for the Master is done under human conditions; the man passes, his work abides. So it will be now; Moody has ceased to live in the flesh, but he lives in his work, and the results of his wonderful teaching will be felt by succeeding generations."—*Christian Work.*

"Mr. Moody was a wonderful leader of men. Everywhere he went he set others to work for Christ. No one was so bad as to be repulsive to him, and no one was so wise or good that he did not venture to approach and use him to further his service for Christ. Thousands of waifs rescued from rags and wretchedness are useful men and women because Mr. Moody put his arms of love around them and lifted them up. He has builded many structures in many cities, where young men and women gather to work for and worship God. But his noblest monument is made of living stones builded together for an habitation of God through the Spirit. His life can best be summed up in one sentence: He was a wise winner of souls."—*The Congregationalist.*

"Mr. Moody was not only sincere; he was intensely in earnest. He not only implicitly believed in the truth of the doctrines which he expounded, but he was firmly convinced that the acceptance of those doctrines by the men and women whom he addressed was the most important thing in the world; that every other interest was in comparison trivial and without consequence. He believed, moreover, and he believed it in all humility, that he had been commissioned from above to go about the world delivering the message of the Gospel. He felt himself to be a Heaven-appointed minister to convince humanity of sin and point out the way of salvation."—*The Philadelphia Inquirer*.

"He commanded the respect and confidence of men of other religious faiths and beliefs, and even of the non-religious classes, by his sturdy common sense, his geniality and whole-heartedness, and by his freedom from all cant and affectation. He lived the religion he professed, and practiced what he preached. In speech and manner he was simple, clear, and direct; he understood the common people because he was always one of them in thought and feeling, and among them his greatest and most enduring work was done. The world is a far better and happier world to-day because of the life of Dwight L. Moody. He will live long in the grateful and tender memory of mankind."—*Leslie's Weekly*.

"He never made any serious mistakes. There was no flaw in his character. He commanded an absolutely universal respect. Rich and poor, high and low, learned and illiterate, cherished almost exactly the same feelings toward him. The kind of influences which he began to put forth in Chicago forty years ago went on growing and extending to the day of his death—and to-day, as tidings of his death are borne to every part of the English-speaking world, his influence will seem to be greater than ever. It is not an exaggeration to say that the coming century will be in certain pervasive and vital respects appreciably different from what it would have been were it not for the distinctive spiritual and moral forces which Moody imparted and put forth."—*The Chicago Record*.

"A rugged simplicity and absolute sincerity were the chief elements in his character. No one ever detected in him a suspicion of cant. It might have been said of him, as Mirabeau said of Robespierre, 'That is a dangerous man; he believes every word he says.' For the 'drill and pipe clay' of the clerical profession, as Robertson phrased it, Mr. Moody had nothing but contempt, and his own unconventional ways, in the pulpit and out of it, did a great deal to break down the stilted ministerial tradition. Nor were the changes in his own style of work, as the years passed by, without great significance. From being a mere evangelist, going from city to city to address vast and emotional audiences, he became, by chief intention and main use of time and strength, a Christian educator. His educational institutions at Northfield, so remarkably planned and endowed, he regarded as the crowning work of his life."—*The New York Nation.*

"'By their fruits shall ye know them.' Judged thus, Mr. Moody's career takes saintly rank. Possessed of a marvelous personal magnetism, an earnestness that was irresistible, and an enthusiasm that defied the flight of time, he took his faith in Divine guidance in one hand and his faith in mankind in the other, and, so armed, hurled the full force of his splendid powers against the cohorts of evil. He could not fail. The measure of his revealed success will challenge the admiration of posterity.

"'The measure of his revealed success.' But what of the unrevealed? Its measure was never known, even to himself. It remains a mystery lodged beyond the stars. He drew the scoffer. He startled the dormant conscience of carelessness, and stirred the soul of the evil-doer. He wrought blessings innumerable in garret and in mansion. He labored apart from the church, yet impelled toward the Church hundreds of thousands whom the Church had not reached."—*The New York Mail and Express.*

"No one could visit North America within recent years without feeling that Mr. Moody was one of the great personalities of the continent—and that not only as an evangelist or the representative of evangelical religion, nor even as an organizer of education, but for his own self's sake as a man who lived his faith, and who lived it with extraordinary force of character and wisdom. * * What I feel to be our sorest loss in the death of this great and good man is that we shall no more have his large heart and large mind in the reconciliation of those divisions of opinion among Christian men which are so strong and in some quarters so bitter at the present day. No one could have assisted reconciliation so much as D. L. Moody. Yet it seems wrong to be envious even to this extent, when we have so very much to thank God for in the influence and results of His servant's life."—*Prof. George Adam Smith, in The British Weekly.*

"The death of D. L. Moody is an almost irreparable loss to evangelical Christianity. He was probably the greatest religious revivalist of the present century. Yet that fact hardly gives a true indication of the widespread influence he exerted over the lives of multitudes of men and women in the Old World as well as the New. Even as a revivalist he differed widely from the old-time revivalists of the last generation, who terrified the sinner into repentance by holding him over the precipice where he could see the lurid fires of the pit seemingly eager to envelop him. Mr. Moody doubtless held exactly the same beliefs as to the character and duration of future punishment as his predecessors did. But, without, perhaps, being exactly conscious of the fact, the seeming harness of this dogma was softened by his profound belief in the goodness and love of God. It was upon that thought he most often dwelt, never failing to bring it in even when he referred to the certainty of future punishment. This characteristic of his exhortations separated him widely from the revivalists of the past, and gave his teachings a much more general acceptance than was accorded to previous evangelists."—*The New York Tribune.*

"He was very simple, absolutely earnest, without self-conceit or pretence or cant. He had power; he used it with all his might according to his knowledge and his lights. Nearly all of us came in time to see that the work was good and the results very valuable; that Moody, however he did it, took hold of the people that needed attention, stirred them up to good purpose, and brought them something that made them better. The English-speaking world long ago recognized him as a great force, and one that made for righteousness and the essentials of true religion. Not all of us are desirous to be good ourselves, but most of us are at least in favor of other persons being good. So, nearly all of us have been in favor of Mr. Moody, and respected him and his work, and honor his memory now that he has gone. He was one of the pre-eminently successful men of the century, and what he accomplished he did without much help from education, and without favor or aid save what his manifest deserts won for his work. He simply forgot himself, and took hold. He never let go, and he never remembered himself enough to distract his attention from the work his heart was in."—*Harper's Weekly*.

"Mr. Moody was not a man to whom theological subtleties had any charm. But his convictions never halted. What he believed, he believed with heart and soul. He might have been wrong in premise and deduction, he might have been old-fashioned in theory, but in spirit he was always right and strong, and he had almost a prophet's gift in the potency of his messages. No one could long be in contact with his honesty of purpose, his unqualified self-consecration, his boundless zeal and prophetic spirit without being moved by these qualities. His influence was not only national, but international. He was as notable a force in Great Britain as in the United States. He possessed great personal magnetism, which, combined with his religious enthusiasm, whose sincerity no one questioned, gave him a power of persuasiveness which was wellnigh irresistible.

"While not reckoned among the clergy, or caring to be, he was yet a powerful inspiration to the profession. He will be missed and mourned by the churches as profoundly as by the common people, who regarded him almost as their Moses. His educational work in his native town might well stand as a monument of noble achievement. But that was among the least of the things that he did in his Master's name and for His cause. He was a living Gospel, and his death, with its peace and joy, seemed to partake of the beauty and splendor and awe of a transfiguration."—*The Boston Transcript.*

"Mr. Moody was a great evangelist, and he did a great work. An unordained and essentially popular preacher, who felt that his commission to win souls was in his love for Christ and his desire to serve Him—he reached thousands who were not likely to come under the influence of others, whose belief in Christianity he quickened from a dull acceptance of doctrine into a living power. Earnest in his own convictions, and gifted with a remarkable talent for enlisting the interest and sympathy of his hearers, he was a speaker of unusual effectiveness. Direct and simple in his utterances; not always grammatical; fond of anecdote and homely illustration; emotional, sometimes to an extreme—such was Dwight L. Moody as the leader of countless public meetings. He filled churches and audience-rooms because the people believed he had a message to deliver; as for himself, he believed that that message was of tremendous consequence. His methods have been criticized, but, certainly, he was not open to the charge of being insincere. His whole life was given to doing what he felt to be his highest duty. To this task he brought native ability, and a constantly increasing knowledge of the ways to make that ability count for the most."—*The Hartford Courant.*

"Men are also asking the secret of Mr. Moody's power. Four words sum it up: Common Sense and Consecration. He had many striking characteristics, but through them all shone his spirit of consecration. He was simple; a child could understand his sermons. He believed in the power of stories; if they caused laughter or weeping, he took advantage of the smiles or the tears to press home the Gospel message. He was a man of faith, faith in God and man. He looked for the best in men, and they responded by giving him their best. No one could hear him in private conversation or on the platform without recognizing his intense earnestness. Whatever he did, he did with all his heart, and he was able to inspire others to similar devotion. Some people called him narrow; they little knew that, if he had used his powers in other directions, he would have been as successful in conducting a great financial venture, or planning a military campaign, as he was in leading men to accept Christ as their Saviour.

"Mr. Moody believed the Bible from cover to cover, and he believed in the fundamental doctrines of Christ. 'People ask me,' he said one time, 'If I believe in the "higher criticism". How can I when I don't know what it is? They ask me if I think there were two Isaiahs. Before taking up that question seriously, I believe we should try to see what the prophecy itself contains.' 'Why do you go to hear Moody?' said a scoffer contemptuously to a fellow club member. 'You don't believe what he preaches.' 'No, but he believes it with all his heart, and it is refreshing to meet such a man in these days of doubt and uncertainty.'

"Mr. Moody was an optimist. Elijah on Carmel was his ideal; he had little patience with the prophet under the juniper tree. He was a sincere man. While looked upon as a leader, his daily prayer was that God would keep him humble. To know him was to love him; thousands of people in every part of this country and in Europe, and hundreds of missionaries in foreign lands, have lost a personal friend in his death. He was a good man. and faithfully served his generation."—*The New York Observer*.

"Mr. Moody was not only reverential, but humble. He was not only humble, but tolerant. He improved very much under travel, under intercourse with able minds, and under the study of vast throngs, as so many units. The consequence was that from a lone exhorter he became a great leader, from a great leader he rose to be an organizer of much skill, and he topped both functions with that of an educator on distinct lines, at needed work, and upon a vast scale. We are regarding him entirely from the human point of view, for the purpose of this consideration, and we are noting in him exactly the qualities which would have made him successful in other undertakings. His qualities were not unusual. His use of them was extraordinary. The high purpose to which he applied them was ennobling and uplifting. The singular simplicity, candor and gentleness of his spirit were remarkable, considering the power he wielded, the influence which he commanded, the support which he received and the praise, whether interested or disinterested, of which he was the subject. * * * His field was the world, and to do good his religion.

"He made haste slowly. He died on the heights, but he started on the plains and had a hard passage through valleys and up mountain steeps, before he walked with God. Without more than elementary education, utterly without training, destitute of experience, simply aflame with spiritual purpose, he had to vindicate himself, he had to create for himself a way, and he had to do so against a critical, cultivated and combined class, the reverend clergy. They did not relish an unlettered lay intruder. They were justified in their instinctive disrelish. Of most lay intruders the note is arrogance, the method burglarious, the self-confidence unabashable and the ignorance unteachable. Of this lay intruder nothing like that could be said. He was altruistic, he was modest, he was hungry to learn, he was deferential to knowledge, what he acquired he held, what he held he increased, and what he increased and made his own he made also the precious possession of others. The greatest of lay workers became the master of lay workers, their monitor and their model, and this at first uneducated man established institutions for Christian instruction which taught the use of the tools of spiritual knowledge as aptly and as thoroughly as the use of the tools of any other knowledge is anywhere taught."—*The Brooklyn Eagle.*

CHAPTER XXXII.

The Personal Side of Mr. Moody.

HE was a remarkable man in all ways, not the least of which was his appearance. He was not a striking figure so far as stature was concerned, for he was rather below the average in height, but he was a marked man in a crowd, and every one turned to look at him because the very atmosphere that surrounded him was commanding. He has been likened to Garfield, in his massive frame; they had the same smiling features, the same facility of anecdote, and the same effect of sincerity in everything they said or did. Their style of oratory was almost identical, and both possessed the rare gift of captivating people at first sight.

Mr. Moody was very quick at repartee. An interesting incident is related of his meeting with Mr. Gladstone. Heartily grasping Mr. Moody's hand the old statesman said, "I wish I had your body." Mr. Moody replied, "I wish I had your head." Mr. Gladstone responded, "I mean I wish I had your lungs;" to which Mr. Moody again replied, "I wish I had your brains," and with hearty good wishes they parted.

Personal Characteristics

Mr. Moody had a wonderful voice. He could easily hold the attention of thousands, and yet in conversation there was a pathos and tenderness in his inflections that was most fascinating. He had a most attractive face; it was kindly and helpful in its every expression.

He was fond of telling how his picture once did duty for that of Rutherford B. Hayes. During the Hayes campaign a big Republican rally was held in Fort Wayne, Ind. Everything was ready, when it was suggested that the meeting would be incomplete without a picture of General Hayes. This brought out the discovery that, although around the walls of the room were hung the pictures of many celebrities of the day, that of Hayes was not among them, nor could a picture of him be found. One of the members of the committee on arrangements, a sign painter, who had a natural gift of drawing, found a copy of *Harper's Magazine* on the table in which was a small cut of Mr. Moody. He decided it was enough like Hayes to make a copy from, and in half an hour he had a good sized sketch, and labeled the product "Rutherford B. Hayes". It was hung on the stage, and the speakers of the evening pointed to it as they referred to "that statesman," etc. Finally the joke leaked out in the crowd, and almost resulted in breaking up the meeting. Mr. Moody was informed of the affair, and told it to President Hayes.

His Hold Upon His Friends

It has been said that he was dictatorial, sometimes extremely so, and it must be confessed that he did insist on his own way; but then, he had studied his work; he knew men, and he knew what would tell with them, and it was a rare thing ever to find him mistaken in his judgment. But even though he was brusque, sometimes almost to the point of rudeness, it is a mighty tribute to the power of his influence over men that he instinctively drew them about him. One of his English friends said of him, "He may make doorkeepers of us, or even door-mats, if he likes, and we will love him." And another has said of him, "Dear old Moody! We all love him, but some of us don't like him." He was, however, the most tender-hearted man I have ever known. Dr. George F. Pentecost has well said of him, "Intentionally he never wounded any one; he simply lacked perception, and did not put himself in the other man's place."

His heart was big enough to take in the whole world, and his sympathy with mankind was genuine. An instance of this occurred in New York. While he was in the midst of a sermon a baby commenced to cry, much to the annoyance of some of the audience, who darted cruel looks at the innocent child and the embarrassed mother. The mother waited for a favorable opportunity to go out, but Mr. Moody told her to remain where she was; he guessed his lungs were stronger than the baby's, and if any didn't like it, they could go out.

At the close of the service he made the unique announcement that the next afternoon he would preach to mothers with babies in their arms, and no one unaccompanied by a baby would be admitted. Never before was there such a gathering. The scene touched the heart of the great preacher, and his words the hearts of the mothers. Mr. Moody said afterward that a good many of the women present must have borrowed babies for the occasion.

His Charming Social Side

He was perfectly delightful socially; he was as genial a man as I have ever known. He would laugh till the tears rolled down his face at some story which he might have heard again and again. He found his recreation in helping others, for he was a tireless worker in one form or another, yet he was never so happy as when he was making others' burdens easier to bear.

From the very day that D. L. Moody came before the eyes of the Christian world, the same characteristics that made him great in later days, were exhibited. He was one of the most conscientious men I have ever known, and if he felt that anything was his duty, nothing in the world would make him so miserable as to feel that he must leave it undone, and nothing made him so happy as to feel that he could perform it quickly whatever the cost. If he ever wronged any one, he was the first to make that wrong right.

Mr. Moody seldom preached a sermon without emphasizing the fact that true happiness and the richest blessings will never be realized by a professed Christian, if at any time he has wronged a fellow-man and has not made an honest attempt to clear up the wrong, or if he does not perform, willingly and promptly, known duties. That the great evangelist made this teaching one of the cardinal principles of his own life is clearly demonstrated by the following incident, related by him in an address to a body of students at Northfield.

A Singular Instance of His Kindliness

"You can never accomplish much in your Christian life until you get right with your fellow-men as well as with God, and until you perform your duty as it comes to you. Let me give you an experience that I had a few mornings ago. I always get up early, and devote the first hour of the day to my Bible. This morning I sat down at my desk to study as usual. In a few minutes I chanced to look out of the window, and I saw a young fellow with a heavy valise on his back, walking toward the railroad station three miles away. If I thought about it at all, I thought he was one of the students going for an early train. I turned my eyes to my Bible, but, try as hard as I might, I could not fix my mind on what I read with my eyes.

"I looked out of the window again. Something said, 'You ought to take that boy to the station.' I tried to persuade myself that it was not my duty. I made another effort to study, but it was of no use. I jumped up and hurried to the stables, hitched up a horse, and drove rapidly until I came up to the boy. I took him and his baggage in and drove to the station. After giving the boy Godspeed and receiving hearty thanks for my kindness, I drove home, and went to my study. I took up my Bible, and I didn't have the slightest trouble in fixing my mind on my work."

I drove with him one morning while he was making some final preparation for the coming of the students to their annual conference, when we stopped at a little patch of corn, and he said, "I hoed two rows of corn here this morning before you were up." I have never been able to get out of my mind the imaginary picture of D. L. Moody, with coat and vest off, hoeing corn at Northfield.

His Extreme Modesty

With all his greatness he was one of the most modest men that you could possibly find. Other men might have been turned with the flattery of the people, but extreme modesty was a striking characteristic of the evangelist's personality. His phenomenal successes in many lines left him a man devoid of all desire for notoriety and fame.

Although thousands of persons would travel long distances to hear him preach, still he invariably maintained that there were any number of ministers who could excel him as a preacher, and he was always willing and eager to give place to others. During the Northfield Conferences, at which, in the minds of the people in attendance, he was the central figure, Mr. Moody seldom preached, unless to take the place of some speaker who was unable to meet his appointment, or unless urgent requests from the audience were repeatedly sent to him. Asked once why he did not speak more often at the conferences, the evangelist replied:

"Oh, you can hear me any time. I want you to hear these noted men that I have brought from over the sea."

Again, when urged to preach, he made this announcement from the rostrum one morning:

"I don't want to take the time of these dear brothers who have come so far to speak to us. I have received a good many requests to preach. If you really want to hear me you will be willing to get up early for the privilege. Meet me here in the auditorium at 7 o'clock to-morrow morning, and we will have a Bible talk together."

Despite the numerous other sessions during the day, these sunrise services were continued during the rest of the conference, and each session was largely attended by those eager to catch every syllable that fell from Mr. Moody's lips.

His Wonderful Unselfishness

He was absolutely unselfish. During the first visit of Messrs. Moody and Sankey to Great Britain they were in need of a book of songs to use at the meetings. No publisher would bring out the book, although Mr. Moody offered to give it to any one who would print it and give him what copies he wanted to use. Finally he was compelled to have the book printed at his own expense. It has since attained a larger circulation than any other publication except the Bible, and is one of the best paying literary properties in the world. Every dollar of the profits of the book has gone to charity in one form or another.

Mr. Fleming H. Revell has said: "Some years ago, some of the papers began to say that Mr. Moody was making a good thing financially of his reputation. As a rule Mr. Moody never paid no attention to criticism. He was wont to say that no two people thought alike of everything or received always the same impression.

TODD B. HALL. The celebrated Detective and Evangelist, converted in the meetings conducted by Mr. Moody in Baltimore, in 1878.

He was friendly toward the public press, claiming that it was a great educator and a great power in the spreading of both secular and religious knowledge. But he was deeply grieved at this. He referred to the criticisms one day in the pulpit here in Chicago. There were tears in his eyes, and his voice quivered as he spoke. 'As I know my heart before God,' he said, 'I have never let the desire for money determine my conduct in any way. I know I am weak and sinful in many ways, but the devil has not that hold upon me. I have never profited personally by a single dollar that has been raised through my work. It hurts me, above all other things, to be charged with this. May God forgive those who say this of me.'"

Mr. Revell added, that though Moody received over $125,000 from royalties on his work, he had never used a penny of it for personal purposes, reserving it all to further his work. "Mr. Moody was a good financier," he said. "He took great care of his money, but not to save it and build a fortune. Rather he desired it to use in his work. I fully believe he died a poor man."

Anecdotes of His Earlier Years of Service

Dr. Edward Eggleston has told the following stories about Mr. Moody: "I have heard Mr. Moody tell how while in the Christian Commission service he was propounding his thorough question to a Tennesee planter, but, as the man was deaf, the repeated vociferation of 'Are you a Christian?' failed to bring a reply. Turning to the black man who stood by he asked, 'Is your master a Christian?' 'No, Massa, he is a Presbyterian.'

"It was not uncommon in those days for Mr. Moody to assail suddenly a strange young man with this blank query. Of course, he soon became noted for his zeal and eccentricity. A young man from the country who had held a situation in the city for just three weeks, was thus accosted by him in the street, 'Are you a Christian?' He replied, 'It is none of your business.' 'Yes it is.' 'Then you must be D. L. Moody,' said the stranger.

"'Madam,' said Moody to an Irishwoman, 'Won't you go to church to-night?' 'Whose is it? Is it Moody's Church?' 'No, it is God's Church, but Moody goes there.' 'Troth, thin I won't go.' With this she began to charge Moody with divers crimes, not knowing to whom she spoke. 'You better be careful,' said he presently, 'my name is Moody.' 'Tut, tut', said she with Irish dexterity and effrontery, 'I know'd Moody afore you was born.'"

A volume could be written of the things which the friends of this mighty man of God have said since his death. The words of two representative men may, however, with peculiar appropriateness be presented.

The Simplicity of His Habits and Tastes

The Rev. George F. Pentecost has said: "Had he lived in the early days of Israel's trials, he should have judged Israel, and delivered them out of the hand of their enemies. He was like Gideon, and his latent powers were known only to God. He was the most reticent man I ever knew. One of his marked characteristics was his strong, practical common sense and fine knowledge of men. Once in the Boston Tabernacle, just before going on the platform, some one came to see him. 'There is a man outside wishes to see you.' 'Well,' said the evangelist, 'I have no time to see him.' 'But,' replied the usher, 'He says he must see you.' 'What kind of a man is he?' 'He is tall and thin, with long hair.' 'That settles it," said Mr. Moody, 'I don't want to see any long-haired men nor short-haired women.' It was a rare thing for him to make a mistake in any of the men gathered about him.

"He had the simplest habits and tastes. He spent money lavishly on other people—almost none on himself. I consider him the world's greatest evangelist, and he has influenced more people for God than any other man in modern times."

The Rev. G. Campbell Morgan has said of him: "My personal acquaintance with Dwight Lyman Moody was not of long duration according to the measure of the calendar. If, however, 'we could count time by heart throbs,' then I might claim to have known him; for it has been one of the greatest privileges of my life to have come very near him in the ripest years of his life.

"I first saw him in 1883 during his second visit to Birmingham. Bingley Hall was being crowded by day with eager crowds who had come by train from the whole surrounding district. The city was moved to its very centre. The impression of those days, therefore, is that of the man in the midst of the rush of work. He was keen, alert, forceful. No detail of arrangement escaped his notice. A vacant seat, the opening and closing of doors, a tendency to drag the singing, all these he noted and uttered directions about. Yet he was by no means a man who cared for detail's sake. The greater was ever the reason for the less, and the less was important only as part of the greater. The supreme passion of his life was the winning of men for Christ, and no detail that would hinder or help was too small for consideration.

How He Appeared in His Native Town

"In 1896 I visited the States for the first time. Among other work, I had promised Mr. Moody to speak at the Chicago Institute to his students. The Northfield Conference was in session, and I managed to get a few hours there. Arriving late at night, I found my quarters and retired. The next day was a field day for me, and a revelation. I attended meetings from morning till night. Everywhere Mr. Moody was the moving spirit. Bright, cheery, and yet in dead earnest, he seemed to make everything go before him. In the intervals of the meetings he gave me a drive round the campus in his buggy. Every point of interest was pointed out, and in a few brief words the story of how the different buildings were erected was told. Passing one house, he said, 'People sometimes ask me how I found Northfield? I tell them it found me. I was born there.' Suddenly he pulled up his horse to speak to a group of children. 'Have you had any apples to-day?' said he. 'No, Mr. Moody,' they replied. 'Then go down to my house, and tell them to give you all you want.' Away they went, and so did he, both happier. Down a narrow lane he drove next, and through a gate to where a man was at work in a field. 'Biglow,' said Mr. Moody, 'it's too hot for you to work much. Half a day's work for a day's pay, you know, while this heat lasts.' I sat by his side and watched, and began to understand the greatness of the man whose life was so broad that it touched sympathetically all other phases of life.

Mr. Moody as Host

"After the evening meeting, at his invitation, I gathered with the speakers at his house. Then, for the first time, I saw him in a new role, that of the host. He sat in his chair at the head of the table and helped the ice-cream, directed the conversation, and listened with the patience and simplicity of a child to every word that others spoke. That night the talk turned on the most serious subjects, the inner life of the people of God and its bearing on the work of the churches among the people. As we broke up I went to bid him good-bye, as I was to depart by an early train on the morrow. 'O!' said he, 'I shall see you in the morning; you are to preach at ten o'clock.' That was my first notice. What did I do? I preached, as he told me, as others and better men have ever been glad to do. That was his way. He printed no programme of the Northfield Conferences. He gathered around him a band of teachers and speakers, and then as the days moved on he manipulated them according to the necessities of the case. After speaking next morning I hurried away, but in that brief stay Moody had become much to me. Strong, tender, considerate, from that day I more than reverenced him, I loved him."

In the summer of 1897 I was asked to go to Kinsman, Ohio, to fill an engagement which properly belonged to Mr. Moody, but he was so busily engaged with his own Northfield work, and was so fearful of taking a long journey in the heat of summer, that Professor James McGranahan insisted that I should come to Kinsman to speak to thousands of people who gathered every summer on the Fair grounds. Mr. Moody had started this meeting two or three years before, and he insisted that it should not be given up.

'Prayer Saved the Ship'

When I reached the beautiful home of Mr. and Mrs. McGranahan I found that my helper in the meeting was to be that grand old hero of many a battle-field and devoted soldier of the cross, General O. O. Howard. Sitting together with the friends who had come in from the surrounding country to attend the meeting, the name of Mr. Moody was mentioned, and General Howard said, "I was with him on the steamship *Spree*, when, Mr. Moody says, 'God heard our prayer and saved the ship.' A good many people have criticised this statement," said General Howard, "and there was much controversy in the newspapers; but Moody always believed it. Over 700 people were with us on the ship. One morning, about daybreak, I was awakened by a sound like an explosion, and I heard the people rushing along the halls, and then some one said the main shaft had been snapped asunder, and falling down had made a break in the ship. The passengers were terror-stricken. The bulkheads were quickly closed, and the bailing and the pumping began, but when they reached the third compartment of the ship, they found it almost impossible to clear it, and the aft part of the ship was sunk to the gunwale. Mr. Moody, with his son, I found on deck. He was lying back in a chair looking very ill, but after a moment he said, 'General Howard, won't you come with me?' And followed by his son we made our way to the state-room, and there he fell upon his knees and prayed as only he knew how to pray. He told the Lord that He was the God of the sea, and asked Him that, like as He had stilled the Sea of Galilee, He might save these people in peril on the ship. He asked the Lord to send him a ship to take them safe home that they might finish their work; and when he had prayed, and his son had followed, he opened his Bible and read the ninety-first Psalm, and then said, 'This Psalm is just made for this occasion, isn't it?'

A Service of Praise on the Steamer

"After that he was always surrounded by a company of people, giving help wherever help could be given. When Sunday morning came he gathered the people in the dining saloon, and conducted the service in his own inimitable style, and after forty-eight hours of drifting, a ship came hurrying over to us to take us safe home. Mr. Moody led a service of thanksgiving and praise, and preached as I never had heard him preach before. That is the story of his sending the cable 'Prayer saved the ship.'"

There was a hush on the little assembly, and I know of one at least who offered up a prayer of thanksgiving that D. L. Moody had not only helped save the people on board the Spree, but had been used of God to save thousands of others just as truly drifting, and whose case was just as apparently hopeless.

The Rev. F. B. Meyer, of Christ Church, London, knew Mr. Moody most intimately, and loved him not only for his work's sake, but also because of the peculiar charm and fascination of his great personality. He has recently said in an English paper:

"To have known D. L. Moody, and come within the range of his strong personality, has been to many men one of the most influential factors in their character and life-work; and it is not easy for such to imagine a world from which the inspiration of his presence has been withdrawn. It is still less easy under the immediate sorrow of such a bereavement to characterize this natural prince and leader of men.

How Mr. Moody First Blessed Mr. Meyer's Work

"I met him first in York, in 1873, on his arrival with Mrs. Moody and his two eldest children. Accompanied by Mr. and Mrs. Sankey, they had come to our country, as it appeared, by a divine prompting, and had just landed at Liverpool. Some time before, the secretary of the Y. M. C. A. had impressed upon him the two words, "Bennett, York;" and not knowing where else to turn, two of his friends having suddenly died, Moody telegraphed to Mr. Bennett, saying, 'I will be in York to-night.'

"This was Saturday. On the following day he preached at the chapel built for the Rev. James Parsons, and then occupied by the Rev. John Hunter (now of Glasgow). During the following week he held evening services in the old Londal Chapel, and noon prayer meetings at the Y. M. C. A. After two or three days with the Wesleyans, he came to the Baptist Chapel, of which I was minister, and conducted meetings there for about a fortnight, with ever-increasing numbers and marvelous results. He and Mr. Sankey have often spoken of that little vestry, where we three spent much time in prayer, little weening that the earnestness of our desires and intercessions were the travail pangs of so great a spiritual movement as followed.

"All who have heard him will recall the quiver in his voice when he told some pathetic story; but I never guessed the intensity of his tenderness till I saw him with his grandchildren. He used to drive them about in his carriage, or carry them in his arms.

"One of the most striking incidents in my memory was when he stood with them beside his mother's grave, in a summer sunset, and asked us to pray that they might be in the coming century what she had been in this. And when little Irene was dying, he used to be on the watch below her window to keep all quiet, would steal down from the meetings to hear the latest news, would be the nurse and playmate of her little cousin, that all might devote themselves to the chamber of sickness.

Mr. Moody's Sure Faith

"He never wavered in his attachment to the great fundamentals of the Gospel. His sermons on the Blood, the Holy Spirit, the Love of God in Jesus Christ, were great testimonies to the mighty truths which have been the theme of every revival of evangelical religion. There was no uncertain sound in the Gospel as he preached it, and it was the power of God unto salvation to tens of thousands.

"What a welcome he must have received as he entered Heaven! Surely an abundant, a choral entrance must have been ministered unto him by myriads who are there, because of the message uttered in burning acccents by his lips."

I am delighted thus to quote Mr. Meyer. I know of few men better qualified to speak than he. While in conversation the other day with Mr. Fleming H. Revell (Mr. Moody's brother-in-law),

REV. H. M. WHARTON, D.D., author of "A Month with Moody, in Chicago," and for many years a most intimate friend and co-worker with Mr. Moody.

he said to me. "If you would like to find in print a good description of Mr. Moody's last hours and his triumphant entrance into the presence of God, you have only to read the closing lines of Bunyan's Pilgrim's Progress, for in the passing over of Mr. Stand-fast, there is the most striking description of the passing away of Mr. Moody." For the help of my readers I here quote it.

"When Mr. Stand-fast had thus set things in order, and the time being come for him to haste him away, he also went down to the river. Now, there was a great calm at that time in the river; wherefore Mr. Stand-fast, when he was about half-way in, stood a while, and talked to his companions that had waited upon him thither. And he said, 'This river has been a terror to many; yea, the thoughts of it have also frighted me; but now methinks I stand easy; my foot is fixed upon that on which the feet of the priests that bare the ark of the covenant stood while Israel went over Jordan. The waters, indeed, are to the palate bitter, and to the stomach cold; yet the thought of what I am going to, and of the conduct that waits for me on the other side, doth lie as a glowing coal at my heart. I see myself now at the end of my journey; my toilsome days are ended; I am going to see that head which was crowned with thorns, and that face which was spit upon for me. I have formerly lived by hearsay and faith; but now I go where I shall live by sight, and shall be with Him in whose company I delight myself. I have loved to hear my Lord spoken of; and wherever I have seen the print of His shoe in the earth, there I have coveted to set my foot, too. His name has been to me as a civet-box; yea, sweeter than all perfumes. His voice to me has been most sweet, and His countenance I have more desired than they that have most desired the light of the sun. His Word I did use to gather for my food, and for antidotes against my faintings.

He hath held me, and hath kept me from mine iniquities; yea, my steps hath He strengthened in His way.'

" Now, while he was thus in discourse, his countenance changed, his strong man bowed under him; and, after he had said, 'Take me, for I come unto Thee!' he ceased to be seen of them."

And so I bring my tribute to a close, thanking God, now, as I thanked Him at the beginning, that I have had the privilege of writing; and saying of Mr. Moody yet again—he was the best friend I ever had, and more helpful to me than any other man that ever lived in all my knowledge of the world. Other men have known him longer than I, but no one, I am sure, could ever have been more helped by him. I say of him as Paul said of the Philippians, "I thank my God upon every remembrance of you."

CHAPTER XXXIII.

Personal Reminiscences of D. L. Moody

By Rev. H. M. Wharton, D. D.

ABOUT twenty years ago, having just concluded in the city of Alexandria, Virginia, the second evangelistic meeting I had ever held, I determined to go to Baltimore in order to hear Mr. Moody, whose fame as a worker for Christ in the salvation of men was filling the world. Mr. Moody was spending the winter in the city of Baltimore, and I found difficulty, being an entire stranger, to gain access to the crowded building the one afternoon it was my privilege to hear him.

By good fortune, I met a minister with whom I had become acquainted some months before. He took me through the pastor's study to the platform. It was in this study that I saw Mr. Moody walking back and forth, his hands behind him, and apparently in deep thought. He shook hands with me, and with hardly an exchange of words put into my hands several circulars which he asked me to give to others as I went home. I found it to be a call to Christian workers to go forth into the harvest field. He preached that afternoon on Repentance, and I well remember something of the sermon, and especially his illustrations.

The years passed on and I became pastor in the City of Baltimore. One afternoon, I think it was in, 92, I was standing in front of Mr. Moody in the great Cyclorama Building, where thousands had assembled for services, the choir was singing, and I think the Scriptures had been read. I did not, of course, suppose that he would recognize me, and was surprised when he looked down and said suddenly, "Come up on the platform." As I was sure he did not know me, I turned to a minister at my side, a prominent pastor of the city, and said, "He is calling you." He started to the platform when Mr. Moody said he wanted me, and as soon as I walked up, he said, "I want you to speak to the people right away." With hardly any notice at all I made some remarks, and before I left that afternoon he had asked me to go to Chicago. It occurred to me afterwards that he had possibly heard that I had been doing some evangelistic work and, being told that I was in the audience, called me up, and was taking a sample to find if I would do as a Chicago worker.

A Closer Personal Acquaintance

It did not take him long to make a decision when facts were before him. Upon my arrival at Chicago it was a great privilege to know that one of the blessings in store for me was a closer personal acquaintance with Mr. Moody. Three times a day, with few exceptions, I sat by his side at the table, and was often in his room, which was regarded as headquarters. Every night when we came in from our places of preaching—halls, churches, tents, theatres, we would meet around a large table in his room and enjoy refreshments and a most delightful social hour, as we discussed the work of the Master, or indulged in innocent jest and merriment. Mr. Moody was fond of a joke. He would tell a good story, and no man had a keener relish for it than he.

It is said of Spurgeon that there was such a hearty good humor about him, and over all and through all such an atmosphere of genuine piety, that, though he had convulsed a party by a lively joke, he could turn at once and say, "Now let us have a word of prayer," and all go smiling into the father's presence.

It would seem altogether the right thing to do. The same may be said of Mr. Moody. And it mattered little if the laugh turned on himself, he enjoyed it just the same.

A Good Story

Here is one I heard him tell one day at the table. First speaking in complimentary terms of the "Mountain Evangelist," George O. Barnes, of Kentucky, he said: "I got him here to preach once many years ago. We worked hard and lived on bread and cheese. One night when I was absent he preached a sermon on 'The Devil!' I insisted that he must repeat it for my benefit, and I worked up a crowd for Saturday night. I had been out all day trying to raise money, and came home at five o'clock tired and hungry. In addition to the crackers and cheese I bought some bologna sausage. I never tasted anything better than that bologna, and I just ate it until I didn't want any more. That night I was to preside and I sat behind Barnes. He hadn't been preaching long before I got so sleepy I could not hold my eyes open any way I could fix it. I got out a pin and stuck myself with it, but nothing would do. I had been banging the people a good deal for going to sleep, and when they saw me it was all they wanted. They would not keep still. Barnes saw something was the matter. He could not get hold of them, and by and by he turned and looked at me, and saw what was up. The next day someone said something to Barnes about it, he said, 'Well, Moody is pretty hard to down; but last night the devil and bologna did the work for him.'" It was comforting to hear Mr. Moody say that he also put people to sleep sometimes. Well, so did Paul, and may be you have also. If you are a preacher, then you know yourself.

Mr. Moody was a great general. He was a great thinker, and planned his work even to the smallest details. He looked after the food and rest and recreation of his workers. Even his carriage horse must have at least one day's rest in seven. It did not matter to him what day you took as Sabbath or rest day, but it must be one in seven. He was the only one who did not rest as much as he should. I organized a strike one day, and informed him that if he did not take a day in seven we would go out on a strike and walk the streets until he gave in. When we came from our work that night we found he had rested, and I told him the threatened strike was having good effect.

Always Ready for a Pleasant Word

Everybody loved him, men, women and children. Although he had enough on his mind to keep a dozen men busy, he so arranged that the work was easily divided out, and he stood at the helm. But he was always ready to have a pleasant word with man, woman or child as they chanced to come his way. Nothing could be more enjoyable than his evening chats with the workers as they came in from their fields in all parts of the city to give an account of their labors. —a picture in minature of the time when we shall all go from the harvest field home to meet our great Leader and Commander, and tell him of the joys and sorrows, the trials and triumphs of our life work on earth.

Mr. Moody was a wise level-headed man. He had a great deal of common sense. You could hardly get an off-hand expression of opinion from him. He heard what others had to say, but reserved his judgment until all the facts were before him; then when he spoke it was worth hearing. His conduct with reference to the Congress of Religions was a noticeable instance. When this ecclesiastical menagerie, gathered from all quarters of the globe, made its appearance, Mr. Moody was asked again and again to take part. He only replied that he had his hands full of work, and declined to go. When it seemed to some of us that our Lord was belittled and disgraced by the motley crew who disported themselves upon the platform day by day in the wonderful "Parliament," we suggested that we should attack them all along the line. Mr. Moody was very emphatic in his instructions. "Preach Christ," said he, "hold up Christ; let the Parliament of Religions alone, preach Christ." And he was right. The many-colored bubble burst, and went to thin air. It will hardly be known in history. Christ lives and reigns; let us live for Him and preach His blessed Gospel.

Mr. Moody Was a Fine Business Man

Mr. Moody was a fine business man. If he had turned his attention to earthly, instead of heavenly things, he would have been a millionaire many times over. He had the happy faculty of dispatching business with great ease and rapidity, and was wise in the selection of his assistants. Over each department there is a head, whom he has chosen for that special work, and the work goes on well through and through. He looked after the smallest matters. The seating of the congregation, ventilation, arrangement of the singers, collections, all passed under his observation and direction. He was a great advertiser. He was one of the children of light, who have learned from the children of this world. The newspapers, street cars, bill posters and ticket distributors were all brought into requisition. One night when he was going to preach in the Standard Theatre—one of the hardest places—he went into barrooms and said, "Moody is going to preach in the theatre to-night, come in." They recognized him and prepared to go. The results proved his wisdom. Some Christian people seem to think that it is only necessary to open the church doors, and the outside world will break its neck trying to get in. Not so. The most attractive thing to the common mind is a circus. Men, women and children, old and young, white and colored, will run after it, and spend their last dimes; and yet, when the circus comes, they plaster the country and paint the towns red with their advertisements. Let the people of God learn a lesson.

Mr. Moody had a great deal of "snap,"—I hardly know what else to call it. If he could not *make* things, like his Master, *he could make things move*, and that comes next to making them. He never allowed a service to drag,—no, not for an instant. No awkward pauses, nor weary moments of inordinate suspense. He went right on from one thing to another even unto the end. I have gone with him to a great theatre building, when we were the first in the house, except the employees who look after the building. As soon as the people came rushing in, he was ready to start the singing. Not that he sang himself. He could make "a joyful noise unto the Lord," and as a gentleman remarked when asked what he thought of his singing, "I could at least say I never heard anything like it." He would call out the numbers of the hymns, and he well knew when the singing was good. Sometimes he would call for one part of the congregation to sing, then another, then all, till they would make the house fairly tremble with the thunder tones of praise. Then several prayers, then his own sermon, usually from twenty to thirty minutes, and then close with prayer. Perhaps he would have one or two sermons more of similar length, as was often the case in Chicago meetings.

His Great Faith

And what faith he had! He believed in the Bible from "back to back" to use his own expression. One night I heard him preach on the ark. "Come thou, and all thy house into the ark." He said some infidel perhaps has come in here, and will say, 'What does Mr. Moody want to talk about that for? Nobody believes the ark story now.' Well, if you don't, you can't believe Christ. The Son of God endorsed it. 'As it was in the days of Noah, so shall it be at the coming of the Son of Man.' A good many preachers these days are trying to cut certain things out of the Bible; they had better leave the pulpit. They are doing more harm than good. Some say, 'I don't believe the fish story about the whale swallowing Jonah.' There is no trouble if you bring God on the scene. He who made the earth could make a whale big enough to swallow a man or a man big enough to swallow a whale."

Mr. Moody believed in the constant presence and guidance of the Holy Spirit. He was a worker together with God in everything. It was thrilling to hear some of his prayers with those who worked with him. On Sunday morning he would call to God for a blessing, and when the day was done, and all met in his room, how sweet it was to kneel and be led by him in a prayer of thanksgiving for the victories of the day. With happy hearts we said "Good night," and sought our rest, rejoicing that we had been engaged in the best and most glorious work on earth.

A Day of Help and Refreshing

A few summers ago, while preaching in New London, Conn., I concluded one Monday morning to go and spend a few hours at Northfield, without letting Mr. Moody know it, my sole purpose being to get a day of help and refreshing from the services he was conducting at that time. It was August, and one of his most important conferences was in session. About ten o'clock I went to the auditorium, and took a seat far back in the great congregation, just inside the door in fact, and enjoyed one of his delightful and helpful addresses. He seemed unusually well, and full of wholesome truth, which he imparted to the great joy of his large audience. After the services were over, I stepped outside the door and went to the Northfield Inn, intending to get my dinner and go back to the auditorium for a little while, then take the five o'clock train for New London, and on to Baltimore; when after dinner some one came to me and said that I was wanted at the telephone.

The well-known voice of Mr. Fitt greeted me with the startling information that Mr. Moody sent his regards, and said he wanted me to speak on the platform at four o'clock, at Roundtop at six, and again at eight in the auditorium. He would not listen though I urged that I must leave on the five o'clock train. Finally, however, he made a compromise by Mr. Moody proposing to send his carriage and take me out driving, bring me back to the auditorium in time for the services, and then to the train if I must go. To one who has been through the vales, and over the hills of beautiful Northfield, it is needless to say that in company with my good friend, Mr. Fitt, we had a charming drive, and a little after four o'clock made our way to the auditorium. When we entered, Mr. Moody called me to the platform saying, "I have been trying to get Dr. Wharton here for some time. He is here now, and we will keep him." Turning to Mr. Stebbins, he said, "You look out for that side of the platform, and I will take care of this, so he shall not get away to-day." He then announced that I would speak at six o'clock, and again at eight. There was only one thing to do, and that was as all others who came within his reach had to do, obey his commands; and it was always for the best that we did it.

The six o'clock meeting at "Roundtop," known as the open-air meeting, was largely attended, and to me exceedingly enjoyable. Mr. Moody sat beside me on the grass, and led in prayer just before the address. Elijah on Mount Carmel, pleading with his God was not nearer the heart of his Father in faith and acceptableness, I am sure, than he, as he led us all in prayer that beautiful evening. We had a fine meeting that night in the auditorium and several interesting addresses were made, after which, at Mr. Moody's kind invitation, we went to his house, where, in company with a number of others, a social hour was much enjoyed.

Mr. Moody was not easily discouraged, nor unduly elated. With all the activity of his great soul, there was still a calmness and courage characteristic of him that at once inspired hope, and kept us all at our best all the days and nights of toil. It was my privilege to be associated with him in the Central Palace Hall, in New York City, where thousands of people assembled every day to listen to his preaching. It was an unusual meeting in many respects, beginning in the early morning and continuing without intermission, throughout the day, until ten o'clock at night. There were many interesting conversions in those meetings, and the words which went abroad throughout the land must have accomplished great things. At the hotel many of his co-workers were entertained, and the brief intervals of personal intercourse were always heartily enjoyed. He would invite us to his room in the morning where, with Mrs. Moody and his daughter and others, he engaged in a daily worship before beginning the duties of the day. Handing me one of Henry Drummond's books one day with an inscription in his own hand to Mrs. Wharton, he turned the leaves rapidly and said, "Look at this," and showed me a paragraph where Drummond speaks of passing to the end of a journey of life, and then, "Isn't that good, Wharton, going to the Father, going to the Father." He has gone to the Father; he went before we wanted him to go, and as it seems to us the burning and shining light was consumed all too soon. Still the Father called, and when he went away, he said we must not call him back, and we will not. He cannot return to us, but we may go to Him, and in that blessed land we shall meet to part no more. Thanks be unto God, who giveth us the victory through our Lord Jesus Christ.

CHAPTER XXXIV

A Month with Mr. Moody in Chicago

By Rev. H. M. Wharton, D. D.

IT was a magnificent opportunity. The year of 1893 would find Chicago, the great city of the West, crowded day by day with hundreds of thousands of people coming and going from all parts of our own country, and from every nation under the sun. Mr. Moody was no prophet, but he was quick to see an opening for usefulness, and ever ready to grasp an opportunity for doing good. He saw before him an occasion similar to the Pentecost at Jerusalem, but on a much larger scale. In fact, the wonderful event at Jerusalem, when the Spirit descended upon the assembled disciples, and they went forth to meet and preach to the crowds coming up to the Holy City was but a prophecy of that which came to pass in the city of Chicago. Mr. Moody laid his plans with unusual wisdom and foresight. When the World's Fair opened, and the people poured in from all quarters of the earth, he was there to meet them with a force adequate to the demands of that teeming multitude. A brief outline of this plan will be of interest.

Outline of His Plan.

Wherever it was practicable, he grouped the churches, including as many as possible in the arrangement; the members were asked to come together in one of the largest of the group, and there met for worship and work. Services were held at night, and visitors who were staying in the neighborhood had ample notice that they might attend an interesting Gospel meeting. All available public places, halls, theatres, and other buildings, which could be used for public worship, were secured without regard to cost. When the theatres could not be had for the afternoons and evenings, they were secured for noonday services, and for Sunday meetings. The people of the great city seemed not only willing but anxious to do everything in their power to add to this wonderful movement for the Gospel of Christ, and for the salvation of souls. Perhaps one of the most interesting features was the tent work. This may be better understood by a simple description of a tent service.

Description of a Tent Service

After supper in the men's department of the Bible Institute, about 100 men are on their knees for a few minutes. Brief, burning, pointed prayers ascend. God is counted on to stand by them in their work. Then, rising, they scatter to mission and tent, going in some cases four, five, and even six miles, each with his Bible and little package of tracts, those containing plenty of Scripture being preferred. Meanwhile, in the Ladies' Home, fifty young women have been making similar preparations. One party is going to the big tent on Milwaukee Avenue, where Mr. Schiverea is holding meetings. On the street cars no time is lost. A young woman opposite speaks to the tired shop-girl at her side, opens her Bible, and points her to Him who said, "Come unto Me, all ye that labor and are heavy laden, and I will give you rest;" but the girl must get off at the next block. She slips the tract "God's Word to You," into her hand with a kind pressure, and asks her to read it. A pleasant smile, and a Good Night, and the seed is sown. Meanwhile, the young men are not idle. A tract is handed to a fellow-passenger—a kind word is spoken—and soon they, too, are talking of that wonderful

Saviour. A man on the platform has secured the attention of the conductor, who seemed under conviction. But we have reached our destination, and step from the cars.

Before us is the tent, brilliantly lighted. We enter, and overhead is a great arch of canvass, supported by three centre-poles and smaller ones about the sides—an auditorium accommodating 1,300 people, and seated with canvas benches.

The little party kneel in prayer for the presence and power of the Holy Spirit. Then some take their places upon the platform, to sing the Gospel, some stand ready to welcome and seat the audience, and others go out upon the streets, with cards of invitation to bring in the passers-by.

From our seat on the platform we watch the audience come in. First, a hesitating group of ragged little ones, then some young "toughs," with mischief in their faces are passed from one usher to another, who will keep his eye upon them. Next a mother with a baby in her arms, a laboring man in gingham shirt and no collar, fathers and mothers with their little ones—so they gather—largely an audience of respectable working people, for this is the character of the neighborhood; but the "tough" element is not wanting. The blue coat of a policeman seen at the door makes it easy to preserve order. The police of Chicago have proved good friends of this work, and some of their hearts have been found tender as well as brave.

A Graphic Address

A Gospel hymn opens the meeting, and how these people sing! A solo from an Institute lady, full of the Gospel message, more hymns, a duet, prayer, and the evangelist begins to speak. Tenderly, lovingly he deals with the people—unsparingly he deals with their sins. The trace of the actor still lingers in his graphic illustrations, largely drawn from his own experience; but so anxious is he that all be to the glory of God that he uses these with more and more care every year.

The address is short, and a hymn of invitation to Christ is sung by the same soloist as before, and then the speaker begins to ask those who wish to turn from a life of sin to God, to rise. Here and there they rise to their feet, the Institute workers marking them carefully. Then the leader says that all may go who wish to do so, but that a short after-meeting will be held for those, who choose to remain. A large part of the audience stay, and the workers thread their way among them, sitting down by those who have risen, and trying from the Word of God to show the way of salvation, often finding among those who linger, deep conviction of sin without the courage to rise and manifest the interest felt. At a late hour the party are once more on the cars, singing the Lord's songs as they take the long ride home.

The Working Force.

From a very wide acquaintance all over the Christian world, Mr. Moody selected his helpers. He secured men of experience, who had been blessed in other work without regard to age, denomination or education. What he wanted was men who believed the Gospel with all their hearts, who worked under the power of the Spirit of God, and who could tell plainly and simply the story of redeeming love. Mr. Moody always attached fully as much importance to the singing as to the preaching of the gospel, and in arranging his plans, sought out the best Gospel singers he could find, whether men or women, and applying the same rules to them as to the preachers, his selections were along the same line. The great purpose of his heart was to put before the people the way of life, and in the inquiry meetings, never to give up a soul while it yet remained in darkness, but to labor on until the seeker had found his Saviour. Without comment as to the wisdom of his plan, the results testified in unmistakable terms, that it was the one way to reach and save the many who came under the preaching of the Word, and there is no question that the results of the campaign during the World's Fair in Chicago were far more extended than at Pentecost in Jerusalem, for while hundreds and even thousands returned from the Holy City to their homes with a blessing, tens of thousands went from Chicago to all parts of the earth, not to tell simply of the wonders of the World's Fair, but the glories and the joys of redeeming love. I might relate many incidents of this work if time and space would allow. Let it be said, however, that from the lowest dens of vice in the slums of the city, to the highest in culture and position, the burning words of the evangelist reached the hearts of the people, whether these words were said or sung, and the whole city throbbed with the blessed impulse of Divine power.

My Arrival in Chicago

Many months before the beginning of the campaign, I met Mr. Moody and he engaged my services. During the spring of 1893, while holding meetings in the state of Texas, a telegram from him was received, announcing a number of appointments for me in Chicago on the following Sunday, according to our agreement made some time before. I had planned my arrangements to suit so that my meetings were closing at the time his message was received. Leaving immediately for Chicago, I arrived on Saturday night, and stopped at the Palmer House, and notified Mr. Moody that I was on hand and ready for duty.

Sunday morning early, I was informed that a gentleman wished to see me in the office of the hotel, and on coming down I met a handsome, young, blue-eyed Irishman. who said he had come

A MONTH WITH MR. MOODY IN CHICAGO

to take me to preach at Haymarket Theatre. It was my first meeting with one who became my genial and fast friend at that time, and such has been our relation ever since. He informed me that he was in this country a brief time, as he then thought, but soon changed his mind, for he succeeded in winning the heart of Miss Moody, and is now one of the leading workers in the great institutions which were established by her father. All of us know Mr. A. P. Fitt, who for years has been at the head of some of the most important branches of a great work.

My First Services in Chicago

On arrival at the Haymarket Theatre that Sunday morning the crowd seemed to be as great in the street as in the house, and it was with difficulty that I could get to the platform, where Mr. Moody greeted me most cordially, and in a few minutes introduced me, and requested me to speak. Immediately upon conclusion of my sermon, he again took the great audience in hand, and turning to me said, "Please go across to the Empire Theatre, and address an overflow meeting there. I will join you in a few minutes." It was quite as difficult to get out as in, but I soon found myself landed on my feet upon the stage in the Empire Theatre, where the people were already joyfully singing under the leadership of my good friend George C. Stebbins. In due time Mr. Moody came on the platform, having spoken in the Haymarket Theatre, and preached in the Empire Theatre with unabated power and zeal.

The meeting over, we went to a convenient hotel, where we had a hasty lunch, and from there up Michigan Avenue to Immanuel Church at three o'clock where another large audience was assembled, and we spoke again, I first, Mr. Moody following. The service here ended, and with but little rest we went for refreshment, then made our way along State Street to Central Music Hall, arriving before any of the audience. Soon after we walked upon the platform, Mr. Moody began to arrange for the service. The doors were opened, the people came pouring in, and a few of the singers had arrived and were on the stage. There was no organist, and no leader for the time, but our great evangelist, never waiting a moment for anything when there was work to do, turned to me, and said, "Wharton, can't you start a hymn?" Taking up some familiar hymn, we sang while the people crowded the building. In a few minutes the choir had assembled, the leader was present, and the great throng joined heartily in praising God. At this service, the order was reversed, Mr. Moody preaching first, and I am sure that, never in my life, have I listened to a more powerful sermon than was preached by him on that occasion to the great waiting throng.

A Most Powerful Sermon

His theme was "Daniel," and he carried us by the wonderful power of his imagination through all the scenes of that remarkable life, culminating with the miraculous delivery from the den of lions. Who can have forgotten his impersonation of the king, as looking down into the den of lions, he calls to Daniel, "O Daniel, servant of the living God, is thy God, whom thou servest continually, able to deliver thee from the lions?" And then the reply of Daniel that comes up from the lions' den, "O king, live for ever.

"My God hath sent His angel, and hath shut the lions' mouths that they have not hurt me, forasmuch as before Him innocency was found in me; and also before thee, O king, have I done no hurt." The whole audience was subdued under the mighty power of the Holy Ghost, and their hearts were melted in sweet fellowship and love. We went away feeling that we had been close to the throne, and had heard and seen strange things that blessed Sabbath day.

It will be for others to tell of his great achievements, and to account, if they can, for the secret of his power and his wonderful success. To me the great personality was the incarnation of love, and although he might at times impress one with a brusqueness which was almost abrupt, back of it all was still beating a great loving heart.

The Chicago Bible Institute

Our headquarters during this campaign were at the Bible Institute, one of the well-known schools already referred to for teaching and training in the Scriptures and evangelistic work. This Institute was the outgrowth of many years' thought on Mr. Moody's part upon the needs of the working people and the poor outcast. He saw that men and women were needed to go among these people and do heart to heart work, so that by the Word of God and the power of the Spirit, they might, by their sympathy and love, bring them to Christ and to nobler lives. These must be searched out and trained, and material was abundant, but it required a vast deal of wisdom in one to select the proper material, and to secure workmen to prepare this material for successful service. There are also many who have been called of God into the Christian work at a period of life too late to take a regular college course, but who could, by the help of the Bible Institute, be qualified for great usefulness; and then there are persons who wish to devote their time to Gospel work while pursuing some other calling.

Its Aim and Method of Work

It was to meet all these demands that the Institute was established. It has sought to send out men and women who have a thorough consecration, intense love for souls, a good knowledge of God's Word, and especially how to use it in leading them to Christ, untiring energy, and the baptism of the Holy Spirit. The method of training is by the study of the Bible and music, and actual work in leading men to Christ. The Institution is located in the heart of Chicago, and has from its beginning been under the management of Rev. R. A. Torrey, a man in every way qualified for this important work. When I reached the Institute the Monday following the day I have been describing, they sent me to a room which was to be my home for the next month. As I entered this pleasant little "Prophet's Chamber," I looked around for pictures, but discovered only one little motto on the wall, neatly framed, and these were the simple words, "GET RIGHT WITH GOD." My first impulse was to kneel down and ask God's blessing that I might be right with Him, and that He would use me in the work upon which it had been my privilege to enter. The very atmosphere of this place is one of worship and work. You can hear the songs of praise at almost any hour of the day. Little meetings are held in the rooms, or a special sermon or lecture in the chapel, and sweet social seasons when they are gathered around the tables in the dining-rooms, or in Mr. Moody's great reception room. It was always sweet and restful during the hours between the times of actual service.

THOUSANDS SAVED

The Institute is a hive, where the workers are coming and going, the difference being the bees go out, gather their honey and bring it home, while here the honey is gathered and carried abroad, where it is dispensed to those who will receive. The workers went forth every day and gave what they had gotten, to return in the evening all full of the sweet consolation that "It is more blessed to give than to receive."

I count it one of the greatest blessings of my life to have participated in the great battle among the multitude that filled Chicago during the most successful Exposition the world has ever known; and when the glorious end shall come, I believe it will be found that during this period of six months' work thousands were saved by the preaching of Christ in these meetings, and not only this, but that Christians from all parts of the earth went back to their homes strengthened and blessed, clothed anew with powers of the unseen world, to work for the Kingdom of God more earnestly and faithfully than ever before. And besides all this, the evil influences that were counteracted, and the good influences that went forth, will bless the world to the end of time. God be praised for this true believer and consecrated Christian man, who, like his Master, loved the world, and gave himself for it, and now, having finished his work, has passed through the gates of glory, and wears a crown of righteousness and victory forever.